Social Cognition and Schizophrenia

**Books are to be returned on or before
the last date below.**

LIBREX —

Social
Cognition
and
Schizophrenia

Edited by
Patrick W. Corrigan
and David L. Penn

American Psychological Association
Washington, DC

Published by
American Psychological Association
750 First Street, NE
Washington, DC 20002
www.apa.org

To order:
APA Order Department
P.O. Box 92984
Washington, DC 20090-2984

Tel: (800) 374-2721, Direct: (202) 336-5510
Fax: (202) 336-5502, TDD/TTY: (202) 336-6123
Online: www.apa.org/books/
Email: order@apa.org

In the U.K., Europe, Africa, and the Middle East, copies may be ordered from
American Psychological Association
3 Henrietta Street
Covent Garden, London
WC2E 8LU England

Typeset in Meridien by EPS Group Inc., Easton, MD

Printer: Data Reproductions, Auburn Hills, MI
Cover Designer: Naylor Design, Washington, DC
Technical/Production Editor: Emily I. Welsh

The opinions and statements published are the responsibility of the authors, and such opinions and statements do not necessarily represent the policies of the APA.

Library of Congress Cataloging-in-Publication Data

Social cognition and schizophrenia / edited by Patrick W. Corrigan and David L. Penn.—
    1st ed.
        p.   cm.
    Includes bibliographical references and index.
    ISBN 1-55798-774-2 (cb: acid-free paper)
        1. Schizophrenia.   2. Social perception.   I. Corrigan, Patrick W.   II. Penn, David L.

    RC514 .S59 2001
    616.89'82—dc21   00-054824

British Library Cataloguing-in-Publication Data
A CIP record is available from the British Library.

Printed in the United States of America
First Edition

To my wife Georgeen M. Carson
P. W. C.

And to my wife Leah Groehler and parents
Murray and Sheila Penn
D. L. P.

Contents

Part III: Future Directions

11

Contributors

Morris D. Bell, PhD, VA Connecticut Health Care System and Yale University, New Haven, CT

Richard P. Bentall, PhD, Department of Psychology, University of Manchester, England

Dennis Combs, PhD, Department of Psychology, Louisiana State University, Baton Rouge

Rhiannon Corcoran, PhD, Department of Psychology, University of Manchester, England

Patrick W. Corrigan, PsyD, Center for Psychiatric Rehabilitation, University of Chicago

Jane Edwards, PhD, Departments of Psychology & Psychiatry, University of Melbourne and MH-SKY, Australia

Kevin L. Holtzman, PsyD, Illinois School of Professional Psychology, Chicago Northwest

Henry J. Jackson, PhD, Department of Psychology, University of Melbourne and MH-SKY, Australia

Peter Kinderman, PhD, Department of Clinical Psychology, University of Liverpool, England

Christoph Leonhard, PhD, Illinois School of Professional Psychology, Chicago Northwest

Patrick D. McGorry, PhD, Department of Psychiatry, University of Melbourne and MH-SKY, Australia

Somaia Mohamed, PhD, Department of Veterans Affairs Medical Center, Cincinnati, OH

Leonard S. Newman, PhD, Department of Psychology, University of Illinois at Chicago

David L. Penn, PhD, University of North Carolina at Chapel Hill

Jeffrey S. Poland, PhD, University of Nebraska, Lincoln

William D. Spaulding, PhD, Department of Psychology, University of Nebraska, Lincoln

Preface

From its earliest conceptions, schizophrenia has been viewed as both a cognitive and a social disorder. Kraepelin, Bleuler, and others first described schizophrenia as a cognitive disorder that undermines almost all thought processes. Conversely, the depth of disabilities in schizophrenia stems largely from the havoc the illness wreaks on almost all interpersonal functions. Although the two domains are well known to researchers and practitioners familiar with schizophrenia, a rapprochement between perspectives has been difficult. How, exactly, do deficits in cognition disrupt social functioning? What impact does interpersonal interaction have on a person's cognitive abilities? We have asked ourselves those questions for the past decade; failures at earlier answers led to our interest in *social cognitive* paradigms and their relevance for schizophrenia.

We noticed that one of the problems with integration stems from the different ways in which cognitive and social researchers approach the questions. Much of the research on the cognitive deficits of schizophrenia defines concepts and theories in the terms of experimental psychopathology and information processing. The good news is that those approaches bring exceptionally rigorous methods and well-considered models to the arena of research on cognitive deficits. The bad news is that many of the internally valid theories yield research techniques and study results that are not readily meaningful for explaining how a person understands social situations. What does key-punching a computer joystick after observing degraded sevens have to do with responding to a clerk's request for ID at the nearby convenience store?

We noticed that much of the research on social functioning represents the pragmatic concerns of clinical researchers. As such, the studies are strong on ecological validity and practical value. Social skills training, for example, teaches people with schizophrenia how to process and respond to the clerk's demand for identification. Unfortunately, those approaches are far removed from the carefully developed heuristics that explain schizophrenia and its associated dysfunctions. What does teaching basic conversation skills have to do with the unique symptoms and disabilities of schizophrenia (as opposed to generic behavioral problems that many other groups also manifest)?

One way in which a marriage between the social and the cognitive has been attempted is by making information-processing models of schizophrenia primary and using those theories to explain components of social perception, understanding, and response. We, along with many others, joined this effort, completing a series of studies that examined the associations between specific deficits in attention, memory, and executive functioning and measures of problem solving, assertiveness, and dating skills. For example, we might describe ways in which a person acts in the local convenience store by using ideas that emerge from laboratory-based computer simulations.

As Rhiannon Corcoran has said, "Cognition *is* fundamentally social!" The leap between laboratory-based tasks and real-world behavior is huge. Some information-processing constructs may be "hijacked" to address more abstract, social information, but they do so less efficiently— much as the left hand, in most right-handed people, is less able to complete fine motor skills. Social cognition is neither an isolated part of the brain nor an adaptation of processing mechanisms. It is the fundamental way in which all information is understood. Fortunately, researchers with interest in schizophrenia need not despair. Over the past 50 years, social psychologists developed a paradigm that merges the social and the cognitive. Moreover, clinical researchers adapted their theories and methods to examine how people with schizophrenia know their social world and respond to this knowledge accordingly.

This book brings together distinguished colleagues from Australia, Great Britain, and the United States who have developed and tested social cognitive models of schizophrenia. It was designed to accomplish two goals: (1) to outline the basic theoretical and conceptual issues related to social cognition in schizophrenia, and (2) to describe some of the clinical applications of those theories—strategies that practitioners might add to their armamentarium to better serve people with schizophrenia. The book ends with a summary of what we have learned thus far and, more important, what research is needed to further our knowledge about social cognition and schizophrenia.

This book was written for students of schizophrenia as well as clinicians and investigators who wish to better understand the breadth of disabilities that impede people with schizophrenia and the explanatory constructs that may identify the causes of those disabilities. This group consists mainly of psychologists, but it includes other mental health practitioners: psychiatrists, social workers, occupational therapists, and psychiatric nurses. The book also is relevant for those interested in social cognition, such as social psychologists, who aim to understand the intellectual process as it is fundamentally anchored within the interpersonal context. One way to understand social cognition is to understand it dysfunctionally; a review of people with schizophrenia and their social cognitive abilities opens this door slightly.

Acknowledgments

We are grateful to several colleagues who read earlier drafts of chapters in this book. They include Carl Baremboim, Richard P. Bentall, Daniel Cervone, Faith Dickerson, Paul Lysaker, Alice Medalia, Neal Roese, and Steven Silverstein.

We also wish to acknowledge Amy Green, who helped us greatly in compiling the final chapters. Finally, we wish to thank our families for their understanding during this project. It is always easier and more fulfilling to be productive when we have the unconditional support of our wives, parents, and children.

Social Cognition and Schizophrenia

Introduction: Framing Models of Social Cognition and Schizophrenia

Patrick W. Corrigan and David L. Penn

Schizophrenia is an especially troublesome disorder because it causes disabilities across most social functioning domains—disabilities that prevent people from achieving their life goals. People with schizophrenia have difficulty attaining good jobs, earning a meaningful income, living in comfortable housing, finding a mate, and generally enjoying life. Researchers, treatment providers, and consumers all have sought explanatory models for what causes and maintains those disabilities in the hope that the models will lead to viable programs for helping people overcome their disabilities so that they can achieve their life goals. Prominent among those models have been neurophysiological and morphological understandings of deficit, leading to essentially medical interventions for schizophrenia. Although the models have yielded significant improvements in symptoms and disabilities, they provide an incomplete picture of the disease's impact. Scientists also have searched for a psychology of schizophrenia to augment the biological perspective. In this book, we propose social cognition as a viable model for this purpose.

Social cognition is defined as the processes and functions that allow a person to understand, act on, and benefit from the interpersonal world. As we and others argue in this book, "social" cognition is distinct from an equally impressive research paradigm based on information process-

Many thanks to Steven Silverstein for helpful comments on an earlier draft of this chapter.

3

ing. The latter heuristic has uncovered several brain–behavior correlates in schizophrenia, which, in turn, have guided the development and evaluation of useful interventions. However, the process of recognizing and interacting with social information is wholly different from the more passive data displays used within information-processing studies. Note the bidirectional nature of our definition of social cognition: The person acts on social information that reciprocally acts on the person. This definition is in contrast to traditional cognitive and perceptual research paradigms. As a result, social cognitive models provide a different picture of schizophrenia, one that we would argue is more relevant to the interpersonal disabilities associated with the disorder.

Social cognition has been shown to be useful for describing disorders and developing treatments, especially for depression and anxiety disorders (Abramson, 1988; Dobson & Kendall, 1993). The authors in *Social Cognition and Schizophrenia* argue that social cognition provides an equally useful model for schizophrenia.

Before describing the chapters that constitute each part of the book, it is important to sum up what is broadly known (from diverse perspectives) about the disabilities that arise from schizophrenia and the services that help people manage those problems. Central to this discussion is a list of the methods and strategies that have proved useful in previous research. This summary will help the reader place social cognition within the larger body of knowledge about schizophrenia. A second goal of this chapter is to briefly describe the line of research that has examined cognitive deficits and corresponding remediation strategies. Understanding the strengths and limitations of this research points to social cognition as a reasonable psychology for schizophrenia.

The Disabilities of Schizophrenia

Many people with schizophrenia experience disabilities in several domains of social functioning, such as interpersonal relationships, self-care skills, education, work and personal achievement, finances, housing, recreation, physical health and wellness, mental health and drug abuse, spirituality, and legal matters. The disorder is especially disabling because its impact is rarely limited to one or two domains; for example, many people with schizophrenia report a poor quality of life because of their inability to get good jobs, live independently in nice areas, generate sufficient finances, and develop lasting relationships. The deficits associated with schizophrenia have been measured in a variety of ways; research on those measures is summarized in Exhibit I.1. As is evident

EXHIBIT I.1

Some Measures of the Deficits and Disabilities of Schizophrenia

Needs
Camberwell Assessment of Needs (Phelan et al., 1995)
Cardinal Needs Schedule (Marshall et al., 1995)
Medical Research Council's Needs for Care Assessment (Brewin et al., 1987; Brewin & Wing, 1993)
Needs and Resources Assessment (Corrigan et al., 1995)

Symptoms
Brief Psychiatric Rating Scale (Lukoff et al., 1986)
Positive and Negative Symptom Scale (Kay et al., 1987)
Schedule for Assessment of Negative Symptoms (Andreasen, 1983)
Schedule for Assessment of Positive Symptoms (Andreasen, 1984)

Functional Skills
Assessment of Interpersonal Problem-Solving Skills (Donahoe et al., 1990)
Community Competence Scale (Oliver & Searight, 1988; Searight & Goldberg, 1991)
Community Psychiatric Clinic Level of Functioning Assessment (Uehara et al., 1994)
Disability Rating Form (Hoyle et al., 1992)
Independent Living Skills Survey (Wallace, 1986)
Life Skills Profile (Rosen et al., 1989)
Multnomah Community Ability Scale (Barker et al., 1994a, 1994b)
Rehabilitation Evaluation (Baker & Hall, 1988)
Role Activity Performance Scale (Good-Ellis et al., 1987)

Social–Adaptive Functioning Evaluation (Harvey et al., 1997)
Social Behavior Schedule (Wykes & Sturt, 1986)
Social Dysfunction Index (Munroe-Blum et al., 1996)
Social Problem-Solving Assessment Battery (Sayers et al., 1995)
St. Louis Inventory of Community Living Skills (Evenson & Boyd, 1993)

Social Roles
Personal Adjustment and Role Skills Scale (Ellsworth et al., 1968)
Role Functioning Scale (Goodman et al., 1993)
Social Adjustment Scale II (Schooler et al., 1979)
Social Functioning Scale (Birchwood et al., 1990)

Quality of Life
Client's Quality of Life Instrument (Pinkney et al., 1991)
Quality of Life Checklist (Malm et al., 1981)
Quality of Life Enjoyment and Satisfaction Questionnaire (Endicott et al., 1993)
Quality of Life Interview (Lehman, 1983, 1988)
Quality of Life Profile (Huxley & Warner, 1992)
Quality of Life Questionnaire (Thapa & Rowland, 1989)
Quality of Life Questionnaire (Bigelow et al., 1991)
Quality of Life Scale (Heinrichs, Hanlon, & Carpenter, 1984)
Quality of Life Self-Assessment (Skantze et al., 1992)

Note. For more complete descriptions of these measures, see Scott & Lehman, 1998; Dickerson, 1997; Corrigan, 1989; and Wallace, 1986.

from the exhibit, extensive research has been completed on strategies that assess disabilities and deficits arising from schizophrenia. The strategies include self-report measures, structured interviews, and observations of people with the disorder. Research measures can be been divided into five domains representing different approaches to conceptualizing disability: needs, symptoms, functional skills, social roles, and quality of life.

Measures of psychosocial *need* assess the person's perceptions of life goals. What do people want to attain for themselves in the near future (frequently defined as the next few months) as well as for the long term (defined as 3–5 years)? This approach acknowledges that the person with mental illness has the best perspective on what the relevant disabilities are and what the corresponding treatments are for those disabilities. The needs assessments in Exhibit I.1 typically approach the measurement question broadly, seeking to identify goals across the breadth of life domains.

The next three sets of measures attempt to identify barriers to obtaining life goals: the disabilities per se. One approach is to identify *psychiatric symptoms* that interfere with social goals. Researchers have distinguished positive from negative symptoms (Andreasen, Roy, & Flaum, 1995). Positive symptoms are the obvious, psychotic signs of the disorder: hallucinations, delusions, formal thought disorder, and agitation. Negative symptoms represent a reduction in reactive, affective, and interpersonal functioning, such as flattened affect, social autism, and alogia. The positive–negative distinction also refers to neurophysiological correlates: Positive symptoms represent a neurochemical disinhibition, whereas negative symptoms suggest dissolution of higher cortical functions. Generally, research has found negative symptoms to be the better predictor of both current social problems as well as future outcomes (Breier, Schreiber, Dyer, & Pickar, 1991; Keefe, Mohs, Losonczy, & Davidson, 1987; Pogue-Geile & Harrow, 1984); however, this finding could be tautological because measurement of negative symptoms involves assessment of social functioning.

A more direct way to measure social and community disability is to assess *functional skills*. This approach is fundamentally behavioral, resting on the assumption that life goals are achieved when people have mastered the skills needed to achieve these goals. Researchers have adopted a variety of sampling procedures to identify the range of functional skills relevant to psychiatric disability (Corrigan & Holmes, 1994; Goldsmith & McFall, 1975; Holmes, Corrigan, Knight, & Flaxman, 1995). These domains include interpersonal (e.g., basic conversation, assertiveness, problem solving, and dating), coping (e.g., medication and symptom management), and self-care (e.g., hygiene, money management, nutrition, work, and wellness) skills. Typically, functioning is tabulated as the total number of exhibited skills in the measure. Some researchers add an assessment of the person's level of distress about functional deficits (Eisen, Wilcox, Leff, Schaefer, & Culhane, 1999).

An alternative way to examine psychiatric disabilities is to determine whether the person has achieved *social roles*. According to social role theory, people achieve various roles as they age and develop (Cohler & Ferrono, 1987). Although specific theme and time issues vary across cultures, consensus exists about common social roles within a group. For example, Western adults (between ages 20 and 30) are expected to find a vocation and become successful in it, find and settle down with a life mate, and establish a household that is independent from their family of origin. Social role theory is especially useful because it gives meaning to the discrete skills that make up a role. Hence, rather than assessing whether a person can get out of bed on time, ride public transportation, communicate clearly with others, and obey authority, assessing social roles can indicate whether that person is likely to achieve goals related to work.

Absence of symptoms, presence of functional skills, and achievement of social roles is not sufficient to determine whether a person's life is fulfilling. Consequently, investigators have borrowed the concept of *quality of life* from medical researchers to measure this last domain related to psychiatric disability. Measures of quality of life attempt to assess this construct by asking people to rate their satisfaction with the variety of domains that comprise a full life in the community.

Psychosocial Treatments for the Deficits of Schizophrenia

A variety of psychosocial treatments have been developed to address the deficits identified by the measures in Exhibit I.1; they are listed in Exhibit I.2 along with citations to controlled research that have demonstrated their efficacy. We do not mean to imply that research has unequivocally supported these interventions for psychiatric disabilities. In fact, several of the studies are significant because they failed to support hypotheses in favor of the corresponding treatment. The weight of evidence for the six interventions, however, suggests the treatment priorities that dominate contemporary practice. Continued research is needed to determine how those interventions combine with individual interests and deficits to yield significant improvements.

The treatments listed in Exhibit I.2 suggest specific factors that help people address their disabilities. Interpersonal support is one of those factors. *Case management* is defined as the provision of interpersonal sup-

EXHIBIT 1.2

Controlled Studies of Psychosocial Services for Schizophrenia

**Management
(Assertive Community Treatment)**
Aberg-Wistedt et al., 1995
Bond et al., 1988, 1990
Bush et al., 1990
Chandler et al., 1996
Curtis et al., 1992
Essock & Kontos, 1995
Franklin et al., 1987
Godley et al., 1994
Hampton et al., 1992
Hoult et al., 1983
Jerrell & Hu, 1989
Lehman et al., 1993, 1997
Macias et al., 1994
Marks et al., 1994
Merson et al., 1992
Modrcin et al., 1988
Morse et al., 1992, 1997
Muijen et al., 1994
Mulder, 1982
Quinlivan et al., 1995
Rosenheck et al., 1994
Shern et al., 1996
Solomon & Draine, 1995
Stein & Test, 1980
Susser et al., 1997
Test, 1992

Skills Training
Bellack et al., 1984
Dobson et al., 1995
Hayes et al., 1995
Hogarty et al., 1986
Liberman et al., 1986
Liberman et al., 1998

Incentive Therapies
Atthowe & Krasner, 1968

Ayllon & Azrin, 1968
Banzett et al., 1984
Paul & Lentz, 1977

**Vocational Rehabilitation/
Supported Employment**
Bond et al., 1995
Chandler et al., 1996
Danley et al., 1994
Drake et al., 1996
Fabian, 1992
Gervey & Bedell, 1994
Kirszner et al., 1991
McFarlane et al., 1995
Mowbray et al., 1995
Nichols, 1989
Shafer & Huang, 1995
Trotter et al., 1988

Family Interventions
Falloon et al., 1982, 1985
Glick et al., 1985, 1990
Goldstein et al., 1978
Leff et al., 1982, 1985, 1990
McFarlane et al., 1995
Mingyuan et al., 1993
Randolph et al., 1994
Tarrier et al., 1988, 1989
Telles et al., 1995
Xiong et al., 1994

**Self-Help/Mutual Help Groups and
Psychosocial Clubhouses**
Galanter, 1988
Kennedy, 1990
Maton, 1988
Schubert & Borkman, 1994
Stein et al., 1995
Young & Williams, 1988

Note. For more complete descriptions of these studies, see Bond et al., 1997; Mueser et al., 1998; and Penn & Mueser, 1996.

port (i.e., providing warmth and unconditional regard for a person) and instrumental support (i.e., actively helping the person meet his or her needs) in the home and community so that the person can attain his or her life goals. Seminal research by Stein and Test (1980) showed that one form of case management, assertive community treatment, helped most people with schizophrenia stay out of the hospital and live successfully in their community. Work by this group suggests that people who could rely on a support team to help them shop, manage finances, deal with work, and address recreational concerns were able to cope with psychiatric symptoms and attain several social roles.

Sometimes people are unable to attain their goals because they lack important social and coping skills. *Skills training* strategies help people with schizophrenia learn such skills; training strategies combine vicarious and operant methods. Results of three meta-analyses suggest that gains from skills training are fairly robust and seem to persist over time (Benton & Schroeder, 1990; Corrigan, 1991a; Dilk & Bond, 1996).

Incentive therapies, like token economies, are another set of strategies that help people perform appropriate social and coping skills. Research by Paul and Lentz (1977) showed that inpatients who participated in incentive programs were discharged from the hospital more quickly and stayed out much longer than a comparison group. Although incentive therapies have frequently been criticized as having limited utility because they are only practical in hospital settings, some researchers have reviewed their effectiveness for community settings (Corrigan, 1991b, 1995).

Employment is an important goal for many people with schizophrenia. Attaining this goal frequently requires *vocational rehabilitation* to help the person get back to work. Two kinds of vocational programs have proven their success for people with schizophrenia (Bond, Drake, Mueser, & Becker, 1997). In train-then-place programs, people receive extensive instruction in work adjustment skills (e.g., how to manage a schedule, work alongside co-workers, and follow a supervisor) and specific trades (e.g., accounting, housekeeping, food preparation, or secretarial) before being placed on the job. Some rehabilitation researchers have argued that train-then-place programs may undermine the person's readiness for work (Becker & Drake, 1994; Wehman, 1988). Those investigators refer to surveys suggesting that trainees are dissatisfied with long prevocational programs that forestall actual job placement. Place-then-train programs have developed as an alternative to the more traditional train-then-place, supported employment (Wehman, 1986, 1988). In place-then-train programs, the person is placed in competitive employment after a short orientation, which sometimes lasts no more than a week. This orientation provides time for the person to determine which jobs most interest him or her (Danley, Rogers, & Nevas, 1989).

The person then learns work adjustment and job-specific skills *in vivo* with follow-along support and guidance from the job coach and supervisor. The real-world necessities of on-the-job work demands make skill learning and adjustment much more compelling.

Families are important resources for many people with schizophrenia. Two kinds of treatment seem to help families contend with the burden of a relative with severe mental illness, thereby becoming a better resource for the person (Mueser & Glynn, 1995). *Educational* programs inform family members about the course of the disorder and effective treatments. They also teach problem-solving skills so the family and the person with disability are better able to cope with disagreements when they recur. *Support* programs typically occur in multiple-family groups. The interaction with other families provides shared experience and resources that reduce the burden over time.

Frequently, people with schizophrenia are robbed of a sense of personal power. A stigmatizing society makes them think they are incapable of personal success even if their disability would not prevent them from work or independent-living opportunities (Corrigan & Penn, 1998). The mental health system has been guilty of adopting those attitudes and developing an authoritarian approach to service. For these reasons, psychosocial treatments need to foster the person's sense of personal empowerment. Two treatments are particularly notable in this area. First, *psychosocial clubhouses* are programs in which staff and people with schizophrenia have equal status. Although clubhouse programs are becoming more widespread, few carefully controlled research projects have examined their effectiveness.

Second, *self-help* programs have been developed by people with mental illness for people with mental illness. Professionals per se have no formal role in those settings. Actually, self-help tends to be a misnomer; it suggests an ethos of rugged individualism in which people borrow coping ideas and support from others in order to make it on their own (Humphreys & Rappaport, 1994). *Mutual help* is a more appropriate term that recognizes an important element provided by the groups: People benefit from helping each other. This kind of help extends beyond sharing information about coping skills or ways to manage the mental health system. The experience of both giving and receiving helps enhance the person's sense of place in the community and well-being (Maton, 1988). Research on mutual help programs has been mostly retrospective, although the Substance Abuse and Mental Health Services Administration is conducting a multicenter study with a randomized design.

The complex problems of mental illness are best treated by some combination of services that is based on the specific needs and treatment preferences of the consumer. Many interventions were developed out of necessity—the treatment system was searching for effective ways to help people with schizophrenia accomplish their goals—and thus do not necessarily represent the evolution of basic models of mental illness. However, since the development of psychosocial treatments, researchers have come to understand the interventions through various psychological models. Perhaps paramount among the models has been a cognitive approach to understanding the disabilities of schizophrenia and corresponding treatments (Green, 1996, 1998).

Cognitive Models of Deficit and Treatment

Cognitive models have yielded some interesting hypotheses about the breadth of psychosocial deficits and the impact of effective treatments; these models have held up to empirical scrutiny. Cognitive models have been popular ever since early conceptualizations about schizophrenia. Emil Kraepelin (1919), summarizing the views of his time, believed that the "annihilation of intrapsychic coordination" engendered by schizophrenia could be attributed in large part to disorders of cognitive associations. Eugen Bleuler (1911/1950) elaborated further, saying that the loss of associations among thoughts was central to the diagnosis of schizophrenia. Since that time, a variety of paradigms has emerged to describe the form and nature of cognitive dissociations. Table I.1 summarizes four models that have been fairly well developed for schizophrenia: intellectual functioning, abstract thinking, syntactical deficits, and information processing. It includes references to review articles and book chapters that summarize the literature in this area.

Research has shown people with schizophrenia to have lower than average *intellectual functioning,* suggesting that the primary cognitive deficit is intellectual in form. Low IQ scores are apparent even when compared with groups that are matched for gender and educational/socioeconomic status. Nor can this finding be explained away by the deleterious effects of institutionalization and medication experienced by adults with schizophrenia. Children who are later diagnosed with schizophrenia have lower IQ scores than members of matched comparison groups. Intellectual paradigms have diminished in popularity, however, because they offer little promise as explanatory models or heuristics for treatment (Corrigan, 1996).

Some researchers have argued that the cognitive deficits of schizophrenia are exacerbated when people have to process *abstract* information. Researchers typically use proverbs to assess abstract thinking: "What does this saying mean: Shallow brooks are noisy." Compared

TABLE 1.1

Five Paradigms That Have Described the Cognitive Deficits of Schizophrenia

Model	Description of Model and Relevant Findings	Reviews of Related Research
1. Low intelligence	People with schizophrenia have lower IQ than matched comparison groups.	Bilder et al., 1992; Frith, 1996; MacPherson et al., 1996
2. Poor abstraction	Cognitive functions diminish when the task involves understanding abstract information like proverbs.	Harrow et al., 1987
3. Loss of syntax	Dissociations result from poor syntax and semantics, as evidenced in speech and written communication.	Maher, 1991
4. Poor information	People with severe mental illness have processing deficits in discrete processing stages or factors that affect those stages.	Kern & Green, 1998; Green, 1998
5. Social cognition	(The introduction to this volume describes the social cognition model.)	

with more concrete tasks, like simple arithmetic and information learning, people with schizophrenia exhibit pronounced inability to understand and respond to abstract information. Moreover, research suggests that deficits in abstraction interfere with social perception and problem solving (Corrigan & Green, 1993; Corrigan & Toomey, 1995).

A third approach to understanding cognitive deficits has carefully examined the syntax and semantics exhibited in speech and written communication. This model has led to two research programs. The first examined the roles of violations of syntax and semantics in the speech and writings of people with mental illness. For example, various algorithms have been developed for quantifying tangential thought, derailments, and neologisms in speech (Andreasen, 1979a, 1979b). Other researchers have used linguistic models to explain the speech dissociations of people with schizophrenia, focusing on language utterances (Maher, 1991).

INFORMATION-PROCESSING MODELS FOR SCHIZOPHRENIA

Perhaps the most popular approach to understanding cognitive deficits is an information-processing model. According to this model, the macroexperience of sensory input is divided into discrete information bytes;

the macro-circumstances of human cognition are divided into composite functions (such as attention, memory, and response selection) that interact in some meaningful order (Corrigan & Stephenson, 1994). Hence, the process of knowing can be understood by studying the various components of the information process individually and together. Early models of information processing framed composite processes in a stepwise linear fashion (e.g., 1. attention; 2. encoding; 3. short-term memory; 4. consolidation; and 5. long-term memory). Subsequent models have proposed parallel distributed processing.

From a methodological standpoint, breaking down information and cognition into theoretical elements greatly enhances the study of those phenomena. Researchers ask questions such as, Which information process seems to be uniquely deficient in people with schizophrenia? Answers to such questions have significant implications for developing phenomenological and etiological models of the disorder and appropriate treatments (Storzbach & Corrigan, 1996). Unfortunately, researchers have not been able to identify a single deficient information process that is characteristic of the thought disturbance of schizophrenia. Instead, broader theories have explained the *pattern* of deficits found in the information processing of people with schizophrenia (Spaulding, Reed, Poland, & Storzbach, 1996).

Correlates With Social Functioning

Information processing also has been a fruitful model because corresponding research has shown repeated associations between measures of specific information processes (e.g., selective attention, verbal memory, and executive functioning) and social functioning. Research in this area, summarized in Exhibit I.3, has found that deficits in attention, memory, and executive functioning account for performance in four social domains:

1. *Program behavior*. People with information-processing deficits show fewer interpersonal skills and greater behavior problems within treatment programs.
2. *Community outcome*. People report a better quality of life and higher occupational functioning when they demonstrate more competent information processes.
3. *Interpersonal problem solving*. People are better able to understand and resolve interpersonal problems when they have fewer information-processing deficits.
4. *Skill learning*. People are able to better learn social and coping skills when they demonstrate fewer processing deficits.

EXHIBIT 1.3

Research Studies That Have Found Significant Associations Among Specific Information Processes and Various Domains of Functioning

Program Behavior
Dickerson et al., 1991
Penn et al., 1996
Spaulding, 1978

Community Outcome
Addington & Addington, 1999
Buchanan et al., 1994
Goldman et al., 1993
Jaeger & Douglas, 1992
Johnstone et al., 1990
Lysaker et al., 1995
Wykes et al., 1990
Wykes et al., 1992

Interpersonal Problem Solving
Addington & Addington, 1999
Bellack et al., 1994
Bowen et al., 1994
Corrigan & Toomey, 1995
Penn et al., 1993
Penn et al., 1995

Skills Learning
Bowen et al., 1994
Corrigan et al., 1994
Kern et al., 1992
Lysaker et al., 1995
Mueser et al., 1991
Weaver & Brooks, 1964

Note. For more complete descriptions of these studies, see Green, 1998 and Penn et al., 1997.

These associations are especially promising for helping to focus rehabilitation programs. They suggest which cognitive rehabilitation strategy may best improve community outcome and facilitate skill learning and problem solving.

Limits to Information-Processing Models

Although information-processing models have contributed to our understanding of schizophrenia, they are not without limits. First, the association between measures of information processing and social functioning generally is modest (Green, 1996; Penn, Corrigan, Bentall, Racenstein, & Newman, 1997). This finding suggests that a fair amount of the variance in social outcome (e.g., social skills, community functioning) may remain unexplained, even after considering factors such as symptomatology. Similarly, the search for the "primary processing" deficit of schizophrenia, the "holy grail" of schizophrenia research (Cromwell, 1984), has not proven to be successful (see Spaulding, 1997). Consequently, other domains of functioning, in addition to cognitive factors, must be considered.

A second limitation of purely cognitive models of schizophrenia is that focusing on processes relatively devoid of social context leads to incomplete frameworks of functioning. In other words, social behavior, whether it is demonstrated by someone with schizophrenia or a person without a psychiatric disorder, is likely to be a function of numerous factors, some of which are information processes. For example, forming an impression of someone certainly will depend on the ability to accurately "perceive" that person. Impression formation, however, also may be influenced by the perceiver's history with that person, whether the target's behavior is constrained by the situation, and the attributions the perceiver makes about the target's behavior (Gilbert, 1995). Thus, observing that someone is ill-tempered may not necessarily lead to the impression that she is "cantankerous" if you find out that she was recently robbed; our initial impression may be "corrected" by situational factors.

The effect of context on cognitive processes is further illustrated by Tversky and Kahneman's (1974) representativeness heuristic. They showed that people ignore base-rate information when provided with additional, "diagnostic" information. For example, research participants in one study were told that 90% of the men in a particular community were from a particular profession, such as a farmer, whereas the remaining 10% were librarians. The participants then were given information about a specific person, such as that he paints in his spare time, is into the arts, and likes to read. The participant was asked to estimate the probability that the target person is a farmer or librarian. One could argue that purely cognitive models would predict that base-rate information will influence probability judgments. However, findings typically show that research participants are influenced by context as well as knowledge about the typical characteristics of farmers and librarians; thus, they overestimate the probability that the target is a librarian rather than farmer. These types of biases fall under the rubric of "social cognition."

Despite these limitations, new generations of processing models have attempted to bridge comprehension of social phenomena with the nonsocial stimuli that tend to be the focus of information-processing paradigms (Knight & Silverstein, 1998; Silverstein, Bakshi, Chapman, & Nowlis, 1998). For example, Andreasen and colleagues (1998) hypothesized that a disruption in circuitry involving the thalamus, cerebellum, and prefrontal cortex produces "cognitive dysmetria." This concept refers to difficulty in prioritizing, processing, coordinating, and responding to information and is applicable to a number of cognitive deficits that have been viewed as independent. Cohen and others (1992, 1999) have developed a model in which a number of cognitive deficits can be seen as a manifestation of a broader impairment in context processing that stems from dopaminergic dysfunction. In our opinion, it is likely that these types of integrative models will have greater relevance for understanding social cognitive deficits in schizophrenia than have past cognitive models.

Toward a Social Cognition of Schizophrenia

Definitions of social cognition are quite varied and range from the relatively brief (e.g., "Social cognition is simply thinking about people"; Fiske, 1995, p. 151) to the more extended (e.g., "A domain of cognition that involves the perception, interpretation, and processing of social information"; Ostrom, 1984, p. 176). We generally prefer a definition offered by Brothers (1990b), which links social cognition with behavior: "The mental operations underlying social interactions, which include the human ability to perceive the intentions and dispositions of others" (p. 28). With respect to schizophrenia, Brothers' definition is consistent with the approaches of Bentall, Kinderman, and colleagues' work on attributional style, and Corcoran and Frith's research on theory of mind (discussed in subsequent chapters of this book). Furthermore, explicitly tying social cognition to behavior compels researchers to understand the functional significance of social cognition in schizophrenia (e.g., behavior and symptoms) and not fall victim to studying social cognition in a functional vacuum (Berkowitz & Devine, 1995).

Social cognition differs from nonsocial cognition in a number of ways, the most salient being the target of information processing. Unlike nonsocial stimuli (e.g., letters, numbers, and inanimate objects), social stimuli tend to be mutable over time, are personally relevant, and act as their own causal agents (Fiske, 1995; Fiske & Taylor, 1991). Furthermore humans tend to be more concerned with the unobservable characteristics of social stimuli (compared with nonsocial stimuli), leading us to search for the causes behind others' behavior (e.g., forming attributions; Fiske, 1995). Finally, the relationship between the perceiver and social object tends to be bidirectional; the object can think about the perceiver, which in turn, can influence the perceiver's impression of the social object. This process, described by Fiske (1995) as "mutual perception," is less likely to occur in the processing of nonsocial stimuli.

In addition to differences between the types of processed stimuli, nonsocial and social cognition differ with respect to how performance is evaluated. For example, performance on nonsocial cognitive tasks among people with schizophrenia typically is indexed in terms of "deficits." Thus, a group with schizophrenia will be compared with a control sample (or, less frequently, normative data) on a task (e.g., Wisconsin Card Sorting Task or Span of Apprehension), and their relative performance assessed. In this sense, the person with schizophrenia either does or does not have a particular skill. This approach clearly has a number of advantages, including the ability to compute subjects' accuracy across a range of tests. The emphasis on accuracy and deficits, however, tends to be at the cost of examining other indices of performance, such as biases, which are of greater interest to the social cognition researcher.

As discussed in Penn et al. (1997), biases refer to a characteristic response style that does not necessarily indicate impaired performance. For example, a recent study showed that undergraduate students high in social anxiety were more likely to interpret an ambiguous passage about a blind date in a negative manner, compared with subjects low in social anxiety (Constans, Penn, Ihnen, & Hope, 1999). Although the response style of the socially anxious subjects may be maladaptive in terms of their characteristic way of approaching the social environment, it is not necessarily deficient or incorrect. In fact, in some situations, interpreting an ambiguous situation negatively may be a conservative, yet beneficial, behavioral strategy (e.g., deciding not to walk down a particular street in which a group of youths have congregated). Thus, a focus on biases in schizophrenia will lead to a better understanding of a characteristic response style, the adaptiveness of which may be understood only in reference to the situation in which it occurs.

The distinction between social and nonsocial cognition also has been made in other areas of inquiry, including clinical neurology, evolutionary biology, primate behavior, and developmental psychology (Ostrom, 1984; Penn et al., 1997; Silverstein, 1997). For example, data indicating dissociations between disorders of face recognition and object recognition imply some (but not complete) specialization of functioning for interpersonal stimuli (Farah, 1992). In the area of evolutionary biology, Cosmides and Tooby (Cosmides, 1989; Cosmides & Tooby, 1989, 1994) argued that natural selection has influenced how people reason and that reasoning for adaptive problems involves specific cognitive mechanisms. In other words, cognitive processes are not "content-free" but are tied to specific social and adaptive functions (Cosmides & Tooby, 1994). Similarly, Brothers (1990a, 1990b) argued that certain behaviors, such as primates trying to deceive or comfort other members of their group, may reflect an ability to make inferences regarding the disposition of others, a social cognitive ability. Finally, Ostrom (1984) reviews evidence suggesting that children may understand causality for social events before physical events and that person permanence may develop before object permanence. Thus, solid evidence appears to indicate that social cognition represents a construct that is not redundant with nonsocial cognition. However, the degree of overlap between the domains, especially as applied to the study of schizophrenia, has not been well examined (Silverstein, 1997).

SOCIAL COGNITION
AND SCHIZOPHRENIA

The study of social cognition in schizophrenia has a rich history. Early work focused on the role of stimulus content (i.e., either social or affective versus neutral) on task performance (Buss & Lang, 1965; Cromwell & Spaulding, 1978; Neale, Held, & Cromwell, 1969; Strauss, Foureman, & Parwatikur, 1974). Findings from those studies were generally mixed, with some studies showing greater performance deficits for social stimuli than for nonsocial stimuli (Gillis, 1969; Whiteman, 1954) and others showing no such differential deficit (Chapman & Chapman, 1975). A different approach to studying social cognition was taken by researchers who examined the role of interpersonal context in task performance. For example, censure, both of a social and nonsocial nature, was manipulated, with the findings indicating that censure improves performance of people with schizophrenia on a variety of tasks (e.g., paired-associate learning; Atkinson & Robinson, 1961; Cavanaugh, Cohen, & Lang, 1960; Frieswyk, 1977; Van Dyke & Routh, 1973). The role of social context on task performance also has been investigated in terms of the presence of the experimenter (Gelburd & Anker, 1970), the role of peer or nonpeer group task performance (i.e., using the Asch conformity paradigm; Schooler & Spohn, 1960), and whether another person is observing or cooperating with the research participant (Schooler & Zahn, 1968). Findings from the studies generally indicate that people with schizophrenia are sensitive to changes in their social environment, suggesting that their social isolation is not a result of a lack of responsiveness to others (Schooler & Spohn, 1960; Schooler & Zahn, 1968).

One could argue that this important early research on social context and schizophrenia laid the groundwork for subsequent work in expressed emotion (EE). In particular, research on EE shifted the idea of social context from that of a nonpersonal stranger (i.e., an experimenter or confederate) to family members. Furthermore, the consequences of context no longer were evaluated in terms of task performance (e.g., discrimination learning) but in terms of symptomatology and relapse rate. In both paradigms, the emphasis of the social context and the person with schizophrenia's reaction to it were of primary importance. Interestingly, EE research itself has become more socially cognitive by exploring the attributions family members make about their ill relatives and how such attributions relate to a more benign or critical family environment (Barrowclough, Johnston, & Tarrier, 1994; Brewin, MacCarthy, Duda, & Vaughn, 1991; Hooley, 1987; Weisman, Lopez, Karno, & Jenkins, 1993; Weisman, Nuechterlein, Goldstein, & Snyder, 1998).

Implications of Social Cognition for Understanding and Treating Schizophrenia

Thus far, we have only hinted about the unique ways in which social cognition describes the disabilities related to schizophrenia and suggests interventions to remediate those disabilities. The remainder of the book specifies the benefits of the social cognitive paradigm in detail. The book is divided into three parts, in a manner akin to texts on related subjects. Part I reviews the body of research that supports our contention; namely, that social cognition is useful for understanding schizophrenia and its disabilities. Part II summarizes the treatments that have emerged from these models, and Part III caps the book with a summary of future directions suggested by a social cognitive paradigm.

Part I reviews the theories relevant to schizophrenia that emerged from a social cognitive perspective. Mainstream research conducted on "normal" populations has much to offer the student of schizophrenia. Hence, we asked social psychologist Leonard S. Newman to summarize the field of social cognition vis-à-vis schizophrenia. Newman makes some fine-grained distinctions in chapter 1, separating the literature into cognitive social psychology, social cognition of psychology, social cognition, and evolved social psychological mechanisms. These distinctions have implications for developing research on schizophrenia.

The next two chapters summarize research that describes the basic social cognitive deficits of schizophrenia. In chapter 2, Christoph Leonhard and Patrick W. Corrigan focus their discussion on the social perceptual deficits found in schizophrenia. The authors differentiate between studies that examined molecular deficits and studies that focused on attention to and encoding of molar stimuli. In chapter 3, David L. Penn, Dennis Combs, and Somaia Mohamed take the review of social cognitive deficits one step further by examining the relationship between discrete social cognitive deficits and limitations in interpersonal skills or social goal attainment.

British colleagues have significantly added to our understanding of social psychology and schizophrenia. Richard Bentall, from the University of Manchester, has developed an intriguing model of delusions based on social cognition; he describes this model in chapter 4. Noting that delusions are not necessarily distinct qualities from normal cognition, he outlines several cognitive elements that, when dysfunctional, may lead to delusions. In chapter 5, Rhiannon Corcoran reviews the theory of mind, a model that she and Christopher Frith developed from its basic social psychological roots. Their theory assumes that successful interpersonal negotiations rest on the knowledge that other people have minds and act according to their contents. Given that we are aware of other's minds, humans are constantly considering what others are thinking, intending, or believing. People with schizophrenia may lack this ability in that they are unable to predict a peer's actions based on ignorance of the other's mind. Corcoran thoroughly explores the significance of this absence of mind for the disabilities of schizophrenia.

Many of the approaches to social cognition presume that deficits in this area represent a primary neurodevelopmental dysfunction brought on by the disease of schizophrenia. We end Part I by providing an alternative view; that is, a discussion of environmental factors that influence or otherwise exacerbate cognitive deficits. In chapter 6, Patrick W. Corrigan and Kevin L. Holtzman consider the evidence that social cognitive deficits might represent the result of stereotype threat. Namely, people with schizophrenia may perform poorly on some measures of social cognition as a result of the impact of societal stigma. They admit that the theory needs to be supported by direct experimental data and outline a research program for examining its hypotheses.

Part II reviews the clinical applications that have developed out of the social cognitive models of schizophrenia. These practical implications outline a research program to further develop treatment and rehabilitation services related to social disabilities. In chapter 7, Peter Kinderman develops strategies that ameliorate attributional abnormalities. Using models of "normal" social psychological functioning, he reviews the data on causal attributions and then juxtaposes this literature against psychotherapy process research examining changes in causal attributions that evolve during therapy. Kinderman then considers implications of this relationship for treatment.

Several therapies have been developed specifically for social cognitive deficits related to schizophrenia. William D. Spaulding and Jeffrey S. Poland review the strengths of integrated psychological therapy (IPT), on which Spaulding has recently completed a thorough study. In chapter 8, they contrast aspects of IPT to cognitive enhancement therapy, a rehabilitation strategy developed by Gerald Hogarty and colleagues that has a strong focus on social cognition. Henry J. Jackson, Patrick D. McGorry, and Jane Edwards from Australia review their cognitive-oriented psychotherapy program in chapter 9. Their program meets the special needs of people early in the course of their psychosis and is based on the idea that intervention at the earliest opportunity offers the best chance for positive outcomes.

Chapter 10, by Morris D. Bell, combines perspectives on ego psychology and reality testing to address the question of social cognition and schizophrenia. Bell asks in his chapter whether consideration of object relations has a place in a book on social cognition. His chapter answers the question by asserting that the assessment of object relations supplies the student of social cognition with a method that captures the essential features of human relatedness and serves a complementary role in the exploration and exposition of that relatedness.

Part III ends the book with a brief summary of what social cognitive models have accomplished thus far. In chapter 11, David L. Penn and Patrick W. Corrigan review the salient issues that have emerged from both theoretical and practical research to date. The authors outline a future research agenda to guide studies that will extend the ideas outlined in this book. We are confident that research programs that are based on the paradigm outlined in this text will significantly advance knowledge about the disabilities of schizophrenia and help develop interventions to effectively remediate them.

References

Aberg-Wistedt, A., Cressell, T., Lidberg, Y., Liljenberg, B., & Osby, U. (1995). Two-year outcome of team-based intensive case management for patients with schizophrenia. *Psychiatric Services, 46,* 1263–1266.

Abramson, L. Y. (1988). *Social cognition and clinical psychology.* New York: Guilford Press.

Addington, J., & Addington, D. (1999). Neurocognitive and social functioning in schizophrenia. *Schizophrenia Bulletin, 25,* 173–182.

Andreasen, N. C. (1979a). Thought, language, and communication disorders. I. Clinical assessment, definition of terms, and evaluation of their reliability. *Archives of General Psychiatry, 36,* 1315–1321.

Andreasen, N. C. (1979b). Thought, language, and communication disorders. II. Diagnostic significance. *Archives of General Psychiatry, 36,* 1325–1330.

Andreasen, N. C. (1983). *The Scale for the Assessment of Negative Symptoms (SANS).* Iowa City: University of Iowa.

Andreasen, N. C. (1984). *The Scale for the Assessment of Positive Symptoms (SAPS).* Iowa City: University of Iowa.

Andreasen, N. C., Paradiso, S., & O'Leary, D. (1998). Cognitive dysmetria as an integrative theory of schizophrenia: A dysfunction in cortical-subcortical-cerebellar circuitry. *Schizophrenia Bulletin, 24,* 203–218.

Andreasen, N. C., Roy, M. A., & Flaum, M. (1995). Positive and negative symptoms. In S. R. Hirsch & D. R. Weinberger (Eds.), *Schizophrenia* (pp. 28–45). Oxford, England: Blackwell Science.

Atkinson, R. L., & Robinson, N. M. (1961). Paired-associate learning by schizophrenic and normal subjects under conditions of personal and impersonal reward and punishment. *Journal of Abnormal Psychology, 62*, 322–326.

Atthowe, J. M., & Krasner, L. (1968). Preliminary report on the application of contingent reinforcement procedures (token economy) on a "chronic" psychiatric ward. *Journal of Abnormal Psychology, 73*, 37–43.

Ayllon, T., & Azrin, N. H. (1968). *The token economy.* New York: Appleton-Century-Crofts.

Baker, R., & Hall, J. N. (1988). REHAB: A new assessment instrument for chronic psychiatric patients. *Schizophrenia Bulletin, 14*, 97–111.

Banzett, L. K., Liberman, R. P., Moore, J. W., & Marshall, B. D. (1984). Long-term follow-up of the effects of behavior therapy. *Hospital and Community Psychiatry, 35*, 277–279.

Barker, S., Barron, N., McFarland, B. H., & Bigelow, D. A. (1994a). A community ability scale for chronically mentally ill consumers. I. Reliability and validity. *Community Mental Health Journal, 30*, 363–383.

Barker, S., Barron, N., McFarland, B. H., & Bigelow, D. A. (1994b). A community ability scale for chronically mentally ill consumers. II. Applications. *Community Mental Health Journal, 30*, 459–472.

Barrowclough, C., Johnston, M., & Tarrier, N. (1994). Attributions, expressed emotion, and patient relapse: An attributional model of relatives' response to schizophrenic illness. *Behavior Therapy, 25*, 67–88.

Becker, D. R., & Drake, R. E. (1994). Individual placement and support: A community mental health center approach to vocational rehabilitation. *Community Mental Health Journal, 30*, 193–206.

Bellack, A. S., Sayers, M., Mueser, K. T., & Bennett, M. (1994). Evaluation of social problem solving in schizophrenia. *Journal of Abnormal Psychology, 103*, 371–378.

Bellack, A. S., Turner, S. M., Hersen, M., & Luber, R. F. (1984). An examination of the efficacy of social skills training for chronic schizophrenic patients. *Hospital and Community Psychiatry, 35*, 1023–1028.

Benton, M. K., & Schroeder, H. E. (1990). Social skills training with schizophrenics: A meta-analytic evaluation. *Journal of Consulting and Clinical Psychology, 58*, 741–747.

Berkowitz, L., & Devine, P. G. (1995). Has social psychology always been cognitive? What is cognitive anyway? *Personality and Social Psychology Bulletin, 21*, 696–703.

Bigelow, D. A., McFarland, B. H., & Olson, M. M. (1991). Quality of life of community mental health program clients: Validating a measure. *Community Mental Health Journal, 27*, 43–55.

Bilder, R. M., Lipschutz-Broch, L., Reiter, G., & Geisler, S. H., Mayerhoff, D. I., & Lieberman, J. A. (1992). Intellectual deficits in first-episode schizophrenia: Evidence for progressive deterioration. *Schizophrenia Bulletin, 18*, 437–448.

Birchwood, M., Smith, J., Cochrane, R., Wetton, S., & Copestake, S. (1990). The Social Functioning Scale: The development and validation of a new scale of social adjustment for use in family intervention programmes with schizophrenic patients. *British Journal of Psychiatry, 157,* 853–859.

Bleuler, E. (1950). *Dementia praecox of the group of schizophrenias.* (J. Zinkin, Trans.). New York: International Universities Press. (Original work published 1911).

Bond, G. R., Dietzen, L. L., McGrew, J. H., & Miller, J. D. (1995). Accelerating entry into supported employment for persons with severe psychiatric disabilities. *Rehabilitation Psychology, 40,* 75–94.

Bond, G. R., Drake, R. E., Mueser, K. T., & Becker, D. R. (1997). An update on supported employment for people with severe mental illness: A review. *Psychiatric Services, 48,* 335–346.

Bond, G. R., Miller, L. D., Krumwied, R. D., & Ward, R. S. (1988). Assertive case management in three CMHC's: A controlled study. *Hospital and Community Psychiatry, 39,* 411–418.

Bond, G. R., Witheridge, T. F., Dincin, J., Wasmer, D., Webb, J., & De Graaf-Kaser, R. (1990). Assertive community treatment for frequent users of psychiatric hospitals in a large city: A controlled study. *American Journal of Community Psychology, 18,* 865–891.

Bowen, L., Wallace, C. J., Glynn, S. M., Nuechterlein, K. H., Lutzker, J. R., & Kuehnel, T. G. (1994). Schizophrenic individuals' cognitive functioning and performance in interpersonal interactions and skills training procedures. *Journal of Psychiatric Research, 28,* 289–301.

Breier, A., Schreiber, J., Dyer, J., & Pickar, D. (1991). National Institute of Mental Health longitudinal study of chronic schizophrenia: Prognosis and predictors of outcome. *Archives of General Psychiatry, 48,* 239–246.

Brewin, C. R., MacCarthy, B., Duda, K., & Vaughn, C. E. (1991). Attribution and expressed emotion in the relatives of patients with schizophrenia. *Journal of Abnormal Psychology, 100,* 546–554.

Brewin, C. R., & Wing, J. K. (1993). The MRC Needs for Care Assessment: Progress and controversies. *Psychological Medicine, 22,* 837–841.

Brewin, C. R., Wing, J. K., Mangen, S. P., Brugha, T. S., & MacCarthy, B. (1987). Principles and practice of measuring needs in the long-term mentally ill: The MRC Needs for Care Assessment. *Psychological Medicine, 17,* 971–981.

Brothers, L. (1990a). The neural basis of primate social communication. *Motivation and Emotion, 14,* 81–91.

Brothers, L. (1990b). The social brain: A project for integrating primate behavior and neurophysiology in a new domain. *Concepts in Neuroscience, 1,* 27–61.

Buchanan, R. W., Strauss, M. E., Kirkpatrick, B., Holstein, C., Breier, A., & Carpenter, W. T. (1994). Neuropsychological impairments in deficit versus nondeficit forms of schizophrenia. *Archives of General Psychiatry, 51*, 804–811.

Bush, C. T., Langford, M. W., Rosen, P., & Gott, W. (1990). Operation outreach: Intensive case management for severely psychiatrically disabled adults. *Hospital and Community Psychiatry, 41*, 647–649.

Buss, A., & Lang, P. (1965). Psychological deficit in schizophrenia: Affect reinforcement and concept attainment. *Journal of Abnormal Psychology, 70*, 2–24.

Cavanaugh, D. K., Cohen, W., & Lang, P. J. (1960). The effect of "social censure" and "social approve" on psychomotor performance of schizophrenics. *Journal of Abnormal and Social Psychology, 60*, 213–218.

Chandler, D., Meisel, J., McGowen, M., Mintz, J., & Madison, K. (1996). Client outcomes in two model capitated integrated service agencies. *Psychiatric Services, 47*, 175–180.

Chapman, L. J., & Chapman, J. P. (1975). Schizophrenic reasoning about affect-laden material. *Archives of General Psychiatry, 32*, 1233–1236.

Cohen, J. D., & Servan-Schreiber, D. (1992). Context, cortex, and dopamine: A connectionist approach to behavior and biology in schizophrenia. *Psychological Review, 99*, 45–77.

Cohen, J. D., Barch, D. M., Carter, C., & Servan-Schreiber, D. (1999). Context-processing deficits in schizophrenia: Converging evidence from three theoretically motivated cognitive tasks. *Journal of Abnormal Psychology, 108*, 120–133.

Cohler, B. J., & Ferrono, C. L. (1987). Schizophrenia and the adult life-course. In N. E. Miller & G. D. Cohen (Eds.), *Schizophrenia and aging: Schizophrenia, paranoia, and schizophreniform disorders in later life* (pp. 189–199). New York: Guilford Press.

Constans, J., Penn, D. L., Ihnen, G., & Hope, D. A. (1999). Interpretation biases in social anxiety. *Behaviour Research and Therapy. 37*, 643–651.

Corrigan, P. W. (1989). Rehabilitation research methods for schizophrenia. *Schizophrenia Research, 2*, 425–437.

Corrigan, P. W. (1991a). Social skills training in adult psychiatric populations: A meta-analysis. *Journal of Behavior Therapy and Experimental Psychiatry, 22*, 203–210.

Corrigan, P. W. (1991b). Strategies that overcome barriers to token economies in community programs for severe mentally ill adults. *Community Mental Health Journal, 27*, 17–30.

Corrigan, P. W. (1995). Use of a token economy with seriously mentally ill patients: Criticisms and misconceptions. *Psychiatric Services, 46*, 1258–1263.

Corrigan, P. W. (1996). Models of "normal" cognitive functioning. In P. W. Corrigan & S. C. Yudofsky (Eds.), *Cognitive rehabilitation for neu-*

ropsychiatric disorders (pp. 3–51). Washington, DC: American Psychiatric Press.

Corrigan, P. W., Buican, B., & McCracken, S. (1995). The Needs and Resources Assessment Interview for severely mentally ill adults. *Psychiatric Services, 46,* 504–505.

Corrigan, P. W., & Green, M. F. (1993). Schizophrenic patients' sensitivity to social cues: The role of abstraction. *American Journal of Psychiatry, 150,* 589–594.

Corrigan, P. W., & Holmes, E. P. (1994). Patient identification of "Street Skills" for a psychosocial training module. *Hospital and Community Psychiatry, 45,* 273–276.

Corrigan, P. W., & Penn, D. L. (1998). *Stigma-busting and stereotype: Lessons from social psychology on discrediting psychiatric stigma.* Manuscript submitted for publication.

Corrigan, P. W., & Stephenson, J. A. (1994). Information processing and clinical psychology. In V. S. Ramachandran (Ed.), *Encyclopedia of human behavior* (Vol. 2, pp. 645–654). Orlando, FL: Academic Press.

Corrigan, P. W., & Toomey, R. (1995). Interpersonal problem solving and information processing in schizophrenia. *Schizophrenia Bulletin, 21,* 395–404.

Corrigan, P. W., Wallace, C. J., Schade, M. L., & Green, M. F. (1994). Learning medication self-management skills in schizophrenia: Relationships with cognitive deficits and psychiatric symptoms. *Behavior Therapy, 25,* 5–15.

Cosmides, L. (1989). The logic of social exchange: Has natural selection shaped how humans reason? Studies with the Wason selection task. *Cognition, 31,* 187–276.

Cosmides, L., & Tooby, J. (1989). Evolutionary psychology and the generation of culture, Part II. Case study: A computational theory of social exchange. *Ethology and Sociobiology, 10,* 51–97.

Cosmides, L., & Tooby, J. (1994). Beyond intuition and instinct blindness: Toward an evolutionarily rigorous cognitive science. *Cognition, 50,* 41–77.

Cromwell, R. L. (1984). Preemptive thinking and schizophrenia research. In W. D. Spaulding & J. K. Cole (Eds.), *Theories of schizophrenia and psychosis* (pp. 1–46). Lincoln: University of Nebraska Press.

Cromwell, R. L., & Spaulding, W. D. (1978). How schizophrenics handle information. In W. Fann, I. Karacan, & A. D. Pokorny (Eds.), *The phenomenology and treatment of schizophrenia* (pp. 127–162). New York: Spectrum.

Curtis, J. L., Millman, E. J., Struening, E., & D'Ercole, A. (1992). Effect of case management on rehospitalization and utilization of ambulatory care services. *Hospital and Community Psychiatry, 43,* 895–899.

Danley, K. S., Rogers, E. S., MacDonald-Wilson, K., & Anthony, W. A. (1994). Supported employment for adults with psychiatric disability: Results of an innovative demonstration project. *Rehabilitation Psychology, 39*, 269–276.

Danley, K. S., Rogers, E. S., & Nevas, D. B. (1989). A psychiatric rehabilitation approach to vocational rehabilitation. In M. D. Farkas & W. A. Anthony (Eds.), *Psychiatric rehabilitation programs: Putting theory into practice. The Johns Hopkins series in contemporary medicine and public health* (pp. 81–131). Baltimore, MD: Johns Hopkins University Press.

Dickerson, F. B. (1997). Assessing clinical outcomes: The community functioning of persons with serious mental illness. *Psychiatric Services, 48*, 897–902.

Dickerson, R. B., Ringel, N. B., & Boronow, J. J. (1991). Neuropsychological deficits in chronic schizophrenics: Relationship with symptoms and behavior. *Journal of Nervous and Mental Disease, 179*, 744–749.

Dilk, M. N., & Bond, G. R. (1996). Meta-analytic evaluation of skills training research for persons with severe mental illness. *Journal of Consulting and Clinical Psychology, 64*, 1337–1346.

Dobson, K. S., & Kendall, P. C. (Eds.). (1993). *Psychopathology and cognition.* San Diego, CA: Academic Press.

Dobson, D. J. G., McDougall, G., Busheikin, J., & Aldous, J. (1995). Effects of social skills training and social milieu treatment on symptoms of schizophrenia. *Hospital and Community Psychiatry, 46*, 376–380.

Donahoe, C. P., Carter, M. J., Bloem, W. D., Hirsch, G. L., Laasi, N., & Wallace, C. J. (1990). Assessment of interpersonal problem-solving skills. *Psychiatry, 53*, 329–339.

Drake, R. E., McHugo, G. J., Becker, D. R., Anthony, W. A., & Clark, R. E. (1996). The New Hampshire study of supported employment for people with severe mental illness: Vocational outcomes. *Journal of Consulting and Clinical Psychology, 64*, 390–398.

Eisen, S. V., Wilcox, M., Leff, H. S., Schaefer, E., Culhane, M. A. (1999). Assessing behavioral health outcomes in outpatient programs: Reliability and validity of the BASIS-32. *The Journal of Behavioral Health Services and Research, 26*, 5–17.

Ellsworth, R. B., Foster, L., Childers, B., Arthur, G., & Kroeker, D. (1968). Hospital and community adjustment as perceived by psychiatric patients, their families, and staff. *Journal of Consulting and Clinical Psychology, 32*, 1–41.

Endicott, J., Nee, J., Harrison, W., & Blumenthal, R. (1993). Quality of life enjoyment and satisfaction questionnaire: A new measure. *Psychopharmacology Bulletin, 29*, 321–326.

Essock, S. M., & Kontos, N. (1995). Implementing assertive community treatment teams. *Psychiatric Services, 46*, 679–683.

Evenson, R. C., & Boyd, M. A. (1993). The St. Louis Inventory of Community Living Skills. *Psychosocial Rehabilitation Journal, 17,* 93–99.

Fabian, E. S. (1992). Supported employment and the quality of life: Does a job make a difference? *Rehabilitation Counseling Bulletin, 36,* 84–97.

Falloon, I. R. H., Boyd, J. L., McGill, C. W., Razani, J., Moss, H. B., & Gilderman, A. M. (1982). Family management in the prevention of exacerbations of schizophrenia: A controlled study. *New England Journal of Medicine, 306,* 1437–1440.

Falloon, I. R. H., Boyd, J. L., McGill, C. W., Williamson, M., Razani, J., Moss, H. B., Gilderman, A. M., & Simpson, G. M. (1985). Family management in the prevention of morbidity of schizophrenia: Clinical outcome of a two-year longitudinal study. *Archives of General Psychiatry, 42,* 887–896.

Farah, M. J. (1992). Is an object an object? Cognitive and neuropsychological investigations of domain specificity in visual object recognition. *Current Directions in Psychological Science, 1,* 164–169.

Fiske, S. T. (1995). Social cognition. In A. Tesser (Ed.), *Advanced social psychology* (pp. 149–193). New York: McGraw-Hill.

Fiske, S. T., & Taylor, S. E. (1991). *Social cognition* (2nd ed.). New York: McGraw-Hill.

Franklin, J. L., Solovitz, B., Mason, M., Clemons, J. R., & Miller, G. E. (1987). An evaluation of case management. *American Journal of Public Health, 77,* 674–678.

Frieswyk, S. H. (1977). Schizophrenic discrimination learning as a function of aversive social and physical reinforcement. *Journal of Abnormal Psychology, 86,* 47–53.

Frith, C. (1996). Neuropsychology of schizophrenia: What are the implications of intellectual and experiential abnormalities for the neurobiology of schizophrenia? In E. C. Johnstone (Ed.), *Biological psychiatry. British Medical Journal* (pp. 618–626). London, England: Royal Society of Medicine Press.

Galanter, M. (1988). Zealous self-help groups as adjuncts to psychiatric treatment: A study of Recovery, Inc. *American Journal of Psychiatry, 145,* 1248–1253.

Gelburd, A., & Anker, J. M. (1970). Humans as reinforcing stimuli in schizophrenics' performance. *Journal of Abnormal Psychology, 75,* 195–198.

Gervey, R., & Bedell, J. R. (1994). Supported employment. In J. R. Bedell (Ed.), *Psychological assessment and treatment of persons with severe mental disorders* (pp. 151–175). Washington, DC: Taylor & Francis.

Gilbert, D. T. (1995). Attribution and interpersonal perception. In A. Tesser (Ed.), *Advanced social psychology* (pp. 99–147). New York: McGraw-Hill.

Gillis, J. S. (1969). Schizophrenic thinking in a probabilistic situation. *Psychological Record, 19,* 211–224.

Glick, I., Clarkin, J., Spencer, J., Haas, G., Lewis, A., Peyser, J., DeMane, N., Good-Ellis, M., Harris, E., & Lestelle, V. (1985). A controlled evaluation of inpatient family intervention, I: Preliminary results of a 6-month follow-up. *Archives of General Psychiatry, 42,* 882–886.

Glick, I. D., Spencer, J. H., Clarkin, J. F., Haas, G. L., Lewis, A. B., Peyser, J., DeMane, N., Good-Ellis, M., Harris, E., & Lestelle, V. (1990). A randomized clinical trial of inpatient family intervention. IV. Follow-up results for subjects with schizophrenia. *Schizophrenia Research, 3,* 187–200.

Godley, S. H., Hoewing-Roberson, R., & Godley, M. D. (1994). *Final MISA report: Technical report.* Bloomington, IL: Chestnut Health System.

Goldman, R. S., Axelrod, B. N., Tandon, R., Ribeiro, S. C. M., Craig, K., & Berent, S. (1993). Neuropsychological prediction of treatment efficacy and one-year outcome in schizophrenia. *Psychopathology, 126,* 122–126.

Goldsmith, J. B., & McFall, R. M. (1975). Development and evaluation of an interpersonal skill-training program for psychiatric inpatients. *Journal of Abnormal Psychology, 84,* 51–58.

Goldstein, M., Rodnick, E., Evans, J., May, P., & Steinberg, M. (1978). Drug and family therapy in the aftercare of acute schizophrenia. *Archives of General Psychiatry, 35,* 1169–1177.

Good-Ellis, M. A., Fine, S. B., Spencer, J. H., & DiVittis, A. (1987). Developing a Role Activity Performance Scale. *American Journal of Occupational Therapy, 41,* 232–241.

Goodman, S. H., Sewell, D. R., Cooley, E. L., & Leavitt, N. (1993). Assessing levels of adaptive functioning: The Role Functioning Scale. *Community Mental Health Journal, 29,* 119–131.

Green, M. F. (1996). What are the functional consequences of neurocognitive deficits in schizophrenia? *American Journal of Psychiatry, 153,* 321–330.

Green, M. F. (1998). *Schizophrenia from a neurocognitive perspective: Probing the impenetrable darkness.* Boston: Allyn & Bacon.

Hampton, B., Koor, W., Bond, G., Mayes, J., & Havis, P. (1992). *Integration service system approach to avert homelessness: CSP homeless prevention project for HMI Adults.* Unpublished manuscript, State of Illinois Department of Mental Health and Developmental Disabilities, Chicago.

Harrow, M., Westermeyer, J. F., Lanin-Kettering, I., Grinker, R. R., Catriona, M., & Carone, B. J. (1987). Disordered cognition and outcome in schizophrenia. In R. R. Grinker & M. Harrow (Eds.), *Clinical research in schizophrenia: A multidimensional approach* (pp. 348–372). Springfield, IL: Charles C Thomas.

Harvey, P. D., Davidson, M., Mueser, K. T., Parrella, M., White, L., & Powchik, P. (1997). Social-adaptive functioning evaluation (SAFE): A rating scale for geriatric psychiatric patients. *Schizophrenia Bulletin, 23,* 131–139.

Hayes, R. L., Halford, W. K., & Varghese, F. T. (1995). Social skills training with chronic schizophrenic patients: Effects on negative symptoms and community functioning. *Behavior Therapy, 26,* 433–449.

Heinrichs, D. W., Hanlon, T. E., & Carpenter, W. T. (1984). The Quality of Life Scale: An instrument for rating the schizophrenic deficit syndrome. *Schizophrenia Bulletin, 10,* 388–398.

Hogarty, G. E., Anderson, C. M., Reiss, D. J., Kornblith, S. J., Greenwald, D. P., Javna, C. D., & Madonia, M. J. (1986). Family psychoeducation, social skills training, and maintenance chemotherapy in the aftercare of schizophrenia. I. One-year effects of a controlled study on relapse and expressed emotion. *Archives of General Psychiatry, 43,* 633–642.

Holmes, E. P., Corrigan, P. W., Knight, S., & Flaxman, J. (1995). Development of a sleep management program for consumers with severe mental illness. *Psychosocial Rehabilitation Journal, 19,* 9–15.

Hooley, J. (1987). The nature and origins of expressed emotion. In K. Hahlweg & M. Goldstein (Eds.), *Understanding major mental disorder: The contribution of family interaction research* (pp. 176–194). New York: Family Process.

Hoult, J., Reynolds, I., Charbonneau-Powis, M., Weekes, P., & Briggs, J. (1983). Psychiatric hospital versus community treatment: The results of a randomized trial. *Australian and New Zealand Journal of Psychiatry, 17,* 160–167.

Hoyle, R. H., Nietzel, M. T., Guthrie, P. R., Baker-Prewitt, J. L., & Heine, R. (1992). The Disability Rating Form: A brief schedule for rating disability associated with severe mental illness. *Psychosocial Rehabilitation Journal, 16,* 77–94.

Humphreys, K., & Rappaport, J. (1994). Researching self-help/mutual aid groups and organizations: Many roads, one journey. *Applied and Preventive Psychology, 3,* 217–231.

Huxley, P. J., & Warner, R. (1992). Case management, quality of life, and satisfaction with services of long-term psychiatric patients. *Hospital and Community Psychiatry, 43,* 799–802.

Jaeger, J., & Douglas, E. (1992). Adjunctive neuropsychological remediation in psychiatric rehabilitation: Program description and preliminary data. *Schizophrenia Research, 4,* 304–305.

Jerrell, J., & Hu, T.-W. (1989). Cost-effectiveness of intensive clinical and case management compared with an existing system of care. *Inquiry, 26,* 224–234.

Johnstone, E. C., Macmillan, J. F., Frith, C. D., Benn, D. K., & Crow, T. J. (1990). Further investigation of the predictors of outcome following first schizophrenic episodes. *British Journal of Psychiatry, 157,* 182–189.

Kay, S. R., Fiszbein, A., & Opler, L. A. (1987). The Positive and Negative Syndrome Scale (PANSS) for schizophrenia. *Schizophrenia Bulletin, 13,* 261–276.

Keefe, R. S., Mohs, R. C., Losonczy, M. F., & Davidson, M. (1987). Characteristics of very poor outcome schizophrenia. *American Journal of Psychiatry, 144,* 889–895.

Kennedy, M. (1990). *Psychiatric hospitalizations of GROWers.* Paper presented at the Second Biennial Conference on Community Research and Action, East Lansing, MI.

Kern, R. S., & Green, M. F. (1998). Cognitive remediation in schizophrenia. In K. T. Mueser & N. Tarrier (Eds.), *Handbook of social functioning in schizophrenia* (pp. 342–354). Boston: Allyn & Bacon.

Kern, R. S., Green, M. F., & Satz, P. (1992). Neuropsychological predictors of skills training for chronic psychiatric patients. *Journal of Psychiatric Research, 43,* 223–230.

Kirszner, M. L., McKay, C. D., & Tippett, M. L. (1991). *Homelessness and mental health: Replication and adaptation of the PACT model in Delaware.* Proceedings from the Second Annual Conference on State Mental Health Agency Services Research. Alexandria, VA: National Association of State Mental Health Program Directors Research Institute.

Knight, R. A., & Silverstein, S. M. (1998). The role of cognitive psychology in guiding research on cognitive deficits in schizophrenia. In M. Lenzenweger & R. H. Dworkin (Eds.), *Origins and development of schizophrenia: Advances in experimental psychopathology* (pp. 247–295). Washington, DC: American Psychological Association.

Kraepelin, E. (1919). *Dementia praecox and paraphrenia.* Edinburgh, Scotland: E. S. Livingston.

Leff, J. P., Kuipers, L., Berkowitz, R., Eberlein-Fries, R., & Sturgeon, D. (1982). A controlled trial of intervention with families of schizophrenic patients. *British Journal of Psychiatry, 141,* 121–134.

Leff, J., Kuipers, L., Berkowitz, R., & Sturgeon, D. (1985). A controlled trial of suicidal intervention in the families of schizophrenic patients: Two year follow up. *British Journal of Psychiatry, 146,* 594–600.

Leff, J. P., Berkowitz, R., Shavit, A., Strachan, A., Glass, I., & Vaughn, C. E. (1990). A trial of family therapy v. relatives' groups for schizophrenia: Two year follow up. *British Journal of Psychiatry, 157,* 571–577.

Lehman, A. F. (1983). The effects of psychiatric symptoms on quality of life assessments among the chronic mentally ill. *Evaluation and Program Planning, 6,* 143–151.

Lehman, A. F. (1988). A quality of life interview for the chronically mentally ill. *Evaluation and Program Planning, 11,* 51–62.

Lehman, A. F., Dixon, L. B., Kernan, E., & Desforge, B. (1997). A randomized trial of assertive community treatment for homeless persons with severe mental illness. *Archives of General Psychiatry, 54,* 1038–1043.

Lehman, A. F., Herron, J. D., Schwartz, R. P., & Myers, C. P. (1993). Rehabilitation for adults with severe mental illness and substance use disorders: A clinical trial. *Journal of Nervous and Mental Disease, 181,* 86–90.

Liberman, R. P., Mueser, K. T., & Wallace, C. J. (1986). Social skills training for schizophrenic individuals at risk of relapse. *American Journal of Psychiatry, 143,* 523–526.

Liberman, R. P., Wallace, C. J., Blackwell, G., Kopelowicz, A., Vaccaro, J. V., & Mintz, J. (1998). Skills training versus psychosocial occupational therapy for persons with persistent schizophrenia. *American Journal of Psychiatry, 155,* 1087–1091.

Lukoff, D., Liberman, R. P., & Nuechterlein, K. H. (1986). Manual for the expanded Brief Psychiatric Rating Scale (BPRS). *Schizophrenia Bulletin, 12,* 594–602.

Lysaker, P., Bell, M., & Beam-Goulet, J. (1995). Wisconsin card sorting test and work performance in schizophrenia. *Schizophrenia Research, 56,* 45–51.

Macias, C., Kinney, R., Farley, O. W., Jackson, R., & Vos, B. (1994). The role of case management within a community support system: Partnership with psychosocial rehabilitation. *Community Mental Health Journal, 30,* 323–339.

MacPherson, R., Jerrom, B., & Hughes, A. (1996). Relationship between insight, educational background and cognition in schizophrenia. *British Journal of Psychiatry, 168,* 718–722.

Maher, B. A. (1991). Language and schizophrenia. In S. R. Steinhauer, J. H. Gruzelier, & J. Zubin (Eds.), *Handbook of schizophrenia: Neuropsychology, psychophysiology and information processing* (Vol. 5, pp. 437–464). Amsterdam: Elsevier Science.

Malm, U., May, P. R. A., & Dencker, S. J. (1981). Evaluation of the quality of life of the schizophrenic outpatient: A checklist. *Schizophrenia Bulletin, 9,* 477–487.

Marks, I. M., Connolly, J., Muijen, M., Audini, B., McNamee, G., & Lawrence, R. (1994). Home-based versus hospital-based care for people with serious mental illness. *British Journal of Psychiatry, 165,* 179–194.

Marshall, M., Hogg, L. I., Gath, D. H., & Lockwood, A. (1995). The Cardinal Needs Schedule: A modified version of the MRC Needs for Care Assessment Schedule. *Psychological Medicine, 25,* 603–617.

Maton, K. I. (1988). Social support, organizational characteristics, psychological well-being, and group appraisal in three self-help group populations. *American Journal of Community Psychology, 16,* 53–77.

McFarlane, W. R., Lukens, E., Link, B., Dushay, R., Deakins, S., Newmark, M., Dunne, E. J., Horen, B., & Toran, J. (1995). Multiple family groups and psychoeducation in the treatment of schizophrenia. *Archives of General Psychiatry, 52,* 679–687.

Merson, S., Tyrer, P., Onyett, S., Lack, S., Birkett, P., Lynch, S., & Johnson, T. (1992). Early intervention in psychiatric emergencies: A controlled clinical trial. *Lancet, 339,* 1311–1314.

Mingyuan, Z., Hequin, Y., Chengde, Y., Jianlin, Y., Qingfeng, Y., Peijun, C., Lianfang, G., Jizhong, Y., Guangya, Q., Zhen, W., Jianhua, C., Minghua, S., Junshan, H., Longlin, W., Yi, Z., Buoying, Z., Orley, G., & Gittelman, M. (1993). Effectiveness of psychoeducation of relatives of schizophrenic patients: A prospective cohort study in five cities of China. *International Journal of Mental Health, 22,* 47–59.

Modrcin, M., Rapp, C. A., & Poertner, J. (1988). The evaluation of case management services with the chronically mentally ill. *Evaluation and Program Planning, 11,* 307–314.

Morse, G. A., Calsyn, R. J., Allen, G., Tempelhoff, B., & Smith, R. (1992). Experimental comparison of the effects of three treatment programs for homeless mentally ill people. *Hospital and Community Psychiatry, 43,* 1005–1010.

Morse, G. A., Calsyn, R. J., Klinkenberg, W. D., Trusty, M. L., Gerber, F., Smith, R., Tempelhoff, B., & Ahmad, L. (1997). An experimental comparison of three types of case management for homeless mentally ill persons. *Psychiatric Services, 48,* 497–503.

Mowbray, C. T., McCrohan, N. M., & Bybee, D. (1995). Integrating vocational services into case management: Implementation analysis of Project WINS. *Journal of Vocational Rehabilitation, 5,* 89–102.

Mueser, K. T., Bellack, A. S., Douglas, M. S., & Wade, J. H. (1991). Prediction of social skill acquisition in schizophrenic and major affective disorder patients from memory and symptomatology. *Psychiatry Research, 37,* 281–296.

Mueser, K. T., Bond, G. R., Drake, R. E., & Resnick, S. G. (1998). Models of community care for severe mental illness: A review of research on case management. *Schizophrenia Bulletin, 24,* 37–74.

Mueser, K. T., & Glynn, S. M. (1995). *Behavioral family therapy for psychiatric disorders.* Needham Heights, MA: Allyn & Bacon.

Muijen, M., Cooney, M., Strathdee, G., Bell, R., & Hudson, A. (1994). Community psychiatric nurse teams: Intensive support versus generic care. *British Journal of Psychiatry, 165,* 211–217.

Mulder, R. (1982). *Evaluation of the Harbinger Program.* Unpublished manuscript, Grand Rapids, MI.

Munroe-Blum, H., Collins, E., McCleary, L., & Nuttall, S. (1996). The social dysfunction index (SDI) for patients with schizophrenia and related disorders. *Schizophrenia Research, 20,* 211–219.

Neale, J. M., Held, J. M., & Cromwell, R. L. (1969). Size estimation in schizophrenics: A review and reanalysis. *Psychological Bulletin, 71,* 210–221.

Nichols, M. (1989). *Demonstration study of a supported employment program for persons with severe mental illness: Benefits, costs, and outcomes.* Unpublished master's thesis, Indiana University–Purdue University, Indianapolis.

Oliver, J. M., & Searight, H. R. (1988). The Community Competence Scale: A preliminary short form for residential placement of deinstitutionalized psychiatric patients. *Adult Foster Care Journal, 2,* 176–188.

Ostrom, T. M. (1984). The sovereignty of social cognition. In R. S. Wyer & T. K. Skrull (Eds.), *Handbook of social cognition* (Vol. 1, pp. 1–37). Hillside, NJ: Erlbaum.

Paul, G. L., & Lentz, R. J. (1977). *Psychosocial treatment of chronic mental patients: Milieu versus social-learning programs.* Cambridge, MA: Harvard University Press.

Penn, D. L., Corrigan, P. W., Bentall, R. P., Racenstein, J. M., & Newman, L. S. (1997). Social cognition in schizophrenia. *Psychological Bulletin, 121,* 114–132.

Penn, D. L., & Mueser, K. T. (1996). Research update on the psychosocial treatment of schizophrenia. *American Journal of Psychiatry, 153,* 607–617.

Penn, D. L., Mueser, K. T., Spaulding, W. D., Hope, D. A., & Reed, D. (1995). Information processing and social competence in chronic schizophrenia. *Schizophrenia Bulletin, 21,* 269–281.

Penn, D. L., Spaulding, W. D., Reed, D., & Sullivan, M. (1996). The relationship of social cognition toward behavior in chronic schizophrenia. *Schizophrenia Research, 20,* 327–335.

Penn, D. L., van der Does, A. J. W., Spaulding, W. D., Garbin, C. P., Linszen, D., & Dingemans, P. (1993). Information processing and social cognitive problem solving in schizophrenia: Assessment of interrelationships and changes over time. *Journal of Nervous and Mental Disease, 181,* 13–20.

Phelan, M., Slade, M., Thornicroft, G., Dunn, G., Holloway, F., Wykes, T., Strathdee, G., Loftus, L., McCrone, P., & Hayward, P. (1995). The Camberwell Assessment of Need: The validity and reliability of an instrument to assess the needs of people with severe mental illness. *British Journal of Psychiatry, 167,* 589–595.

Pinkney, A. A., Gerber, G. J., & Lafave, H. G. (1991). Quality of life after psychiatric rehabilitation: The client's perspective. *Acta Psychiatrica Scandinavica, 83,* 86–91.

Pogue-Geile, M. F., & Harrow, M. (1984). Negative and positive symptoms in schizophrenia and depression: A follow-up. *Schizophrenia Bulletin, 10,* 371–387.

Quinlivan, R., Hough, R., Crowell, A., Beach, C., Hofstetter, R., & Kenworthy, K. (1995). Service utilization and costs of care for severely mentally ill clients in an intensive case management program. *Psychiatric Services, 46,* 365–371.

Randolph, E. T., Eth, S., Glynn, S., Psaz, G. G., Leong, G. B., Shaner, A. L., Strachan, A., van Vort, W., Escobar, J. L., & Liberman, R. P. (1994). Behavioral family management in schizophrenia: Outcome from a clinic-based intervention. *British Journal of Psychiatry, 164,* 501–506.

Rosen, A., Hadzi-Pavlovic, D., & Parker, G. (1989). The Life Skills Profile: A measure assessing function and disability in schizophrenia. *Schizophrenia Bulletin, 15,* 325–337.

Rosenheck, R., Neale, M., & Frisman, M. (1994). Issues in estimating the cost of innovative mental health programs. *Psychiatric Quarterly, 66,* 1–23.

Sayers, M. D., Bellack, A. S., Wade, J. H., Bennett, M. E., & Fong, P. (1995). An empirical method for assessing social problem solving in schizophrenia. *Behavior Modification, 19,* 267–289.

Schooler, N., Hogarty, G., & Weissman, M. M. (1979). Social Adjustment Scale II (SAS-II). In W. A. Hargreaves, C. C. Attkisson, & J. E. Sorenson (Eds.), *Resource materials for community mental health program evaluators* (No. ADM 79-328, pp. 290–330). Washington, DC: U.S. Government Printing Office.

Schooler, C., & Spohn, H. E. (1960). The susceptibility of chronic schizophrenics to social influence in the formation of perceptual judgments. *Journal of Abnormal and Social Psychology, 61,* 348–354.

Schooler, C., & Zahn, T. P. (1968). The effect of closeness of social interaction on task performance and arousal in chronic schizophrenia. *Journal of Nervous and Mental Disease, 147,* 394–401.

Schubert, M. A., & Borkman, T. (1994). Identifying the experiential knowledge developed within a self-help group. In T. J. Powell (Ed.), *Understanding the self-help organization: Frameworks and findings* (pp. 227–246). Thousand Oaks, CA: Sage Publications.

Scott, J. E., & Lehman, A. F. (1998). Social functioning in the community. In K. T. Mueser & N. Tarrier (Eds.), *Handbook of social functioning in schizophrenia* (pp. 1–19). Boston: Allyn & Bacon.

Searight, H. R., & Goldberg, M. A. (1991). The Community Competence Scale as a measure of daily functional living skills. *Journal of Mental Health Administration, 18,* 128–134.

Shafer, M. S., & Huang, H. W. (1995). The utilization of survival analysis to evaluate supported employment services. *Journal of Vocational Rehabilitation, 5,* 103–113.

Shern, D. L., Tsemberis, S., Anthony, W., Lovell, A. M., Richmond, L., Felton, H. C., Winarski, J., & Cohen, M. (1996). *Serving street dwelling individuals with psychiatric disabilities: Outcomes of a psychiatric rehabili-*

tation clinical trial. Unpublished manuscript, Florida Mental Health Institute, University of South Florida, Tampa.

Silverstein, S. M. (1997). Information processing, social cognition, and psychiatric rehabilitation in schizophrenia. *Psychiatry, 60,* 327–340.

Silverstein, S. M., Bakshi, S., Chapman, R. M., & Nowlis, G. (1998). Perceptual organization of configural and nonconfigural visual patterns in schizophrenia: Effects of repeated exposure. *Cognitive Neuropsychiatry, 3,* 209–223.

Skantze, K., Malm, U., Dencker, S. J., May, P. R., & Corrigan, P. W. (1992). Comparison of quality of life with standard of living in schizophrenic outpatients. *British Journal of Psychiatry, 161,* 797–801.

Solomon, P., & Draine, J. (1995). One-year outcomes of a randomized trial of case management with seriously mentally ill clients leaving jail. *Evaluation Review, 19,* 256–273.

Spaulding, W. D. (1978). The relationships of some information processing factors to severely disturbed behavior. *Journal of Nervous and Mental Disease, 166,* 417–428.

Spaulding, W. D. (1997). Cognitive models in a fuller understanding of schizophrenia. *Psychiatry, 60,* 341–346.

Spaulding, W. D., Reed, D., Poland, J. P., & Storzbach, D. M. (1996). In P. W. Corrigan & S. C. Yudofsky (Eds.), *Cognitive rehabilitation for neuropsychiatric disorders* (pp. 129–166). Washington, DC: American Psychiatric Association.

Stein, C. H., Rappaport, J., & Seidman, E. (1995). Assessing the social networks of people with psychiatric disability from multiple perspectives. *Community Mental Health Journal, 31,* 351–367.

Stein, L. I., & Test, M. A. (1980). Alternative to mental hospital treatment: I. Conceptual model, treatment program, and clinical evaluation. *Archives of General Psychiatry, 37,* 392–397.

Storzbach, D. M., & Corrigan, P. W. (1996). Cognitive rehabilitation for schizophrenia. In P. W. Corrigan & S. C. Yudofsky (Eds.), *Cognitive rehabilitation for neuropsychiatric disorders* (pp. 299–328). Washington, DC: American Psychiatric Association.

Strauss, M., Foureman, W. C., & Parwatikur, S. D. (1974). Schizophrenics' size estimation of thematic stimuli. *Journal of Abnormal Psychology, 83,* 117–123.

Susser, E., Valencia, E., Conover, S., Felix, A., Tsai, W.-Y., & Wyatt, R. J. (1997). Science and homelessness: Critical time intervention for mentally ill men. *American Journal of Public Health, 87,* 256–262.

Tarrier, N., Barrowclough, C., Vaughn, C. E., Bamrah, J.S., Porceddu, K., Watts, S., & Freeman, H. (1988). The community management of schizophrenia: A controlled trial of a behavioral intervention with families to reduce relapse. *British Journal of Psychiatry, 153,* 532–542.

Tarrier, N., Barrowclough, C., Vaughn, C. E., Bamrah, J. S., Porceddu,

K., Watts, S., & Freeman, H. (1989). Community management of schizophrenia: A two-year follow-up of a behavioral intervention with families. *British Journal of Psychiatry, 154,* 625–628.

Telles, C., Karno, M., Mintz, J., Paz, G., Arias, M., Tucker, D., & Lopez, S. (1995). Immigrant families coping with schizophrenia: Behavioural family intervention v. case management with a low-income Spanish-speaking population. *British Journal of Psychiatry, 167,* 473–479.

Test, M. A. (1992). Training in community living. In R. P. Liberman (Ed.), *Handbook of psychiatric rehabilitation* (pp. 153–170). New York: Macmillan.

Thapa, K., & Rowland, L. A. (1989). Quality of life perspectives in long-term care: Staff and patient perceptions. *Acta Psychiatrica Scandinavica, 80,* 267–271.

Trotter, S., Minkoff, K., Harrison, K., & Hoops, J. (1988). Supported work: An innovative approach to the vocational rehabilitation of persons who are psychiatrically disabled. *Rehabilitation Psychology, 33,* 27–36.

Tversky, A., & Kahneman, D. (1974). Judgment under uncertainty: Heuristics and biases. *Science, 185,* 1124–1131.

Uehara, E. S., Smukler, M., & Newman, F. L. (1994). Linking resource use to consumer level of need: Field test of the level of need-care assessment (LONCA) method. *Journal of Consulting and Clinical Psychology, 62,* 695–709.

Van Dyke, W. K., & Routh, D. K. (1973). Effects of censure on reaction time: Critique and reformulation of the Garmezy censure-deficit model. *Journal of Abnormal Psychology, 82,* 200–206.

Wallace, C. J. (1986). Functional assessment in rehabilitation. *Schizophrenia Bulletin, 12,* 604–630.

Weaver, L. A., & Brooks, G. W. (1964). The use of psychometric tests in predicting the potential of chronic schizophrenics. *Journal of Neuropsychiatry, 5,* 170–180.

Wehman, P. (1986). Supported competitive employment for persons with severe disabilities. *Journal of Applied Rehabilitation Counseling, 17,* 24–29.

Wehman, P. (1988). Supported employment: Toward zero exclusion of persons with severe disabilities. In P. Wehman & M. S. Moon (Eds.), *Vocational rehabilitation and supported employment* (pp. 71–93). Baltimore: Brookes.

Weisman, A. G., Lopez, S. R., Karno, M., & Jenkins, J. (1993). An attributional analysis of expressed emotion in Mexican-American families with schizophrenia. *Journal of Abnormal Psychology, 102,* 601–606.

Weisman, A. G., Nuechterlein, K. H., Goldstein, M. J., & Snyder, K. S. (1998). Expressed emotion, attributions, and schizophrenia symptom dimensions. *Journal of Abnormal Psychology, 107,* 355–359.

Whiteman, M. (1954). The performance of schizophrenics on social concepts. *Journal of Abnormal and Social Psychology, 49,* 266–271.

Wykes, T., Katz, R., Sturt, E., & Hemsley, D. (1992). Abnormalities of response processing in a chronic psychiatric group: A possible predictor of failure in rehabilitation programmes? *British Journal of Psychiatry, 160,* 244–252.

Wykes, T., & Sturt, E. (1986). The measurement of social behavior in psychiatric patients: An assessment of the reliability and validity of the SBS schedule. *British Journal of Psychiatry, 148,* 1–11.

Wykes, T., Sturt, E., & Katz, R. (1990). The prediction of rehabilitative success after three years: The use of social, symptom and cognitive variables. *British Journal of Psychiatry, 157,* 865–870.

Xiong, W., Phillips, M. R., Hu, X., Wang, R., Dai, Q., Kleinman, J., & Kleinman, A. (1994). Family-based intervention for schizophrenic patients in China. *British Journal of Psychiatry, 165,* 239–247.

Young, J., & Williams, C. L. (1988). Whom do mutual-help groups help? A typology of members. *Hospital and Community Psychiatry, 39,* 1178–1182.

Basic Theory and Concepts

What Is "Social Cognition"? Four Basic Approaches and Their Implications for Schizophrenia Research

1

Leonard S. Newman

The study of error, failure, and abnormality has long been understood to be a useful way to shed light on normal functioning. The causes of a system's breakdown can reveal a great deal about the processes involved when that system operates smoothly (Bechtel & Richardson, 1993). Among psychologists, the study of psychopathology and errors of perception and cognition has traditionally been seen as an appropriate starting point for the development of models of normal psychological processes (Dyer, 1973; Freud, 1933/1964; Miller, 1989). At the same time, progress in the behavioral sciences also has benefited from a different but complementary scientific strategy: using models of typical and normative psychological processes as frameworks for investigations into maladaptive thought and behavior (e.g., Kowalski & Leary, 1999; Weary & Mirels, 1982). For example, basic social psychological research on causal attribution and knowledge schemata has had profound theoretical and clinical implications for the study of depression and other affective disorders (Dykman & Abramson, 1990; Hollon & Garber, 1990).

This chapter was written in the spirit of the latter approach. The sections that follow define the term *social cognition* and review the different ways in which it has been used. The chapter suggests that mainstream social cognition research conducted with normal populations might have much to offer students of schizophrenia. Those speculations

Completion of this chapter was facilitated by a grant from the National Science Foundation (SBR-9809188). I am grateful to Dan Cervone and Neal Roese for thoughtful comments on an earlier version of this chapter.

rely heavily on the descriptions and illustrations of schizophrenic symptomatology presented by Gottesman (1991) and Keefe and Harvey (1994).

Why social cognition? Penn, Corrigan, Bentall, Racenstein, and Newman (1997) argued that schizophrenia is "inherently an interpersonal disorder in which problems result from faulty construction of the social environment and one's place in it" (p. 114). Indeed, not only are impairments in social functioning more pronounced among people with schizophrenia than in other clinical groups (Bellack, Morrison, Wixted, & Mueser, 1990), but premorbid social competence is possibly the strongest predictor of their outcomes (Strauss & Carpenter, 1977; Tien & Eaton, 1992). Social functioning, in turn, has been shown to be significantly related to the ability of people with schizophrenia to effectively perceive, interpret, and reason about social information (Penn, Spaulding, Reed, & Sullivan, 1996). These findings hint at the promise of a unique perspective on schizophrenia—that is, the perspective represented by the contemporary social cognition literature. Social cognition research traditionally has focused on normative psychological processes, but it may provide a set of conceptual tools for understanding the dysfunctions associated with schizophrenia. A social cognitive approach would not, of course, compete with or provide alternative explanations for genetic and neurophysiological analyses. Instead, it would complement those analyses. The psychological processes that social cognition researchers investigate could suggest new ways of conceptualizing the adjustment problems of people with schizophrenia.

The purpose of this chapter is to set the stage for those that follow in this volume by defining this important perspective—that is, by answering the question, What is social cognition? That question does not have a single, unambiguous, or consensual answer because in the 25 years or so since the term has come into common use, it has taken on at least four distinct meanings (see Table 1.1). This chapter describes all of those meanings because all arguably have something to offer the study of social cognition in schizophrenia.

Cognitive Social Psychology

Isen and Hastorf (1982) defined *social cognition* as "an approach that stresses understanding of cognitive processes as a key to understanding complex, purposive, social behavior" (p. 2). Similarly, Manis (1977) identified social cognition as that branch of social psychology characterized by "an emphasis on personal beliefs and hypotheses as the immediate determinants of behavior" (p. 550). The two definitions capture

TABLE 1.1

What Is "Social Cognition"? Four Definitions

	Focus	Representative research
Cognitive social psychology	The cognitive processes underlying social behavior	The processes involved in interpreting behavior and mentally representing information about people; the role of affect in those processes
The social psychology of cognition	How the actual or imagined presence of other people affects cognitive processes	Social constraints on the development of the self-concept; how sharing information with different people affects how one mentally represents that information
Social cognition	Coordinated cognitive activity in dyads or groups	How information is distributed among group members and how that information is retrieved, shared, and used
Evolved social psychological mechanisms	The species-general psychological mechanisms that evolved to solve the adaptive problems presented by group living	How certain cognitive processes are reserved specifically for social situations (e.g., "cheater detection")

what is arguably the most common construal of the term: social cognition as *cognitive social psychology*. The basic assumptions of social psychologists conducting research in this category are that people are thinking organisms and that to understand any interesting aspect of social behavior, one needs to understand the thought processes underlying that behavior. Social cognition thus involves investigations of what people notice in their social worlds, how people interpret and evaluate what comes to their attention, what social information they subsequently store in memory, how mental representations of that information are organized, and how those representations are retrieved and to what effect.[1]

As should be apparent, cognitive social psychology is, as Sherman, Judd, and Park (1989) noted, "not a domain of inquiry within social

---

[1]Another distinction occasionally emphasized is the one between active, controlled social information processing, on the one hand, and passive, associationistic (and not typically conscious) processing on the other (Berkowitz & Devine, 1995; Landman & Manis, 1983). This distinction is roughly approximate to the one between automatic and controlled social information processing (Bargh, 1994), but an extended discussion of its implications is beyond the scope of this chapter.

psychology but an approach or set of assumptions guiding research in a variety of traditional substantive domains" (p. 281); or as Schneider (1991) pointed out, it is "less an area of focus than an approach or perspective" (p. 531). In other words, most of the phenomena that historically have been of interest to social psychologists (e.g., aggression, altruism, interpersonal attraction, intra- and intergroup relations, leadership, and social influence) can be studied with a focus on social cognitive mediators (Devine, Hamilton, & Ostrom, 1994).

As many researchers have pointed out (e.g., Fiske & Taylor, 1991) another prominent feature of this kind of social cognition research has been a direct focus on cognitive processes themselves (i.e., how people think about social objects) and not necessarily on the actual social behaviors believed to be affected by those processes. Dependent variables in social cognition experiments are less likely to involve behavior than to consist of inferences, attributions, decisions, memory for social information (e.g., recall, recognition, clustering of information, and order of recollection), and even latency of response to questions about the self or others. More recently, though, the field has seen a renewed focus on actual action and behavior, as opposed to just the thought processes believed to mediate that action and behavior (Gollwitzer & Bargh, 1996).

What follows is a description of some prominent and representative examples of research areas in this tradition. The first section presents on overview of research on *person perception*, the cognitive processes involved in interpreting people's behavior and forming impressions of them. The second section provides an introduction to *person memory*, the study of how people mentally represent social information once they have perceived and interpreted it. Following that is a discussion of research on the cognitive representation of a social entity of particular significance: the *self*. Finally, the important role played by *affect* in directing and constraining social cognitive processes is reviewed. (For a more complete picture, see the now dated but nevertheless broad and accessible review of the literature by Fiske and Taylor, 1991.)

PERSON PERCEPTION

An understanding of person perception long has been seen as necessary for building models of a wide variety of social psychological phenomena, such as aggression, prosocial behavior, persuasion, attraction, and just about any other interesting and significant interpersonal behavior (Newman, in press). Although the study of person perception predates what has been called the "cognitive revolution" of the 1960s, a central focus of cognitive social psychology has always been the study of how people interpret, evaluate, and determine the causes of others' behavior (see D. Gilbert, 1998, for a comprehensive review). In fact, social cognition has been so closely identified with the study of person perception that some sources even define social cognition as "how people think about people" (Wegner & Vallacher, 1977, p. viii) or as "the process of understanding or making sense of people" (Worchel, Cooper, & Goethals, 1989, p. 50). Of particular concern have been the processes involved in trait inference—that is, the processes involved in deciding that a person's behavior reflects a stable underlying disposition. In other words, much research on person perception has been designed to shed light on how one determines that someone acting in a friendly or unfriendly or anxious or confident or some other way actually is a friendly or unfriendly or anxious or confident or some other sort of person.

General models of person perception and social attribution typically have been designed to describe how people integrate information about a person (e.g., his or her past behavior, the behavior displayed by that person, and the social context of that behavior) to reach conclusions about the meaning of the behavior and the characteristics of the person. In a particularly influential treatment, Jones and Davis (1965; cf. Kelley, 1973) argued that the first step in making a trait inference is to determine whether someone's behavior was intentional. If one determines that a person was aware that his or her behavior would bring about certain effects and had the ability to bring about those effects, then it is reasonable to infer intention. The next step is to figure out *what* was intended. This is done by what Jones and Davis call the analysis of noncommon effects, which essentially boils down to determining what was unique about the course of action a person chose relative to other possible courses of action. For example, if a person has many available options for resolving a conflict and chooses the only one of those that involves violence, it might be concluded that violence was the feature that drew the person to that option; similarly, if many interesting courses of study are available to a student and the student selects the one that promises the most in the way of financial rewards, then financial gain is the noncommon effect. Finally, one must take into account the social desirability and normative frequency of the noncommon effects; the less socially desirable and the less common an outcome is, the more informative it is. To return to the previous examples, choosing a course of study with financial rewards is arguably more normative than choosing a course of study for other (e.g., intellectual) rewards, so it might not be seen as especially informative about a person's unique characteristics. In contrast, opting for violent behavior to resolve a conflict would generally be seen as informative, particularly if that behavior took place in the workplace or the classroom and not in a boxing ring. This analysis determines whether one can make a *correspondent inference* about a person (i.e., an inference that an avaricious or aggressive behavior corresponds to an underlying avaricious or aggressive trait).

Although the Jones and Davis (1965) model portrays the process of person perception as a logical, effortful, and careful one, it became apparent early on that the inferences people make about each other often are radically discrepant from what would be predicted by this and other "rational baseline" models. Many systematic biases affect person perception. The most familiar of these is what Jones (1990) argued might be

> the most robust and repeatable finding in social psychology: the tendency to see behavior as caused by a stable personal disposition of the actor when it can be just as easily explained as a natural response to more than adequate situational pressures. (p. 138)

This bias, known as both the *correspondence bias* (Gilbert & Malone, 1995) and the *fundamental attribution error* (Ross, 1977), has been demonstrated in a wide variety of contexts. The most famous of these demonstrations revealed that people infer that speakers truly endorse the arguments they make, even when it is clear that those speakers have been randomly assigned to profess particular attitudes (Jones & Harris, 1967), and that observers assume that people randomly selected to serve as "questioners" in a mock quiz show actually are smarter and more knowledgeable than the people who have been randomly selected to be "contestants" (Ross, Amabile, & Steinmetz, 1977). In sum, when explaining people's behavior (and when predicting it; see Newman, 1996), there is a marked tendency to rely on dispositional causes at the expense of situational ones.

More recent process models of person perception explicitly account for the correspondence bias (Gilbert, 1989; Reeder, 1993; Trope, 1986). They differ in a number of important details, but they all essentially describe a similar sequence of events. Perceivers must initially identify or categorize a behavior (e.g., a facial expression is identified as a smile or a frown, abrupt physical contact as a stumble or a shove, and the offer of an object or money as generosity or bribery). In addition, most models agree that without additional cognitive work, the interpretations made at this early stage will form the basis for a subsequent trait inference. An act of generosity will lead to an inference of personal generosity, an aggressive act will lead one to infer a trait of aggression, and so on. In fact, a sizable body of work on the phenomenon of *spontaneous trait inference* (Uleman, Newman, & Moskowitz, 1996) shows that perceivers will infer traits from others' behavior even when they do not intend to do so, are not aware of doing so, and are not devoting any effort to the person perception process.[2]

---

[2]Both the correspondence bias and spontaneous trait inference, however, might be more pronounced in Western individualistic cultures (Choi, Nisbett, & Norenzayan, 1999; Newman, 1993).

Most influential models of the trait inference process (see especially Gilbert, 1989) also specify a final, more effortful and deliberate stage at which people take into account contextual and other factors so as to correct or adjust their initial trait inferences. This stage (during which people could do the kind of attributional work described by Jones and Davis, 1965), however, is not necessary and will be skipped if a person is lacking in motivation or available cognitive capacity. In other words, people will not reassess a spontaneous trait inference—and will thus be prone to the correspondence bias—if they do not care about or do not have the time or energy to think carefully about the behaviors that they have observed.

The person perception literature could be useful for schizophrenia researchers in a number of ways. People with schizophrenia are notable for misreading other people's intentions, and thus, not surprisingly, for experiencing high, even debilitating levels of paranoia (Bentall, Kinderman, & Kaney, 1994). An understanding of this phenomenon might be informed by more general models of how people infer others' intentions; that, of course, is exactly what the literature on person perception and causal attribution offers. In addition, the models reviewed here might provide a systematic way of thinking about the implications of the difficulties that people with schizophrenia often have with facial-affect perception and emotional recognition (Feinberg, Rifkin, Schaeffer, & Walker, 1986; Mueser et al., 1996). The importance of the mental operations involved in identifying facial affect is quite evident in current models of dispositional inference (see especially Trope, 1986). Affect perception, which occurs early in the general sequential model (the identification or categorization stage), feeds into subsequent inferential process. The attributions that are made at that latter stage, in turn, will have direct implications for one's behavior. An inability to identify facial affect can thus snowball and have disastrous implications for social interaction.

The finding that a consideration of situational information is a process requiring cognitive effort also has important implications. A hallmark of schizophrenia is an inability to concentrate; intimately related to that symptom, of course, is the overstimulation people with schizophrenia experience. As noted by Penn et al. (1996), people with schizophrenia may be less likely than other people to proceed to the adjustment or correction stage. Therefore, they often may not modify their initial impressions and may be highly prone to the correspondence bias. Even more than other people, then, people with schizophrenia could chronically misinterpret others' behavior by failing to take into account situational factors. One of those situational factors, of course, could be *their own behavior*. People in general have a tendency to underestimate the extent to which their own behavior can elicit particular responses from others (Gilbert & Jones, 1986; Jones, 1990). Unfortunately, people with schizophrenia might find it especially difficult to recognize how what they say and do could lead to unwanted reactions from others.

Other person perception phenomena already have proven to be of great interest to schizophrenia researchers. For example, the *self-serving bias* perhaps rivals the correspondence bias as social psychology's most replicable finding. Social cognition researchers have spent a great deal of time developing models of the process that leads people to take credit for their successes and blame others for their failures (Miller & Ross, 1975; Newman, 1999; Trope & Liberman, 1996). People with schizophrenia who have persecutory delusions have been found to demonstrate an exaggerated form of this attributional pattern (Candido & Romney, 1990; Kaney & Bentall, 1989, 1992; Silverman & Peterson, 1993). General models of the self-serving bias could provide frameworks for more systematically pinpointing the cognitive locus of that defensive attributional style.

PERSON MEMORY

Perhaps no area of research is seen as more emblematic of cognitive social psychology than the study of person memory. Whereas person perception researchers focus on how social information (especially behavior) is interpreted, person memory researchers study how information about people—including other people, the self, and groups of people—is then represented in memory. Their concerns include what kinds of social information gets stored, how it is organized in long-term memory, and what information is later most accessible for recall and for use in making social judgments. Essentially, researchers in this area study people's ability to recall and recognize social information (e.g., people's behaviors and traits); how quickly people are able to do so; the order in which they recall pieces of information; and how that information is clustered when retrieved from memory. From these and other data, they attempt to map out the abstract memory structures people use to represent their social worlds.

A detailed description of the many kinds of abstract social representations posited by different models of person memory is beyond the scope of this chapter, as is a discussion of the research paradigms developed to study person memory (for reviews, see Carlston & Smith, 1996; Hastie et al., 1980; Wyer & Carlston, 1994; Wyer & Srull, 1989; for a discussion of the relationship between the person perception and person memory literatures, see Newman & Uleman, 1993). In general, though, such models are based on more general, associative network conceptions of memory. Concepts are represented by nodes, and related nodes are connected by associative links. In addition, person memory models indicate that knowledge about distinct social entities, such as different people, is located in separate locations in long-term memory. The way the pieces of information at each location are organized both reflects past processing operations (e.g., behaviors and traits that one has thought about extensively will have more links in memory to other pieces of information than will facts that are only rarely brought to mind) and affects future thinking about the person or people in question (e.g., a piece of information with links to many others will come to mind more easily and have a significant effect on one's judgments).

Although many of the assumptions made by person memory researchers are compatible with more general models of memory developed by cognitive psychologists, the mental representation of people involves structures and processes that would not be easily derivable from those general models. For example, in one influential model (Srull & Wyer, 1989) information about a given person can be embodied in more than one qualitatively different kind of knowledge structure. Srull and Wyer propose that the location in memory reserved for the representation of a given person will contain both an "evaluative person representation" (i.e., a subset of behaviors clustered together as a separate cognitive entity that allow one to form a general conception of how likable a person is) and any number of "trait–behavior clusters," which each consist of a trait concept and the behaviors exemplifying that concept. Only by assuming such separate structures, Srull and Wyer argue, can one adequately account for the entire pattern of data in the person memory literature—that is, what people remember, how they remember it, and how that information gets combined when they form impressions and make social judgments.

Person memory research has occupied a place of importance in the cognitive social psychology literature because how people cognitively represent information about others in memory will indirectly affect how they *behave* toward those people. Those effects, of course, are mediated by inferences, evaluations, and expectations, but the representations described by the person memory literature make up the cognitive underpinnings of social behavior. In light of that idea, it would be interesting to examine whether unusual social behavior is associated with unusual person memory structures. How, for example, do people with schizophrenia represent information about their social worlds in memory? Unfortunately, little research exists on the topic (see Corrigan, Wallace, & Green, 1992), and none uses the procedures developed by person memory researchers. A particularly provocative issue is how people with schizophrenia represent themselves in memory. In the nonpsychiatric samples typically used in person memory research, information about the self, like information about other people, is hypothesized to be stored in a separate and distinct location in memory. People with schizophrenia, however, have been known to lose track of the self–other distinction and confuse their internal and external worlds. Is this symptom associated with an unusual person memory architecture? Currently, this question cannot be answered.

THE SELF

The representation of the self also has been a topic of great interest to cognitive social psychologists. As noted in the previous section, conceptions of the self as a knowledge structure have been guided by more general associative network models of person memory (see Kihlstrom & Klein, 1994, for a review). Whether or not the self is a *unique* knowledge structure has been a matter of much debate. Rogers, Kuiper, and Kirker's (1977) well-known work on the *self-reference effect* suggested a special status for the self-concept. Rogers et al. found that a particularly effective way to boost recall of a list of items was to consider the relationship of each item to oneself. This highly replicable effect suggested to many that the self was qualitatively different from other social representations in memory. Later analyses (Greenwald & Banaji, 1989; Higgins & Bargh, 1987) suggested that although the self is a highly familiar, accessible, and well-organized knowledge structure, there is no reason to assume that it is unique. In other words, the memory-enhancing effects of self-reference can be produced by thinking about material in terms of any other familiar, accessible, and well-organized knowledge structure.

Nonetheless, as Baumeister (1998) concluded, "the self is one powerful memory system, and things generated by the self do leave especially strong memory traces" (p. 684)—or at least they do in nondisabled populations. The status of the self as a memory structure among people with schizophrenia is more uncertain. Research using the procedures developed by investigators of the self-reference effect could be useful in shedding light on why people with schizophrenia have been known to lose track of the boundaries between themselves and other people and even report not knowing or recognizing themselves. As discussed by Penn et al. (1996), a number of researchers, guided by personal construct theory (Kelly, 1955), have used self-report measures to examine the relationship between schizophrenia and representations of the self. But the experimental procedures used to study the self-reference effect could be used to more directly test the hypothesis that for people with schizophrenia, the role played by the self in information processing is different from the one normally found in studies of nonclinical samples.

Such investigations could be particularly important given speculations that the self-concept may play a central role in mediating the onset of schizophrenia symptomatology. Some have argued that it is no coincidence that the disorder typically develops in adolescence and young adulthood, when people's social worlds become more complex (Carter & Flesher, 1995; Keefe & Harvey, 1994; Penn et al., 1996). Navigating those worlds requires more complex, multifaceted, and elaborated representations of the self. Social complexity could interact with the vulnerabilities of people at risk for developing schizophrenia and either trigger or magnify their symptoms.

AFFECTIVE INFLUENCES ON COGNITION

Social cognition has been caricatured as an approach that treats motivation "as some quaint notion left over from psychoanalytic theory" that has no place in an "information-processor or computer" model of the person (Baumeister, 1992, p. 21). It is true that researchers in the 1970s often self-consciously strove to account for as much social behavior as possible (even self-serving biases) with "cold" cognitive processes (Miller & Ross, 1975; Nisbett & Ross, 1980). But for at least a decade, one of the central projects of cognitive social psychology has been to integrate affective and motivational factors into social cognitive models (for reviews, see Sorrentino & Higgins, 1986, 1996; Higgins & Sorrentino, 1990).

Affect, for example, has been found to have many systematic and profound effects on social cognitive processes (for a review, see Clore, Schwarz, & Conway, 1994). When people make evaluative judgments (e.g., judgments about whether they are happy with their lives or their jobs, whether they care for other people, or whether a particular course of action seems appealing), they naturally will base those judgments on whatever information is accessible to them. That information typically includes knowledge and beliefs about the attributes of the people, places, things, and activities that are the targets of judgment. Affect, it has been shown, plays a role in such judgments by serving as yet another (and important) piece of information. Schwarz and Clore (1983) illustrated this "affect as information" effect by showing that people make more positive global evaluations of their lives when asked to do so on sunny days than when asked on gloomy days. When the researchers purposely directed participants' attention to the weather, however, the effect disappeared. By alerting people to the true source of their affect, it was essentially "discredited" as a valid piece of information for the life-satisfaction judgment (for a review of the affect-as-information model, see Schwarz, 1990).

Another general finding is that affect can have implications for the sheer quantity of processing that people devote to social information. As Frijda (1988) argued, "emotions exist for the sake of signaling states of the world that they have responded to, or that no longer need response or action" (p. 354). Negative affect, in particular, can alert a person to the fact that his or her goals are not being met and thus can signal the need for increased analysis of the environment (Schwarz & Bless, 1991). For example, people exposed to persuasive messages engage in more careful and systematic thinking about those messages and their implications when they are in a depressed as opposed to an elated mood (Schwarz, Bless, & Bohner, 1991). In sum, affective states serve a "tuning function."

Given that one of the main diagnostic criteria for schizophrenia is the negative symptom of blunted or flat affect, these findings have important implications for schizophrenia research. Although the affective influences on judgment often are portrayed as unwanted biases that get in the way of fair and objective judgment and decision making (e.g., Wilson & Brekke, 1994), it is clear that affective considerations play an important and useful role in normative everyday behavior. It is unlikely that people respond differently to friends and family members versus strangers—both in terms of valence and intensity—as a result of a dispassionate accounting of the objective attributes of the different members of their social worlds. But such differential responding is arguably necessary to maintain close relationships. Affect is not just another piece of information: It is vital information that people ignore at their peril. As Damasio (1998) argued in a call for more research on emotions by neuroscientists,

> Emotion is critical for survival in the complex organisms equipped to process it. . . . [It] plays a role in reasoning and decision-making, from the simple decisions that animals make to avert danger or endorse an advantageous encounter, to the more complex decisions that we humans can consider. (p. 84)

If a person with schizophrenia experiences little in the way of emotional feelings, he or she will lack important input into the kinds of judgments and decisions needed to guide behavior. This, in turn, will lead to significant disruptions in their ability to manage relationships and everyday activities.

Diminished affect not only will deprive one of mood as information but also will disrupt the vital tuning function of affective states discussed above (Schwarz & Bless, 1991). People with diminished affect simply may not be able to receive or interpret the signals that normally indicate that a physical or psychological situation needs attending to (i.e., deeper consideration or even an actual behavioral response).[3] For example,

---

[3]It has been observed, however, that schizophrenia often is characterized not so much by an absence of affect as by an inability to communicate or express it. Such a symptom would create difficulties that are more interpersonal than intrapersonal. Expressions of emotion have a signaling function that plays an important role in regulating social interaction (Baumeister & Tice, 1987).

negative affect has been shown to trigger counterfactual thinking (Roese & Hur, 1997). In other words, when people feel bad they often actively generate alternative possible outcomes for the past events that led them to feel the way that they do (see Roese & Olson, 1997, for a review). Hooker, Roese, and Park (1999) had people with schizophrenia and a group of control participants think about the kinds of incidents that have been shown to trigger counterfactuals (e.g., personally experienced unpleasant events). Participants with schizophrenia exhibited significantly less counterfactual thinking than did control participants. The results have important implications because counterfactual thinking can be quite functional. Specifically, thinking about what one might have done and what might have been allows people to plan for similar events in the future (Nasco & Marsh, 1999; Roese & Olson, 1997). In fact, Hooker et al. (1999) also found that counterfactual thinking correlated with social functioning and that low levels of counterfactual thinking partially mediated the difference between people with schizophrenia and control participants in social functioning.

As discussed by Clore et al. (1994), social cognitive analyses of affect also have been influenced by attentional resource models. The main assumption of such models is that intense affective states can reduce the attentional resources available for complex thought. Negative affect has been hypothesized to lead to greater self-focused attention (Ingram, 1990) and might reduce attentional resources by eliciting intrusive thoughts (Ellis & Ashbrook, 1988). In other words, feeling bad can lead to rumination, and that rumination can be difficult to break out of (Wenzlaff, Wegner, & Roper, 1988). At the other extreme, high levels of elation can affect thought by limiting attentional resources and impairing one's ability to respond to social information (Mackie & Worth, 1989; cf. Bless, Bohner, Schwarz, & Strack, 1990). It is thus not surprising that the triggering of affect has been shown to lead to marked disturbances in thinking in people with schizophrenia (Docherty, Evans, Sledge, Seibyl, & Krystal, 1994; Haddock, Wolfenden, Lowens, Tarrier, & Bentall, 1995).

The role of affect in people's thinking about their social worlds is complex. For example, researchers are only beginning to tease apart the effects of different kinds of moods (e.g., depression, anxiety, anger, and fear). Some of the diagnostic criteria for schizophrenia involve abnormal affective states; in fact, it has been suggested that "a reduction in the normal intensity of emotional experiences and expression are actually more foreboding predictors" of long-term pathology than what seem like the more "dangerous and unusual symptoms" (Keefe & Harvey, 1994, p. 57). Schizophrenia researchers therefore might want to avail themselves of the fine-grained analyses of the role of affect in social thought and behavior that is found in the social cognition literature.

The Social Psychology
of Cognition

Every comprehensive review of the literature on social cognition as cognitive social psychology eventually must address a common critique of that entire area of research. Social cognition, some have complained, is nothing more than cognitive psychology as it applies to social objects. According to this view, social cognition is simply a branch of cognitive psychology that contributes nothing unique or fundamental to the study of basic cognitive processes. The attentional, interpretive, encoding, organizational, and retrieval processes involved in making sense of human beings and their behavior, it has been suggested, are perhaps the same ones used to process information about nonsocial categories of objects, such as automobiles, furniture, clothing, and kitchen appliances.

For discussions of why the principles, models, and phenomena described above are not simply straightforward derivations from models of cognitive psychology developed on the basis of research with nonsocial objects, the reader should consult discussions by Fiske and Taylor (1991); Higgins, Kuiper, and Olson (1981); Ostrom (1984); and Schneider, Hastorf, and Ellsworth (1979). More important for present purposes is to emphasize that such a critique would not apply to another perspective on social cognition, which focuses not so much on the cognitive processes underlying behavior as on how social situations and constraints affect cognitive processes. Higgins (1992) termed this broad area of research the *social psychology of cognition* (as opposed to the cognition of social psychology), and Levine and Higgins (1995, p. 183) also describe it as "social cognition as a social science" (as opposed to social cognition as a cognitive science). More specifically, the social psychology of cognition refers to "how the meaning that people assign to the events in their lives (e.g., their representation, interpretation, and evaluation of life events) is transformed because their actions take others into account" (Higgins, 1992, p. 243).

To illustrate how social factors affect cognitive processes, consider a classic finding from the person memory literature (Hastie & Kumar, 1979; Sherman & Hamilton, 1994; Srull, 1981). When people are led to expect a certain kind of behavior from another person (e.g., honesty) and then learn about that person's behaviors, they usually are able to recall behaviors that were inconsistent with their expectations (in this case, behaviors implying dishonesty) better than behaviors consistent with the expectations (i.e., honest behaviors). This effect seems to occur because people devote more time and energy to thinking about the inconsistent behaviors so as to reconcile them with what they believe to be true about the target person's general characteristics. That leads the inconsistent behaviors to become linked to many other pieces of information in memory, a process that in turn facilitates recall (see Srull & Wyer, 1989, and Wyer & Srull, 1989, for reviews). In such studies, information generally is presented to research participants by a neutral experimenter, but in a variation of this basic experimental paradigm, Wyer and his colleagues (Wyer, Budesheim, & Lambert, 1990; Wyer, Budesheim, Lambert, & Swan, 1994) embedded the trait descriptors and accounts of behavior in taped conversations between two people. Their studies revealed memory biases that typically are not found when the transmission of social information is divorced from a naturalistic social context. For example, when participants heard people attribute negative behaviors to other people or positive traits to themselves, recall for those behaviors was enhanced. Apparently, participants were especially attentive when norms to "be modest" and "speak kindly of others" were violated, and the extra processing led those behaviors to be more memorable than others. In sum, the processing, storage, and retrieval of person information varies as a function of social context, a classic example of the social psychology of cognition.

THE "LOOKING-GLASS SELF"

It long has been observed that social relationships and interpersonal experiences affect a particularly important kind of cognitive activity: the construction of a self-concept (see Baumeister, 1998). According to Mead's (1934) symbolic interactionist theory, self-understanding relies on taking other people's standpoints on the self into account. Even earlier than that, Cooley (1902) introduced the term "looking-glass self" as a metaphor for his claim that people's self-concepts are simply reflections of how they believe others see them.

Empirical exploration of these ideas (Shrauger & Schoeneman, 1979) has yielded fairly consistent conclusions. Self-concepts are indeed strongly related to people's perceptions of how they believe others see them. At the same time, people's ability to figure out how they are *really* seen, categorized, and evaluated by others is far from perfect (DePaulo, Kenny, Hoover, Webb, & Oliver, 1987; Felson, 1989). Thus, the effects of other people's beliefs about a person on the contents of that person's self-concept are, to a certain extent, indirect. Nonetheless, in nonclinical populations, the correlations between how people see themselves and how others see them are certainly significantly greater than zero (Funder, 1987).

The situation among people with schizophrenia, however, is unclear. Schizophrenia is associated with unrealistic self-appraisal; sometimes this trait manifests itself in the form of self-aggrandizement. People with schizophrenia, because of problems with perspective, might be even less able than other people to ascertain how others see them; this inability could contribute to the development of their distorted self concepts. In other words, people with schizophrenia may not be governed by the same social factors that constrain the cognitive processes that people without schizophrenia use to construct their self-concepts.

SOCIAL CONTEXT EFFECTS AND ROLE-TAKING

Social influences on cognition are broader than just those that involve self-concept formation. Higgins and his colleagues provided a compelling illustration of such influences in their studies of how people modify their social communications as a function of the attitudes, beliefs, and other characteristics of their listeners (e.g., Higgins & McCann, 1984; Higgins & Rholes, 1978). Higgins et al. found that when their participants described a particular person to other people, the nature of the descriptions differed as a function of whether participants believed that the audience liked or disliked that person. Although this finding is not particularly surprising, more surprising was that providing the biased descriptions actually had long-term effects on participants' memories, impressions, and evaluations of the people they had described. For example, memories for the people whom the audience liked were distorted in a relatively positive direction. These studies confirm that it is common to use one's knowledge of other people's beliefs, preferences, and other internal states as a guide for how to process, organize, and communicate information. In addition, the research by Higgins and his colleagues shows that social context can affect not only the transmission but also the mental representation of information.

Clearly, such social context effects are not unambiguously positive. In fact, Higgins and Rholes (1978) note that "message modification may play a significant role in forming and maintaining false and harmful characterizations, both with respect to other people and social groups (e.g., racial and ethnic stereotypes) and with respect to oneself (e.g., distorted self-perceptions)" (p. 377). In contrast, not being able to take into account other people's attitudes, beliefs, and knowledge also will be associated with costs. Most obviously, being oblivious to others' states of mind can lead to awkward and unpleasant social interactions. But the consequences could be more subtle and far-reaching than even that. Difficulties in appreciating and integrating other people's perspectives on one's social world could exacerbate the development of all sorts of distorted and dysfunctional representations, such as those involving other people and one's relationships with those people. People with schizophrenia, of course, are known to be deficient in role-taking abilities and empathy. Their social adjustment could well be adversely affected by their problems with transforming information to take others into account—that is, by their unusual social psychology of cognition.

INTERNAL AUDIENCES

Although this discussion of the social psychology of cognition has focused primarily on the effects of people or audiences who are in actual physical proximity, internalized representations of other people or groups of people also can guide judgments and evaluations (see Higgins, 1992). For example, Baldwin and Holmes (1987) asked research participants to visualize either two acquaintances from school or two older members of their families. They then read a sexually permissive essay. Participants' reactions to the essay (i.e., their reported enjoyment of the essay) varied as a function of the private audience that had been made more cognitively accessible—specifically, those who visualized the older family members enjoyed the essay less.

Internalized audiences undoubtedly play an important role in self-regulation of behavior. Being directed by *imaginary* internal audiences, however, is certainly not the norm. People with schizophrenia often report hearing imaginary voices that comment on their behavior or even order them to do things. Sometimes those voices are associated with specific people—even dead ones (Gottesman, 1991)—although at other times, they come from an indeterminate source. Often the voices are attributed to external agents (Bentall, 1990). More important, though, is that for people with schizophrenia, auditory hallucinations become "regarded as important elements in their social world" (Penn et al., 1996, pp. 121–122).

Although the self-generated internal audiences of people with schizophrenia may be entirely imaginary, the effects of those audiences could well parallel the general effects of internalized social entities found in nonclinical populations. For example, Baldwin and his colleagues (Baldwin, Carrell, & Lopez, 1990), using a subliminal activation method, found that internal audiences (e.g., the Pope, for Catholic students, or a respected faculty member, in the case of graduate students) can be activated without awareness and affect how people evaluate themselves. The internal voices generated by people with schizophrenia could thus have effects even when the voices are not actively being heard. Baldwin et al.'s work and, more generally, the literature on the social psychology of cognition, could provide a starting point for thinking about those effects.

Social Cognition

Despite the many important differences between cognitive social psychology and the social psychology of cognition, both approaches share an important feature: they focus on the individual as the unit of analysis. In other words, cognition is an individual mental activity, and social cognition is something that takes place in the head of a person when he or she is either in a social context or thinking about social entities. Some researchers, though, prefer to reserve the term social cognition to refer to joint cognitive activity taking place in groups (or even dyads) that is collaborative and mutually goal oriented (e.g., Larson & Christensen, 1993). Others (Ickes & Gonzalez, 1994) highlight a distinction between "social" cognition and *social* cognition. Only the latter, they argue, is truly social, because it refers to phenomena that involve "some sort of interdependence between the contents and processes of two conscious minds" (Ickes & Gonzalez, 1994, p. 298). In sum, people in their daily social interactions often find themselves involved in cognitive activity that is intertwined and coordinated with the cognitive activity of other people. The term *social cognition* is sometimes used to refer specifically to this sort of group-level phenomenon.

Larson and Christensen (1993) focused on group problem-solving and decision-making as prototypical examples of this kind of social cognition. When a person must make decisions or solve problems with other people, they argue, he or she is involved in social processes "that relate to the acquisition, storage, transmission, manipulation, and use of information for the purpose of creating a group-level intellective product" (p. 6). Although Larson and Christensen illustrated their conceptualization of group-level social cognition primarily with relatively formal problem-solving or decision-making teams (e.g., doctors working collectively to arrive at a diagnosis, students trying to solve math problems together, and executives making business decisions), their analysis is more broadly applicable to any situation in which two or more people combine their cognitive resources in order to plan for and generate some common outcome.

As outlined by Larson and Christensen, one of the first steps in any social cognitive activity is the joint conceptualization of the problem or issue requiring the attention of group members. Only then can the relevance and importance of different information, solutions, and other available resources be assessed. For example, if a company experiences a drop in sales, those responsible for attending to the problem must frame the problem in terms of the undesirable features of its products, ineffective advertising, inefficient distribution, or some combination of those factors. Similarly, a family in crisis, to take steps to alleviate its problems, has to figure out how to conceptualize the problems. People with schizophrenia, because of their delusions, distorted social knowledge (Cutting & Murphy, 1990), and poor communication skills (e.g., disorganized speech), are unlikely to be able to contribute constructively to such a joint cognitive process. In fact, they could well derail it. That, in turn, could contribute to an escalation of interpersonal conflict: Without a common conceptualization, it is impossible for a family or other social group to coordinate collective problem-solving.

Once a group successfully identifies and conceptualizes a problem, it also has implicitly identified the kind of knowledge and information that will be needed for solving it. But that knowledge generally will be unevenly distributed among group members (see also Wegner, 1995, on "transactive memory"). In other words, a typical social cognitive challenge is to figure out who knows what. Fortunately, groups usually have a considerable amount of what Larson and Christensen have called *meta-knowledge* at their disposal. One can determine who has access to different facts, memories, or kinds of knowledge in many ways. In formal decision-making groups, members' organizational roles and areas of expertise can serve as simple cues to help index the likely distribution of knowledge. But in any group, meta-knowledge also develops in more informal ways, as a result of conversations with other members or simply knowledge about people's past experiences. For example, family members generally have extensive knowledge about the range of each others' experiences and can take into account factors such as who was present during particular events in the past and who might be reasonably expected to have reached different conclusions or developed particular opinions about various matters. People with schizophrenia, unfortunately, are often characterized by poor role-taking skills and a lack of empathy. Their consequent lack of meta-knowledge is likely to wreak havoc on any group problem-solving activity of which they are a part. As a result, they could contribute to creating a social cognitive environment that is as disordered at the group level as is the thinking occurring at the level of the person with schizophrenia.

The final steps in the creation of any social cognitive product are information retrieval and the use and manipulation of that information by the group. As discussed by Larsen and Christensen, the kind of information that will dominate these stages is *shared information,* which is simply information that is held and retrieved by more than one group member (see Larson, Foster-Fishman, & Keys, 1994). The nonnormative knowledge bases (i.e., unusual or false beliefs) of people with schizophrenia thus will leave them on the periphery of group social cognitive activity; their subjective knowledge is unlikely to be shared. Finally, difficulty in communicating thoughts and feelings—and the difficulty that others often have in reading their nonverbal behavior—will further hinder the abilities of people with schizophrenia to contribute to the thinking that groups do.

The important point is not that people with schizophrenia will have more difficulty than other people integrating themselves into complex group activities—clearly, that is not a novel observation. As discussed above, the purpose of this volume is to highlight the social cognitive dimensions of schizophrenia. Specifically, the goals are to reconceptualize the adjustment problems of such people in terms of social cognitive processes and to suggest that social cognitive deficits might contribute to their distress over and above more general information-processing problems. This literature provides a novel way of approaching that project. What goes on between people in their everyday interactions often involves exchanging and pooling information in the service of joint goals. Effectively managing those interactions requires specific and subtle skills—skills that people with schizophrenia may lack. Models of *social* cognition provide a way of thinking about those skills; thus, they provide tools to systematically analyze what goes wrong for people with schizophrenia when they have to participate in interdependent thinking. In sum, research on group-level cognition offers another unique way to frame the study of the social cognition of schizophrenia.

Social Psychological Mechanisms

As noted above, researchers in the area of social cognition have operated under the assumption that the specific mental representations and phenomena they have been studying could not have been derived from cognitive research on stimuli divorced from their social context. Nonetheless, most researchers probably have agreed with Fiske and Linville (1980), who noted that "it is unlikely that in the process of evolution, qualitatively different knowledge structures or procedures developed for social and nonsocial classes of stimuli" (p. 548). But a burgeoning group of researchers interested in social cognition emphatically disagree. United by an *evolutionary psychology* perspective, they have presented a radically different perspective on what makes a cognition "social." Although cognitive social psychology, the social psychology of cognition, and *social* cognition differ in terms of level of analysis (individual or group) and in terms of whether they emphasize the causes or effects of cognitive processes, all three approaches are comfortably situated within a general information-processing framework. Evolutionary psychologists, however, have adopted an entirely different meta-theory. Guided by models of natural selection, they hypothesize that human beings have developed a set of domain-specific cognitive mechanisms for dealing with social situations. In other words, evolutionary psychologists propose that people possess a distinct "faculty of social cognition" (Tooby & Cosmides, 1992, p. 91).

Buss (1995) presented a particularly clear and comprehensive overview of the evolutionary psychology perspective. As described by Buss, evolutionary psychologists begin with the assumption that all human behavior depends on underlying psychological mechanisms. Those mechanisms are activated by specific contexts (cf. Cervone, 2000), and natural selection is the process that produces the psychological mechanisms. Because human beings, throughout their evolutionary history, faced a great number of diverse adaptive problems in a wide variety of environments, a great many species-general psychological mechanisms evolved. Possible psychological mechanisms that Buss identifies include the fear of snakes, a desire for foods rich in fats and sugar, and a preference for certain kinds of landscapes. But others are more specifically *social* psychological mechanisms: sexual jealousy, different mate preferences for males and females, imitation of high-status models, and even a procedure for detecting cheating so as to avoid being exploited by other people (Cosmides, 1989; Cosmides & Tooby, 1989; see also Sedikides & Skowronski, 1997, for a discussion of evolutionary pressures that might have played a role in the development of the complex representations of the self discussed above).

Buss (1995) predicts that future research will more precisely identify many other evolved social psychological mechanisms; in fact, he states that "because social adaptive problems were so crucial for human survival and reproduction, many of the most important features of our evolved psychological mechanisms will necessarily be social in nature" (p. 9). Adaptive problems include "successful intrasexual competition, mate selection, mate attraction, sexual intercourse, mate retention, reciprocal dyadic alliance formation, coalition building and maintenance, prestige and reputation maintenance, hierarchy negotiation, parental care and socialization, and extraparental kin investment" (p. 9).

In sum, for evolutionary psychologists, social cognition is not simply a matter of the context in which general cognitive processes operate, nor does it involve domain-general mental processes applied to social objects. The concept of social psychological mechanisms goes beyond even cognitive social psychologists' implicit assumption that specialized cognitive operations or representations are necessary to adequately process social information. Buss (1995), for example, proposes that even basic categorization processes involve different mechanisms when the entities to be categorized are social (e.g., people and relationships) or nonsocial (e.g., plants, foods, and features of the natural environment).

The psychological mechanisms investigated by evolutionary psychologists are species-general. People do not vary in terms of whether they do or do not possess the mechanisms. As a result, Buss (1995, p. 19) noted that "the derivation of individual differences is considerably more problematic" than the specification of the general psychological mechanisms (see also Scarr, 1995). Evolutionary psychologists have not been entirely silent on the issue; in general, they argue that as a result of variations in their environments or physical attributes, each person faces different adaptive problems (see Buss, 1991; Gangstead & Simpson, 1990; Tooby & Cosmides, 1990; Wright, 1995). The different challenges (e.g., unpredictable and resource-poor environments or physical weakness), in turn, lead to the triggering of the general psychological mechanisms that have evolved to deal with those problems. Thus, individual differences (e.g., aggressiveness, sociability, and promiscuity) are a reflection of ideographically distinct blends of activated species-typical mechanisms. Mental disorders also can be conceptualized in this way; in P. Gilbert's (1998) words, "many psychological states that we label 'psychopathology' may represent the activation of (previously) adaptive strategies" (p. 353).

Nonetheless, analyses of individual differences from the perspective of evolutionary psychology are currently at the earliest stages of development, so applying those analyses to an understanding of schizophrenia may be premature. More provocative, though, is Buss's (1995, p. 11) speculation that although psychological mechanisms are species-general, it is possible that an "unusual genetic or environmental accident" could lead to the elimination or distortion of a psychological mechanism (just as a genetic or environmental accident could affect a species-general *physical* attribute). For example, he suggests that autism could be the result of impairment of a psychological mechanism devoted to making inferences about other people's thoughts and feelings—that is, autism could be caused by damage to a mechanism responsible for people's "theory of mind" (see also Leslie, 1991). Interestingly, Frith (1992, 1994) has proposed that many people with schizophrenia suffer from a similar impairment. Frith argued that many of the positive symptoms of schizophrenia possibly derive from an inability to take others' perspectives in conversation and social interaction and from a corresponding difficulty in inferring other people's intentions.

Needless to say, the point of this observation is not to suggest that autism and schizophrenia share similar etiologies. The point is to emphasize that from the evolutionary psychology perspective, the term *social cognition* refers to distinct and specialized psychological mechanisms that have evolved to help solve many of the adaptive problems presented by group living. From this perspective, then, schizophrenia is probably the result of damage to one or more of those basic mechanisms (or a breakdown in their integrated functioning; see P. Gilbert, 1998). This analysis is compatible with evidence for a genetic component to schizophrenia, but it further suggests that a more complete and fine-grained understanding of the inherited vulnerabilities associated with schizophrenia will require the more precise identification of the nature of the relevant psychological—including social psychological—mechanisms.

Conclusion

Social cognition has meant many things and been associated with a variety of distinct research programs. For some researchers, social cognition has meant investigating the cognitive process underlying social behavior; others have focused instead on how social situations and relationships alter people's thinking; still others have examined the ways in which dyads or groups of people coordinate their cognitive activities; and most recently, evolutionary psychologists have begun to attempt to specify the psychological mechanisms that have evolved specifically for the purpose of adapting to group living. Similarly, the study of social cognition and schizophrenia could require different levels of analysis for a variety of phenomena. This chapter has included a number of examples of the kinds of research questions that might be promising to pursue. More than that, though, the purpose of this chapter has been to provide a context for such questions and an overview of the different ways in which they could be framed.

Finally, although the main theme of the chapter has been that schizophrenia researchers have much to gain from an appreciation of the work done by students of social cognition, the reverse is also true. In other words, social cognition researchers could benefit from the kind of work represented by the other chapters in this volume. Research on how people with schizophrenia think in and about their social worlds will undoubtedly lead to questions that would not emerge from studies of nonclinical populations and will produce findings that would not be predicted by the researchers who do those studies. Those questions and findings could provide unique opportunities to challenge and extend existing models of social cognition.

References

Baldwin, M. W., Carrell, S. E., & Lopez, D. F. (1990). Priming relationship schemas: My advisor and the pope are watching me from the back of my mind. *Journal of Experimental Social Psychology, 26*, 435–454.

Baldwin, M. W., & Holmes, J. G. (1987). Salient private audiences and awareness of the self. *Journal of Personality and Social Psychology, 52*, 1087–1098.

Bargh, J. A. (1994). The four horsemen of automaticity: Awareness, intention, efficiency, and control in social cognition. In R. S. Wyer, Jr., & T. K. Srull (Eds.), *Handbook of social cognition: Vol. 1. Basic processes* (2nd ed., pp. 1–40). Hillsdale, NJ: Erlbaum.

Baumeister, R. F. (1992). Neglected aspects of self theory: Motivation, interpersonal aspects, culture, escape, and existential value. *Psychological Inquiry, 3*, 21–25.

Baumeister, R. F. (1998). The self. In D. T. Gilbert, S. T. Fiske, & G. Lindzey (Eds.), *The handbook of social psychology* (4th ed., Vol. 1, pp. 680–740). New York: McGraw Hill.

Baumeister, R. F., & Tice, D. M. (1987). Emotion and self-presentation. In R. Hogan & W. H. Jones (Eds.), *Perspectives in personality: Vol. 2. Theory, measurement, and interpersonal dynamics* (pp. 181–199). Greenwich, CT: JAI Press.

Bechtel, W., & Richardson, R. C. (1993). *Discovering complexity: Decomposition and localization strategies in scientific research.* Princeton, NJ: Princeton University Press.

Bellack, A. S., Morrison, R. L., Wixted, J. T., & Mueser, K. T. (1990). An analysis of social competence in schizophrenia. *British Journal of Psychiatry, 156*, 809–818.

Bentall, R. P. (1990). The illusion of reality: A review and integration of psychological research on hallucinations. *Psychological Bulletin, 107*, 82–95.

Bentall, R. P., Kinderman, P., & Kaney, S. (1994). The self, attributional processes and abnormal beliefs: Towards a model of persecutory delusions. *Behaviour Research and Therapy, 32*, 331–341.

Berkowitz, L., & Devine, P. G. (1995). Has social psychology always been cognitive? What is "cognitive" anyhow? *Personality and Social Psychology Bulletin, 21*, 696–703.

Bless, H., Bohner, G., Schwarz, N., & Strack, F. (1990). Mood and persuasion: A cognitve response analysis. *Personality and Social Psychology Bulletin, 16*, 331–345.

Buss, D. M. (1991). Evolutionary personality psychology. *Annual Review of Psychology, 42*, 459–491.

Buss, D. M. (1995). Evolutionary psychology: A new paradigm for psychological science. *Psychological Inquiry, 6*, 1–30.

Candido, C. L., & Romney, D. M. (1990). Attributional style in paranoid vs. depressed patients. *British Journal of Medical Psychology, 63*, 355–363.

Carlston, D. E., & Smith, E. R. (1996). Principles of mental representation. In E. T. Higgins & A. W. Kruglanski (Eds.), *Social psychology: Handbook of basic principles* (pp. 184–210). New York: Guilford Press.

Carter, M., & Flesher, S. (1995). The neurosociology of schizophrenia: Vulnerability and functional disability. *Psychiatry, 58,* 209–224.

Cervone, D. (2000). Evolutionary psychology and explanation in personality psychology: How do we know which module to invoke? *American Behavioral Scientist, 43,* 1001–1014.

Choi, I., Nisbett, R. E., & Norenzayan, A. (1999). Causal attribution across cultures: Variation and universality. *Psychological Bulletin, 125,* 47–63.

Clore, G. L., Schwarz, N., & Conway, M. (1994). Affective causes and consequences of social information processing. In R. S. Wyer, Jr., & T. K. Srull (Eds.), *Handbook of social cognition: Vol. 1. Basic processes* (2nd ed., pp. 323–417). Hillsdale, NJ: Erlbaum.

Cooley, C. H. (1902). *Human nature and the social order.* New York: Charles Scribner's Sons.

Cosmides, L. (1989). The logic of social exchange: Has natural selection shaped how humans reason? Studies with the Wason selection task. *Cognition, 31,* 187–276.

Cosmides, L., & Tooby, J. (1989). Evolutionary psychology and the generation of culture, Part II. Case study: A computational theory of social exchange. *Ethology and Sociobiology, 10,* 51–97.

Corrigan, P. W., Wallace, C. J., & Green, M. F. (1992). Deficits in social schemata in schizophrenia. *Schizophrenia Research, 8,* 129–135.

Cutting, J., & Murphy, D. (1990). Impaired ability of schizophrenics, relative to manics or depressives, to appreciate social knowledge about their culture. *British Journal of Psychiatry, 157,* 355–358.

Damasio, A. R. (1998). Emotion in the perspective of an integrated nervous system. *Brain Research Reviews, 26,* 83–86.

DePaulo, B. M., Kenny, D. A., Hoover, C. W., Webb, W., & Oliver, P. V. (1987). Accuracy of self-perception: Do people know what kinds of impressions they convey? *Journal of Personality and Social Psychology, 52,* 303–315.

Devine, P. G., Hamilton, D. L., & Ostrom, T. M. (1994). *Social cognition: Impact on social psychology.* San Diego, CA: Academic Press.

Docherty, N. M., Evans, I. M., Sledge, W. H., Seibyl, J. P., & Krystal, J. H. (1994). Affective reactivity of language in schizophrenia. *Journal of Nervous and Mental Disease, 182,* 98–102.

Dykman, B. M., & Abramson, L. Y. (1990). Contributions of basic research to the cognitive theories of depression. *Personality and Social Psychology Bulletin, 16,* 42–57.

Dyer, F. N. (1973). The Stroop phenomenon and its use in the study of perceptual, cognitive, and response processes. *Memory and Cognition, 1,* 106–120.

Ellis, H. C., & Ashbrook, P. W. (1988). Resource allocation model of the effects of depressed mood states on memory. In K. Fiedler & J. Forgas (Eds.), *Affect, cognition, and social behavior* (pp. 25–43). Toronto, Ontario, Canada: C. J. Hogrefe.

Feinberg, T. E., Rifkin, A., Schaeffer, C., & Walker, E. (1986). Facial discrimination and emotional recognition in schizophrenia and affective disorders. *Archives of General Psychiatry, 43,* 276–279.

Felson, R. B. (1989). Parents and the reflected appraisal process: A longitudinal study. *Journal of Personality and Social Psychology, 56,* 965–971.

Fiske, S. T., & Linville, P. W. (1980). What does the schema concept buy us? *Personality and Social Psychology Bulletin, 6,* 543–557.

Fiske, S. T., & Taylor, S. E. (1991). *Social cognition.* New York: McGraw-Hill.

Freud, S. (1964). New introductory lectures on psychoanalysis. In J. Strachey (Ed.), *The standard edition of the complete psychological works of Sigmund Freud* (Vol. 22). London: Hogarth Press. (Original work published in 1933)

Frijda, N. H. (1988). The laws of emotion. *American Psychologist, 43,* 349–358.

Frith, C. D. (1992). *The cognitive neuropsychology of schizophrenia.* Hillsdale, NJ: Erlbaum.

Frith, C. D. (1994).Theory of mind. In A. S. David & J. C. Cutting (Eds.), *The neuropsychology of schizophrenia* (pp. 147–151). East Sussex, England: Erlbaum.

Funder, D. C. (1987). Errors and mistakes: Evaluating the accuracy of social judgment. *Psychological Bulletin, 101,* 75–90.

Gangstead, S. W., & Simpson, J. A. (1990). Toward an evolutionary history of female sociosexual variation. *Journal of Personality, 58,* 69–96.

Gilbert, D. T. (1989). Thinking lightly about others: Automatic components of the social inference process. In J. S. Uleman & J. A. Bargh (Eds.), *Unintended thought* (pp. 189–211). New York: Guilford Press.

Gilbert, D. T. (1998). Ordinary personology. In D. T. Gilbert, S. T. Fiske, & G. Lindzey (Eds.), *The handbook of social psychology* (4th ed., Vol. 2, pp. 89–150). New York: McGraw Hill.

Gilbert, D. T., & Jones, E. E. (1986). Perceiver-induced constraint: Interpretations of self-generated reality. *Journal of Personality and Social Psychology, 50,* 269–280.

Gilbert, D. T., & Malone, P. S. (1995). The correspondence bias. *Psychological Bulletin, 117,* 21–38.

Gilbert, P. (1998). Evolutionary psychopathology: Why isn't the mind designed better than it is? *British Journal of Medical Psychology, 71,* 353–373.

Gollwitzer, P. M., & Bargh, J . A. (Eds.). (1996). *The psychology of action.* New York: Guilford Press.

Gottesman, I. I. (1991). *Schizophrenia genesis: The origins of madness.* New York: W. H. Freeman.

Greenwald, A. G., & Banaji, M. R. (1989). The self as a memory system: Powerful, but ordinary. *Journal of Personality and Social Psychology, 57,* 41–54.

Haddock, G., Wolfenden, M., Lowens, I., Tarrier, N., & Bentall, R. P. (1995). The effect of emotional salience on the thought disorder of patients with a diagnosis of schizophrenia. *British Journal of Psychiatry, 167,* 618–620.

Hastie, R., & Kumar, P. A. (1979). Person memory: Personality traits as organizing principles in memory for behaviors. *Journal of Personality and Social Psychology, 37,* 25–38.

Hastie, R., Ostrom, T. M., Ebbesen, E. B., Wyer, R. S., Jr., Hamilton, D. L., & Carlston, D. E. (Eds.). (1980). *Person memory: The cognitive basis of social perception.* Hillsdale, NJ: Erlbaum.

Higgins, E. T. (1992). Social cognition as a social science: How social action creates meaning. In D. N. Ruble, P. R. Costanzo, & M. E. Oliveri (Eds.), *The social psychology of mental health* (pp. 241–278). New York: Guilford Press.

Higgins, E. T., & Bargh, J. A. (1987). Social cognition and social perception. *Annual Review of Psychology, 38,* 369–425.

Higgins, E. T., Kuiper, N. A., & Olson, J. M. (1981). Social cognition: A need to get personal. In E. T. Higgins, C. P. Herman, & M. P. Zanna (Eds.), *Social cognition: The Ontario Symposium* (Vol. 1, pp. 343–392). Hillsdale, NJ: Erlbaum.

Higgins, E. T., & McCann, C. D. (1984). Social encoding and subsequent attitudes, impressions, and memory: "Context-driven" and motivational aspects of processing. *Journal of Personality and Social Psychology, 47,* 26–39.

Higgins, E. T., & Rholes, W. S. (1978). "Saying is believing": Effects of message modification on memory and liking for the person described. *Journal of Experimental Social Psychology, 14,* 363–378.

Higgins, E. T., & Sorrentino, R. M. (Eds.). (1990). *Handbook of motivation and cognition* (Vol. 2). New York: Guilford Press.

Hollon, S. D., & Garber, J. (1990). Cognitive therapy for depression: A social cognitive perspective. *Personality and Social Psychology Bulletin, 16,* 58–73.

Hooker, C., Roese, N. J., & Park, S. (1999). Impoverished counterfactual thinking is associated with schizophrenia. Unpublished manuscript, Northwestern University, Evanston, IL.

Ickes, W., & Gonzalez, R. (1994). "Social" cognition and *social* cognition: From the subjective to the intersubjective. *Small Group Research, 25,* 294–315.

Ingram, R. E. (1990). Self-focused attention in clinical disorders: Review and conceptual model. *Psychological Bulletin, 107,* 156–176.

Isen, A. M., & Hastorf, A. H. (1982). Some perspectives on cognitive social psychology. In A. Hastorf & A. Isen (Eds.), *Cognitive social psychology* (pp. 1–3). New York: Elsevier/North Holland.

Jones, E. E. (1990). *Interpersonal perception.* New York: Macmillan.

Jones, E. E., & Davis, K. E. (1965). From acts to dispositions: The attribution process in person perception. In L. Berkowitz (Ed.), *Advances in experimental social psychology* (Vol. 2, pp. 219–266). New York: Academic Press.

Jones, E. E., & Harris, V. A. (1967). The attribution of attitudes. *Journal of Experimental Social Psychology, 3,* 1–24.

Kaney, S., & Bentall, R. P. (1989). Persecutory delusions and attributional style. *British Journal of Medical Psychology, 62,* 191–198.

Kaney, S., & Bentall, R. P. (1992). Persecutory delusions and the self-serving bias. *Journal of Nervous and Mental Disease, 180,* 773–780.

Keefe, R. S. E., & Harvey, P. D. (1994). *Understanding schizophrenia: A guide to the new research on causes and treatment.* New York: Free Press.

Kelley, H. H. (1973). Processes of causal attribution. *American Psychologist, 28,* 107–128.

Kelly, G. A. (1955). *The psychology of personal constructs.* New York: Norton.

Kihlstrom, J. F., & Klein, S. B. (1994). The self as a knowledge structure. In R. S. Wyer, Jr., & T. K. Srull (Eds.), *Handbook of social cognition: Vol. 1. Basic processes* (2nd ed., pp. 153–208). Hillsdale, NJ: Erlbaum.

Kowalski, R. M., & Leary, M. R. (Eds.). (1999). *The social psychology of emotional and behavioral problems: Interfaces of social and clinical psychology.* Washington, DC: American Psychological Association.

Landman, J., & Manis, M. (1983). Social cognition: Some historical and theoretical perspectives. In L. Berkowitz (Ed.), *Advances in experimental social psychology* (Vol. 16, pp. 49–123). Orlando, FL: Academic Press.

Larson, J. R., Jr., & Christensen, C. (1993). Groups as problem-solving units: Toward a new meaning of social cognition. *British Journal of Social Psychology, 32,* 5–30.

Larson, J. R., Jr., Foster-Fishman, P. G., & Keys, C. B. (1994). Discussion of shared and unshared information in decision-making groups. *Journal of Personality and Social Psychology, 67,* 446–461.

Leslie, A. M. (1991). The theory of mind impairment in autism: Evidence for modular mechanisms in development? In A. Whiten (Ed.), *Natural theories of the mind: Evolution, development, and simulation of everyday mindreading* (pp. 63–78). Oxford, England: Blackwell.

Levine, J. M., & Higgins, E. T. (1995). Social determinants of cognition. *Social Cognition, 13,* 183–187.

Mackie, D. M., & Worth, L. T. (1989). Processing deficits and the mediation of positive affect in persuasion. *Journal of Personality and Social Psychology, 57,* 27–40.

Manis, M. (1977). Cognitive social psychology. *Personality and Social Psychology Bulletin, 3,* 550–566.

Mead, G. H. (1934). *Mind, self, and society.* Chicago: University of Chicago Press.

Miller, D. T., & Ross, M. (1975). Self-serving biases in the attribution of causality: Fact or fiction? *Psychological Bulletin, 82,* 213–225.

Miller, P. H. (1989). *Theories of developmental psychology.* New York: W. H. Freeman.

Mueser, K. T., Doonan, B., Penn, D. L., Blanchard, J. J., Bellack, A. S., Nishith, P., & DeLeon, J. (1996). Emotion perception and social competence in chronic schizophrenia. *Journal of Abnormal Psychology, 105,* 271–275.

Nasco, S. A., & Marsh, K. L. (1999). Gaining control through counterfactual thinking. *Personality and Social Psychology Bulletin, 25,* 556–568.

Newman, L. S. (1993). How individualists interpret behavior: Idiocentrism and spontaneous trait inference. *Social Cognition, 11,* 243–269.

Newman, L. S. (1996). Trait impressions as heuristics for predicting future behavior. *Personality and Social Psychology Bulletin, 22,* 395–411.

Newman, L. S. (1999). Motivated cognition and self-deception. *Psychological Inquiry, 10,* 59–63.

Newman, L. S. (in press). A cornerstone for the science of interpersonal behavior? Person perception and person memory, past, present, and future. In G. B. Moskowitz (Ed.), *Future directions in social cognition.*

Newman, L. S., & Uleman, J. S. (1993). When are you what you did? Behavior identification and dispositional inference in person memory, attribution, and social judgment. *Personality and Social Psychology Bulletin, 19,* 513–525.

Nisbett, R., & Ross, L. (1980). *Human inference: Strategies and shortcomings of social judgment.* Englewood Cliffs, NJ: Prentice-Hall.

Ostrom, T. M. (1984). The sovereignty of social cognition. In R. S. Wyer, Jr., & T. K. Srull (Eds.), *Handbook of social cognition: Vol. 1* (pp. 1–38). Hillsdale, N. J.: Erlbaum.

Penn, D. L., Corrigan, P. W., Bentall, R. P., Racenstein, J. M., & Newman, L.S. (1997). Social cognition in schizophrenia. *Psychological Bulletin, 121,* 114–132.

Penn, D. L., Spaulding, W. D., Reed, D., & Sullivan, M. (1996). The relationship of social cognition to ward behavior in chronic schizophrenia. *Schizophrenia Research, 20,* 327–335.

Reeder, G. D. (1993). Trait-behavior relations and dispositional inference. *Personality and Social Psychology Bulletin, 19,* 586–593.

Roese, N. J., & Hur, T. (1997). Affective determinants of counterfactual thinking. *Social Cognition, 15,* 274–290.

Roese, N. J., & Olson, J. M. (1997). Counterfactual thinking: The intersection of effect and function. In M. P. Zanna (Ed.), *Advances in experimental social psychology,* (Vol. 29, pp. 1–59). San Diego, CA: Academic Press.

Rogers, T. B., Kuiper, N. A., & Kirker, W. S. (1977). Self reference and the encoding of personal information. *Journal of Personality and Social Psychology, 35,* 677–688.

Ross, L. (1977). The intuitive psychologist and his shortcomings: Distortions in the attribution process. In L. Berkowitz (Ed.), *Advances in experimental social psychology* (Vol. 10, pp. 173–220). New York: Academic Press.

Ross, L., Amabile, T. M., & Steinmetz, J. L. (1977). Social roles, social control, and biases in social-perception processes. *Journal of Personality and Social Psychology, 35,* 485–494.

Scarr, S. (1995). Psychology will be truly evolutionary when behavior genetics is included. *Psychological Inquiry, 6,* 68–71.

Schneider, D. J. (1991). Social cognition. *Annual Review of Psychology, 42,* 527–561.

Schneider, D. J., Hastorf, A. H., & Ellsworth, P. C. (1979). *Person perception* (2nd ed.). Reading, MA: Addison-Wesley.

Schwarz, N. (1990). Feelings as information: Informational and motivational functions of affective states. In E. T. Higgins and R. Sorrentino (Eds.), *Handbook of motivation and cognition: Foundations of social behavior* (Vol. 2, pp. 527–561). New York: Guilford Press.

Schwarz, N., & Bless, H. (1991). Happy and mindless, but sad and smart? The impact of affective states on analytic reasoning. In J. Forgas (Ed.), *Emotion and social judgment* (pp. 55–71). Oxford, England: Pergamon.

Schwarz, N., Bless, H., & Bohner, G. (1991). Mood and persuasion: Affective states influence the processing of persuasive communications. In M. Zanna (Ed.), *Advances in experimental social psychology* (Vol. 24, pp. 161–199). San Diego, CA: Academic Press.

Schwarz, N., & Clore, G. L. (1983). Mood, misattribution, and judgments of well-being: Informative and directive functions of affective states. *Journal of Personality and Social Psychology, 45,* 513–523.

Shrauger, J. S., & Schoeneman, T. J. (1979). Symbolic interactionist view of self-concept: Through the looking glass darkly. *Psychological Bulletin, 86,* 549–573.

Sedikides, C., & Skowronski, J. J. (1997). The symbolic self in evolutionary context. *Personality and Social Psychology Review, 1,* 80–102.

Sherman, J. W., & Hamilton, D. L. (1994). On the formation of interitem associative links in person memory. *Journal of Experimental Social Psychology, 30,* 203–217.

Sherman, S. J., Judd, C. M., & Park, B. (1989). Social cognition. *Annual Review of Psychology, 40,* 281–326.

Silverman, R. J., & Peterson, C. (1993). Explanatory style of schizophrenic and depressed outpatients. *Cognitive Therapy and Research, 17,* 457–470.

Sorrentino, R. M., & Higgins, E. T. (Eds.). (1986). *Handbook of motivation and cognition* (Vol. 1). New York: Guilford Press.

Sorrentino, R. M., & Higgins, E. T. (Eds.). (1996). *Handbook of motivation and cognition* (Vol. 3). New York: Guilford Press.

Srull, T. K. (1981). Person memory: Some tests of associative storage and retrieval models. *Journal of Experimental Psychology: Human Learning and Memory, 7,* 440–463.

Srull, T. K., & Wyer, R. S., Jr. (1989). Person memory and judgment. *Psychological Review, 96,* 58–83.

Strauss, J. S., & Carpenter, W. T. (1977). Prediction of outcome in schizophrenia: Five-year outcome and its predictors. *Archives of General Psychiatry, 34,* 159–163.

Tien, A. Y., & Eaton, W. W. (1992). Psychopathologic precursors and sociodemographic risk factors for the schizophrenia syndrome. *Archives of General Psychiatry, 49,* 37–46.

Tooby, J., & Cosmides, L. (1990). On the universality of human nature and the uniqueness of the individual: The role of genetics and adaptation. *Journal of Personality, 58,* 17–68.

Tooby, J., & Cosmides, L. (1992). Psychological foundations of culture. In J. Barkow, L. Cosmides, & J. Tooby (Eds.), *The adapted mind* (pp. 19–136). New York: Oxford University Press.

Trope, Y. (1986). Identification and inferential processes in dispositional attribution. *Psychological Review, 93,* 239–257.

Trope, Y., & Liberman, A. (1996). Social hypothesis testing: Cognitive and motivational mechanisms. In E. T. Higgins & A. W. Kruglanski (Eds.), *Social psychology: Handbook of basic principles* (pp. 239–270). New York: Guilford Press.

Uleman, J. S., Newman, L. S., & Moskowitz, G. B. (1996). People as spontaneous interpreters: Evidence and issues from spontaneous trait inference. In M. Zanna (Ed.), *Advances in experimental social psychology* (Vol. 28, pp. 211–279). San Diego, CA: Academic Press.

Weary, G., & Mirels, H. L. (1982). *Integrations of clinical and social psychology.* New York: Oxford University Press.

Wegner, D. M. (1995). A computer network model of human transactive memory. *Social Cognition, 13,* 319–339.

Wegner, D. M., & Vallacher, R. R. (1977). *Implicit psychology: An introduction to social cognition.* New York: Oxford University Press.

Wenzlaff, R. M., Wegner, D. M., & Roper, D. (1988). Depression and mental control: The resurgence of unwanted negative thoughts. *Journal of Personality and Social Psychology, 55,* 882–892.

Wilson, T. D., & Brekke, N. (1994). Mental contamination and mental correction: Unwanted influences on judgments and evaluations. *Psychological Bulletin, 116,* 117–142.

Worchel, S., Cooper, J., & Goethals, G. R. (1989). *Understanding social psychology* (4th ed.). Pacific Grove, CA: Brooks/Cole.

Wright, R. (1995, March 13). The biology of violence. *The New Yorker,* pp. 68–77.

Wyer, R. S., Jr., Budesheim, T. L., & Lambert, A. J. (1990). The cognitive representation of conversations about persons. *Journal of Personality and Social Psychology, 58,* 128–218.

Wyer, R. S., Jr., Budesheim, T. L., Lambert, A. J., & Swan, S. (1994). Person memory and judgment: Pragmatic influences on impressions formed in a social context. *Journal of Personality and Social Psychology, 66,* 254–267.

Wyer, R. S., Jr., & Carlston, D. E. (1994). The cognitive representation of persons and events. The self as a knowledge structure. In R. S. Wyer, Jr., & T. K. Srull (Eds.), *Handbook of social cognition: Vol. 1. Basic processes* (2nd ed., pp. 41–98). Hillsdale, NJ: Erlbaum.

Wyer, R. S., & Srull, T. K. (1989). *Memory and cognition in its social context.* Hillsdale, NJ: Erlbaum.

Social Perception in Schizophrenia

2

Christoph Leonhard and Patrick W. Corrigan

The presentation and course of severe mental illnesses like schizophrenia may be significantly exacerbated by deficits in interpersonal functioning. In fact, long-term outcome in people with serious psychiatric illness often is judged by whether the person can function appropriately in the community, rather than by the absence of psychiatric symptoms (Harding et al., 1987; McGlashan, 1988). Psychiatric rehabilitation strategies that target the interpersonal deficits of schizophrenia have been developed and evaluated to improve the course of the disorder. Unfortunately, not all people with schizophrenia fully benefit from rehabilitation approaches such as social skills training (see Bellack, Turner, Hersen, & Luber, 1984; Wallace & Liberman, 1985), family communication training (see Anderson, Reiss, & Hogarty, 1986; Falloon, Boyd, & McGill, 1984; Mueser & Glynn, 1995), job training (see Bond, Drake, Mueser, & Becker, 1997; Drake, McHugo, Becker, Anthony, & Clark, 1996), and other therapies.

Researchers have attempted to identify individual variables that may mitigate the effects of psychiatric rehabilitation. Although several variables have been examined (e.g., negative symptoms, comorbid depression, gender, history of illness, comorbid substance abuse, and economic poverty), clinical investigators have been especially interested

Many thanks to Alice Medalia for a helpful review of an earlier version of this chapter and to Janan Reyna and the ISPP/CNW library staff for invaluable help in manuscript preparation.

in the effects of deficient cognition, particularly *social* cognition or rehabilitation.

This chapter reviews research on social perception in schizophrenia. First, it describes social perception in terms of the dominant model for understanding cognitive deficits in schizophrenia: information processing (IP). As argued in chapter 1, IP models are limited for explaining the perception and comprehension of social phenomena. Hence, this chapter reviews the limitations of IP models with special consideration to the discrimination of nonsocial stimuli (which typically are the foci of IP research) from social stimuli.

It may be useful here to differentiate between two IP models: the stage model and the capacity model. The former is the dominant model; it views social perception in a series of steps, beginning with sensation of relevant stimuli, progressing to perception with the help of attention, then adding cognition, finally leading to response production. A complementary model, the capacity model, accounts for cognitive (although not necessarily social cognitive) deficits in terms of IP demands exceeding processing capacity as a result of schizophrenia-related limitations (see Callaway & Naghdi, 1981; Nuechterlein & Dawson, 1984). Because capacity IP models have not been applied widely in social perception research, stage-model work is focal here. The chapter then reviews research on social perception of molecular and molar stimuli. The chapter ends with implications of this research for rehabilitating the social perceptual deficits of schizophrenia.

Information-Processing Models and Deficits in Attention

Information-processing models construe perception and attention as one step in an allopathic etiological cascade (see Spaulding, 1997).[1] Deficits at early stages may lead to poor functioning in subsequent processing (e.g., deficient memory or response selection), as well as diminished ability to understand and react to social situations. Hence, improvement in deficits may lead to generalized augmentation of memory and some interpersonal skills. Attention deficits have been ameliorated in people with schizophrenia using a mix of prompting, corrective feedback, and contingent reinforcement or punishment (Karras, 1962, 1968; Meiselman, 1973; Wagner, 1968). Unfortunately, the positive effects rarely

---

[1]Many of the issues related to limitations of IP models are more thoroughly addressed in chapter 1. Issues specific to IP models related to attention and perception are discussed here.

generalize to more ecologically meaningful abilities (Corrigan & Storz-bach, 1993; Green, 1993). For example, research has failed to show that improved ability to attend to an array of computer-generated letters leads to better perception and understanding of the cues that define social situations. IP models of cognitive deficit and the rehabilitation strategies they have generated therefore may not be sufficient to explain and ultimately remediate the *social* deficits of schizophrenia (see Spauld-ing et al., 1998, however, for contradictory findings).

Cognitive processes involved in social conduct seem to differ from nonsocial cognition in a number of ways (Holyoak & Gordon, 1984; Ostrom, 1984; Penn, Corrigan, Bentall, Racenstein, & Newman, 1997). Stimuli used in IP studies typically are limited to affectively neutral and static phenomena, such as numbers, words, and objects (Corrigan & Toomey, 1995). Social stimuli, in contrast, are personally relevant and affect laden (Fiske & Taylor, 1991). Perception of social stimuli also dif-fers in the relationship of the perceiver to the stimulus. IP research tends to support a unidirectional relationship between perceiver and stimulus (i.e., perceivers see, attend to, process, and finally act on environmental stimuli). Social stimuli and the perceiver, in contrast, are interactive (i.e., the perceiver can be complimented or disparaged by social stimuli; Fiske & Taylor, 1991).

Furthermore, social stimuli are relatively fluid and ever changing, rather than static. For example, even a 3-minute conversation may ex-pose the perceiver to a constantly changing array of facial affect and body language on the part of a conversation partner. What is more, the meaning of stimuli is highly dependent on complex contextual variables involving social status, conversation topics, and goals of interlocutors. For example, the meaning of laughter in response to humorous remarks is very different from the meaning of laughter in response to a social faux pas.

Finally, social situations have a conjugate quality not usually found in nonsocial situations. Social stimulation is not only ever changing and context dependent, but its fluidity is immediately and reciprocally influ-enced by the perceiver's behavior. Conjunction is thus a combination of stimulus fluidity and reciprocity. For example, in order to be socially appropriate, each turn in a conversation has to account for the larger sociocultural context of the interaction, what was said so far in the con-versation, and what was said immediately before.

FURTHER DIFFERENCES BETWEEN SOCIAL AND NONSOCIAL PERCEPTION

Social situations call for attending to and perceiving stimuli that con-stantly change, that are laden with affect, and whose meaning is context dependent. This complexity results in considerably greater demands on IP resources than are required for the processing of nonsocial stimuli. Because of the highly complex nature of the phenomena under investigation, common research and conceptual methods have not yet addressed which of the possible differences between social and nonsocial perception are actually clinically relevant. However, several related research findings can be mined for information to help hypothesize how social and nonsocial cognition may differ. Some of those findings are summarized in Exhibit 2.1.

One reason for poor perception may relate to impaired familiarity with specific cultural knowledge rather than deficits in attention per se (Cutting & Murphy, 1990). In social perception, as in all perception, familiarity with a stimulus significantly enhances correct perception of it. For example, a person who lacks familiarity with the nonverbal expression of social approval in a certain culture may misperceive when a conversation partner is enjoying an interaction. Because the meaning of social stimuli is culture bound, impaired cultural familiarity could be expected to adversely affect social perception, but not nonsocial information processing. Research has shown that a person's familiarity with specific social situations is directly related to the accuracy of his or her perception of that event (Corrigan, Silverman, Stephenson, Nugent-Hirschbeck, & Buican, 1996).

Another vector that differentiates social and nonsocial perception relates to the abstract versus concrete nature of stimuli. The meaning of social stimuli tends to depend more on abstraction (e.g., judgments of intention), whereas nonsocial stimuli often are interpreted in concrete dimensions, such as color or shape. Reich and Cutting (1982), for example, showed that the ability to perceive abstract meaning in a picture is more impaired in schizophrenia than in other mental illnesses. There-

---

EXHIBIT 2.1

Why Social and Nonsocial Stimuli Are Perceived Differently by People With Schizophrenia
- Perception of social stimuli is affected by cultural familiarity with situations; people with schizophrenia may have less familiarity.
- Social stimuli are generally more abstract and therefore are harder for people with schizophrenia to perceive.
- Perception of social stimuli requires greater semantic processing, a process that may be deficient in people with schizophrenia.
- Perception of social stimuli requires perception of emotional parameters, a difficult function for people with schizophrenia.

fore the relevant difference between social and nonsocial stimuli may be that the former require more abstraction than the latter. This point is discussed more fully in the section of this chapter on the perception of molar social stimuli.

A third difference between social and nonsocial perception may be the relative level of semantic involvement. Social tasks, such as perception of emotions, may place higher demands on semantic processing than perception of color or even of more complex geometrical forms. For example, the distinction between love, liking, and infatuation is more semantically based than the distinction between round and square shapes. Research on nonsocial perception in schizophrenia has shown left-hemispheric semantic processing to be relatively more impaired than right-hemispheric visual processing, even though both are impaired in absolute terms (David & Cutting, 1993). Extrapolating those findings, one might assume that the level of semantic involvement may contribute to apparent differences in social and nonsocial perception in people with schizophrenia.

Differences in affective involvement are another possible explanation for the deficits in social and nonsocial perception. Generally, social stimuli convey affective meaning, whereas nonsocial stimuli do not. Research findings indicate, for example, that people with schizophrenia are less able to correctly identify social stimuli that are laden with negative affect (Morrison, Bellack, & Bashore, 1988). The findings are further complicated by the possible moderating effect of the immediacy of affective load. It may be that the effect of chronic affective load on social perception differs from that of immediate load, a finding that would be difficult to examine in a pure laboratory study because chronic load is not manipulable.

ADDITIONAL RESEARCH ISSUES IN SOCIAL PERCEPTION

An implicit assumption in the discussion up to this point has been that social and nonsocial perception is fundamentally different. In part, this assertion is based on research suggesting that social and nonsocial perception account for independent variance in measures of social skill (Corrigan & Toomey, 1995). A competing explanation for these findings, however, may be a function of instrumentation effects. One possible reason why research findings show measures of social cognition to be more ecologically valid is method–trait confounds (i.e., tests of social perception are similar to tests of social functioning). For example, the Social Cue Recognition Test (SCRT; Corrigan & Green, 1993), commonly used in research on social perception and schizophrenia, comprises eight videotaped vignettes of interacting people. Upon viewing each vignette, research participants answer questions about concrete and abstract social cues present in the tape. Similarly, tests of social skill often involve judgments based on videotaped vignettes (Toomey, Wallace, Corrigan, & Schuldberg, 1997). However, tests of nonsocial perception frequently involve nonsense syllables or computer-generated graphical figures and digits (see Spaulding, Garbin, & Crinean, 1989). A higher correlation between social perception and social skill thus may be a result of confounding measurements and traits.

An argument for a method–trait confound is further strengthened by recent research that compared the relationship of self-evaluative statements, (e.g., "I am a good talker.") and SCRT performance with social skills (Ihnen, Penn, Corrigan, & Martin, 1998). Rather than using a video-based procedure, the investigators in this study measured social skill with a role-play test (Penn, Mueser, Doonan, & Nishith, 1995). Self-evaluation was found to be a superior predictor of social skill than the SCRT. Hence, future research needs to include multiple instruments to measure social cue perception, so that method contributions to the overall results can be partialled out.

Simple indices of the correct identification of social cues are biased estimators of perception, confounded by the perceived payoff that affects any decision to overtly report cue perception. Response rates can be increased by reinforcing people for correct identifications and decreased by fining them for errors. Payoff effects suggest that sensitivity to typical cognitive tasks represent not only the person's "cognitive apparatus" but also their motivation to complete the task correctly. For example, the number of correct identifications on the SCRT can be increased by paying participants 5 cents each time they accurately identify a cue. This kind of confound can be statistically estimated and thus eliminated by using a signal-detection model. Signal-detection parameters representing perceptual sensitivity are free of response biases caused by varying payoffs (i.e., for any task, sensitivity remains constant despite fluctuations in conditions that might affect correct identification and false positive rates; Davies & Parasuraman, 1982).

Signal-detection models for analyzing data typically are applied to vigilance tasks. Social cue perception involves a large memory component that may violate some of the assumptions about the distribution of signals and noise. Nonparametric indices of sensitivity have been used to investigate recognition-memory deficits in people without psychiatric illness (Banks, 1970; Lockhart & Murdock, 1970) and people with schizophrenia (Snodgrass & Corwin, 1988). One of these indices, A' (Davies & Parasuraman, 1982), is particularly robust and has been used in several studies on social perception and schizophrenia.

Specific Research on Social Perception and Schizophrenia

Given these conceptual and methodological concerns, what then is known about social perception in schizophrenia? This literature can be partitioned into work on the molar and work on the molecular aspects of social perception. The distinction seems to be both theoretical and methodological. Molecular models focus on the components of social stimuli; models focusing on those building blocks help researchers understand the elements that constitute social perceptual deficits in schizophrenia. Research in this area largely has examined deficits in facial-affect recognition. Researchers have countered, however, that social perception is a molar task that cannot be addressed by dividing the gestalt into pieces (Furnham, 1986; Trower, 1986). Research on molar perception has focused on scripts and schema that define social situations.

DEFICITS RELATED TO MOLECULAR MODELS

Research on the molecular aspects of social perception dates back more than 40 years, when it was empirically demonstrated that people with schizophrenia have greater difficulties perceiving socially relevant stimuli than do controls (Whiteman, 1954). Specific studies examined deficits in judging emotional expressions in audiotaped voices (Turner, 1964) or photographs (Dougherty, Bartlett, & Izard, 1974). These findings have been replicated, extended, and refined in research in the United States (Mueser, Penn, Blanchard, & Bellack, 1997), Japan (Ito, Shiragata, Kanno, Hoshino, & Niwa, 1998), Europe (Archer, Hay, & Young, 1992; Gessler, Cutting, Frith, & Weinman, 1989), and India (Mandal & Rai, 1987). A detailed review of findings in the molecular area is beyond the scope of this chapter; the reader is referred to reviews by Morrison, Bellack, and Mueser (1988) and Mandal, Pandey, and Prasad (1998).

Research generally suggests that compared with nonpatients, people with schizophrenia or schizoaffective disorder are unable to perceive accurately a micro level of social cues (e.g., Mandal et al., 1998; Mandal & Rai, 1987; Muzekari & Bates, 1977; Zuroff & Colussy, 1986). This finding also may apply to comparisons of people with schizophrenia against people with other mental illnesses, such as anxiety (Mandal & Rai) or depression (Gessler et al., 1989; but see Mueser et al., 1997 and Zuroff & Colussy for contradicting findings). It is unclear, however, whether the deficit in social perception is specific or generalized to the perceptual and cognitive deficits found in schizophrenia. Kerr and Neale

(1993), for example, addressed this question by examining the relationships among two neuropsychological measures and indices of facial-affect recognition. Findings indicated no differential deficiency for social perception that would go beyond a generalized perceptual—and, indeed, cognitive—processing deficit. Hence, problems with social perception may represent a deficit in processing information and not a problem specific to social phenomena.

Another conceptual question is whether emotions that vary in valence present similar perceptual challenges. Research in this area has been mixed. Dougherty and colleagues (1974), for example, found perception of shame–humiliation and disgust–anguish to be most diminished in people with schizophrenia, but not perception of enjoyment–joy. Other studies have similarly found that perception of negative affective states is suppressed, whereas perception of positive states is less, or possibly not at all, impaired (Borod, Martin, Alpert, Brozgold, & Welkowitz, 1993; Burch, 1995; Mandal & Rai, 1987; Muzekari & Bates, 1977).

Research also has examined whether the deficit in affect perception is equally evident in chronic and acute stages of schizophrenia. Some studies have indicated that social perception is more impaired during the acute stage of the illness (Gessler et al., 1989). Other investigations, however, have found that at least during the latter stages of hospitalization, the level of symptoms is not associated with affect perception (Bellack, Blanchard, & Mueser, 1996). Conversely, research also has found that the longer a person with schizophrenia has been hospitalized, the worse social perception becomes (Mueser et al., 1997). Interpreting such findings is complicated because the statistical correlation between chronicity (as measured by time spent in hospital) and social perception may result from a long stay in an impoverished social environment, rather than from the illness per se.

Another research question is whether social perceptual difficulties are specific to, or more pronounced in, diagnostic subcategories. Findings suggest that facial-affect perception is more accurate in people with paranoid schizophrenia (Kline, Smith, & Ellis, 1992; Lewis & Garver, 1995), although some early findings, using an emotion-perception task based on audiotaped stimuli, contradict this idea (Turner, 1964).

In addition to the unresolved conceptual issues, methodological questions have been raised (e.g., the issue of confounding emotion perception with skill difficulty). Many studies compare facial-affect perception to a control task, such as recognition of faces. One study found that when controlling for task difficulty, social perceptual deficiency in people with schizophrenia disappeared (Gessler et al., 1989). This finding renews the question of whether what appears to be a social perceptual problem is really just a problem with general perception.

A final methodological concern relates to instrumentation. As previously stated, tests of emotion or affect perception use different tasks and test stimuli. The nature of the task can vary, with some studies asking true–false questions (e.g. Ito et al., 1998) and others requiring research participants to match emotion labels to photos (Addington & Addington, 1998); yet others ask participants to rate videotaped actors on a Likert scale (Morrison, Bellack, & Bashore, 1988). Such variability in measures makes it hard to compare results across studies because different results may merely reflect differences in instruments.

DEFICITS EXPLAINED BY MOLAR MODELS

Molar approaches to understanding social perceptual deficits in schizophrenia have relied on social schema and script theory. According to these models, people make sense of social situations based on preexisting templates that organize the information provided in social situations. Rather than focusing on specific facial expressions or voice tones, this research focuses on macro phenomena, such as the roles, rules, and goals that define social situations.

Much of this research has been completed using the SCRT, which comprises eight videotaped vignettes of two or three people talking. Each vignette is short (2 or 3 minutes) so that performance on the task is not confounded by vigilance deficits. Research participants are instructed to watch each scene carefully, after which they answer several questions about it.

Our first study with the SCRT examined whether cue-recognition scores of people with schizophrenia differed from other groups (Corrigan, Davies-Farmer, & Stolley, 1991). Like most cognitive research, people with schizophrenia were expected to recognize fewer social cues than the comparison groups recognized. However, this distinction does not adequately describe diagnostic subsets of schizophrenia (Magaro, 1981). People with nonparanoid schizophrenia are characteristically hypovigilant, whereas people with paranoid schizophrenia are hypervigilant. The latter group therefore was expected to perform better than people with nonparanoid schizophrenia. The hypotheses were supported in our study.

Several studies used the SCRT to identify variables that may influence the perception of social cues in schizophrenia. Three variables are of particular interest: the level of abstraction required to interpret the cues of a social situation; the emotional tone of the interpersonal situation; and the presence of extraneous stimuli in the situation.

Levels of Abstraction and Cue Perception

Macro social cues are encoded vis-à-vis cognitive representations of the social world called schemata (Argyle, Furnham, & Graham, 1981). In particular, cues that define a social situation may be understood in terms of composite actions (what the actor did in the situation), dialogue (what the actor said in the situation), affect (emotions experienced by the actor in the situation), and goals (what the actor hoped to achieve in the situation). Argyle and colleagues (1978, 1981, 1986) argued that schemata that give meaning to social cues differ in level of abstraction. Abstract information requires greater cognitive resources to process than concrete information does. Actions and dialogue are relatively concrete descriptors, whereas affect and goals must be inferred from the concrete cues and, therefore, are more abstract.

Cognitive research long has suggested that people with schizophrenia perform significantly better on concrete cognitive tasks than on abstract ones because they are overwhelmed by the demands of abstract tasks (Goldstein, 1959). Abstract tasks require more cognitive effort, which frequently exceeds the limited capacity of their IP functions (Nuechterlein & Dawson, 1984). People with schizophrenia are expected to recognize the concrete cues of a situation better than the abstract cues. Research by our group supported this hypothesis; both inpatients and outpatients with *Diagnostical and Statistical Manual of Mental Disorders*, 3rd Edition revised (American Psychiatric Association, 1987) diagnoses of schizophrenia were presented the eight SCRT vignettes and asked several true–false questions about the abstract and concrete cues in the situation (Corrigan, Buican, & Toomey, 1996; Corrigan & Green, 1993; Corrigan & Nelson, 1998). Results showed that they were significantly less sensitive to the abstract cues than to the concrete cues. Hence, people with schizophrenia may show a differential deficit in perceiving abstract and concrete interpersonal cues.

Differential deficit across any two tasks may be confounded by the generalized performance decrements that are characteristic of schizophrenia. Chapman and Chapman (1973, 1978) said that this confound can be diminished by matching items across tasks for difficulty and reliability on samples of control participants who are similar to samples with schizophrenia. Items representing abstract and concrete social cues were matched for difficulty and consistency on standardization and cross-validation samples of control participants in this study (Corrigan & Green, 1993). Moreover, findings have suggested that differences in concrete and abstract cue recognition were not significantly associated with verbal intelligence (Corrigan, 1994). Therefore, the differential perception of social cues is not likely to be a function of psychometric confound or generalized performance decrement.

Cue Perception and Emotional Arousal

Research on facial-affect recognition (reviewed previously in this chapter) was extrapolated to research on cue perception and emotions. In particular, the emotional tone of an interpersonal situation was expected to covary with the psychophysiological arousal of the people experiencing those situations. More specifically, people are expected to be more aroused when observing interpersonal situations with greater emotional tone.

We tested this hypothesis on people with schizophrenia who were shown the eight vignettes of the SCRT. The vignettes were originally written so that four of the situations were considered low emotion and four were of relatively moderate emotion. Yerkes and Dodson (1908) argued that the relationship between psychophysiological arousal and cognitive ability is described by an inverted U. Cognitive abilities like social cue perception are optimal at relatively moderate levels of psychophysiological arousal and diminish as a person approaches low- or high-arousal extremes. This finding suggests that perception of social cues should be greater in situations that are more emotionally arousing as long as situational arousal does not overwhelm the person.

To test this hypothesis, research participants with schizophrenia in two different studies were shown the eight SCRT vignettes (Corrigan, Davies-Farmer, & Stolley, 1991; Corrigan & Green, 1993). Consistent with our hypotheses, people with schizophrenia were more sensitive to social cues when viewing the moderately arousing vignettes versus the low-arousing vignettes. The findings suggest that people with schizophrenia are more attentive to situations that are emotionally poignant rather than sedate. Hence, they are more likely to be responsive to social interactions in emotionally lively situations. Interestingly, control participants in the studies showed no differential sensitivity to social cues as a function of situational arousal.

The findings have implications for training people with schizophrenia on social skills. Training situations should be relatively lively affairs in which people are stimulated to participate fully. However, trainers using active stimulation during skills training should consider the tonic level of a person's arousal. Acutely agitated people should not be further stimulated to participate. More than likely, their perceptual skills are already diminished because of excessive arousal. Instead, they may participate better if they are encouraged to calm down through the use of an appropriate relaxation strategy.

Cue Perception and Extraneous Emotional Stimuli

What would happen if people with schizophrenia were asked to attend to the molar cues of interpersonal situations while extraneous, emotionally arousing stimuli were presented? Findings on the effect of situational arousal suggest that people might perceive social cues better because their level of psychophysiological arousal would increase. However, this finding seems to contradict research showing that external stimuli can be significantly distracting to people with schizophrenia (Corrigan & Green, 1991; Oltmanns & Neale, 1975; Rund, 1983). Presentation of extraneous emotional stimuli might decrease the cue perception of people in this group.

These competing questions were addressed in a study in which 25 people with schizophrenia listened to the SCRT vignettes, half of which were presented with a simultaneous emotionally arousing stimulus (Corrigan & Addis, 1995). The remaining half of the vignettes were presented without the extraneous stimulus. An audiotaped segment from *Star Trek* was selected as the emotionally arousing stimulus because it was believed to be familiar to research participants and because participants rated it as emotionally arousing in a separate pilot study. Results from this study showed that people with schizophrenia were more sensitive to interpersonal cues when the episode was presented simultaneously. Control participants in standardization and cross-validation groups showed no differences in cue sensitivity across conditions.

We concluded that the level of emotional arousal engendered by the extraneous stimuli was the operative factor in enhancing cue perception. Perhaps people with schizophrenia were more aroused and alert as a result. This finding is consistent with our research on emotional arousal, which suggests that cue perception is enhanced in more arousing situations. Still, we are reluctant to suggest that perception of interpersonal situations can be facilitated by, for example, playing inspirational music. The effects of distraction on attention and memory in schizophrenia are robust and not to be overlooked.

COGNITIVE SCHEMATA AS TEMPLATES OF SOCIAL PERCEPTION

Social schemata describe the manner in which perceived interpersonal information is represented; they may be viewed as templates through which incoming social information is encoded or as blueprints by which interpersonal responses are guided. Investigators have identified several classes of schemata that describe self (Rogers, Kuiper, & Kirker, 1977), people (Cantor & Mischel, 1979), and situations (Galambos, Abelson, & Black, 1986; Schank & Abelson, 1977). Because performance of social skills has been shown to be directly related to perception and processing of situational cues (Forgas, 1983; Trower, 1986), situational schemata have particular relevance for understanding the interpersonal functioning deficits of schizophrenia.

Bower, Black, and Turner (1979) showed that Stanford undergraduates were consistently able to identify component actions from a list of behaviors that make up two social situations—eating at a restaurant and visiting a doctor's office. They interpreted the findings as representing the organizational power of schemata that represent social situations. Argyle and his colleagues (1978, 1981, 1986) said that the meaning which situational schemata impart on sensory stimuli are a function of schema components called "features." Consistent with other research, studies by our group showed people with schizophrenia to be less able than controls to recognize the features of interpersonal situations (Corrigan, Wallace, & Green, 1992). Like our research on the SCRT, several studies have been conducted to examine variables that feature detection, including the level of feature abstraction, the familiarity of situations described by features, and the temporal relationships of features.

Feature Abstraction

Of the various features that describe social situations, four have been targeted in research on abstraction: actions, roles, rules, and goals (Argyle, Furnham, & Graham, 1981). Actions are the characteristic behaviors that occur in a situation (e.g., in a restaurant, the customer follows the hostess to his seat, takes the menu, and places an order). Many actions are consistently undertaken by situationally defined characters or roles (e.g., the role or character of a hostess seating a customer, or of a barmaid serving a drink situationally defines a culturally prescribed domain of actions). Rules consist of the subtle interpersonal customs that govern the situation (e.g., customers wait until the hostess calls them to be seated). Goals define the actor's purpose for entering and engaging in the situation (e.g., customers are trying to satisfy their hunger).

Features that describe interpersonal situations vary on a continuum of abstraction; actions and roles represent more concrete schematic representations of situations, and rules and goals represent more abstract features. As described earlier in this chapter, schizophrenia has been viewed classically as a deficit in abstract thinking. Therefore, people with schizophrenia are predicted to better identify the more concrete features of situations, rather than the abstract components. To test this question, the Situational Feature Recognition Test (SFRT) was administered to people with *DSM* diagnoses (III-R, 1987) of schizophrenia or schizoaffective disorder (Corrigan & Green, 1993; Corrigan et al., 1996). The SFRT is a paper-and-pencil measure that requires participants to identify features from a list of descriptors that describe test situations. Research participants are presented four lists of features for each situation corresponding to actions, roles, rules, and goals. Each list includes six features and eight distractors.

Results supported our hypotheses: People with schizophrenia were significantly less sensitive to the relatively abstract features that describe a situation (i.e., goals) than to the more concrete features, like actions and roles. This differential deficit seemed to represent characteristics of the disorder rather than psychometric limitations of the SFRT because items representing abstract and concrete features were matched for difficulty and internal consistency on standardization and cross-validation samples.

Situational Familiarity

Further analyses suggested that feature identification on the SFRT was confounded by the content of situations (Corrigan & Green, 1993). Perhaps the effects of institutionalization diminish the person's familiarity with the content of common interpersonal situations. Many people with chronic mental illness are hospitalized for long periods of time and suffer other forms of social isolation. As a result, the effects of institutionalization, rather than the deficits in processing abstract information, may account for diminished feature recognition.

To test this question, a second version of the SFRT (the SFRT–2) was developed, in which stimulus situations that constitute the measure were selected because pilot samples of severely mentally ill and control participants had rated them reliably as very familiar or unfamiliar (Corrigan et al., 1996). Items representing abstract and concrete (i.e., goals and actions, respectively) features were then written for each situation. Item difficulty and internal consistency of the lists were matched on standardization and cross-validation samples. People with schizophrenia who then completed the SFRT–2 once again recognized concrete features of the situations significantly better than abstract features. Moreover, this group recognized features in the familiar situations better than they did features in the unfamiliar situations. Of the greatest interest, findings showed that difference in action and goal recognition interacted with situational familiarity (i.e., people with schizophrenia were least sensitive to the goals that described lesser known situations).

These findings have implications for remediation of social perceptual deficits; namely, helping people become more familiar with interpersonal situations will help them better recognize situational features. This recommendation, however, requires some information about what "familiar situation" means to a person with schizophrenia. Familiarity, of course, is merely a function of the frequency with which people are present in and interact with various situations. Therefore, opportunities for people with schizophrenia to experience various hitherto unfamiliar situations may improve as they are introduced to them.

Unpublished findings by our group have examined other factors that correlate with a person's ratings of situational familiarity (Corrigan,

1993). Findings from this research suggested that ratings of familiarity of emotionally arousing situations are significantly associated with ratings of comfort in those situations; this association was not found for relatively unarousing situations. Therefore, becoming familiar with "emotional" situations may be, to some extent, a function of becoming comfortable with the situation. Exposing people with schizophrenia to situations may require the inclusion of coping strategies to help them become comfortable with these situations.

Temporal Sequence of Features

Research on situational schemata with control groups has shown that people tend to store and retrieve component actions that describe specific situations in temporal sequences (Abelson, 1981, Galambos, Abelson, & Black, 1986). For example, component actions in a restaurant situation are likely to be recalled as "(1) enter restaurant, (2) be seated by hostess, (3) read menu, (4) order meal, (5) eat meal, and (6) pay bill." Situational information presented out of order appears discordant and tends to be reordered quickly by the observer. The temporal information contained in social sequences is essential for accurate predictions and inferences about the actions of others as people participate in these sequences (Galambos et al., 1986). "Entering the restaurant" and "observing Mary eating dinner" leads to the inference that Mary has already ordered and the prediction that she will soon pay her bill. Inability to recognize social sequences correctly may diminish a person's performance in social situations. Preliminary research by our group found that people with schizophrenia were less able to correctly order actions into a temporal sequence than were participants in a comparison group (Corrigan et al., 1992).

Twenty-six people with schizophrenia then participated in a study to determine how the number of component actions to be ordered in a temporal sequence affected the accuracy of their performance on this social cognitive ability (Corrigan & Addis, 1995). In particular, we wanted to know whether people with schizophrenia are able to use more information (longer sequences) to better understand social situations or whether the increased complexity overwhelms their comprehension of the experience. Researchers have argued that the cognitive functions of people with schizophrenia, compared with similar control groups, are inordinately diminished by the cognitive complexity of a task (Gjerde, 1983; Nuechterlein & Dawson, 1984). For example, people with schizophrenia performed significantly worse than matched control participants on a short-term recall task when an auditory distractor was presented simultaneously (Oltmanns & Neale, 1975).

The Schema Component Sequencing Task (Corrigan & Addis, 1995) is a measure in which research participants are instructed to order short and long sequences. Like previous efforts by our group, this task is matched for item difficulty and internal consistency on standardization and cross-validation groups. The 26 people with schizophrenia who then completed the measure were able to order short sequences significantly better than long sequences. The differential deficit in sequencing actions was found to correlate significantly with the Brief Psychiatric Rating Scale (BPRS; Lukoff, Liberman, & Nuechterlein, 1986) Withdrawal/Retardation factor, a measure of negative symptoms. Positive symptoms did not seem to be significantly associated with the differential deficit.

Information about the effects of cognitive complexity on social sequencing may be especially useful in terms of social and cognitive rehabilitation. In particular, the differential deficit in this study suggests that strategies that assist people with schizophrenia in managing relatively complex cognitive tasks will help them understand social situations better. Such strategies include memory interventions that help people encode information into personally meaningful schemata and using environmental cues to help organize the person's social space.

Conclusion and Implications for Cognitive Rehabilitation

To summarize, research on social perception has investigated both molar and molecular aspects of social cognition. Many methodological challenges need to be overcome in advancing our knowledge, including method–trait confounds, operationalization problems, and confounds between the social and nonsocial nature of a task and its relative difficulty. In spite of the challenges, we know that people with schizophrenia have deficits in social perception both when analyzed in a sequential, molecular IP fashion and when viewed from a more holistic, molar perspective. Factors that relate to such deficits include diagnostic subtype, the affective quality of the situation to be perceived and the emotionality of the person perceiving it, the concrete versus abstract level of perception required, and the familiarity of the social situation.

Our main interest in research on social perception is to see how it can yield richer conceptual findings for the development of cognitive rehabilitation strategies. Of the various findings reported here, one that has been particularly useful is that cue perception of people with schizophrenia is significantly associated with verbal memory deficits and relatively unassociated with deficits in vigilance (Corrigan, Green, & Toomey, 1994). We conclude, therefore, that rehabilitation strategies that enhance memory should have a better effect on cue perception than strategies that enhance attention.

Koh (Koh, Grinker, Marusarz, & Forman, 1981; Koh, Kayton, & Peterson, 1976) showed that deficits in verbal memory in people with schizophrenia can be remediated using encoding strategies. Semantic elaboration is an encoding strategy used by neuropsychologists to improve memory deficits in patients (Gouvier, Webster, & Blanton, 1986); the process instructs people to put new information into their own words. When information is encoded in this fashion, it will more readily be incorporated into existing schemata and thereby more easily recalled later.

Corrigan, Nugent-Hirschbeck, and Wolfe (1995) compared the effects of semantic elaboration with the effects of an attention-focusing strategy on social cue perception in people with schizophrenia. Research participants in the semantic-elaboration condition were instructed to say aloud what was just observed in each of eight vignettes. Directive questions also were asked to assist the person in stating aloud the concrete and abstract cues of each vignette. People in the attention-focusing condition were taught to self-instruct, "I will pay attention to the TV screen."

Results showed that people in the semantic-elaboration condition significantly enhanced their cue perception, whereas no change was observed in the attention-focusing group. In fact, cue perception in the semantic-elaboration condition approached normal levels. Moreover, improvements in cue perception were significantly greater for abstract than for concrete cues.

This research suggests that measuring cue perception is a useful first step in understanding and rehabilitating the social cognitive deficits of schizophrenia. This body of literature seems to be yielding more ecologically valid models of cognition and social functioning than are IP models. However, the ecological validity of social perception and social cognition needs further testing in studies that examine the relationship between those constructs and the social competence of schizophrenic patients. Our assertions will be further supported if deficits in social perception and cognition are found to be significant predictors of interpersonal functioning and social skill learning. In turn, this research will lead to more effective rehabilitation strategies for people with schizophrenia.

References

Abelson, R. P. (1981). Psychological status of the script concept. *American Psychologist, 36,* 715–729.

Addington, J., & Addington, D. (1998). Facial affect recognition and information processing in schizophrenia and bipolar disorder. *Schizophrenia Research, 32,* 171–181.

American Psychiatric Association. (1987). *Diagnostic and statistical manual of mental disorders* (3rd ed. revised). Washington, DC: Author.

Anderson, C. M., Reiss, D. J., & Hogarty, G. E. (1986). *Schizophrenia and the family.* New York: Guilford Press.

Archer, J., Hay, D. C., & Young, A. W. (1992). Face processing in psychiatric conditions. *British Journal of Clinical Psychology, 31,* 45–61.

Argyle, M., Furnham, A., & Graham, J. A. (1981). *Social situations.* New York: Cambridge University Press.

Argyle, M., Henderson, M., Bond, M., & Iizuka, Y. (1986). Cross-cultural variations in relationship rules. *International Journal of Psychology, 21,* 287–315.

Argyle, M., Shimoda, K., & Little, B. (1978). Variance due to persons and situations in England and Japan. *British Journal of Social & Clinical Psychology, 17,* 335–337.

Banks, W. P. (1970). Signal detection theory and human memory. *Psychological Bulletin, 74,* 81–99.

Bellack, A. S., Blanchard, J. J., & Mueser, K. T. (1996). Cue availability and affect perception in schizophrenia. *Schizophrenia Bulletin, 22,* 535–544.

Bellack, A. S., Turner, S. M., Hersen, M., & Luber, R. F. (1984). An examination of the efficacy of social skills training for chronic schizophrenic patients. *Hospital and Community Psychiatry, 35,* 1023–1028.

Bond, G. R., Drake, R. E., Mueser, K. T., & Becker, D. R. (1997). An update of supported employment for people with severe mental illness. *Psychiatric Services, 48,* 335–346.

Borod, J. C., Martin, C. C., Alpert, M., Brozgold, A., & Welkowitz, J. (1993). Perception of facial emotion in schizophrenic and right brain-damaged patients. *Journal of Nervous and Mental Disease, 181,* 494–502.

Bower, G. H., Black, J. B., & Turner, T. J. (1979). Scripts in memory for text. *Cognitive Psychology, 11,* 177–220.

Burch, J. W. (1995). Typicality range deficit in schizophrenics' recognition of emotion in faces. *Journal of Clinical Psychology, 51,* 140–152.

Callaway, E., & Naghdi, S. (1981). An information processing model of schizophrenia. *Archives of General Psychiatry, 39,* 339–347.

Cantor, N., & Mischel, W. (1979). Prototypicality and personality: Effects on free recall and personality impressions. *Journal of Research in Personality, 13,* 187–205.

Chapman, L. J., & Chapman, J. P. (1973). *Disordered thought in schizophrenia.* New York: Appleton-Century-Crofts.

Chapman, L. J., & Chapman, J. P. (1978). When should schizophrenic and normal groups be compared? *Journal of Psychiatric Research,14,* 321–325.

Corrigan, P. W. (1993). Staff stressors at a developmental center and state hospital. *Mental Retardation, 31,* 234–238.

Corrigan, P. W. (1994). Social cue perception and intelligence in schizophrenia. *Schizophrenia Research, 13,* 73–79.

Corrigan, P. W., & Addis, I. (1995). The effects of cognitive complexity on a social sequencing task in schizophrenia. *Schizophrenia Research, 16,* 137–144.

Corrigan, P. W., Buican, B., & Toomey, R. (1996). The construct validity of two tests of social cognition in schizophrenia. *Psychiatry Research, 62,* 251–257.

Corrigan, P. W., Davies-Farmer, R. M., & Stolley, M. R. (1991). Social cue recognition in schizophrenia under variable levels of arousal. *Cognitive Therapy and Research, 14,* 353–361.

Corrigan, P. W., & Green, M. F. (1991). Signal detection analysis of short-term recall in schizophrenia. *Journal of Nervous and Mental Disease, 179,* 495–498.

Corrigan, P. W., & Green, M. F. (1993). The situational feature recognition test: A measure of schema comprehension for schizophrenia. *International Journal of Methods in Psychiatric Research, 3,* 29–36.

Corrigan, P. W., Green, M. F., & Toomey, R. (1994). Cognitive correlates to social cue perception in schizophrenia. *Psychiatry Research, 53,* 141–151.

Corrigan, P. W., & Nelson, D. (1998). Factors that affect social cue recognition in schizophrenia. *Psychiatry Research, 78,* 189–196.

Corrigan, P. W., Nugent-Hirschbeck, J., & Wolfe, M. (1995). Memory and vigilance training to improve social perception in schizophrenia. *Schizophrenia Research, 17,* 257–265.

Corrigan, P. W., Silverman, R., Stephenson, J., Nugent-Hirschbeck, J., & Buican, B. (1996). Situational familiarity and feature recognition in schizophrenia. *Schizophrenia Bulletin, 22,* 153–162.

Corrigan, P. W., & Storzbach, D. (1993). The ecological validity of cognitive rehabilitation for schizophrenia. *Journal of Cognitive Rehabilitation, 11,* 2–9.

Corrigan, P. W., & Toomey, R. (1995). Interpersonal problem solving and information processing in schizophrenia. *Schizophrenia Bulletin, 21,* 395–404.

Corrigan, P. W., Wallace, C. J., & Green, M. F. (1992). Deficits in social schemata in schizophrenia. *Schizophrenia Research, 8,* 129–135.

Cutting, J., & Murphy, D. (1990). Impaired ability of schizophrenics, relative to manics or depressives, to appreciate social knowledge about their culture. *British Journal of Psychiatry, 157,* 355–358.

David, A. S., & Cutting, J. C. (1993). Visual imagery and visual semantics in the cerebral hemispheres in schizophrenia. *Schizophrenia Research, 8,* 263–271.

Davies, D. R., & Parasuraman, R. (1982). *The psychology of vigilance.* New York: Academic Press.

Dougherty, F. E., Bartlett, E. S., & Izard, C. E. (1974). Responses of schizophrenics to expression of the fundamental emotions. *Journal of Clinical Psychology, 30,* 243–246.

Drake, R. E., McHugo, G. J., Becker, D. R., Anthony, W. A., & Clark, R. E. (1996). The New Hampshire study of supported employment for people with severe mental illness. *Journal of Consulting and Clinical Psychology, 64,* 391–399.

Falloon, I. R. H., Boyd, J. L., & McGill, C. W. (1984). *Family care of schizophrenia.* New York: Guilford Press.

Fiske, S. T., & Taylor, S. E. (1991). *Social cognition* (2nd ed.). New York: McGraw-Hill.

Forgas, J. P. (1983). Social skills and the perception of interaction episodes. *British Journal of Clinical Psychology, 22,* 195–207.

Furnham, A. (1986). Response bias, social desirability and dissimulation. *Personality and Individual Differences, 7,* 385–400.

Galambos, J. A., Abelson, R. P., & Black, J. B. (1986). *Knowledge structures.* Hillsdale, NJ: Lawrence Erlbaum.

Gessler, S., Cutting, J., Frith, C. D., & Weinman, J. (1989). Schizophrenic inability in judging facial emotion: A controlled study. *British Journal of Clinical Psychology, 28,* 19–29.

Gjerde, P. F. (1983). Attentional capacity dysfunction and arousal in schizophrenia. *Psychological Bulletin, 93,* 57–72.

Goldstein, K. (1959). Concerning the concreteness in schizophrenia. *Journal of Abnormal and Social Psychology, 59,* 146–148.

Gouvier, W. D., Webster, J. S., & Blanton, P. D. (1986). Cognitive retraining with brain damaged patients. In D. Wedding & A. M. Horton, Jr. (Eds.), *The neuropsychology handbook: Behavioral and clinical perspectives* (pp. 278–324). New York: Springer.

Green, M. F. (1993). Cognitive remediation in schizophrenia: Is it time yet? *American Journal of Psychiatry, 150,* 178–187.

Harding, C. M., Brooks, G. W., Ashikaga, T., Strauss, J. S., & Breier, A. (1987). The Vermont longitudinal study of persons with severe mental illness: I. Methodology, study sample, and overall status 32 years later. *American Journal of Psychiatry, 144,* 718–726.

Holyoak, K. J., & Gordon, P.C. (1984). Information processing and social cognition. In R. S. Wyer & T. K. Srull (Eds.), *Handbook of social cognition: Vol. 1* (pp. 176–201). Hillsdale, NJ: Lawrence Erlbaum.

Ihnen, G. H., Penn, D. L., Corrigan, P. W., & Martin, J. (1998). Social perception and social skill in schizophrenia. *Psychiatry Research, 80,* 275–286.

Ito, M., Shiragata, M., Kanno, M., Hoshino, K.-Y., & Niwa, S.-I. (1998). Social cue perception in Japanese schizophrenic patients. *Schizophrenia Research, 34,* 113–119.

Karras, A. (1962). The effects of reinforcement and arousal on the psychomotor performance of chronic schizophrenics. *Journal of Abnormal Psychology, 65,* 104–111.

Karras, A. (1968). Choice reaction time of chronic and acute psychiatric patients under primary and secondary aversive stimulation. *British Journal of Social Clinical Psychology, 7,* 270–279.

Kerr, S. L., & Neale, J. M. (1993). Emotion perception in schizophrenia: specific deficit or further evidence of generalized poor performance? *Journal of Abnormal Psychology, 102,* 312–318.

Kline, J. S., Smith, J. E., & Ellis, H. C. (1992). Paranoid and nonparanoid schizophrenic processing of facially displayed affect. *Journal of Psychiatric Research, 26,* 169–182.

Koh, S. D., Grinker, R. R., Marusarz, T. Z., & Forman, P. L. (1981). Affective memory and schizophrenia anhedonia. *Schizophrenia Bulletin, 7,* 292–307.

Koh, S. D., Kayton, L., & Peterson, R. A. (1976). Affective encoding and consequent remembering in schizophrenic young adults. *Journal of Abnormal Psychology, 85,* 156–166.

Lewis, S. F., & Garver, D. L. (1995). Treatment and diagnostic subtype in facial affect recognition in schizophrenia. *Journal of Psychiatric Research, 29,* 5–11.

Lockhart, R. S., & Murdock, B. B. (1970). Memory and the theory of signal detection. *Psychological Bulletin, 74,* 100–109.

Lukoff, D., Liberman, R. P., & Nuechterlein, K. H. (1986). Symptom monitoring in the rehabilitation of schizophrenic patients. *Schizophrenic Bulletin, 12,* 578–593.

Magaro, P. A. (1981). The paranoid and the schizophrenic: The case for distinct cognitive style. *Schizophrenia Bulletin, 7,* 632–661.

Mandal, M. K., Pandey, R., & Prasad, A. B. (1998). Facial expressions of emotions and schizophrenia: A review. *Schizophrenia Bulletin, 24,* 399–412.

Mandal, M. K., & Rai, A. (1987). Responses to facial emotion and psychopathology. *Psychiatry Research, 20,* 317–323.

McGlashan, T. H. (1988). A selective review of recent North American long-term follow-up studies of schizophrenia. *Schizophrenia Bulletin, 14,* 515–542.

Meiselman, K. C. (1973). Broadening dual modality cue utilization in chronic non-paranoid schizophrenia. *Journal of Consulting and Clinical Psychology, 41,* 447–453.

Morrison, R. L., Bellack, A. S., & Bashore, T. R. (1988). Perception of emotion among schizophrenic patients. *Journal of Psychopathology and Behavioral Assessment, 10,* 319–332.

Morrison, R. L., Bellack, A. S., & Mueser, K. T. (1988). Deficits in facial-affect recognition and schizophrenia. *Schizophrenia Bulletin, 14,* 67–83.

Mueser, K. T., & Glynn, S. M. (1995). *Behavioral family therapy for psychiatric disorders.* Boston, MA: Allyn & Bacon.

Mueser, K. T., Penn, D. L., Blanchard, J. J., & Bellack, A. S. (1997). Affect recognition in schizophrenia: A synthesis of findings across three studies. *Psychiatry, 60,* 301–308.

Muzekari, L. H., & Bates, M. E. (1977). Judgement of emotion among chronic schizophrenics. *Journal of Clinical Psychology, 33,* 662–666.

Nuechterlein, K. H., & Dawson, M. E. (1984). Information processing and attentional functioning in the developmental course of schizophrenic disorders. *Schizophrenia Bulletin, 10,* 160–203.

Oltmanns, T. F., & Neale, J. M. (1975). Schizophrenic performance when distractors are present: Attentional deficit or differential task difficulty? *Journal of Abnormal Psychology, 84,* 205–209.

Ostrom, T. M. (1984). The sovereignty of social cognition. In R. S. Wyer & T. K. Skrull (Eds.), *Handbook of social cognition* (Vol. 1, pp. 1–37). Hillside, NJ: Lawrence Erlbaum.

Penn, D. L., Corrigan, P. W., Bentall, R. P., Racenstein, J. M., & Newman, L. S. (1997). Social cognition in schizophrenia. *Psychological Bulletin, 121,* 114–132.

Penn, D. L., Mueser, K. T., Doonan, R., & Nishith, P. (1995). Relations between social skills and ward behavior in chronic schizophrenia. *Schizophrenia Research, 16,* 225–232.

Reich, S. S., & Cutting, J. (1982). Picture perception and abstract thought in schizophrenia. *Psychological Medicine, 12,* 91–96.

Rogers, T. B., Kuiper, N. A., & Kirker, W. S. (1977). Self reference and the encoding of personal information. *Journal of Personality and Social Psychology, 35,* 677–688.

Rund, B. R. (1983). The effect of distraction on focal attention in paranoid and non-paranoid schizophrenic patients compared to normals and non-psychotic psychiatric patients. *Journal of Psychiatric Research, 17,* 241–250.

Schank, R. C., & Abelson, R. P. (1977). *Scripts, plans, goals and understanding: An inquiry into human knowledge structures.* Hillsdale, NJ: Lawrence Erlbaum.

Snodgrass, J. G., & Corwin, J. (1988). Pragmatics of measuring recognition memory: Applications to dementia and amnesia. *Journal of Experimental Psychology: General, 117,* 34–50.

Spaulding, W. D. (1997). Cognitive models in a fuller understanding of schizophrenia. *Psychiatry, 60,* 341–346.

Spaulding, W., Garbin, C. P., & Crinean, W. J. (1989). The logical and psychometric prerequisites for cognitive therapy of schizophrenia. *British Journal of Psychiatry, 155*(Suppl. 5), 69–73.

Spaulding, W., Reed, D., Storzbach, D., Sullivan, M., Weiler, M., & Richardson, C. (1998). The effects of a remediational approach to cognitive therapy for schizophrenia. In T. Wykes, N. Tarrier, & S. Lewis (Eds.), *Outcome and innovation in psychological treatment of schizophrenia* (pp. 145–160). Chichester, England: John Wiley & Sons.

Toomey, R., Wallace, C. J., Corrigan, P. W., & Schuldberg, D. (1997). Social processing correlates of nonverbal social perception in schizophrenia. *Psychiatry: Interpersonal and Biological Processes, 60,* 292–300.

Trower, P. (1986). On the ethical basis of "scientific" behavior therapy. In S. Fairbairn & G. Fairbairn (Eds.), *Psychology ethics & change* (pp. 74–90). London, England: Routledge & Kegan Paul.

Turner, J. le B. (1964). Schizophrenics as judges of vocal expressions of emotional meaning. In J. R. Davitz (Ed.), *The communication of emotional meaning* (pp. 129–142). New York: McGraw-Hill.

Wagner, B. R. (1968). The training of attending and abstracting responses in chronic schizophrenia. *Journal of Experimental Research in Personality, 3,* 77–88.

Wallace, C. J., & Liberman, R. P. (1985). Social skills training for patients with schizophrenia: A controlled clinical trial. *Psychiatry Research, 15,* 239–247.

Whiteman, M. (1954). The performance of schizophrenics on social concepts. *Journal of Abnormal and Social Psychology, 49,* 266–271.

Yerkes, R. M., & Dodson, J. D. (1908). The relation of strength of stimulus to rapidity of habit formation. *Journal of Comparative Neurology and Psychology, 18,* 459–482.

Zuroff, D. C., & Colussy, S. A. (1986). Emotion recognition in schizophrenic and depressed inpatients. *Journal of Clinical Psychology, 42,* 411–417.

Social Cognition and Social Functioning in Schizophrenia

3

David L. Penn, Dennis Combs, and Somaia Mohamed

One of the hallmark characteristics of schizophrenia is impairment in social functioning (*DSM–IV;* American Psychiatric Association, 1994). People with schizophrenia, relative to both clinical and nonclinical control subjects, demonstrate deficits in social skills (Bellack, Morrison, Wixted, & Mueser, 1990b) that are fairly stable over time (Mueser, Bellack, Douglas, & Morrison, 1991). Such deficits are related to molar indices of functioning, such as behavior in the treatment setting (Penn, Mueser, Doonan, & Nishith, 1995) and adjustment in the community (Bellack, Morrison, Mueser, Wade, & Sayers, 1990a; Halford & Hayes, 1995). Furthermore, the deficits appear to have, at best, a modest association with current symptomatology (Glynn, 1998). Such impairments in social functioning may partially account for the impoverished social networks often observed for people with schizophrenia (Macdonald, Jackson, Hayes, Baglioni, & Madden, 1998; discussed and reviewed by Randolph, 1998). The social disability associated with schizophrenia is a potentially devastating outcome of this disorder.

Given the profound social impairments resulting from schizophrenia, interventions such as social skills training (SST) have been developed to ameliorate functioning in this area. In general, SST tends to improve specific social skills, but it has less of an effect on community adjustment and symptoms (Mueser, Wallace, & Liberman, 1995; Mueser, Drake, & Bond, 1997; Penn & Mueser, 1996). Concerns regarding generalization and maintenance of social skills training, as well as other interventions that target social functioning, led to hypotheses that functional domains in addition to social skills should be addressed

(Hogarty & Flesher, 1992; Penn, 1991). One such domain is *social cognition,* which refers to the "mental operations underlying social interactions, which include the human ability and capacity to perceive the intentions and dispositions of others" (Brothers, 1990, p. 28). From a treatment perspective, addressing social cognitive functioning in schizophrenia may bridge the gap between learned skills in the treatment setting and application of those skills to novel situations. For example, people with schizophrenia may not apply newly acquired assertiveness skills in the community because they do not perceive the similarities between interpersonal situations in different settings. Thus, interventions that focus on social perceptual skills, a component of social cognition, may be useful in enhancing treatment generalization and maintenance.

It follows that any discussion of social cognition in schizophrenia should be firmly rooted in its implications for social functioning; this approach distinguishes this chapter from the others in this book. In particular, this chapter attempts to link, whenever possible, social cognition in schizophrenia to social behavior, social functioning, or both. Because social cognition is a broad topic, and because of considerations about overlap with other chapters, this chapter focuses on the *perception* and *representation* of social information. This chapter only briefly summarizes the topics of facial-affect perception and general social perception (e.g., perception of multiple people interacting with one another) because those topics are discussed in chapter 2. Likewise, topics of attributional perspectives and theory of mind are covered elsewhere in this book (see chapters 4, 5, and 8) and are only briefly summarized here.

The "representation of social information" comprises knowledge of social situations and social mores as well as aspects of the self (e.g., self-schema). The end of each section therefore provides evidence suggesting a link between the particular domain of social cognition and social functioning. The chapter concludes with a discussion of future directions.

Perception of Social Stimuli

In this section, we discuss different aspects of social perception in schizophrenia (e.g., facial-affect perception) and how performance in this area relates to social functioning.

FACIAL-AFFECT PERCEPTION

An age-old question in schizophrenia research is whether people with this disorder have impairments in their ability to identify the emotional expressions of others and whether such impairment has functional consequences. For example, a person with schizophrenia who misreads someone's face as being open to conversation may end up in an aversive encounter. From a diathesis–stress perspective, an increase in aversive or inadequate social encounters may augment stress levels or reduce social support, which in turn would increase the likelihood of relapse. Furthermore, a number of models of social competence in schizophrenia posit a role for social perception, which includes facial-affect perception (Liberman et al., 1986; McFall, 1982; Morrison & Bellack, 1981; Trower, Bryant, & Argyle, 1978). Thus, understanding the extent of facial-affect perception deficits in schizophrenia is of potential clinical interest.

Over the past 15 years, a number of reviews of the literature on facial-affect perception in schizophrenia have been published (e.g., Edwards, Jackson, & Pattison, 1999; Hellewell & Whittaker, 1998; Mandal, Pandey, & Prasad, 1998; Morrison, Bellack, & Mueser, 1988; Penn, Corrigan, Bentall, Racenstein, & Newman, 1997). On the basis of those and other reviews, one can conclude the following:

- People with schizophrenia generally show deficits in facial-affect perception (i.e., both identification and discrimination) relative to nonclinical control individuals.
- People with schizophrenia typically show deficits in facial-affect perception relative to people with depressive disorder, but the findings are mixed with respect to their impairment relative to control samples with psychotic features (e.g., people with bipolar disorder).
- Deficits in facial-affect perception tend to be greater for negative compared with positive facial displays, with impairment perhaps being greatest for the perception of fear (Edwards et al., 1999).
- Some evidence indicates that people in an acute phase of the disorder perform worse on affect-perception tasks relative to those whose symptoms are in remission (Cutting, 1981; Gessler, Cutting, Frith, & Weinman, 1989), although if one looks at longitudinal designs, this deficit appears fairly stable (Addington & Addington, 1998; Gaebel & Wolwer, 1992).
- The jury is still out regarding whether the facial-affect perception deficits are part of a generalized performance deficit (see Bellack, Blanchard, & Mueser, 1996; Kerr & Neale, 1993; Mueser et al., 1996; Salem, Kring, & Kerr, 1996) or specific to decoding only facial emotions (e.g., Heimberg, Gur, Erwin, Shtasel, & Gur, 1992; Penn et al., 2000).
- Some evidence points to an advantage in facial-affect perception in people with paranoid schizophrenia relative to nonparanoid

subtypes (Kline, Smith, & Ellis, 1992; Lewis & Garver, 1995; see Mandal & Rai, 1987, for an exception), although these limited findings need to be replicated in more studies before valid conclusions can be drawn.

Facial-Affect Perception and Social Functioning

Three published studies have examined the relationship between facial-affect perception and social functioning in schizophrenia (Ihnen, Penn, Corrigan, & Martin, 1998; Mueser et al., 1996; Penn, Spaulding, Reed, & Sullivan, 1996). In the first of these studies, Mueser and colleagues examined the relationship between measures of affect perception (i.e., the Face Emotion Identification Test [FEIT] and the Face Emotion Discrimination Test [FEDT]; Kerr & Neale, 1993) with two measures of social functioning: social skills during unstructured role plays and social behavior in the treatment setting, as measured by the Social Behaviour Schedule (Wykes & Sturt, 1986). The participants were 28 people with chronic schizophrenia who had been hospitalized an average of 9.5 years. The findings showed that both measures of facial-affect perception had a fairly consistent association with ward behavior, especially hygiene and grooming, but were more weakly related to social skills during unstructured interactions.

In a related study, Penn et al. (1996) examined the relationship between a battery of social cognitive tasks, which included facial-affect perception (measured by Ekman's, 1976, pictures of facial affect) and social functioning in the treatment setting, as measured by the Nurse's Observation Scale for Inpatient Evaluation (Honigfeld & Klett, 1966). Like the research participants in Mueser et al. (1996), the research participants were inpatients with chronic schizophrenia, although their length of hospitalization was typically less than 2 years. Correlational analyses revealed that facial-affect perception was significantly associated only with indices of adaptive ward behavior (i.e., social competence, social interest, and neatness). The association of facial-affect perception with maladaptive ward behavior was not significant, although it was in the expected direction.

Ihnen et al. (1998) examined the relationship between multiple measures of social perception, including facial-affect perception (using the FEIT and FEDT), and a measure of social skill in a sample of clinically stabilized outpatients with schizophrenia. Social skill was measured with a pair of unstructured role plays. The results revealed that performance on the emotion identification test, but not the discrimination test, was significantly associated with various indices of social skill (e.g., global social skill). Note, however, that the significant correlations were only modest in size and did not remain significant after applying Bonferroni correction.

Given the small number of studies in this area, conclusions regarding the association between facial-affect perception and social functioning in schizophrenia are preliminary. At this point, however, one can make the following two conclusions: (1) Facial-affect identification is significantly associated with social behavior in the treatment setting among inpatients with chronic schizophrenia and modestly associated with social skill among stabilized outpatients and (2) evidence for an association between facial-affect discrimination and social functioning is limited to social adjustment in the treatment setting.

It is not clear why the association between facial-affect perception and social functioning appears to be more consistent for ward behavior than social skill during interactions. One possibility concerns the parameters of the role plays used to assess social skill. In particular, the role plays are brief (i.e., 3 minutes) and involve research confederates who are trained to be emotionally neutral to ensure standardized performance. The unstructured role plays may have limited the number of affective cues available to decode, thereby reducing the likelihood that perception of facial affect will have an association with social behavior. This raises the interesting issue of how the association between affect perception and social skill would change if confederates were trained to consistently demonstrate a particular emotion across role plays; clearly, this issue warrants future research.

GENERAL SOCIAL PERCEPTION

The observation that social perception is not limited to identifying facial-affective displays has led to the development of tasks that involve more realistic stimuli, such as an individual or a small group either interacting or expressing a particular affect across multiple channels (i.e., vocal and visual). Unlike tests of facial-affect perception, which typically involve presentation of static stimuli, tasks that assess general social perception involve dynamic stimuli (i.e., those that are *active* and mutable over time). Examples of specific tasks include the Social Cue Recognition Test (SCRT; Corrigan, Davies-Farmer, & Stolley, 1991), the Bell–Lysaker Emotion Recognition Test (Bell, Bryson, & Lysaker, 1997), and the Videotape Affect Perception Test (Bellack et al., 1996). These tasks may be considered more "ecologically valid" than tests of facial-affect perception because they tend to better approximate the dynamic nature of affect expressed during social interactions.

In light of the reviews of this literature (Corrigan, 1997; Hellewell & Whitaker, 1998), what can be concluded about general social perceptual skills in schizophrenia? Again, this review will be brief, as the emphasis here is on the functional significance of social perception in schizophrenia. First, people with schizophrenia tend to be impaired in their perception of dynamic emotional displays relative to both nonclinical control subjects (Archer, Hay, & Young, 1994; Cramer, Bowen, & O'Neill, 1992; Cramer, Weegmann, & O'Neil, 1989; Hellewell, Connell, & Deakin, 1994; Muzekari & Bates, 1977) and clinical control participants (e.g., patients with diagnoses of depression or substance abuse; Archer et al., 1994; Bell, Bryson, & Lysaker, 1997), although there have been exceptions (e.g., Bellack, Blanchard, & Mueser, 1996; Joseph, Sturgeon, & Leff, 1992; LaRusso, 1978; Morrison, Bellack, & Bashore, 1988). Interestingly, studies that did not find differences in general social perception between people with schizophrenia and control individuals used people recently recovered from an acute episode (Bellack et al., 1996; Morrison et al., 1988) or those whose symptoms were in remission (Joseph et al., 1992). Thus, deficits in general social perception may be limited to inpatients, people with chronic symptoms, or both.

Second, evidence shows that people with schizophrenia, relative to control participants, have particular difficulty in discerning abstract, rather than concrete cues (as measured with the SCRT; Corrigan, Davies-Farmer, & Stolley, 1991). For example, a person with schizophrenia will have more difficulty identifying the goal of a situation (i.e., an abstract cue) rather than what someone is wearing (i.e., a concrete cue) (Corrigan, 1997; see chapter 2, this volume for a more extensive review). These findings are consistent with the work of others (i.e., Cramer et al., 1989; Hellewell et. al., 1994, discussed in Hellewell & Whittaker, 1998) who found that people with schizophrenia tend to focus on the physical characteristics of actors in scenes rather than on the dominant emotional theme. This suggests that people with schizophrenia have particular difficulty extracting the *meaning* underlying social interactions. This impairment is consistent with the difficulties that people with schizophrenia have in comprehending metaphors (deBonis, Epelbaum, Deffez, & Feline, 1997) as well as with Frith's work on Theory of Mind in schizophrenia (Frith, 1994; see chapter 5).

A number of unanswered questions regarding the social perception of people with schizophrenia remain unanswered, especially questions regarding the use of dynamic stimuli. First, some evidence indicates that deficits in social perception are especially pronounced for negative, rather than neutral or positive, emotional displays (Bell et al., 1997; Bellack, Mueser, Wade, Sayers, & Morrison, 1992; Morrison et al., 1988; see Joseph et al., 1992, for an exception). These findings certainly have implications for issues such as sensitivity to expressed emotion and threshold for relapse, but they need to be more consistently replicated, with similar stimuli, before confident conclusions can be drawn. A second question concerns whether deficits in dynamic social perception are

a function of a specific or generalized performance deficit. In two studies, using different dynamic stimuli as well as different research methodologies (i.e., a differential deficit design [Archer et al., 1994] and a
correlational design [Bryson, Bell, & Lysaker, 1997]), evidence was
found in support of a specific deficit in emotion perception. Again, however, the small number of studies, as well as the limited number of
female participants in the Bryson et al. study (2 of 63 participants),
suggests an interesting trend rather than a valid conclusion.

A final unanswered question concerns whether some subtypes of
schizophrenia are associated with greater impairment in social perception than other subtypes. For example, mixed support exists for greater
deficits in emotion perception occurring in people with predominantly
negative symptoms (Cramer et al., 1989) as well as inconclusive findings
regarding correlations between performance on social perception tasks
and negative symptoms (Bellack et al., 1992, 1996). Furthermore, the
relative advantage in static facial-affect perception observed for people
with paranoid schizophrenia relative to nonparanoid subtypes (i.e.,
Kline et al., 1992; Lewis & Garver, 1995) has not been well investigated
with dynamic stimuli. Therefore, it is still not clear whether performance
on dynamic stimuli varies as a function of diagnostic subtype in
schizophrenia.

General Social Perception and Social Functioning

Some evidence indicates that social perception is associated with social
behavior in people with schizophrenia. Specifically, Fingeret, Monti, and
colleagues performed a series of studies in the 1980s examining social
perception and social skill among psychiatric inpatients and day-hospital
patients comprising a variety of psychiatric diagnoses. In one particular
study, Fingeret, Monti, and Paxson (1983) reported a positive association between identifying appropriate responses from a videotaped interaction and social skill as measured during a brief conversation with
a confederate. In a subsequent study, performance on a task of nonverbal social perception, the Profile of Nonverbal Sensitivity (PONS; Rosenthal, Hall, DiMatteo, Rogers, & Archer, 1979) was found to be associated
with social skill in a diagnostically heterogeneous sample of psychiatric
inpatients (Fingeret, Monti, & Paxson, 1985). A similar pattern emerged
in a third study, which found that relative to both clinical and nonclinical controls, people with schizophrenia were less socially skillful and
more impaired in nonverbal social perception, although a direct (i.e.,
correlational) relationship between the variables was not assessed
(Monti & Fingeret, 1987). The findings generally converge with those
of Toomey, Wallace, Corrigan, Schuldberg, and Green (1997), who
found that performance on the PONS was associated with interpersonal

problem-solving skill as measured with the Assessment of Interpersonal Problem Solving Skills (AIPSS; Donahoe, Carter, Bloem, Hirsch, Laasi, & Wallace, 1990).

The relationship between social perception and social skill also was examined in two studies using the SCRT (Corrigan et al., 1991). The SCRT comprises eight videotaped vignettes of two or three people interacting with one another and, as mentioned earlier, is scored for accuracy in identifying abstract and concrete interpersonal cues. In the first study, Corrigan and Toomey (1995) compared the relationships between measures of nonsocial information processing (e.g., the Wisconsin Card Sorting task) and performance on the SCRT with the AIPSS task used in the Toomey et al. (1997) study. Corrigan and Toomey found that performance on the SCRT was significantly associated with interpersonal problem-solving skills, even after applying Bonferroni correction. The relationships were generally stronger than the bivariate associations between nonsocial information processing and interpersonal problem solving, suggesting a unique contribution of social cognition to social behavior. However, in a second study, Ihnen et al. (1998) found that the SCRT had a generally weak relationship with social skill among outpatients with schizophrenia. In fact, in terms of the number of significant bivariate correlations, the SCRT had the weakest relationship relative to measures of facial-affect perception and self-perception.

It is difficult to reconcile the contradictory findings of Corrigan and Toomey (1995) and Ihnen et al. (1998). One possibility is that the two studies used research participants in a different phase of their illness; Corrigan and Toomey's research participants were chronically ill inpatients, whereas Ihnen et al. used stabilized outpatients. The subjects in Ihnen et al. may have had higher functioning, which could have produced range restriction in their data. In fact, Ihnen et al. had to transform the data on the SCRT because of extreme negative skewness, which would be consistent with ceiling effects. An alternative possibility concerns the test used to measure social skill. Corrigan and Toomey relied on the AIPSS, which produces an index of social skill (termed "sending skills") that is based on the research participant's response to a single query or statement from a confederate. Conversely, Ihnen et al. assessed social skill with a series of unstructured role plays, each of 3-minute duration. As noted earlier in this chapter, in these role plays, the research confederate is instructed to be emotionally neutral and ask only specific probe questions. Thus, the skills needed to discern concrete and abstract cues might not be relevant to performing adequately in these unstructured role plays, given the limited stimulus information provided by the confederate. Therefore, the findings are mixed regarding the relationship of social cue perception to social behavior in schizophrenia.

Bellack et al. (1992) examined the relationship between social perception and social skill in a sample of people with schizophrenia during the latter stages of hospitalization for acute exacerbation of symptoms. For this study, Bellack et al. developed the Social Perception Test (SPT). The SPT is comprised of 12 videotaped interactions, which are viewed by the research participant. Each interaction involves a person in the research participant's role, who is off-camera, and an individual playing a significant other of the research participant (i.e., mother or friend). In half of the interactions, the person playing the mother or friend depicts high expressed emotion; in the other half, the affective display is neutral. Following the social perception assessment, social skill is then measured with a series of structured role-plays between the research participant and a research confederate. As in the videotaped SPT interactions, the research confederate portrays a significant other depicting other hostile or neutral affect. The comprehensive nature of the social skill and social perception assessment in this study is definitely an improvement over the other studies described in this section. The results showed that better social perception of negative affect scenes was associated with better social skills during interactions with a hostile interaction partner and negatively associated with likelihood of lying during the role play.

The research suggests that various measures of social perception are associated with socially skillful behavior during brief interactions. A number of issues, however, should be addressed in future research. Specifically, it remains to be evaluated whether this association persists when behavior is assessed at a more general level (e.g., behavior in the treatment setting or in the community). Addington and Addington (1999) took an important step in this direction by reporting the associations among various measures of social functioning in outpatients with schizophrenia (within the context of a broader study on neurocognitive processes and social behavior). They found that receiving skills on the AIPSS, which likely taps into social perceptual skills, was positively associated with quality of life among outpatients with schizophrenia.

Along the same lines, no studies, to our knowledge, have examined the association of multiple measures of social perception with multiple measures of social functioning. Research in this area has concentrated predominantly on single-task assessments rather than social perception batteries and social skill measures. Similarly, the association between social perception and social functioning has been limited largely to visual perceptual measures, with scant attention to the role of prosody perception in social functioning. This situation may be a function of the few studies that have investigated auditory social perception in schizophrenia (relative to those investigating visual or multichannel social perception; see Edwards et al., 1999; Hellewell & Whittaker, 1998). This area therefore warrants further study as a possible correlate or contributor to social behavior in schizophrenia. Finally, the studies reviewed above used cross-sectional designs, which limit conclusions regarding how the relationship between social perception and social functioning changes over time. For example, in a recent study on the correlates of instrumental functioning, it was found that the association between instrumental functioning (i.e., social and work) and thought disorder differed as a function of when this relationship was assessed (Racenstein, Penn, Harrow, & Schleser, 1999). This finding underscores the need to assess relationships among different domains of functioning across multiple time periods, an especially powerful design when the relationships can be assessed in both acute and remitted states (e.g., Addington & Addington, 1998; Penn et al., 1993).

Representation of Social Information

In this section, we review research on how persons with schizophrenia represent social information (i.e., about others, themselves, social situations) and how this relates to their social functioning.

KNOWLEDGE OF SOCIAL SITUATIONS

Social cognition is not limited to the perception of others, but it comprises our knowledge of social situations as well as the rules describing appropriate behavior in those situations. It seems that people have consensual knowledge regarding the behaviors that can be expected to occur in various social situations (Cantor, Mischel, & Schwartz, 1982). For example, although it is appropriate to laugh and cheer during a sporting event, such behavior is inappropriate during a funeral or in a classroom. This knowledge of behavior-situation relationships likely affects social skills in any given setting. Therefore, social competence may be a function, in part, of a person's knowledge of the rules concerning situation-specific behaviors. This perspective long has been embraced by social psychologists in their work on scripts (i.e., the actions that compose social situations; Abelson, 1981; Schank & Abelson, 1977). Research in this area has shown that people without a psychiatric disorder are able to accurately identify the steps making up a variety of social situations (e.g., going to a doctor; Bower, Black, & Turner, 1979). This research has led to the hypothesis that people with schizophrenia may be socially impaired because of deficits in their representation of social situational information (Trower, Bryant, & Argyle, 1978).

A common method for studying the representation of situational information in schizophrenia is to use the Picture Arrangement (PA) subtest from the Wechsler intelligence scales (Wechsler, 1997) or some variation of this measure. Erlenmeyer-Kimling and colleagues have examined the performance of children and adolescents at risk for schizophrenia and other psychopathology on the PA subtest. Lipsitz, Dworkin, and Erlenmeyer-Kimling (1993) found that in participants at risk for schizophrenia or major affective disorder and in a control group (during both childhood and adolescence) PA-scaled scores were not significantly associated with either hostility or premorbid social adjustment. In a second study, Ott et al. (1998) reported that performance on the PA subtest did not significantly differ between at-risk (for either schizophrenia or major affective disorder) and control participants, during either childhood or adolescence. These findings cast doubt on the role of impaired ability to represent social sequential information in the development of schizophrenia.

The representation of social situational information also has been investigated in adults with schizophrenia. Using the PA subtest, Toomey et al. (1997) reported deficits in adult inpatients relative to a sample of nonclinical control participants. Griggs and Green (1983) examined the ability of people with schizophrenia to describe (either orally or in writing) the steps required to prepare and serve tea. People with schizophrenia showed impairments, relative to individuals with other psychiatric disorders, in their verbal description of tea-preparation steps, with the difference approaching statistical significance for the written descriptions. Interestingly, when examining the oral description of tea serving, thought-disordered participants with schizophrenia outperformed non-thought-disordered participants with schizophrenia. No group differences were found in the order in which the steps comprising tea preparation or serving were reported. The authors also conducted post hoc analyses concerning "necessary" and "optional" steps (e.g., boiling water vs. letting the tea brew) and found that for tea preparation, thought-disordered participants provided more necessary than optional steps, whereas the opposite pattern emerged for tea serving. Finally, Corrigan and colleagues found that relative to nonclinical controls, people with schizophrenia were less sensitive to the abstract features of social situations (especially for unfamiliar situations and for inpatients) and were impaired in their ability to sequence social situations (particularly for long sequences; reviewed in Corrigan, 1997, and chapter 2 of this book).

Based on the foregoing, it appears that deficits in the ability to represent information about the steps of social situations are impaired in adults with schizophrenia. It is not clear, however, whether this performance deficit is unique to social sequencing tasks or reflects the tendency of people with schizophrenia to perform more poorly than control individuals on any cognitive task. Furthermore, this impairment does not appear evident in children at risk for the disorder, although this result also may be a function of the limitations of using the PA subtest to measure social cognitive abilities (discussed in Lipsitz et al., 1993). Consistent with the findings reported for general social perception tests, people with schizophrenia have particular difficulty with the abstract features of social situations, such as the goals and rules of a particular setting. These difficulties are especially salient for unfamiliar social situations; consequently, efforts to "remediate" these impairments may need to incorporate experiential as well as psychological interventions. Finally, little evidence exists on whether the deficits vary as a function of phase of the disorder, although they may be more profound in inpatients, and whether particular subgroups of patients (e.g., people with the deficit symptom) are especially impaired in this area.

KNOWLEDGE OF SOCIAL SITUATIONS AND SOCIAL FUNCTIONING

Few studies have examined the relationship between knowledge of social situations and social behavior in people with schizophrenia. Appelo et al. (1992) administered the PA subtest to 39 inpatients and assessed social skill during a brief role play (i.e., the Simulated Social Interaction Test; Curran, 1982). Furthermore, behavior in the treatment setting was coded by staff using the general behavior subscale from the Rehabilitation Evaluation instrument (Baker & Hall, 1988). Results of multiple regression analyses showed that performance on the PA subtest accounted for the most variance in the measure of ward functioning (relative to symptomatology). However, performance on the PA subtest did not significantly predict social skill.

Penn et al. (1996) extended the findings of Appelo and colleagues by examining the relationship of a measure of "social scripts" with behavior in the treatment setting. (See the section on facial-affect perception and social functioning for a description of the study.) The Scripts task comprised six social situations, each describing the steps that underlie various social situations (e.g., going to work or school or going grocery shopping). The participants, 26 inpatients with chronic schizophrenia, were presented with the steps in random order and were instructed to the put them in the correct order as quickly as possible. Performance on the Scripts task was coded for the time to complete the task and the number of steps in the correct order. Results showed that a faster completion time was associated with less irritability on the ward. This association remained significant even after other cognitive and social cognitive variables were included in the regression analyses. Performance on the Scripts task, however, was not significantly associated with the other five indices of ward behavior.

Because of the limited number of studies, it is difficult to draw any conclusions regarding the association of knowledge of social situations and social behavior in people with schizophrenia. Some evidence, albeit preliminary, shows that this social cognitive skill may relate to behavior in the treatment setting. It is possible that knowledge of the steps comprising social situations has a bearing on how people with schizophrenia structure and organize their own social environment. For example, people with schizophrenia who struggle on a "scripts task" may have difficulty anticipating problems in their environment, thus getting easily frustrated or thwarted in achieving their goals. Until further research is conducted, however, this idea is merely speculation; it certainly is an issue worthy of investigation.

KNOWLEDGE OF SOCIAL CONVENTION AND SOCIAL JUDGMENT

Another way to examine the social cognitive underpinnings of social impairment in schizophrenia is to consider the person with schizophrenia's understanding of social rules and conventions—what might also be called "common sense." According to this view, people with schizophrenia are socially unskilled because they lack information about what is considered appropriate behavior according to their particular culture. Some evidence indicates that people with schizophrenia have impairments in social judgment. Specifically, Ott et al. (1998) reported that children at risk for schizophrenia scored significantly lower on the Comprehension subtest from the Wechsler scales relative to at-risk subjects for affective disorder; this pattern was not evident in adolescents (the mean age was 15.2 years). In adults, Toomey et al. (1997) reported that inpatients with schizophrenia performed significantly lower on the Comprehension subtest relative to nonclinical control participants.

Cutting and Murphy (1988, 1990) took a different approach for assessing social judgment, or common sense, in schizophrenia. They developed the Social Knowledge Questionnaire (SKQ) which is a multiple-choice test that assesses a person's knowledge of how someone should act in various situations (e.g., "What do you think would be the most sensible thing to say if you came across two strangers having a fight in the streets?"). In a series of studies, Cutting and Murphy showed that people with schizophrenia showed greater impairment on the SKQ (and an early version of it) than on nonsocial tests relative to clinical control subjects. Outpatients with schizophrenia also perform worse on the SKQ relative to control participants (Munoz, Munoz, Blas, & Ruiz, 1992). However, Munoz et al. (1992) noted that the difference between control participants and outpatients with schizophrenia was not great, and that the participants with schizophrenia performed at a level comparable to that of the control participants (who had manic disorder) in Cutting and Murphy (1990). This finding suggests, albeit tentatively, that social knowledge may vary as a function of phase of the disorder.

Social Judgment and Social Functioning

As in the previous section, little research exists in the area of social judgment and social functioning. Interestingly, most of the research that has examined the functional significance of the Comprehension subtest has taken place when using it as a tool to evaluate thought disorder and its association with outcome or psychosocial adjustment (e.g., Marengo & Harrow, 1997; Racenstein et al., 1999). Findings from the New York high-risk project revealed an association between performance on the Comprehension subtest (Wechsler, 1997) and Premorbid Social Adjustment scale among the research participants at risk for schizophrenia at both childhood and adolescence (Lipsitz et al., 1993). However, as Lipsitz et al. pointed out, this subtest was but one of many intelligence subtests correlated with social adjustment in the at-risk sample (although it was the only subtest associated with social adjustment in childhood for the "normal" comparison group). Regarding Cutting and Murphy's Social Knowledge Questionnaire, no studies, to our knowledge, have assessed its relationship with social behavior.

KNOWLEDGE OF THE SELF AND OTHERS

Although the construct of social cognition implies thinking about others, one cannot ignore perceptions of the self in this process. In *Mind, Self, and Society,* Mead (1934) argued that the self develops in the context of interacting with others. For example, when children engage in role playing (e.g., playing "house"), they incorporate characteristics of others (e.g., the "mommy") into the self. Furthermore, the playing of games helps the child learn broader societal rules and how to fit in with others. The social nature of the self, according to Mead, is underscored by his conceptualization of the self as comprising two parts: the *I,* which initiates action, and the *me,* which is the self as an object of attention. Relatedly, evidence from social psychology shows that the perceptions of the self influence one's perceptions of others (discussed in Kenny, 1988, 1993; see also Levesque, 1997). Therefore, the nature of the "self" in schizophrenia may have implications for both social cognition and behavior (see Carter & Flesher, 1995, for a further discussion of the self, socialization, and schizophrenia).

The role of the self in schizophrenia has been evaluated in a number of experimental contexts. In particular, using methodology drawn from personal construct theory, people with schizophrenia, especially those with thought disorder, have been shown to have "loose" or inconsistently applied personal constructs, which may reflect lower self-complexity, phasic aspects of the disorder, or periods of disattention (e.g., Bannister, Fransella, & Agnew, 1971; Dingemans, Space, & Cromwell, 1983; Livesay, 1984; van den Bergh, de Boeck, & Claeys, 1981; see Pierce, Sewell, & Cromwell, 1992, for a review). Furthermore, relative to nonclinical controls, people with schizophrenia tend to produce a greater number of physical constructs but fewer emotional–personality trait constructs (discussed in Pierce et al., 1992).

Using somewhat different methodology, Gara and colleagues investigated "self-structure" in schizophrenia, which refers to the "hierarchically organized interrelationships among the several selves (of a person) in terms of their separate and overlapping features" (Robey, Cohen, & Gara, 1989, p. 436). In a series of studies, it was found that the self-structures of people with schizophrenia were less elaborated relative to clinical and nonclinical controls (Gara, Rosenberg, & Mueller, 1989; Robey, Cohen, & Gara, 1989). Furthermore, the impairments evident for the self-structures of people with schizophrenia did not generalize to their constructs of others (Robey et al., 1989). This latter finding is especially interesting in light of work showing "impaired perspective" among people with schizophrenia: Their ability to discriminate between appropriate and inappropriate verbalizations and behavior is impaired for ratings of themselves but not others (Carini & Nevid, 1992; Harrow, Lanin-Kettering, & Miller, 1989; but see Fingeret et al., 1985, and Monti & Fingeret, 1987, for evidence that self-ratings of social skill can be fairly accurate in schizophrenia).

Bentall and Kinderman, in their research on paranoia, have taken a different approach to understanding the role of the self in schizophrenia (see chapter 4 in this volume). Much of the work in this area has focused on the role of attributions in paranoia, with findings indicating that people with persecutory delusions tend to externalize blame for negative outcomes, particularly to other people rather than to situations (reviewed in Garety & Freeman, 1999). Less support, however, has been found for the hypothesis that this attributional style serves the defensive or protective function of reducing discrepancies between self-representations (i.e., how one sees oneself) and self-ideals (i.e., what one would like to be; Garety & Freeman, 1999).

Another social cognitive approach to understanding the role of the self in paranoia has been the work on attentional focus and paranoia. In particular, increased paranoia in samples of undergraduate students is associated with focusing attention on the experimenter following feedback that they failed various experimental tasks (Bodner & Miku-lineer, 1998), a finding consistent with Kinderman and Bentall's model. Others have used the construct of "self-consciousness" to investigate paranoia. Self-consciousness refers to dispositional awareness of the self (Fenigstein, 1987), a concept that is based on Duval and Wicklund's (1972) construct of objective self-awareness. People who are high in private self-consciousness tend to be aware of their own thoughts and feelings, whereas those high in public self-consciousness are focused on themselves as a social object—how they appear to others. One could argue that private and public self-consciousness correspond to Mead's constructs of the I and me, respectively. Unfortunately, results have been inconsistent regarding the relationship between self-consciousness and paranoia. Specifically, although Fenigstein and Vanable (1992) reported an association between paranoia and public self-consciousness among nonclinical research participants, the findings were not replicated in a sample of people with schizophrenia (Smari, Stefansson, & Thorgilsson, 1994). In fact, Smari et al. (1994) found that private, rather than public, self-consciousness was related to paranoia. Smari and colleagues speculate that the difference in findings across the two studies may be a reflection of studying paranoia in clinical and subclinical samples.

The Self and Social Functioning

Evidence indicates that perceptions of the self are associated with social functioning in schizophrenia. In their study on self-structure, Robey et al. (1989) reported that elaboration of the self as a psychiatric patient was positively associated with functioning on the Global Assessment Scale (APA, 1994). In two studies investigating self-perception, it was found that research participants' post hoc ratings of their own social skills were associated with social skill ratings made by either their role-play partners or independent judges (Appelo et al., 1992; Ihnen et al., 1998). Finally, Penn et al. (1999) examined the role of self-monitoring in the sample of research participants from Ihnen et al. (1998). Self-monitoring refers to a stable personality characteristic involving the ability to control expressive behavior and self-presentation (Snyder & Gangestad, 1986). High self-monitors tend to regulate their behavior across social situations and be concerned with impression management. Conversely, low self-monitors are relatively consistent in their behavior across situations. Penn et al. (1999) administered the modified form of the Self-Monitoring Scale (Snyder & Gangestad, 1986) to outpatients with schizophrenia and assessed social skill with two role plays differing in impression-management demands: Research participants were told either that they had to make a good impression on the research confederate or that the research confederate was supposed to make a good impression on them. The results revealed that high self-monitors with schizophrenia (based on a median split) had significantly better paralinguistic social skills (e.g., speech fluency) than low self-monitors, but the two groups did not differ with respect to nonverbal or general social skills. Penn et al. suggest that by having their conversations videotaped, the high self-monitors in this study may have felt the need to manage impressions in both role plays, thus rendering the role of context relatively unimportant.

Conclusion

This chapter has reviewed the literature on the relationship between social cognition and social behavior. Evidence indicates that certain domains of social perception, such as facial-affect recognition, perception of dynamic social stimuli, and self-perception, are related to social functioning in schizophrenia. The absolute number of studies is quite small, however, so the conclusions here are tentative, at best. Furthermore, no evidence reveals how those relationships change over time or whether they are stronger in some subgroups of schizophrenia versus others. Those issues need to be addressed in future research.

Social psychology can provide further direction for research examining the relationship between social cognition and social functioning. In particular, research from the area of attitude–behavior consistency shows that attitudes best predict behavior when measured at the same level of specificity (Krauss, 1995). For example, attitudes toward garbage recycling would better predict recycling behavior than a range of conservation behaviors, in general. Along the same lines, the behaviors assessed in schizophrenia should match the social cognitive construct being measured. Therefore, if one were interested in the functional consequences of Theory-of-Mind performance in schizophrenia, it would be best to assess behavior in a situation in which the research participant has to interpret hints or humor from another person, rather than examining social behavior during a generic role play. Research on the relationship between the content of hallucinations or delusions and violent behavior is a good example of measuring social cognition and behavior at similar levels of specificity (Buchanan & Wessely, 1998; Juninger, 1996; Juninger, Parks-Levy, & McGuire, 1998; Link, Monahan, Stueve, & Cullen, in press; Swanson, Borum, Swartz, & Monahan, 1996).

In closing, investigation of social cognition may help advance our understanding of the mechanisms underlying interpersonal dysfunction in schizophrenia. It is critical, however, to always assess the functional consequences of social cognition and not to assume that social cognitive impairment always reflects behavioral failures. Otherwise, schizophrenia research, by focusing predominantly on social cognition, stands the risk of developing intrapersonal, rather than interpersonal, models of the disorder; this problem apparently has occurred in social psychology as a result of its emphasis on social cognition (Berkowitz & Devine, 1995). Therefore, a comprehensive *psychological* model of social dysfunction in schizophrenia needs to use both social cognitive and *behavioral* (e.g., Haynes, 1986) perspectives; neither alone are likely to account for the extreme impairment associated with schizophrenia.

References

Abelson, R. P. (1981). The psychological status of the script concept. *American Psychologist, 36,* 715–729.

Addington, J., & Addington, D. (1998). Facial affect recognition and information processing in schizophrenia and bipolar disorder. *Schizophrenia Research, 32,* 171–181.

Addington, J., & Addington, D. (1999). Neurocognitive and social functioning in schizophrenia. *Schizophrenia Bulletin, 25,* 173–182.

American Psychiatric Association. (1994). *Diagnostic and statistical manual of mental disorders* (4th ed.). Washington, DC: Author.

Appelo, M. T., Woonings, F. M. J., van Nieuwenhuizen, C. J., Emmelkamp, P. M. G., Sloof, C. J., & Louwerens, J. W. (1992). Specific skills and social competence in schizophrenia. *Acta Psychiatrica Scandinavica, 85,* 419–422.

Archer, J., Hay, D. C., & Young, A. W. (1994). Movement, face processing, and schizophrenia: Evidence of a differential deficit in expression analysis. *British Journal of Clinical Psychology, 33,* 517–528.

Baker, R., & Hall, J. N. (1988). A new assessment instrument for chronic psychiatric patients. *Schizophrenia Bulletin, 14,* 97–110.

Bannister, D., Fransella, F., & Agnew, J. (1971). Characteristics and validity of the Grid Test of thought disorder. *British Journal of Social and Clinical Psychology, 10,* 144–151.

Bell, M., Bryson, G., & Lysaker, P. (1997). Positive and negative affect recognition in schizophrenia: A comparison with substance abuse and normal control subjects. *Psychiatry Research, 73,* 73–82.

Bellack, A. S., Blanchard, J. J., & Mueser, K. T. (1996). Cue availability and affect perception in schizophrenia. *Schizophrenia Bulletin, 22,* 535–544.

Bellack, A. S., Morrison, R. L., Mueser, K. T., Wade, J. H., & Sayers, S. L. (1990a). Role-play for assessing the social competence of psychiatric patients. *Psychological Assessment, 2,* 248–255.

Bellack, A. S., Morrison, R. L., Wixted, J. T., & Mueser, K. T. (1990b). An analysis of social competence in schizophrenia. *British Journal of Psychiatry, 156,* 809–818.

Bellack, A. S., Mueser, K. T., Wade, J., Sayers, S., & Morrison, R., (1992). The ability of schizophrenics to perceive and cope with negative affect. *British Journal of Psychiatry, 160,* 473–480.

Berkowitz, L., & Devine, P. G. (1995). Has social psychology always been cognitive? What is "cognitive" anyhow? *Personality and Social Psychology Bulletin, 21,* 696–703.

Bodner, E., & Mikulineer, M. (1998). Learned helplessness and the occurrence of depressive-like and paranoid-like responses: The role of attentional focus. *Journal of Personality and Social Psychology, 74,* 1010–1023.

Bower, G. H., Black, J. B., & Turner, T. J. (1979). Scripts in memory for text. *Cognitive Psychology, 11,* 177–220.

Brothers, L. (1990). The social brain: A project for integrating primate behavior and neurophysiology in a new domain. *Concepts in Neuroscience, 1,* 27–61.

Bryson, G., Bell, M., & Lysaker, P. (1997). Affect recognition in schizophrenia: A function of global impairment or a specific cognitive deficit. *Psychiatry Research, 71,* 105–113.

Buchanan, A., & Wessely, S. (1998). Delusions, action, and insight. In X. F. Amador & A. S. David (Eds.), *Insight and psychosis* (pp. 241–268). Oxford, England: Oxford University Press.

Cantor, M., Mischel, W., & Schwartz, J. (1982). A prototype analysis of psychological situations. *Cognitive Psychology, 14,* 45–77.

Carini, M. A., & Nevid, J. S. (1992). Social appropriateness and impaired perspective in schizophrenia. *Journal of Clinical Psychology, 48,* 170–177.

Carter, M., & Flesher, S. (1995). The neurosociology of schizophrenia: Vulnerability and functional disability. *Psychiatry, 58,* 209–224.

Corrigan, P. W. (1997). The social perceptual deficits in schizophrenia. *Psychiatry, 60,* 309–326.

Corrigan, P. W., Davies-Farmer, R. M., & Stolley, M. R. (1991). Social cue recognition in schizophrenia under variable levels of arousal. *Cognitive Therapy and Research, 14,* 353–361.

Corrigan, P. W., & Toomey, R. (1995). Interpersonal problem solving and information processing in schizophrenia. *Schizophrenia Bulletin, 21,* 395–403.

Cramer, P., Bowen, J., & O'Neill, M. (1992). Schizophrenics and social judgment: Why do schizophrenics get it wrong? *British Journal of Psychiatry, 160,* 481–487.

Cramer, P., Weegmann, M., & O'Neill, M. (1989). Schizophrenia and the perception of emotions: How accurately do schizophrenics judge the emotional states of others? *British Journal of Psychiatry, 155,* 225–228.

Curran, J. P. (1982). A procedure for the assessment of social skills: The simulated social interaction test. In J. P. Curran & P. M. Monti (Eds.), *Social skills training: A practical handbook for assessment and treatment* (pp. 348–373). New York: Guilford Press.

Cutting, J. (1981). Judgement of emotional expression in schizophrenia. *British Journal of Psychiatry, 139,* 1–6.

Cutting, J., & Murphy, D. (1988). Schizophrenic thought disorder: A psychological and organic interpretation. *British Journal of Psychiatry, 1988,157,* 310–319.

Cutting, J., & Murphy, D. (1990). Impaired ability of schizophrenics, relative to manics or depressives, to appreciate social knowledge about their culture. *British Journal of Psychiatry, 157,* 355–358.

deBonis, M., Epelbaum, C., Deffez, V., & Feline, A. (1997). The comprehension of metaphors in schizophrenia. *Psychopathology, 30,* 149–154.

Dingemans, P., Space, L. G., & Cromwell, R. L. (1983). How general is the inconsistency in schizophrenic behavior? In J. Adams-Webber & J. Mancuso (Eds.), *Applications of personal construct theory.* Ontario, Canada: Academic Press.

Donahoe, C. P., Carter, M. J., Bloem, W. D., Hirsch, G. L., Laasi, N., & Wallace, C. J. (1990). Assessment of interpersonal problem solving skills. *Psychiatry, 53,* 329–339.

Duval, S., & Wicklund, R. A. (1972). *A theory of objective self-awareness.* New York: Academic Press.

Edwards, J., Jackson, H. J., & Pattison, P. (1999). *Emotion recognition via facial expression and affective prosody in schizophrenia: A methodological review.* Manuscript submitted for publication.

Ekman, P. (1976). *Pictures of facial affect.* Palo Alto, CA: Consulting Psychologists Press.

Fenigstein, A. (1987). On the nature of public and private self-consciousness. *Journal of Personality, 55,* 543–554.

Fenigstein, A., & Vanable, P. A. (1992). Paranoia and self-consciousness. *Journal of Personality and Social Psychology, 62,* 129–138.

Fingeret, A. L., Monti, P. M., & Paxson, M. A. (1983). Relationships among social perception, social skill, and social anxiety of psychiatric patients. *Psychological Reports, 53,* 1175–1178.

Fingeret, A. L., Monti, P. M., & Paxson, M. A. (1985). Social perception, social performance, and self-perception. *Behavior Modification, 9,* 345–356.

Frith, C. D. (1994). Theory of mind. In A. S. David & J. C. Cutting (Eds.), *The neuropsychology of schizophrenia* (pp. 147–161). East Sussex, England: Erlbaum.

Gaebel, W., & Wolwer, W. (1992). Facial expression and emotional face recognition in schizophrenia and depression. *European Archives of Psychiatry and Clinical Neuroscience, 242,* 46–52.

Gara, M. A., Rosenberg, S., & Mueller, D. (1989). The perception of self and other in schizophrenia. *International Journal of Personal Construct Psychology, 2,* 253–270.

Garety, P. A., & Freeman, D. (1999). Cognitive approaches to delusions: A critical review of theories and evidence. *British Journal of Clinical Psychology, 38,* 113–154.

Gessler, S., Cutting, J., Frith, C. D., & Weinman, J. (1989). Schizophrenic ability in judging facial emotion: A controlled study. *British Journal of Clinical Psychology, 28,* 19–29.

Glynn, S. M. (1998). Psychopathology and social functioning in schizophrenia. In K. T. Mueser & N. Tarrier (Eds.), *Handbook of social functioning in schizophrenia* (pp. 66–78). Boston: Allyn & Bacon.

Griggs, S. A., & Green, D. W. (1983). How to make a cup of tea: Exploring the scripts of thought- and non-thought-disordered patients. *British Journal of Medical Psychology, 56,* 125–133.

Halford, W. K., & Hayes, R. L. (1995). Social skills in schizophrenia: Assessing the relationship between social skills, psychopathology, and community functioning. *Social Psychiatry and Psychiatric Epidemiology, 30,* 14–19.

Harrow, M., Lanin-Kettering, L., & Miller, J. G. (1989). Impaired perspective and thought pathology in schizophrenic and psychotic disorders. *Schizophrenia Bulletin, 15,* 605–623.

Haynes, S. N. (1986). A behavioral model of paranoid behaviors. *Behavior Therapy, 17,* 266–287.

Heimberg, C., Gur, R. E., Erwin, R. J., Shtasel, D. L., & Gur, R. C. (1992). Facial emotion discrimination: III. Behavioral findings in schizophrenia. *Psychiatry Research, 42,* 253–265.

Hellewell, J. S. E., Connell, J., & Deakin, J. F. W. (1994). Affect judgment and facial recognition memory in schizophrenia. *Psychopathology, 27,* 255–261.

Hellewell, J. S. E., & Whitaker, J. F. (1998). Affect perception and social knowledge in schizophrenia. In K. T. Mueser & N. Tarrier (Eds.), *Handbook of social functioning in schizophrenia* (pp. 197–212). Boston: Allyn & Bacon.

Hogarty, G., & Flesher, S. (1992). Cognitive remediation in schizophrenia: Proceed . . . with caution! *Schizophrenia Bulletin, 18,* 51–57.

Honigfeld, R., & Klett, J. C. (1966). NOSIE-30: A treatment sensitive ward behavior scale. *Psychological Reports, 19,* 180–182.

Ihnen, G. H., Penn, D. L., Corrigan, P. W., & Martin, J. (1998). Social perception and social skill in schizophrenia. *Psychiatry Research, 80,* 275–286.

Joseph, P. L. A., Sturgeon, D. A., & Leff, J. (1992). The perception of emotion by schizophrenic patients. *British Journal of Psychiatry, 161,* 603–609.

Juninger, J. (1996). Psychosis and violence: The case for a content analysis of psychotic experience. *Schizophrenia Bulletin, 22,* 91–103.

Juninger, J., Parks-Levy, & McGuire, L. (1998). Delusions and symptom-consistent violence. *Psychiatric Services, 49,* 218–220.

Kenny, D. A. (1988). Interpersonal perception: A social relations analysis. *Journal of Social and Personal Relationships, 5,* 247–261.

Kenny, D. A. (1993). A coming-of-age for research on interpersonal perception. *Journal of Personality, 61,* 789–807.

Kerr, S. L., & Neale, J. M. (1993). Emotion perception in schizophrenia: Specific deficit or further evidence of generalized poor performance? *Journal of Abnormal Psychology, 102,* 312–318.

Kline, J. S., Smith, J. E., & Ellis, H. C. (1992). Paranoid and nonparanoid schizophrenic processing of facially displayed affect. *Journal of Psychiatric Research, 26,* 169–182.

Krauss, J. J. (1995). Attitudes and the prediction of behavior: A meta-analysis of the empirical literature. *Personality and Social Psychology Bulletin, 21,* 58–75.

LaRusso, L. (1978). Sensitivity of paranoid patients to nonverbal cues. *Journal of Abnormal Psychology, 87,* 463–471.

Levesque, M. J. (1997). Meta-accuracy among acquainted individuals: A social relations analysis of interpersonal perception and meta-perception. *Journal of Personality and Social Psychology, 72,* 66–74.

Lewis, S. F., & Garver, D. L. (1995). Treatment and diagnostic subtype in facial affect recognition in schizophrenia. *Journal of Psychiatric Research, 29,* 5–11.

Liberman, R. P., Mueser, K. T., Wallace, C. J., Jacobs, H. E., Eckman, T., & Massell, H. K. (1986). Training skills in the psychiatrically disabled: Learning coping and competence. *Schizophrenia Bulletin, 12,* 631–647.

Lipsitz, J. D., Dworkin, R. H., & Erlenmeyer-Kimling, L. (1993). Wechsler comprehension and picture arrangement subtests and social adjustment. *Psychological Assessment, 5,* 430–437.

Link, B. G., Monahan, J., Stueve, A., & Cullen, F. T. (in press). Real in their consequences: A sociological approach to understanding the association between psychotic symptoms and violence. *Journal of Health and Social Behavior.*

Livesay, J. R. (1984). Cognitive complexity-simplicity and inconsistent interpersonal judgment in thought-disordered schizophrenia. *Psychological Reports, 54,* 759–768.

Macdonald, E. M., Jackson, H. J., Hayes, R. L., Baglioni, A. J., & Madden, C. (1998). Social skill as a determinant of social networks and perceived social support in schizophrenia. *Schizophrenia Research, 29,* 275–286.

Mandal, M. K., Pandey, R., & Prasad, A. B. (1998). Facial expressions of emotions and schizophrenia: A review. *Schizophrenia Bulletin, 24,* 399–412.

Mandal, M. K., & Rai, A. (1987). Responses to facial emotion and psychopathology. *Psychiatry Research, 20,* 317–323.

Marengo, J., & Harrow, M. (1997). The longitudinal courses of thought disorder in schizophrenia and schizoaffective disorder. *Schizophrenia Bulletin, 23,* 273–285.

McFall, R. M. (1982). A review and reformulation of social skills. *Behavior Assessment, 4,* 1–33.

Mead, G. H. (1934). *Mind, self, and society.* Chicago: University of Chicago Press.

Monti, P. M., & Fingeret, A. L. (1987). Social perception and communication skills among schizophrenics and nonschizophrenics. *Journal of Clinical Psychology, 43,* 197–205.

Morrison, R. L., & Bellack, A. S. (1981). The role of social perception in social skill. *Behavior Therapy, 12,* 69–79.

Morrison, R. L., Bellack, A. S., & Bashore, T. R. (1988). Perception of emotion among schizophrenic patients. *Journal of Psychopathology and Behavioral Assessment, 10,* 319–332.

Morrison, R. L., Bellack, A. S., & Mueser, K. T. (1988). Deficits in facial-affect recognition and schizophrenia. *Schizophrenia Bulletin, 14,* 67–83.

Mueser, K. T., Bellack, A. S., Douglas, M. S., & Morrison, R. L. (1991). Prevalence and stability of social skill deficits in schizophrenia. *Schizophrenia Research, 5,* 167–176.

Mueser, K. T., Doonan, R., Penn, D. L., Blanchard, J. J., Bellack, A. S., & Nishith, P. (1996). Emotion recognition and social competence in chronic schizophrenia. *Journal of Abnormal Psychology, 105,* 271–275.

Mueser, K. T., Drake, R. E., & Bond, G. R. (1997). Recent advances in psychiatric rehabilitation for patients with severe mental illness. *Harvard Review of Psychiatry, 5,* 123–137.

Mueser, K. T., Wallace, C. J., & Liberman, R. P. (1995). New developments in social skills training. *Behavior Change, 12,* 31–40.

Munoz, R. A., Munoz, L. A., Blas, M., & Ruiz, D. (1992). Use of the Social Knowledge Scale (SKS) among patients treated for schizophrenia and psychology students. *Annals of Clinical Psychiatry, 4,* 267–273.

Muzekari, L. H., & Bates, M. E. (1977). Judgment of emotion among chronic schizophrenics. *Journal of Clinical Psychology, 33,* 662–666.

Ott, S. L., Spinelli, S., Rock, D., Roberts, S., Amminger, G. P., & Erlenmeyer-Kimling, L. (1998). The New York high-risk project: Social and general intelligence in children at risk for schizophrenia. *Schizophrenia Research, 31,* 1–11.

Penn, D. L. (1991). Cognitive rehabilitation of social deficits in schizophrenia: A direction of promise or following a primrose path? *Psychosocial Rehabilitation Journal, 15,* 27–41.

Penn, D. L., Combs, D., Ritchie, M., Francis, J., Cassisi, J., Morris, S., & Townsend, M. (2000). Emotion recognition in schizophrenia: Further investigation of generalized versus specific deficit models. *Journal of Abnormal Psychology, 109,* 512–516.

Penn, D. L., Corrigan, P. W., Bentall, R. P., Racenstein, J. M., & Newman, L. S. (1997). Social cognition in schizophrenia. *Psychological Bulletin, 121,* 114–132.

Penn, D. L., Corrigan, P. W., Martin, J., Ihnen, G., Racenstein, J. M., Nelson, D., Cassisi, J., & Hope, D. A. (1999). Social cognition and social skills in schizophrenia: The role of self-monitoring. *Journal of Nervous and Mental Disease, 187,* 188–190.

Penn, D. L., & Mueser, K. T. (1996). Research update on the psychosocial treatment of schizophrenia. *American Journal of Psychiatry, 153,* 607–617.

Penn, D. L., Mueser, K. T., Doonan, R., & Nishith, P. (1995). Relations between social skills and ward behavior in chronic schizophrenia. *Schizophrenia Research, 16,* 225–232.

Penn, D. L., Spaulding, W. D., Reed, D., & Sullivan, M. (1996). The relationship of social cognition to ward behavior in chronic schizophrenia. *Schizophrenia Research, 20,* 327–335.

Penn, D. L., van der Does, A. J. W., Spaulding, W. D., Garbin, C. P., Linszen, D., & Dingemans, P. (1993). Information processing and social-cognitive problem solving in schizophrenia: Assessment of inter-relationships and changes over time. *Journal of Nervous and Mental Disease, 181,* 13–20.

Pierce, D. L., Sewell, K. W., & Cromwell, R. L. (1992). Schizophrenia and depression: Construing and constructing empirical research. In R. Neimeyer & G. Neimeyer (Eds.), *Advances in personal construct psychology* (Vol. 2, pp. 151–184). Greenwich, CT: JAI Press.

Racenstein, J. M., Penn, D. L., Harrow, M., & Schleser, R. (1999). Thought disorder and instrumental functioning in schizophrenia: The concurrent and longitudinal relationships. *Journal of Nervous and Mental Disease, 187,* 281–287.

Randolph, E. T. (1998). Social networks and schizophrenia. In K. T. Mueser & N. Tarrier (Eds.), *Handbook of social functioning in schizophrenia* (pp. 238–246). Boston: Allyn & Bacon.

Robey, K. L., Cohen, B. D., & Gara, M. A. (1989). Self-structure in schizophrenia. *Journal of Abnormal Psychology, 98,* 436–442.

Rosenthal, R., Hall, J. A., DiMatteo, M. R., Rogers, P. L., & Archer, D. (1979). *Sensitivity to nonverbal communication: The PONS test.* Baltimore: Johns Hopkins University Press.

Salem, J. E., Kring, A. M., & Kerr, S. L. (1996). More evidence for generalized poor performance in facial emotion performance in schizophrenia. *Journal of Abnormal Psychology, 105,* 480–483.

Schank, R. C., & Abelson, R. P. (1977). *Scripts, plans, goals, and understanding: An inquiry into human knowledge structures.* Hillsdale, NJ: Erlbaum.

Smari, J., Stefansson, S., & Thorgilsson, H. (1994). Paranoia, self-consciousness, and social cognition in schizophrenics. *Cognitive Therapy and Research, 18,* 387–399.

Snyder, M., & Gangestad, S. (1986). On the nature of self-monitoring: Matters of assessment, matters of validity. *Journal of Personality and Social Psychology, 51,* 125–139.

Swanson, J. W., Borum, R., Swartz, M. S., & Monahan, J. (1996). Psychotic symptoms and disorders and the risk of violent behaviour in the community. *Criminal Behaviour and Mental Health, 6,* 309–329.

Toomey, R., Wallace, C. J., Corrigan, P. W., Schuldberg, D., & Green, M. F. (1997). Social processing correlates of nonverbal social perception in schizophrenia. *Psychiatry, 60,* 292–300.

Trower, P., Bryant, B., & Argyle, M. (1978). *Social skills and mental health.* Pittsburgh, PA: University of Pittsburgh Press.

van den Bergh, O., de Boeck, P., & Claeys, W. (1981). Research findings on the nature of constructs in schizophrenics. *British Journal of Clinical Psychology, 20,* 123–130.

Wechsler, D. (1997). *Wechsler Adult Intelligence Scale, Third Edition (WAIS III).* San Antonio, TX: Psychological Corporation.

Wykes, T., & Sturt, E. (1986). The measurement of social behaviour in psychiatric patients: An assessment of the reliability and validity of the SBS. *British Journal of Psychiatry, 148,* 1–11.

Social Cognition and Delusional Beliefs

See Lecture Slides

Richard P. Bentall

Abnormal beliefs are a common symptom observed in a variety of psychotic conditions. Until recently, however, they were not subjected to intensive psychological research. Indeed, in an edited book reviewing a number of theoretical accounts of delusions published a little more than 10 years ago, Oltmanns and Maher (1988) were able to cite few empirical studies of the psychological mechanisms that might be responsible for these kinds of beliefs. In the decade since that book was published, a number of lines of research have proven fruitful. These have highlighted, in particular, the role of social cognition in certain kinds of delusions. This chapter reviews this work, focusing in particular on our own studies of paranoid patients.

Characteristics of Delusional Beliefs

Following Karl Jaspers (1913/1963), most clinicians have assumed that delusions are qualitatively different from normal beliefs; this assumption may partially account for their neglect by psychologists. Attempts to operationalize the distinction between delusions and ordinary beliefs have not been entirely successful, however.

Although a wide variety of delusions are reported by psychiatric patients, they tend to reflect a small range of themes. Persecutory (sometimes called "paranoid") delusions are most commonly observed, but grandiose delusions also are quite common and often occur in association with paranoid beliefs (Garety, Everitt, & Hemsley, 1988; Sims, 1995). Other, less often studied delusional beliefs include ideas of reference (in which apparently innocuous events are believed to have some special significance for the person), somatic delusions (in which the person entertains fantastic beliefs about his or her own body), and delusional jealousy (in which the person irrationally believes that a loved one is being unfaithful). A few rare but colorful delusional systems have received detailed attention from researchers, such as the Cotard syndrome (first described by Cotard, 1882), in which the person denies the existence of the external world or even claims that she is dead, and the Capgras delusion (described by Capgras & Reboul-Lachaux, 1923/1994), in which the person believes that a loved one has been replaced by an impostor, robot, or doppelganger. Some commentators have noted that the themes of these delusions reflect common existential dilemmas (Musalek, Berner, & Katschnig, 1989) or concerns about the person's place in the social universe (Bentall, 1994).

Jaspers held that all delusional beliefs are *ununderstandable,* by which he meant that they are meaningless and cannot be understood in the context of individual personality or experience. However, this perspective can be criticized as highly subjective. Most modern definitions of delusions have emphasized characteristics of abnormal beliefs other than ununderstandability. For example, in the *Diagnostic and Statistical Manual of Mental Disorders* (*DSM–IV;* American Psychiatric Association, 1994) a *delusion* is defined as "a false personal belief based on incorrect inference about external reality and firmly sustained in spite of what almost everyone else believes and in spite of what usually constitutes incontrovertible and obvious proof or evidence to the contrary" (p. 765). Social constructionists have pointed out that this definition begs questions about what is meant by "incorrect inference," "external reality," and "incontrovertible and obvious proof" (Harper, 1992). Wary that the definition does not sufficiently exclude the extreme beliefs of religious leaders and politicians, the authors of *DSM–IV* go on to add, "[It] is not ordinarily accepted by other members of the person's culture or subculture" (p. 765).

Much of the difficulty in defining delusional beliefs can be resolved if it is accepted that they exist on a continuum with ordinary beliefs and attitudes. Strauss (1969) studied psychotic patients' accounts of their symptoms and argued that they could be classified along four dimensions: the strength of the patient's conviction in the objective reality of the experience; the extent to which the experience seems to be independent of stimuli or cultural determinants; the patient's preoccupation with the experience; and its implausibility. Subsequent research has confirmed that delusions vary along a number of dimensions, including conviction, extension (the degree to which the belief has implications for different areas of life), bizarreness, disorganization, and preoccupation (Kendler, Glazer, & Morgenstern, 1983). Although some delusions persist for many years (Harrow, MacDonald, Sands, & Silverstein, 1995), contrary to the conventional view that they are incorrigible, patients' conviction in their delusional beliefs may vary considerably from day to day (Brett-Jones, Garety, & Hemsley, 1987; Garety, 1985).

Delusions and Affect

Despite the dearth of research, early psychologists and psychiatrists felt free to speculate about the psychological mechanisms responsible for delusions. Freud (1911/1950) proposed an influential theory of paranoia in a speculative analysis of the autobiography of Daniel Schreber (1903/1955), a German judge who suffered from a severe paranoid illness. Skillfully piecing together various strands of evidence, Freud leads his readers to a conclusion that, to many minds, will seem rather implausible. In brief, he maintained that Schreber harbored homosexual feelings for his father, which he had defensively displaced on to his physician, Paul Flechsig. According to Freud, in a further series of defensive maneuvers, Schreber's love for his physician was then transformed into the physician's supposed hatred of Schreber.

Later psychoanalytically inspired theorists continued to assume that paranoid ideas serve a defensive function, but their accounts were rather more straightforward. Bleuler (1911/1950) regarded all delusions as attempts to attribute unacceptable ideas to external agencies, but believed that the ideas were not necessarily homoerotic in origin. More recently, Colby, Weber, and Hilf (1971) created a primitive computer simulation of paranoid thinking, which assumed that people who are paranoid are highly sensitive to threats to their self-esteem but protect themselves from feelings of personal inadequacy by blaming disappointments on malevolent others.

Colby et al.'s model implies that the mechanisms involved in some delusional systems may be similar to those in depression, an idea that Zigler and Glick (1988) developed further. They noted that grandiose and paranoid delusions often occur together and observed that they are found not only in patients with schizophrenia but also in patients suffering from affective psychoses. They argued that preoccupation with the self is a central feature of depression, paranoia, and mania (in depression and mania, the person is overly preoccupied by self-esteem, whereas in paranoia, the person is preoccupied by slights to the self).

Finally, they observed that premorbid social functioning is usually good in people who later suffer from paranoid delusions or disorders of mood, in contrast to people who later develop other schizophrenia symptoms, particularly negative symptoms. They therefore concluded that both paranoid schizophrenia and delusional disorder should be viewed as camouflaged forms of depression.

Zigler and Glick's (1988) theory takes Kraepelin's distinction between schizophrenia and the affective psychoses for granted, but it draws the line between the two types of disorder in a novel way. A rather different approach to understanding the relationship between paranoia and mood disturbance was proposed by sociologists Mirowsky and Ross (1989), who conducted a community survey of psychiatric symptoms in El Paso, Texas, and Juarez, Mexico. A total of 463 randomly selected English-speaking and Spanish-speaking residents living in the two cities were interviewed about whether they had experienced a range of psychiatric symptoms over the past 12 months. The data on 91 symptoms were then subjected to multidimensional scaling. The symptoms formed a two-dimensional circumplex in which paranoid symptoms fell between extreme symptoms of depression, on the one hand, and grandiose symptoms and symptoms normally attributed to schizophrenia, on the other.

A Framework for Understanding Delusions

Given that delusions exist on a continuum with ordinary beliefs, a psychological model of delusion formation might well begin with a model of the processes involved in acquiring ordinary beliefs. Although no agreed-upon and comprehensive account of this process exists, Figure 4.1 shows a simple "heuristic" model of belief formation proposed by Bentall (1990), which highlights some of the stages that may be involved. According to this model, beliefs about the world are usually based on events in the world (i.e., data). The events have to be perceived and attended to—those which the person fails to notice cannot influence thinking. Once data have been perceived, a person can make inferences about their importance and meaning, leading to a set of beliefs. Finally, the person may seek further information to either support or refute the beliefs, and so the cycle is repeated. Note that this is *not* a model of delusions per se; however, by considering each part of the model in turn, it is possible to see how different factors may act together to cause beliefs that appear strange or unusual.

FIGURE 4.1

A simple "heuristic" model of belief formation (Bentall, 1990).

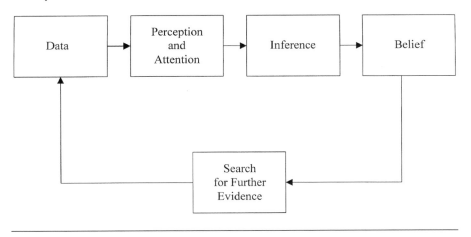

THE IMPACT OF EVENTS

We can begin by considering whether delusions sometimes reflect real events. Of course, if patients' accounts of their lives were completely realistic, it would be wrong to regard them as delusional. However, even if unrealistic, it remains possible that delusions contain a nugget of truth that is somehow distorted by the delusional process.

Clinical evidence consistent with this hypothesis has emerged from modern research into the case of Daniel Schreber. Following up on Freud's insight that Schreber's delusions had something to do with his father, Niederland (1960) and Schatzman (1973) investigated the judge's family. Schreber's father was a well-known physician who had unusual views about childrearing, which he proselytized in a series of books. Believing that children should learn to adopt rigid postures when sitting, walking, or even sleeping, he devised a series of braces to force them to adopt the desired positions. It seems likely that Schreber spent much of his childhood restrained in this way, and the contents of the bizarre ideas he developed later in his life seem to reflect these experiences. For example, a delusion about a "chest compression miracle" seems to reflect his father's practice of securing the child to his bed by means of a specially designed chest strap. Similarly, a delusion about a "head compressing machine" seems much more understandable when it is known that his father invented a *kopfhalter* (head-holder) consisting of a strap, one end of which was clamped to the child's hair and the other to his underwear, so that his hair was pulled if he did not hold his head straight.

The Schreber story is a single case study. It is difficult to gauge the extent to which most delusions reflect real experiences, because it is hard to verify deluded patients' accounts of their lives. However, two lines of research provide tentative evidence of an environmental contribution to delusion formation.

The first line of evidence is epidemiological. Mirowsky and Ross (1983) studied the distribution of persecutory beliefs, assessed by a brief interview, in their survey of residents of El Paso and Juarez. They assumed that objective circumstances that would encourage feelings of external control would engender paranoid thinking. Such circumstances would include experiences of victimization and powerlessness which, previous research had shown, were associated with low socioeconomic status and a lack of educational opportunities. Mirowski and Ross were able to show that external control, mistrust, and persecutory beliefs were connected to socioeconomic status and educational attainment in roughly the manner they had expected.

The second line of evidence has emerged from research into the role of life events in psychosis. In a recent review of this literature, Bebbington, Bowen, Hirsch, and Kuipers (1995) noted many inconsistencies but concluded that, on balance, the evidence suggests that life events do play some role in precipitating episodes of psychosis. Harris (1987) provided tentative evidence that life events specifically involving "outsider intrusiveness" (i.e., attempted interference or control by others) are associated with psychotic breakdowns. Clearly, intrusive events are precisely those that are likely to form the basis of paranoid delusions. Unfortunately, this observation has not been adequately followed up in subsequent research.

Perceptual Processes

THE ANOMALOUS PERCEPTION MODEL

Kraepelin (1907) suggested that delusions might be the product of rational attempts to make sense of unusual experiences. This theory has been developed at length more recently in a series of papers by Maher (1974, 1988, 1992). Maher's account, in fact, consists of two separate hypotheses: first, that delusions are always a reaction to some kind of anomalous perception or experience, and second, that delusions are *never* the product of abnormal reasoning processes. Clearly, the second of these hypotheses does not follow inevitably from the first.

Maher and Ross (1984) pointed to case study evidence that appears to support the first part of the theory (e.g., they interpreted Schreber's delusions as attempts to explain unusual bodily sensations). However, empirical studies have shown that anomalous perceptions play a role in only some delusions. For example, although it has been suggested that paranoid ideas might follow the slow onset of deafness (leading patients to incorrectly infer that others are talking about them), early studies that seemed to show the expected association between deafness and the onset of paranoid symptoms (Kay, Cooper, Garside, & Roth, 1976) were not replicated by later, more carefully conducted investigations (Moore, 1981; Watt, 1985).

Evidence favors the anomalous perception model as the basis for the Capgras delusion. Although this type of delusion sometimes has been attributed to the patient's emotional ambivalence toward the person who is believed to have been substituted, Ellis and de Pauw (1994) have listed a number of reasons for questioning this kind of account. For example, a motivational account implies that the delusion should exclusively concern people who have a close relationship with the patient, whereas this is not invariably the case. Also, patients with Capgras syndrome usually express no fears about the genuineness of voices heard over the telephone, suggesting that some difficulty in processing visual information is involved. Most important, about one third of Capgras patients are known to have suffered from some kind of brain damage that predates their illness.

Ellis and Young (1990) proposed that the Capgras syndrome is caused by damage to the brain systems responsible for face perception. Neuropsychological studies indicate that face recognition involves two pathways in the brain. A ventral pathway through the visual cortex to the limbic system allows retrieval of specific information about people (e.g., name and occupation). A second pathway, which passes through the inferior parietal lobe, enables an emotional reaction to a face and the accompanying feeling of familiarity. Ellis and Young proposed that in people with Capgras syndrome, the second pathway is disrupted, so the sense of familiarity is lost. They argued that the delusion is an attempt to explain this experience.

On the basis of their theory, Ellis and Young (1990) suggested that patients with Capgras syndrome would show little emotional response when meeting people who are well known to them. Consistent with this prediction, it has been shown that the electrodermal response that normally occurs when encountering a familiar person is absent in Capgras patients (Ellis, Young, Quale, & de Pauw, 1997).

It seems likely that delusions in general are rarely the product of anomalous perceptions. Chapman and Chapman (1988) interviewed students who scored high on questionnaire measures of schizotypal traits, finding that some expressed delusional ideas but reported no anomalous experiences, whereas others reported anomalous experiences in the absence of delusional ideas. In only a minority of cases did there appear to be an obvious causal connection between anomalous experiences and unusual beliefs.

SELECTIVE ATTENTION

Despite the disappointing evidence for Maher's theory, it remains possible that perceptual and especially attentional processes play a role in *maintaining* delusional ideas once they have been formed.

Ullmann and Krasner (1969) suggested that selective attention to relevant stimuli would lead deluded patients to notice information that especially supported their beliefs. In an attempt to test this hypothesis, Bentall and Kaney (1989) conducted a study that exploited the emotional Stroop effect, in which people show slowed color-naming of emotionally salient words. Four types of stimuli were used in the study: paranoia-related words (e.g., "deceit" and "follow"), depression-related words (e.g., "defeat" and "failure"), neutral words (e.g., "bud" and "recipe"), and meaningless strings of Os. The words and strings were printed in five different ink colors, and the participants had to name the colors as quickly as possible. Patients with paranoid delusions took much longer to color-name the paranoia-related words than the neutral words. This effect, which has been replicated by Fear, Sharp, and Healy (1996), was not found for a group of ordinary people or for a control group of depressed patients.

In an interesting variant of the Stroop experiment, Leafhead, Young, and Szulecka (1996) studied a woman who was experiencing the Cotard delusion (she believed that she was dead) as well as a Capgras delusion that her brother and mother were impostors. The patient was tested on three occasions, using words relating to death (e.g., "coffin" and "dead"), depression-related words, words relating to duplicates (e.g., "copy" and "double"), paranoia-related words, anxiety-related words, and emotionally neutral words. When acutely ill, the woman was slow to color-name both the death-related and the duplicate-related words. On a second assessment, when she was beginning to improve, only the duplicate-related words caused her difficulty. By the third test, when she was nearly recovered, color-naming was not impaired for any of the words.

If people attend excessively to information relating to their delusions, they also should preferentially recall this kind of information. Kaney, Wolfenden, Dewey, and Bentall (1992) presented a group of paranoid patients and a group of control participants with a series of stories describing threatening and nonthreatening social interactions, observing that the paranoid patients specifically recalled the threatening elements from the stories, despite recalling less information. In a later study, Bentall, Kaney, and Bowen-Jones (1995) asked patients to read a mixed list of words, some of which were paranoia-related, some of which were depression-related, and some of which were emotionally neutral. The paranoid patients showed preferential recall of the paranoia-related words, an effect that was absent in depressed patients and ordinary people.

Interestingly, these attentional and memory effects may not be caused by patients spending more time looking at stimuli relating to their delusions. Philips and David (1997a, 1997b) studied the eye movements of patients as they looked at various pictures, some of which showed people making threatening gestures. They measured the amount of time that the participants spent visually scanning different parts of the pictures. Compared with patients with other symptoms, patients with paranoid delusions spent less time looking at the threatening parts.

Paranoia and Social Cognition

We can now move onto the third box in the crude model of belief acquisition shown in Figure 4.1. Although Maher argued that delusions are never the product of abnormal reasoning processes, he was able to cite only one study in which patients with schizophrenia were observed to perform normally on a logical reasoning task (Williams, 1964). No evidence was presented to show that the patients in the study actually were deluded. More recent research has provided clear evidence that deluded patients make abnormal inferences, especially when they are asked to think about social situations.

DEFENSIVE ATTRIBUTIONS

Many delusional beliefs have the characteristics of unusual explanations for troubling events. Attribution theory provides an appropriate framework for exploring this aspect of delusions. In the first study to attempt this kind of analysis, Kaney and Bentall (1989) used Peterson et al.'s (1982) Attributional Style Questionnaire (ASQ) to compare patients with paranoia, patients with depression, and participants with no psychiatric diagnosis. The ASQ requires respondents to describe likely causes of hypothetical positive and negative events (e.g., earning a raise or going on a date that turns out badly) and then to rate their own causal judgments on three scales: internal versus external (caused by self versus caused by other people or circumstances); stability (whether the cause is likely to be present in the future); and globalness (whether the cause will affect other areas of life).

The patients with paranoia, like those with depression, tended to make excessively global and stable explanations for negative events. As earlier researchers have found (Robins & Hayes, 1995), the depressed patients had lower internality scores for hypothetical positive events than for negative events. Again, as observed by other researchers, the participants without a psychiatric diagnosis made a greater number of internal attributions for positive events than for negative events. This "self-serving bias" was significantly exaggerated in the paranoid patients. Similar findings were reported by other investigators in Great Britain (Fear et al., 1996), Canada (Candido & Romney, 1990), and Korea (Lee & Won, 1998), and a partial replication has been reported from Australia (Kristev, Jackson, & Maude, 1999).

The abnormal self-serving bias in paranoid patients also has been demonstrated using other methods. Kaney and Bentall (1992) asked participants to play a computer game in which they were required to discover a rule. On each of 40 trials, two pictures were presented on the computer screen; participants could choose one or the other by pressing button 1 or button 2. The participants started with 20 points, and when they made a correct choice, another point was awarded; when they made an incorrect choice, a point was deducted. In fact, the outcome of the games was predetermined at the outset. No matter what the participants did, one game (i.e., the "win game") awarded more points than it deducted, whereas the other (i.e., the "lose game") deducted more points than it awarded. After each game the participants were asked to complete a questionnaire indicating the extent to which they believed they had controlled the outcomes. The depressed patients who took part were sadder but wiser and claimed little control over either of the games (their judgments were therefore relatively accurate). The control participants showed a robust self-serving bias, claiming control when they were winning but not when they were losing. Again, the paranoid patients showed this self-serving bias to a greater degree.

Despite these generally consistent findings, it appears that attributional style is not abnormal in all deluded patients. Sharp, Fear, and Healy (1997) assessed the attributional styles of patients who avowed a variety of unusual beliefs. They observed an abnormal self-serving bias in patients with persecutory or grandiose delusions, but not in those who reported other kinds of delusional ideas.

DELUSIONS AND THE SELF

A possible explanation of paranoid patients' extreme self-serving bias is that it reflects excessive attempts to maintain self-esteem. This hypothesis is similar to some of the simpler psychoanalytic accounts of paranoia (e.g., Colby's theory). However, it is quite difficult to devise experiments to empirically test this theory.

The processes involved in self-representation are complex, and for this reason simple questionnaire measures of self-esteem can be misleading. Kinderman and Bentall (1996b) therefore decided to measure several different kinds of self-representation, using the method developed by Higgins (1987). Participants in the study (i.e., paranoid patients, depressed patients, and participants without a psychiatric diagnosis) were asked to describe themselves as they actually were (the actual self), the self as they would like to be (the ideal self) and how they believed their parents saw them (the parent-actual self). A quantitative measure of the discrepancies between the different descriptions then was calculated. As observed in previous research (Strauman, 1989; Strauman & Higgins, 1988), the descriptions were fairly consistent in the control group, who believed that they were more or less the sort of people they would like to be and that their parents shared their positive opinions about themselves. Also consistent with previous research, the depressed group showed marked discrepancies between how they saw themselves and how they said they would like to be. In contrast, the group of paranoid patients showed little discrepancy between their self-actual and self-ideal concepts but marked discrepancies between their self-actual concepts and their beliefs about how their parents saw them. In general, they seemed to believe that their parents harbored extremely negative attitudes toward them. The findings are consistent with the proposal that the external attributions for negative events that patients with paranoia create function to minimize discrepancies between self-actual representations and self-ideals, but because they implicate the actions of malevolent others, the attributions increase discrepancies between self-actual representations and the perception of the self they believe others have (Bentall, Kinderman, & Kaney, 1994).

Self-discrepancies reflect conscious and thoughtful judgments about the self. Some kinds of self-representation, however, are more implicit. In an attempt to measure those kinds of self-representations, Kinderman (1994) devised an approach that exploited the Stroop effect. Reasoning that people who are unhappy about themselves should be slow to color-name self-descriptive words, he showed paranoid patients, depressed patients, and participants with no psychiatric diagnosis a questionnaire consisting of high self-esteem words (e.g., "capable" and "wise") and low self-esteem words (e.g., "childish" and "lazy"). The participants were asked to indicate whether the words described themselves. As expected, normal people endorsed most of the positive words but few of the negative words. The depressed patients, in contrast, ticked about equal numbers of positive and negative words. The paranoid patients ticked mostly positive words but slightly more negative words than did the control participants. In the second stage of the study, the participants completed a Stroop task in which they were asked to color-name the same words. Kinderman found that the control participants had little difficulty with this task and color-named both the high self-esteem and the low self-esteem words about as fast as they color-named a list of emotionally neutral words. However, the depressed patients showed slowed color-naming for the high self-esteem words, and even slower color-naming for the low self-esteem words; this effect was even more pronounced for the paranoid patients.

A second approach has involved studying *implicit attributions*. The ASQ requires people to make explicit and deliberate judgments about the causes of events, and it is therefore unsurprising that paranoid patients' responses on it are rather defensive. If patients could be led to make more implicit judgments, perhaps their responses would be more concordant with any underlying self-esteem problems. To test this prediction, Lyon, Kaney, and Bentall (1994) used an implicit measure of attributional style devised by Winters and Neale (1985), known as the Pragmatic Inference Task (PIT). Participants are asked to listen to a series of brief stories describing themselves taking part in various successful or unsuccessful activities. After each story, participants are asked to answer a number of multiple-choice questions. One question after each story asks listeners to recall which of two causes (one internal and one external) was responsible for the good or bad outcome. The stories are constructed so that neither answer is more obviously correct than the other. Therefore, Winters and Neale argued, the answers chosen will reflect participants' implicit self-evaluations.

Lyon et al. (1994) asked paranoid patients, depressed patients, and control participants to complete the PIT as well as a conventional attributional style questionnaire that was similar to the ASQ but which was devised especially for the study. (We were unable to use the ASQ because its items are too similar to those in the PIT.) As we expected, the control participants showed a self-serving bias on both measures. In contrast, both deluded and depressed patients responded similarly on the PIT, choosing a greater number of internal attributions for negative than for positive events. In the case of the depressed patients, this pattern corresponded with their scores on the ASQ-like questionnaire. On the conventional attributional style questionnaire, however, the paranoid patients made a greater number of external attributions for negative than for positive events, a style that was consistent with previous findings but completely at variance with their pattern of responding on the PIT. This discrepancy between the paranoid patients' responses on the two measures presumably reflected the influence of underlying negative beliefs about the self, which determined their implicit attributions, as assessed by the PIT, but not their explicit attributions, which were more defensive.

A final indirect approach to assessing the self concerns self-schemata, which are the enduring standards of self-evaluation. Depressed patients typically embrace overly perfectionistic standards and therefore inevitably judge themselves to be inadequate (Olinger, Kuiper, & Shaw, 1987; Williams, Healy, Teasdale, White, & Paykel, 1990). To measure these standards in paranoid patients, Bentall and Kaney (1996) used the Dysfunctional Attitudes Scale (Weissman & Beck, 1978). Because paranoid patients often complain of being depressed, two groups of deluded patients were recruited: one with concurrent depression and a smaller group, who were not depressed at the time of testing. In fact, both groups scored similarly to a group of depressed patients who were not suffering from delusions, showing high scores on the questionnaire. Similar results were obtained in a study by Fear et al. (1996). Because perfectionistic self-schemata presumably make people vulnerable to negative self-evaluations, the findings are a further indication that sensitivity to these types of evaluations is a characteristic of paranoid patients.

Despite the findings, not all research has supported the hypothesis that paranoia may be a product of defensive processes. One peer reviewer noted that the empirical support for causality was not strong. For example, Freeman et al. (1998) administered a self-esteem questionnaire to their patients, finding that only about 30% of those with paranoid symptoms scored within the normal range. They therefore concluded that defensive processes play a role in only a minority of patients. An alternative interpretation of this finding, however, is that paranoid attributions do not always succeed in protecting the person against low self-esteem.

ATTRIBUTIONS AND OTHER MINDS

The evidence we have outlined so far suggests that paranoia is associated with abnormal attributions. The most widely used assessment of attributional style, the ASQ, assumes that the internality of attributions can be measured on a one-dimensional scale running from internal to external. In fact, many people find the distinction between "internal" and "external" difficult to comprehend (White, 1991), so it is not surprising that the reliability of the ASQ internality scale is poor (Reivich, 1995).

Part of the problem would seem to be that the ASQ and similar measures fail to distinguish between two types of external attributions: explanations that implicate circumstances ("external-situational attributions") and those that implicate other people ("external-personal attributions"). The importance of this distinction becomes evident if we think about a common situation that provokes attributions in ordinary people: being late for a meeting. Most people in those circumstances (at least in Great Britain) explain their lateness in situational terms ("I'm sorry, but the traffic was dreadful"). This commonsensical analysis suggests that external-situational attributions may be psychologically benign because they allow us to avoid blaming ourselves while blaming no one else, either. (Presumably, this is why they are the essence of a good excuse.) External-personal attributions, in contrast, appear to be much more psychologically toxic: They allow us to avoid blaming ourselves only at the expense of blaming someone else.

Kinderman and Bentall (1996a) found that when categorized this way, attributions could be assessed much more reliably than with the ASQ, suggesting that the distinction between the two types of external attributions has some validity. When Kinderman and Bentall (1997) compared paranoid, depressed, and control participants, they found that the depressed patients who took part in the study uniquely blamed themselves for negative events and that the paranoid patients uniquely blamed others for negative events (Figure 4.2). Although external-

FIGURE 4.2

Number of internal (left panel), external-personal (center panel), and external-situational (right panel) attributions made by paranoid, depressed, and control participants for hypothetical positive (+ ive) and negative (− ive) events (from Kinderman & Bentall, 1997).

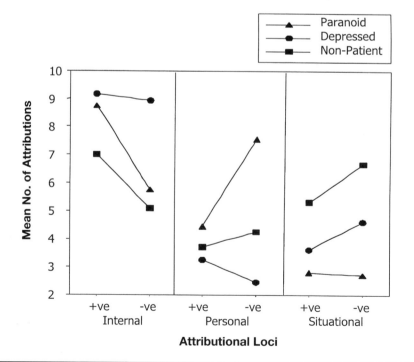

situational attributions may seem unimportant on first consideration, the paranoid patients who took part in the study also were unusual in that they made few explanations of this kind, either for positive or for negative events. Their excessive use of external-personal (other-blaming) explanations can be understood in the light of this apparent deficit.

This finding suggests a possible connection between the attributional model of paranoid symptoms and an alternative model proposed by Frith (1994). Because this theory is discussed in detail in chapter 5 of this book, we will deal with it only briefly here. The theory has been inspired by studies of autism, a developmental disorder that severely disrupts relationships with other people and which therefore prevents the child from becoming a fully functioning member of society. An impressive series of studies carried out by a number of psychologists, most notably Baron-Cohen (1995), have suggested that the core deficit responsible for the difficulties is an inability to think about the mental states of other people. This ability is said to require possession of a "theory of mind" (ToM).

Frith (1994) proposed that ToM deficits with a course and etiology different from those found in autism could lead to paranoid symptoms. He argued that paranoid beliefs occur when people lose their theory of mind and therefore suddenly experience difficulties inferring the intentions of other people. According to this model, the difficulties are attributed to deliberate acts of deception by others—hence the assumption that others harbor malevolent intentions toward the patient. On its own, this theory is clearly incomplete, because it is not obvious why a person who becomes unskilled at understanding others' minds will automatically assume that their intentions are evil.

In practice, it can be quite difficult to test for theory of mind. However, in a series of studies, Frith and Corcoran (Corcoran, Cahill, & Frith, 1997; Corcoran, Frith, & Mercer, 1995; Frith & Corcoran, 1996) found that two groups of patients with schizophrenia experience problems with questions of this sort: patients with paranoia and patients with predominantly negative symptoms. In the latter group, ToM performance correlated strongly with IQ, suggesting that their poor performance was probably caused by general cognitive deficits. In the paranoid patients, however, poor performance on the ToM questions seemed to be unrelated to low IQ. Interestingly, patients recovered from paranoia performed normally, indicating that ToM deficits are present only in episodes of illness.

Not all studies have shown a clear link between theory of mind and paranoia (Drury, Robinson, & Birchwood, 1998), so these findings should be considered tentative. Nonetheless, it is possible that ToM skills are involved in the generation of certain kinds of attributions. When ordinary people experience some kind of slight from others, the slight often is attributed to circumstances affecting the other person (e.g., "She's having a bad day" or "She's worried about something"). These kinds of explanations require taking the other person's point of view. In the absence of the ability to do this, and given the kind of attributional biases described earlier, the slight is likely to be attributed to some kind of simple disposition or trait "She's selfish and unreliable").

This argument suggests that defensive attributional biases and ToM deficits may work together to generate paranoid delusions, in the manner shown in the flow diagram in Figure 4.3. As the figure suggests, Gilbert, Pelham, and Krull (1988) found that people without psychiatric diagnoses are more likely to make dispositional attributions and less likely to make situational attributions when they are affected by a cognitive load.

In a preliminary attempt to test this theory, Kinderman, Dunbar, and Bentall (1998) assessed a large group of students on a ToM measure and on a measure of attributional style. As predicted by the theory, students who performed poorly on our ToM task made more paranoid-style, external-personal attributions than did students who performed

FIGURE 4.3

Defensive attributional biases and ToM deficits may work together to generate paranoid delusions. On the left, defensive processes, which buffer a person against negative opinions about the self, lead to a tendency to make external attributions when threatened by negative events (e.g., failure or rejection). On the right, a failure of ToM, occurring perhaps when the person is under stress, ensures that the external attributions are other-blaming rather than situational.

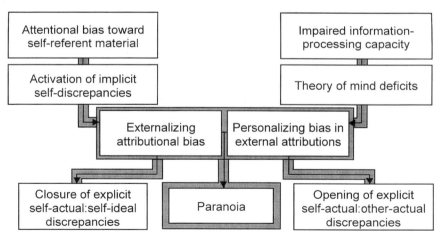

well. However, this study was limited by its use of students rather than participants who were mentally ill, so it would be wrong to place too much weight on it. Clearly, further research is needed to more adequately explore the relationship between attributions and theory of mind.

Deluded Patients' Use of Evidence

To conclude our discussion, we now consider the final part of the simple model of belief acquisition shown in Figure 4.1. When people try to work out what is going on around them, a number of hypotheses usually are available. Of course, the evidence rarely points in one direction. A person struggling to make sense of a difficult relationship with an employer might have to weigh her employer's irritable manner in one meeting against her cheerful and encouraging manner in another.

The ability of deluded patients to evaluate inconsistent evidence was first studied by Huq, Garety, and Hemsley (1988) and Garety, Hemsley, and Wessely (1991). Like most researchers who have later addressed this issue, they studied patients with a variety of delusional beliefs, not just paranoia. The participants taking part in the experiments were shown two jars, each containing beads of two colors. In one jar, one color far outnumbered the other (by a ratio of 85:15), whereas in the other, the proportions were reversed. The jars were then hidden away; the participants then were shown a predetermined sequence of beads and were asked to guess which jar the beads had been drawn from. In their first study, Huq et al. demonstrated that the patients with delusional beliefs made guesses on the basis of less evidence and with greater confidence, compared with a mixed group of psychiatric patients without delusions. Garety et al. obtained a more surprising result, in which the sequence of beads shown to participants was carefully designed so that it favored one jar early in the sequence, but the other jar later in the sequence. Garety et al. found that her patients with delusions were quicker to change their mind about the jar of origin than were her control participants. At first sight, this observation seems paradoxical because it implies that patients with delusions can sometimes be excessively flexible in their beliefs.

The studies provoked a series of further experiments by other investigators that have, by and large, supported this finding. For example, John and Dodgson (1994) tested deluded patients and controls using a variant of the well-known 20-questions game, in which participants pose a series of yes/no questions (e.g., "Is it a vegetable?") until they have enough evidence to guess the nature of a hidden object. When taking part in this game, deluded patients asked fewer questions than ordinary people before making their first guess.

It is also clear, however, that the content of the stimulus material affects performance on these kinds of measures. Dudley, John, Young, and Over (1997a) asked participants to make guesses about whether a series of statements had been made by a person who had mostly negative or mostly positive opinions about someone similar to the participant. In a similar study, Young and Bentall (1997a) asked participants to guess whether a list of personality traits described someone who had mainly positive traits or someone who had mainly negative traits. In both studies, all who took part made more hasty and extreme judgments in the emotionally salient conditions than on the original beads task used by Garety and her colleagues. Evidence also indicated that the difference between patients with delusions and control participants was greater when they were thinking about the emotionally salient problems versus the emotionally neutral problems.

Although the finding that people with delusions perform abnormally when evaluating evidence is one of the most consistent reported by researchers, it might be explained in several ways. One possibility is that people with delusions respond only to recently presented information. This explanation would be consistent with a theory of schizophrenia Salzinger (1973) proposed, arguing that many of the cognitive deficits that patients experience are caused by their tendency to respond to the most immediate stimuli in their environment. Dudley, John, Young, and Over (1997b) and Young and Bentall (1997b) carried out experiments to test whether this kind of deficit could explain the results of Garety's experiments; their research examined how patients reacted when the balance of the evidence was less clear-cut. Both studies found that deluded patients, like ordinary people, became more cautious in their judgments as the ratio of the colors approached 50:50.

Another possibility is that deluded people do not know how to go about testing their hypotheses. Popper (1963) famously argued that the most logical way of evaluating a theory is to look for evidence against it; in principle, a single piece of disconfirmatory evidence can be enough to refute a theory to its knees, whereas confirmatory evidence may be equally consistent with rival theories.

Until recently it was believed that ordinary people fail to reason logically because they pay attention exclusively to confirmatory evidence (Wason & Johnson-Laird, 1972). More recently, it has become obvious that people use "sensible reasoning" strategies, which may not be entirely logical but often are highly effective. When some kind of manipulation is believed to have produced a positive outcome (e.g., when it is believed that a cake is particularly nice because honey was used instead of sugar), it is sensible to test the hypothesis by looking for confirmatory evidence (e.g., by baking another cake with honey but changing some of the other ingredients) because the result of the test is likely to be a further positive outcome (another nice cake). However, if the outcome is negative (e.g., if it is believed that a cake is indigestible because margarine was used instead of butter), it is sensible to devise a disconfirmatory test (e.g., by baking a cake with butter) because doing so will reduce the possibility of another negative result. Studies show that both children and adults vary their hypothesis-testing strategies according to outcome in just this way (Farris & Revlin, 1989; Tschirgi, 1980). Bentall and Young (1996) found that paranoid patients, when given a choice between different ways of evaluating hypotheses, used similar sensible reasoning strategies.

It appears that the epistemological impulsiveness of deluded patients cannot be attributed to biased attention to recent evidence or to a failure to reason sensibly about hypotheses. A final possible explanation of this tendency implicates motivational processes. Perhaps deluded patients have a strong emotional need to reach definite ideas about the world and an inability to tolerate uncertainty. Kruglanski has described this kind of motivation as "a desire for a definite answer on some topic, any answer compared to confusion and ambiguity" (Kruglanski, 1989, p. 14). In a series of experiments, Kruglanski and his colleagues have demonstrated that people vary in the need for closure, which appears to be an important dimension of personality (Kruglanski & Webster, 1996). However, they also have shown that this need can be enhanced by particular circumstances (e.g., when people have to work against time). Interestingly, they observed that people who have a high need for closure make excessively stable and global attributions for failure experiences, rather like depressed and deluded patients.

Until recently, there has been no direct evidence that indicates this kind of motivation is especially strong in deluded patients, but one piece of indirect evidence has indicated that it might be. Using a measure of the need for meaning in one's life, Roberts (1991) compared currently ill deluded patients, patients whose delusions were in remission, people who were training to become Anglican priests, and ordinary people, using a measure of their need for meaning in their lives. Both the Anglican trainees and the currently ill patients, but not the remitted patients or control participants, produced high scores on this measure. In the same study, the patients were asked whether they would welcome evidence that their delusions—which often were associated with considerable distress—were false. Surprisingly, most said that they would not. Roberts interpreted this finding as evidence that for many patients, their delusional worlds constituted a preferred reality, embraced perhaps because they are less fraught with uncertainty than the real world.

In a recent study, Bentall and Swarbrick (2001) measured need for closure in currently deluded paranoid patients, remitted paranoid patients, and normal control participants, using a highly simplified version of Kruglanski's questionnaire. As we had predicted, both the currently ill and remitted patients scored higher on this measure than the controls.

Conclusion

This chapter has tried to show how psychological research has shed light on the mechanisms responsible for delusional beliefs. The evidence suggests that delusional beliefs, far from being ununderstandable, can be readily understood as products of psychological mechanisms that influence the acquisition of ordinary beliefs and attitudes.

Four mechanisms seem to be important. Some delusions appear to result from attempts to explain unusual experiences. Others, especially paranoid and grandiose beliefs, seem to be the product of attributional processes, although whether the processes function to defend the person against feelings of low self-esteem remains a hypothesis requiring further investigation. Evidence also shows that patients with paranoia experience difficulty when attempting to understand the mental states of other people, leaving them vulnerable to misinterpreting other people's actions. Finally, people with delusions generally appear to be epistemologically impulsive, perhaps because they have a strong emotional need for certainty. At present it is not obvious which, if any, of those processes is the most important, or whether delusional beliefs are products of complex interactions between these processes.

References

American Psychiatric Association. (1994). *Diagnostic and statistical manual for mental disorders* (4th ed.). Washington, DC: Author.

Baron-Cohen, S. (1995). *Mindblindness: An essay on autism and theory of mind*. Cambridge, MA: MIT Press.

Bebbington, P. E., Bowen, J., Hirsch, S. R., & Kuipers, E. A. (1995). Schizophrenia and psychosocial stresses. In S. R. Hirsch & D. R. Weinberger (Eds.), *Schizophrenia* (pp. 587–604). Oxford, England: Blackwell.

Bentall, R. P. (1990). The syndromes and symptoms of psychosis: Or why you can't play 20 questions with the concept of schizophrenia and hope to win. In R. P. Bentall (Ed.), *Reconstructing schizophrenia* (pp. 23–60). London: Routledge.

Bentall, R. P. (1994). Cognitive biases and abnormal beliefs: Towards a model of persecutory delusions. In A. S. David & J. Cutting (Eds.), *The neuropsychology of schizophrenia* (pp. 337–360). London: Lawrence Erlbaum.

Bentall, R. P., & Kaney, S. (1989). Content-specific information processing and persecutory delusions: An investigation using the emotional Stroop test. *British Journal of Medical Psychology, 62,* 355–364.

Bentall, R. P., & Kaney, S. (1996). Abnormalities of self-representation and persecutory delusions. *Psychological Medicine, 26,* 1231–1237.

Bentall, R. P., Kaney, S., & Bowen-Jones, K. (1995). Persecutory delusions and recall of threat-related, depression-related and neutral words. *Cognitive Therapy and Research, 19,* 331–343.

Bentall, R. P., Kinderman, P., & Kaney, S. (1994). The self, attributional processes and abnormal beliefs: Towards a model of persecutory delusions. *Behaviour Research and Therapy, 32,* 331–341.

Bentall, R. P., & Swarbrick, R. (2001). The best laid schemas of paranoid patients: Sociotropy, autonomy and need for closure. Manuscript submitted for publication.

Bentall, R. P., & Young, H. F. (1996). Sensible-hypothesis-testing in deluded, depressed and normal subjects. *British Journal of Psychiatry, 168,* 372–375.

Bleuler, E. (1950). *Dementia praecox or the group of schizophrenias* (E. Zinkin, Trans.). New York: International Universities Press. (Original work published 1911)

Brett-Jones, J., Garety, P., & Hemsley, D. (1987). Measuring delusional experiences: A method and its application. *British Journal of Clinical Psychology, 26,* 257–265.

Candido, C. L., & Romney, D. M. (1990). Attributional style in paranoid vs depressed patients. *British Journal of Medical Psychology, 63,* 355–363.

Capgras, J., & Reboul-Lachaux, J. (1923/1994). L'illusion des 'sosies' dans un delire systematise chronique. *History of Psychiatry, 5,* 117–130.

Chapman, L. J., & Chapman, J. P. (1988). The genesis of delusions. In T. F. Oltmanns & B. A. Maher (Eds.), *Delusional beliefs* (pp. 167–183). New York: John Wiley.

Colby, K., Weber, S., & Hilf, F. D. (1971). Artificial paranoia. *Artificial Intelligence, 2,* 1–25.

Corcoran, R., Cahill, C., & Frith, C. D. (1997). The appreciation of visual jokes in people with schizophrenia: A study of "mentalizing" ability. *Schizophrenia Research, 24,* 319–327.

Corcoran, R., Frith, C. D., & Mercer, G. (1995). Schizophrenia, symptomatology and social inference: Investigating "theory of mind" in people with schizophrenia. *Schizophrenia Research, 17,* 5–13.

Cotard, J. (1882). Du delire des negations. *Archives de Neurologie, 4,*152–170, 282–295.

Drury, V. M., Robinson, E. J., & Birchwood, M. (1998). "Theory of mind" skills during an acute episode of psychosis and following recovery. *Psychological Medicine, 28,* 1101–1112.

Dudley, R. E. J., John, C. H., Young, A. W., & Over, D. E. (1997a). The effect of self-referent material on the reasoning of people with delusions. *British Journal of Clinical Psychology, 36,* 575–584.

Dudley, R. E. J., John, C. H., Young, A. W., & Over, D. E. (1997b). Normal and abnormal reasoning in people with delusions. *British Journal of Clinical Psychology, 36,* 243–258.

Ellis, H. D., & de Pauw, K. W. (1994). The cognitive neuropsychiatric origins of the Capgras delusion. In A. S. David & J. C. Cutting (Eds.), *The neuropsychology of schizophrenia* (pp. 317–335). Hove, England: Erlbaum.

Ellis, H. D., & Young, A. W. (1990). Accounting for delusional misidentifications. *British Journal of Psychiatry, 157,* 239–248.

Ellis, H. D., Young, A. W., Quale, A. H., & de Pauw, K. W. (1997). Reduced autonomic responses to faces in Capgras delusion. *Proceedings of the Royal Society of London, 264,* 1085–1092.

Farris, H. H., & Revlin, R. (1989). Sensible reasoning in two tasks: Rule discovery and hypothesis evaluation. *Memory and Cognitive, 17,* 221–232.

Fear, C. F., Sharp, H., & Healy, D. (1996). Cognitive processes in delusional disorder. *British Journal of Psychiatry, 168,* 61–67.

Freeman, D., Garety, P., Fowler, D., Kuipers, E., Dunn, G., Bebbington, P., & Hadley, C. (1998). The London-East Anglia randomized controlled trial of cognitive-behaviour therapy for psychosis IV: Self-esteem and persecutory delusions. *British Journal of Clinical Psychology, 37,* 415–430.

Freud, S. (1950). Psychoanalytic notes upon an autobiographical account of a case of paranoia (Dementia Paranoides). In *Collected papers* (Vol. III, pp. 387–466). London: Hogarth Press. (Original work published 1911)

Frith, C. (1994). Theory of mind in schizophrenia. In A. S. David & J. C. Cutting (Eds.), *The neuropsychology of schizophrenia* (pp. 147–161). Hove, England: Erlbaum.

Frith, C., & Corcoran, R. (1996). Exploring "theory of mind" in people with schizophrenia. *Psychological Medicine, 26,* 521–530.

Garety, P. A. (1985). Delusions: Problems in definitions and measurement. *British Journal of Medical Psychology, 58,* 25–34.

Garety, P. A., Everitt, B. S., & Hemsley, D. R. (1988). The characteristics of delusions: A cluster analysis of deluded subjects. *European Archives of Psychiatry and Neurological Sciences, 237,* 112–114.

Garety, P. A., Hemsley, D. R., & Wessely, S. (1991). Reasoning in deluded schizophrenic and paranoid patients. *Journal of Nervous and Mental Disease, 179*(4), 194–201.

Gilbert, D. T., Pelham, B. W., & Krull, D. S. (1988). On cognitive busyness: When person perceivers meet persons perceived. *Journal of Personality and Social Psychology, 54,* 733–740.

Harper, D. J. (1992). Defining delusions and the serving of professional interests: The case of "paranoia." *British Journal of Medical Psychology, 65,* 357–369.

Harris, T. (1987). Recent developments in the study of life events in relation to psychiatric and physical disorders. In B. Cooper (Ed.), *Psychiatric epidemiology: Progress and prospects* (pp. 81–102). London: Croom Helm.

Harrow, M., MacDonald, A. W., Sands, J. R., & Silverstein, M. L. (1995). Vulnerability to delusions over time in schizophrenia and affective disorders. *Schizophrenia Bulletin, 21,* 95–109.

Higgins, E. T. (1987). Self-discrepancy: A theory relating self and affect. *Psychological Review, 94,* 319–340.

Huq, S. F., Garety, P. A., & Hemsley, D. R. (1988). Probabilistic judgements in deluded and nondeluded subjects. *Quarterly Journal of Experimental Psychology, 40A,* 801–812.

Jaspers, K. (1963). *General psychopathology* (J. Hoenig & M. W. Hamilton, Trans.). Mancheste, England: Manchester University Press. (Original work published 1913)

John, C. H., & Dodgson, G. (1994). Inductive reasoning in delusional thought. *Journal of Mental Health, 3,* 31–49.

Kaney, S., & Bentall, R. P. (1989). Persecutory delusions and attributional style. *British Journal of Medical Psychology, 62,* 191–198.

Kaney, S., & Bentall, R. P. (1992). Persecutory delusions and the self-serving bias. *Journal of Nervous and Mental Disease, 180,* 773–780.

Kaney, S., Wolfenden, M., Dewey, M. E., & Bentall, R. P. (1992). Persecutory delusions and the recall of threatening and non-threatening propositions. *British Journal of Clinical Psychology, 31,* 85–87.

Kay, D. W., Cooper, A. F., Garside, R. F., & Roth, M. (1976). The differentiation of paranoid from affective psychoses by patients' premorbid characteristics. *British Journal of Psychiatry, 129,* 207–215.

Kendler, K. S., Glazer, W., & Morgenstern, H. (1983). Dimensions of delusional experience. *American Journal of Psychiatry, 140,* 466–469.

Kinderman, P. (1994). Attentional bias, persecutory delusions and the self concept. *British Journal of Medical Psychology, 67,* 53–66.

Kinderman, P., & Bentall, R. P. (1996a). The development of a novel measure of causal attributions: The Internal Personal and Situational Attributions Questionnaire. *Personality and Individual Differences, 20,* 261–264.

Kinderman, P., & Bentall, R. P. (1996b). Self-discrepancies and persecutory delusions: Evidence for a defensive model of paranoid ideation. *Journal of Abnormal Psychology, 105,* 106–114.

Kinderman, P., & Bentall, R. P. (1997). Causal attributions in paranoia: Internal, personal and situational attributions for negative events. *Journal of Abnormal Psychology, 106,* 341–345.

Kinderman, P., Dunbar, R. I. M., & Bentall, R. P. (1998). Theory of mind deficits and causal attributions. *British Journal of Psychology, 71,* 339–349.

Kraepelin, E. (1907). *Textbook of psychiatry* (7th ed., A.R. Diefendorf, Trans.). London: Macmillan.

Kristev, H., Jackson, H., & Maude, D. (1999). An investigation of attributional style in first-episode psychosis. *British Journal of Clinical Psychology, 88,* 181–194.

Kruglanski, A. W. (1989). *Lay epistemics and human knowledge: Cognitive and motivational bases.* New York: Plenum.

Kruglanski, A. W., & Webster, D. M. (1996). Motivated closing of the mind: "Seizing" and "freezing." *Psychological Review, 103,* 263–283.

Leafhead, K. M., Young, A. W., & Szulecka, T. K. (1996). Delusions demand attention. *Cognitive Neuropsychiatry, 1,* 5–16.

Lee, H. J., & Won, H. T. (1998). The self-concepts, the other-concepts, and attributional style in paranoia and depression. *Korean Journal of Clinical Psychology, 17,* 105–125.

Lyon, H. M., Kaney, S., & Bentall, R. P. (1994). The defensive function of persecutory delusions: Evidence from attribution tasks. *British Journal of Psychiatry, 164,* 637–646.

Maher, B. A. (1974). Delusional thinking and perceptual disorder. *Journal of Individual Psychology, 30,* 98–113.

Maher, B. A. (1988). Anomalous experience and delusional thinking: The logic of explanations. In T. F. Oltmanns & B. A. Maher (Eds.), *Delusional beliefs* (pp. 15–33). New York: Wiley.

Maher, B. A. (1992). Models and methods for the study of reasoning in delusions. *Revue Europeenne de Psychologie Appliqee, 42,* 97–102.

Maher, B. A., & Ross, J. S. (1984). Delusions. In H. E. Adams & P. Suther (Eds.), *Comprehensive handbook of psychopathology* (pp. 383–408). New York: Plenum.

Mirowsky, J., & Ross, C. E. (1983). Paranoia and the structure of powerlessness. *American Sociological Review, 48,* 228–239.

Mirowsky, J., & Ross, C. E. (1989). *Social causes of psychological distress.* New York: Aldine de Gruyter.

Moore, N. C. (1981). Is paranoid illness associated with sensory defects in the elderly? *Journal of Psychosomatic Research, 25,* 69–74.

Musalek, M., Berner, P., & Katschnig, H. (1989). Delusional theme, sex and age. *Psychopathology, 22,* 260–267.

Niederland, W. G. (1960). Schreber's father. *Journal of the American Psychoanalytic Association, 8,* 492–499.

Olinger, L. J., Kuiper, N. A., & Shaw, B. F. (1987). Dysfunctional attitudes and stressful life events: An interactive model of depression. *Cognitive Therapy and Research, 11,* 25–40.

Oltmanns, T. F., & Maher, B. A. (Eds.). (1988). *Delusional beliefs.* New York: John Wiley.

Peterson, C., Semmel, A., Von Baeyer, C., Abramson, L., Metalsky, G. I., & Seligman, M. E. P. (1982). The Attributional Style Questionnaire. *Cognitive Therapy and Research, 3,* 287–300.

Philips, M., & David, A. S. (1997a). Abnormal visual scan paths: A psychophysiological marker of delusions in schizophrenia. *Schizophrenia Research, 29,* 235–254.

Philips, M., & David, A. S. (1997b). Visual scan paths are abnormal in deluded schizophrenics. *Neuropsychologia, 35,* 99–105.

Popper, K. (1963). *Conjectures and refutations: The growth of scientific knowledge.* London: Routledge.

Reivich, K. (1995). The measurement of explanatory style. In G. M. Buchanan & M. E. P. Seligman (Eds.), *Explanatory style* (pp. 21–48). Hillsdale, NJ: Lawrence Erlbaum.

Roberts, G. (1991). Delusional belief systems and meaning in life: A preferred reality? *British Journal of Psychiatry, 159*(Suppl. 14), 19–28.

Robins, C. J., & Hayes, A. H. (1995). The role of casual attributions in the prediction of depression. In G. M. Buchanan & M. E. P. Seligman (Eds.), *Explanatory Style* (pp. 71–98). Hillside, NJ: Lawrence Erlbaum.

Salzinger, K. (1973). *Schizophrenia*: Behavioral aspects. New York: John Wiley.

Schatzman, M. (1973). *Soul murder: Persecution in the family.* London: Penguin Books.

Schreber, D. (1955). *Memoirs of my nervous illness* (I. Macalpine & R. A. Hunter, Trans.). London: Dawsons. (Original work published 1903)

Sharp, H. M., Fear, C. F., & Healy, D. (1997). Attributional style and delusions: An investigation based on delusional content. *European Psychiatry, 12,* 1–7.

Sims, A. (1995). *Symptoms in the mind* (2nd ed.). London: W. B. Saunders.

Strauman, T. J. (1989). Self-discrepancies in clinical depression and social phobia: Cognitive structures that underlie emotional disorders? *Journal of Abnormal Psychology, 98*(1), 14–22.

Strauman, T. J., & Higgins, E. T. (1988). Self-discrepancies as predictors of vulnerability to distinct syndromes of chronic emotional distress. *Journal of Personality, 56*(4), 685–707.

Strauss, J. S. (1969). Hallucinations and delusions as points on continua function: Rating scale evidence. *Archives of General Psychiatry, 21,* 581–586.

Tschirgi, J. E. (1980). Sensible reasoning: A hypothesis about hypothesis. *Child Development, 51,* 1–10.

Ullmann, L. P., & Krasner, L. (1969). *A psychological approach to abnormal behaviour.* Englewood Cliffs, NJ: Prentice-Hall.

Wason, P. C., & Johnson-Laird, P. (1972). *Psychology of reasoning.* Cambridge, MA: Harvard University Press.

Watt, J. A. (1985). The relationship of paranoid states to schizophrenia. *American Journal of Psychiatry, 142*(12), 1456–1458.

Weissman, A. N., & Beck, A. T. (1978). *Development and validation of the Dysfunctional Attitude Scale.* Paper presented at the Annual Meeting of the Association for the Advancement of Behavior Therapy, Chicago, IL.

White, P. A. (1991). Ambiguity in the internal/external distinction in causal attribution. *Journal of Experimental Social Psychology, 27,* 259–270.

Williams, E. B. (1964). Deductive reasoning in schizophrenia. *Journal of Abnormal and Social Psychology, 69,* 47–61.

Williams, J. M. G., Healy, D., Teasdale, J. D., White, W., & Paykel, E. S. (1990). Dysfunctional attitudes and vulnerability to persistent depression. *Psychological Medicine, 20,* 375–381.

Winters, K. C., & Neale, J. M. (1985). Mania and low self-esteem. *Journal of Abnormal Psychology, 94,* 282–290.

Young, H. F., & Bentall, R. P. (1997a). Probabilistic reasoning in deluded, depressed and normal subjects: Effects of task difficulty and meaningful versus nonmeaningful materials. *Psychological Medicine, 27,* 455–465.

Young, H. F., & Bentall, R. P. (1997b). Social reasoning in individuals with persecutory delusions: The effects of additional information on attributions for the behaviour of other. *British Journal of Clinical Psychology, 36,* 569–573.

Zigler, E., & Glick, M. (1988). Is paranoid schizophrenia really camouflaged depression? *American Psychologist, 43,* 284–290.

Theory of Mind and Schizophrenia | 5

Rhiannon Corcoran

n all gregarious creatures, the brain has evolved in such a way as to maximize our fitness for living with those of our own kind. Because creatures aim to enhance only their own (and direct kin's) survival, this can make for circumstances when the outdoing of others, to whom the individual bears no direct relation, can be extremely advantageous. For example, an animal might deceive and trick another out of its food or reproductive opportunities. Such instances have been documented many times over in field studies of chimpanzees, for example (Whiten & Byrne, 1988), although some skepticism surrounds this issue. The ability to deceive a conspecific can be achieved only if one holds an implicit theory that others (with whom the creature lives and shares certain characteristics) have minds and act according to the contents of their minds.

In the human species this so-called mentalizing, or theory of mind (ToM), ability is believed to be at its most advanced. We effortlessly and constantly set our minds to consider what other people are thinking, intending, or believing. We demonstrate this facility every time we infer veiled or hidden intentions behind speech acts or whenever we appreciate states of false belief and predict the behavioral consequences of those false beliefs. Lying, cheating, weaving stories, imagining, pretending, sharing humor, tricking, or using and understanding nonverbal ges-

The research reported here was funded by a project grant awarded to Christopher Frith from the Medical Research Council and by a Wellcome Trust project grant awarded to Rhiannon Corcoran and Christopher Frith.

149

tures can be achieved only if we have a theory of mind. All of these skills demonstrate that our knowledge of the existence of other minds is central to the smooth running of everyday human performance. If we had to live without this amazing "mind-reading" skill, life would be rather two-dimensional; furthermore, daily life would be, at the very least, extremely mysterious. Wellman (1985) describes such a case:

> Imagine a hypothetical being who knows nothing of internal mental states. . . . Such a being might be able to remember, know and learn, but it would possess no understanding of these activities. The social world, the world of self and others, would be an impoverished place for such a creature. . . . Persons would be seen and heard but there would be no notion of a backlog of ideas and beliefs organizing their actions and personalities. Indeed, for this hypothetical being, no one could be construed as possessing private persona; public present behavior would have no deeper meaning. The concept of a lie would be inconceivable, as would . . . notions such as illusions, beliefs, hunches, mistakes, guesses, or deceptions. It is almost impossible to imagine what such a perspective would be like, how such a creature would view the world. (Wellman, 1985, pp. 169–170)

Wellman's description, although given before the ToM model of autism was widely accepted, depicts accurately what life must be like for a person with autism. It is quite widely believed that people with autism or Asperger's syndrome lack a ToM that enables them to function effortlessly within a social world (see Baron-Cohen, Tager-Flusberg, & Cohen, 2000). It is argued that such people do not recognize that others have minds or work with the contents of their minds. This state of affairs, it seems, results from a failure of neurodevelopment. Many elegant empirical studies have been conducted that support this assertion (see Baron-Cohen, 1995, for a review). The studies have shown that children with a diagnosis of autism who otherwise seem cognitively intact tend, on the whole, to fail both first-order (i.e., representing someone else's mental state) and second-order (i.e., representing someone else's thoughts about another's mental state) ToM tasks. It was argued that this failure of theory of mind was specific and exclusive to autism.

Any observer of human behavior, however, knows that mentalizing is not an all-or-nothing skill. This fact, in itself, implies that a theory of mind is not something that is either absent or present. We have all met people who lack tact, are "thick-skinned," literal, lacking in humor, or who seem to pick up the wrong messages from those around them. Indeed, a case may exist for arguing sex differences in the origins of the skill (see Skuse et al., 1997). Furthermore, other neurological, psychiatric, and sensory conditions that affect ToM skill have been documented (see Corcoran, 2000). Those conditions include schizophrenia, where arguably, there is most evidence indicating mentalizing problems outside the field of autism. The interest in this social inference skill as it relates to schizophrenia began in 1992 with Chris Frith's book *The Cognitive Neuropsychology of Schizophrenia.*

Schizophrenia as a Disorder of Metarepresentation (Frith, 1992)

Like autism, strong evidence from various sources supports a neurodevelopmental etiology for chronic schizophrenia, even though the illness itself only becomes manifest during early adulthood. This evidence includes that accrued from epidemiological studies such as those conducted at the Institute of Psychiatry (e.g., Murray & Lewis, 1987; Jones et al., 1993). It seems that those who are diagnosed as suffering from chronic deficit state schizophrenia show clear signs of dysfunction during childhood, one of the chief aspects of which is social in nature. Such children are described as loners, having few, if any, friends. This information, along with the supporting findings from other disciplines, has considerable significance for the development of sociocognitive skills, particularly theory of mind.

The thesis put forward by Chris Frith (1992) fits well with those findings. He argued that schizophrenia could be understood as a disorder of the representation of mental states. The single most important thing to appreciate about Frith's model is the precise way in which it deals with the different signs and symptoms of schizophrenia. Like others before him (e.g., Persons, 1986; Bentall, 1990), he sought a way forward toward an understanding of the illness by considering the psychotic signs and symptoms that are most characteristic of it. Using the metarepresentational framework, he argued that the signs and symptoms of schizophrenia reflected the precise nature and location of the dysfunction within a cognitive system devoted to the recognition and monitoring of one's own intentions and the attribution of intentions, thoughts, and beliefs to others.

According to the model, *abulia*, or lack of will, arises as a result of an early disruption to the system causing a complete inability to represent intentional behavior. Passivity phenomena, such as delusions of control, thought insertion or withdrawal, and auditory hallucinations, arise as a result of a failure at a point within the system when one's own intentions to act ought to be monitored. Certain features of formal thought disorder are believed to arise from a failure to take account of other people's state of knowledge. Finally, certain delusions, such as delusions of reference, misinterpretation, and persecution, as well as delusions of thoughts being read (henceforth referred to as delusions of a paranoid nature) arise from a system dysfunction that disables the representation of other people's thoughts, beliefs, and intentions.

Frith and colleagues' studies examining the cognitive accounts of propositions related to negative features and passivity phenomena met with a good deal of success (see Frith, 1987; Frith & Done, 1989; Mlakar, Jensterle, & Frith, 1994); the studies presented in the following section are those which Chris Frith and I conducted to explore the ToM hypotheses. Before describing those studies, it is necessary to elaborate on the rationale behind the ToM hypotheses, particularly on how certain signs and symptoms are thought to result from a ToM deficit.

Negative signs are thought to be the consequence of an early and wide-ranging breakdown in the ability to represent intention. Such a hypothesis has the potential to explain the poverty of action that is so characteristic of people with schizophrenia as well as the social withdrawal and blunted affect that are typical signs of chronic deficit-state schizophrenia. The inability to represent intentional mental states may apply not only to one's own mental states but also to those of others. The extent to which awareness of one's own mental state is intertwined with awareness of others' is largely unknown, but Frith's model suggests that the two abilities are indeed related and enveloped within a single metarepresentational mechanism. It is suggested that the inability to fathom the mental states of others leads to an exclusion from society, evidenced in social withdrawal and the blunting of affective responses. Because people with schizophrenia cannot think about other people's mental states, they cannot behave appropriately. Affective responding therefore will be noticeably lacking.

Certain features of formal thought disorder, such as the use of neologisms and the overuse of pronominal referents (see Rochester & Martin, 1979), are indicative of a failure to consider the knowledge state of listeners. The thought-disordered speaker who uses idiosyncratic vocabulary or who refers to people or objects as *he*, *she*, or *it* without having first introduced them presents the listener with a problem of interpretation. The listener cannot know what the speaker is talking about. The "fault" lies with the thought-disordered speaker, who apparently does not recognize a difference between his or her knowledge state of a topic and the knowledge state of the listener; consequently, the speaker does not consider the extent of the listener's knowledge of the topic. This failure to separate the two states of knowledge reflects a fundamental failure of theory of mind.

A number of delusions typical of schizophrenia are proposed to result from a ToM disorder. For the sake of brevity, as mentioned earlier, those delusions are referred to here as delusions of a paranoid nature.

I am happy to adopt this shorthand because if we think about the contents of these delusions, it is clear that they have something to do with misinterpretation of other people's mental states. For example, the falsely held belief that people on television are talking about you or that gestures or certain speech acts have veiled meanings is called a *delusion of reference*. The extension of this type of delusion is the *delusion of misinterpretation* or *misidentification*, wherein the patient believes that situations or objects have special significance and that they have been arranged by others to test the patient. The apparently unjustified belief that others intend you harm is a *delusion of persecution*. Finally, there is the delusion that others can read your thoughts when, in fact, all they are probably doing is using their intact theory of mind. One question that relates to persecutory delusions in particular is why the misinterpretation of others' intentions toward the self are so negative. Frith (1992) has argued that the negativity is a predictable consequence of a de novo malfunction in a system that, up to the point of early adulthood, functioned effortlessly. The acutely ill person who can no longer infer others' intentions may well reasonably assume that the problem has arisen because others are trying to hide their intentions. One reason for hiding intentions would be because they are not good. An alternative explanation for the negative quality of persecutory delusions is presented later in this chapter.

The Original Studies

In a series of four investigations, Frith and I set out to test the hypothesis that certain people with schizophrenia have difficulty inferring the thoughts, beliefs, and intentions of other people. Based on Frith's cognitive model of the disease, we expected to find mentalizing problems in patients with negative behavioral signs, formal thought disorder, and paranoid-type delusions. Normal performance was expected in patients with other symptoms and in those in remission, because the breakdown in the cognitive mechanism is thought to be primary and to give rise to the signs and symptoms. The theory is that if the malfunction is repaired, mentalizing will improve, and as a result, the signs and symptoms will remit. Given the specificity of our predictions, we devised a subgrouping technique, based upon the signs and symptoms present at the time of testing, that was best able to test the model. Thus, everyone with schizophrenia whom we tested was placed into one of six mutually exclusive groups. Table 5.1 describes the precise symptoms considered within each subgroup. Group 1 consisted of any patient who displayed the negative behavioral signs of social withdrawal or blunted affect;

TABLE 5.1

Symptoms and Signs in Patient Subgroups

Subgroup	Signs and Symptoms
1. Negative signs	Social withdrawal, blunted affect (poverty of speech, abulia)
2. Positive signs	Formal thought disorder (disorganized behavior, incongruous affect)
3. Paranoid delusions	Delusions of persecution, reference, misinterpretation and thoughts being read (third-person auditory hallucinations)
4. Passivity features	Delusions of control, delusions of influence, thought insertion, thought withdrawal, second-person auditory hallucinations
5. Other symptoms	Musical hallucinations; grandiose, sexual, and hypochondriacal delusions, etc.
6. Remission	Minimum 2-week period free of signs and symptoms

these typically arise in conjunction with other signs of poverty. Group 2 comprised patients with formal thought disorder, commonly seen with disorganization. Any patients with paranoid-type delusions but without behavioral signs were cast into Group 3. Patients who described passivity phenomena at the time of testing but no paranoid-type delusions or behavioral signs went into Group 4. Group 5 comprised patients who displayed or described none of the signs or symptoms but who described other, less typical symptoms. Finally Group 6 consisted of patients with a *DSM–III–R* or *–IV* diagnosis of schizophrenia (American Psychiatric Association, 1989, 1994) but who appeared well and symptom free at the time of testing and had been so for at least the previous 2 weeks.

The judgments about signs and symptoms were arrived at using the Present State Examination, version 9 (Wing, Cooper, & Sartorius, 1974). All patients were tested for their abilities to infer the intentions, beliefs, and thoughts of others before they were assigned to a subgroup. Up to four paradigms designed to be appropriate for an adult sample of differing ability and motivational levels were used to assess this skill. Ability level was established using the Quick Test (Ammons & Ammons, 1962), a word-to-picture matching test giving an estimate of full-scale Wechsler Adult Intelligence Scale (WAIS; 1955) IQ. No patients who were assessed to function below a full-scale IQ of 85 were included in the investigations.

UNDERSTANDING HINTS
(Corcoran, Mercer, & Frith, 1995)

The Hinting Task (Corcoran, Mercer, & Frith, 1995) was devised as an ecologically valid way of looking at ToM abilities within our clinical sample, who often describe problems with this kind of veiled speech act. The task comprises 10 vignettes involving two characters, one of whom drops a heavy hint at the end of each story. Some examples of the vignettes are as follows:

> Rebecca's birthday is approaching, so she says to her dad, "I love animals, especially dogs."
> *Question*: What does Rebecca really mean when she says this?
> *Add*: Rebecca goes on to ask, "Is the pet shop open on my birthday, Dad?"
> *Question*: What does Rebecca want her dad to do?

> Paul has to go to an interview, and he's running late. While he is cleaning his shoes, he says to his wife Jane, "I want to wear my blue shirt, but it's very creased."
> *Question*: What does Paul really mean when he says this?
> *Add*: Paul goes on to say, "It's in the ironing basket."
> *Question*: What does Paul want Jane to do?

The stories are read to the participants as often as they request, and they are asked what the person really means by his or her utterance. A correct response involves inferring, from the limited context given in the vignette, the intention behind the speech act, which is always clearly different from what is actually said. The task is scored out of 20 possible points, with 2 points given for a correct response to the first hint. If a participant fails to infer a reasonable meaning from the first hint, a further, even more obvious hint is added to the story, and the participant is asked what the character wants the other to do. A correct response at this stage is given 1 point, and an incorrect response scores zero. Either way, the next item is introduced.

Fifty-five people with a *DSM–III–R* or *–IV* diagnosis of schizophrenia performed this task for us. We also collected data from 30 "normal" adults and 14 nonpsychotic psychiatric control adults suffering from anxiety or depression. The symptom-specific findings were independent of levels of functioning. Our patients with negative behavioral signs performed this task significantly more poorly than did patients with passivity features, patients in remission, and the two control groups. The patients with paranoid delusions performed significantly worse than the two control groups, as did the small group of patients with positive signs. As expected, the patients with passivity features and those in remission

[handwritten marginal note: who does bad u on Tom tests remission]

[handwritten note at bottom: remission same as control groups ie 'normal' people.]

TABLE 5.2

Summary of the Performance on the Hinting Task

Symptom Subgroup	Number	Mean Hinting Task Score (0–20)[a]	Standard Deviation
Negative feature	10	12.8	4.5
Formal thought disorder	3	12.7	5.7
Paranoid delusions	23	15.4	3.6
Passivity features	7	18.6	1.7
Other symptoms	4	16.5	2.6
Remission	8	18.0	2.6
Psychiatric control	14	18.6	1.6
Normal sample	30	18.1	1.6

[a]Patients with negative signs scored lower than those in the passivity, remitted, psychiatric, and normal control groups. Patients in the paranoia and formal thought disorder groups scored lower than those in the psychiatric and normal control groups.

performed at a level with the control groups. Table 5.2 summarizes the findings.

UNDERSTANDING FALSE BELIEF AND DECEPTION (Frith & Corcoran, 1996)

For this investigation we used simple stories with accompanying line drawings to examine the ability of 46 patients to understand the concept of false belief and the practice of deception to the second-order level. Examples of the first- and second-order false belief stories are given below:

First-order level

John has five cigarettes left in his packet. He puts the packet on the table and goes out of the room. Meanwhile, Janet comes in, takes one of John's cigarettes, and leaves the room without John knowing.

ToM question: When John comes back for his cigarettes, how many does he think he has left?

Memory/reality question: How many cigarettes are really left in John's packet?

Second-order level

Sally and Ian are at the station because Sally has to catch a train home. Sally lives in Homesville, but the train doesn't stop at Homesville station. Sally will have to get off at Neartown and walk. Sally goes to buy a magazine to read on her journey before she buys her ticket. While she is gone, there is an alteration to the timetable, and the train is now going to stop at Homesville. The guard tells Ian about this change, and Ian sets off to find Sally to tell her, but before Ian finds her, the guard meets Sally and tells her, "the train will now stop at Homesville." Ian eventually finds Sally, who has just bought her ticket.

ToM question: Which station does Ian think that Sally has bought her ticket for?

Memory/reality question: Where has Sally really bought her ticket for?

Compared with 22 normal control and 13 psychiatric control participants, the patients with paranoid delusions were impaired on the questions requiring an inference to be made about one of the characters' belief state at first- and second-order levels. The patients with behavioral signs (a combined group of positive and negative but mostly negative) had problems not only with questions of this type but also those requiring them to remember a factual aspect of the story. In other words, patients in this group had ToM difficulties coexisting with other, more general cognitive problems, whereas patients with paranoid delusions seemed to have a more specific mentalizing difficulty. In this study it was again noted that patients with passivity features as well as those in remission behaved normally. Table 5.3 summarizes the findings.

UNDERSTANDING JOKES
(Corcoran, Cahill, & Frith, 1997)

In this study we explored the mentalizing skill using a task that incorporated visual as well as linguistic information, giving it greater real-life validity. We chose visual jokes because the understanding of intention is clearly involved in some forms of humor, but not others; therefore, parallel tasks could be developed to look at physical versus ToM jokes. Two sets of 10 cartoons were shown to participants. In one set, it was necessary to infer the mental state of one of the characters in order to get the jokes, whereas the other set needed only a physical or behavioral appreciation. Data was collected from 44 patients with schizophrenia, 40 normal control participants, and 7 psychiatric control patients. We found that our control groups and our patients in remission understood both types of joke equally well. However, the patients with behavioral signs and those with paranoid delusions obviously found the ToM jokes more difficult. Contrary to our earlier findings, the group with passivity features also had problems with this type of mentalizing, although the problem was not as marked for them. Table 5.4 summarizes the findings.

TABLE 5.3

Summary of the Performance on the First- and Second-Order False Belief and Deception Stories

Symptom Subgroup	% Correct on the First-Order Stories (n)[a]	% Correct on the Second-Order Stories (n)[b]
Behavioral signs	63 (10)	25 (8)
Paranoid delusions	76 (23)	46 (21)
Passivity features	100 (10)	58 (10)
Remission	65 (9)	67 (9)
Psychiatric control	100 (13)	69 (13)
Normal sample	98 (22)	95 (22)

Note. Table includes only those participants who answered the reality question correctly.
[a]Participants in the behavioral signs and paranoia groups scored lower on first-order stories than did those in the passivity, remission, psychiatric, and normal control groups.
[b]Participants in the behavioral signs and paranoid groups scored lower than participants in the remission, psychiatric and normal control groups on second-order stories.

COMMUNICATIVE RULES VERSUS PROTOCOL (Corcoran & Frith, 1996)

In 1975, Grice proposed five maxims as guiding principles of conversation (Table 5.5). They are hard-and-fast rules that were thought to apply cross-culturally to ensure that acts of communication were as meaningful as possible. We suggested that, in contrast to the maxims, the *politeness protocol* or convention is much more flexible. Its appropriate use depends on an ability to detect important contextual variables that change, often subtly, from instance to instance. We expected to see our

TABLE 5.4

Summary of the Performance on the Physical and Theory of Mind Jokes

Symptom Subgroup	n	Mean (SD) Correct Physical Jokes	Mean (SD) Correct ToM Jokes	Significance of the Difference Score
Behavioral signs	7	5.4 (2.8)	3.3 (2.5)	Significant
Paranoid delusions	16	6.8 (2.2)	5.4 (1.8)	Significant
Passivity features	8	7.0 (2.6)	4.9 (3.1)	Significant
Remission	13	6.5 (2.2)	6.2 (2.7)	Not significant
Psychiatric controls	7	7.6 (2.5)	6.1 (1.7)	Not significant
Normal sample	40	7.7 (1.8)	7.6 (1.8)	Not significant

SD = standard deviation.

TABLE 5.5

The Gricean Maxims and Politeness Convention

Maxim	Rule	Example
Maxim of quantity 1	Say enough to be informative.	Joe is in the tobacconist's. The assistant asks him what he would like. Joe replies, 1. A packet of cigarettes please. 2. Twenty Benson and Hedges please.
Maxim of quantity 2	Don't say too much.	Geoff has a pet dog Bugsy, whom he is very fond of. One day Sylvia comes over to Geoff's house while Bugsy is out with Geoff's sister. Sylvia asks, 1. Where is Bugsy? 2. Where is your pet dog Bugsy?
Maxim of quality	Be truthful.	Thomas is about to sit a maths test but feels very ill. His teacher comes over and asks him how he is. Thomas replies, 1. I'm fine thank you. 2. I feel dreadful. May I go home please?
Maxim of relation	Be relevant.	Tony and David are traveling home from work together. They have been chatting about the work they have both been doing on their houses. Tony says, 1. I wonder what's for dinner? 2. The wife is very pleased with the front room.
Politeness/tact	Choose a level of politeness to fit the individual occasion.	Bill and Fergus are having a business lunch at a Chinese restaurant. Bill likes to try all kinds of food, but Fergus is much less adventurous and prefers to stick to what he knows. When Fergus orders steak and chips, Bill says, 1. You can't go wrong with steak and chips. I'm sure you will enjoy that. 2. For goodness sake Fergus, that's a bit boring isn't it?

paranoid patients having problems appreciating the correct use of this context-specific convention while having no difficulty with the maxims. In our patients with behavioral signs, we thought it more likely that an across-the-board problem would exist, pointing to a widespread ignorance of social rules. The summary data in Table 5.6 demonstrates that this is what we found. Again, normal performance was seen in our remitted subgroup.

TABLE 5.6

A Summary of Performance on the Gricean Maxims and the Politeness Convention Task

Symptom Subgroup	n	Mean (SD) Total Maxims Score	Mean (SD) Politeness Score
Behavioral signs	10	13.7 (1.6)	2.2 (0.9)
Paranoid delusions	17	16.6 (3.0)	2.8 (1.3)
Passivity features	11	15.4 (2.1)	3.2 (1.7)
Remission	11	17.3 (1.9)	3.8 (1.2)
Psychiatric control	10	17.5 (2.3)	4.4 (0.7)
Normal sample	13	18.5 (1.1)	4.2 (1.0)

Note. Participants in the behavioral signs group do poorly on social rules across the board; those with paranoia do poorly on politeness only.

INTERPRETING THE FINDINGS

Using the four experimental paradigms, we clearly demonstrated the existence of ToM problems in people with schizophrenia. It also seemed likely that the extent of the problem was related to the presence of certain signs and symptoms, in a manner predicted by Frith's model. We had shown severe mentalizing problems in those with negative features, where the dysfunction is thought to exist at the level of representing intentional acts and where, therefore, we also would expect to find more widespread cognitive problems on tests that require volitional behavior. We also had demonstrated the existence of more circumscribed problems of theory of mind in our patients with paranoid symptoms, where the model proposes a malfunction within the system at a stage devoted to the mental states of others. The four studies did not address other predictions and implications of the model, including a proper test of ToM functioning in patients with formal thought disorder, of whom too few were tested to enable a strong case. Sarfati, Hardy-Bayle, Nadel, Chevalier, and Widlocher (1997) addressed the deficit seen in relation to the presence of formal thought disorder more thoroughly, as described in the next section.

Another aspect that remained unclear was the performance of the patients with passivity phenomena. The performance of this group on the visual jokes and the maxims test indicated that some subtle difficulties with social inference may exist in these patients. In the maxims test, they seemed to find it more difficult to recognize a speech act that was clearly verbose and therefore flouted the maxim of quantity. According to Frith's model, the metarepresentational difficulty experienced by people with this type of symptom lies in monitoring their own intentions to act. It is unknown to what extent a deficit of this kind would affect the ability to reflect on others' mental states. This issue of mutual exclusivity, or double dissociation, is one of the questions Langdon et al. (1997) addressed in a comprehensive study.

Further Studies

Since Frith's original thesis, a good deal of interest has been generated in the metarepresentational model of the illness and, in particular, the idea that schizophrenic thought can be understood as resulting from an inability to accurately reflect on other people's mental states. The areas explored include the relationship of the dysfunction to signs and symptoms as well as to other cognitive skills. The studies reviewed in this section deal in a meticulous and comprehensive way with issues that were left unclear by the original studies. Note that not all the follow-up studies have found ToM dysfunction in patients with paranoid delusions (see Garety & Freeman, 1999, for a review). It is reasonable to assume that this failure to replicate reflects differences in the categorization of symptoms. In our own studies (Corcoran et al., 1995; Corcoran & Frith, 1996; Frith & Corcoran, 1996; Corcoran et al., 1997), we used a theory-driven if somewhat atypical classification of paranoid-type delusions. A follow-up study looking at individual delusions within this broad paranoid category would be worthwhile, as would an exploration of the grandiose delusions that often are considered a feature of "paranoid schizophrenia."

MENTAL AND NON-MENTAL-STATE REPRESENTATION AND THEIR RELATIONSHIP TO EXECUTIVE DYSFUNCTION IN SCHIZOPHRENIA

It is probably indisputable that one aspect of the ability to contemplate others' mental states involves reasoning about various contextual variables in the setting within which the behavior to be considered takes place. Such conditional reasoning is among the skills referred to by cognitive neuropsychologists as "executive." In the autism literature on ToM dysfunction, some writers believe that this sociocognitive failure is related to executive skill difficulties (see, e.g., Ozonoff, Pennington, & Rogers, 1991). Given this fact , it is necessary to explore the relationship that might exist between theory of mind and executive skills in people with schizophrenia, in whom separate investigations have shown both types of difficulty to exist (see Shallice, Burgess, & Frith, 1991, for evidence pointing to executive underfunctioning). It is also important to establish the extent of the representational deficit in schizophrenia: Frith's thesis argues that the representation of mental states gives rise to the illness, but it is not clear whether non-mental-state representation also is affected.

In his doctoral thesis, Graham Pickup (1997) set about exploring those issues. He used the same sign-and-symptom grouping methodology that was devised for the original studies (Corcoran et al., 1995; Corcoran & Frith, 1996; Frith & Corcoran, 1996; Corcoran et al., 1997) and used matched mental state and non-mental-state representation tasks drawn from the autism literature. He found no evidence of difficulty with first-order tasks in his participants with schizophrenia compared with control participants, but he found highly significant differences on second-order, false-belief tasks between the behavioral-signs group and his normal and psychiatric controls as well as in his group of patients with schizophrenia in remission. This difference in performance was not seen in the matched second-order non-mental-state task, however. When Pickup looked at within-group differences, it became clear that although the two control groups and the group in remission found the two types of task equally challenging, the behavioral-signs group and the paranoid group found the mental state task more difficult. Composite scores of both types of task using first- and second-order performance also indicated that the participants in the paranoid and behavioral-signs groups were performing mental-state tasks more poorly than were control participants. However, when Pickup considered the role of general intellectual functioning, the difference between the paranoid group and the controls was reduced to a trend when current IQ was controlled for but remained significant if premorbid IQ was considered.

In his study of executive functions, Pickup (1997) used the same composite mental-state scores. He showed that although the behavioral-signs group made more perseverative errors on a two-stage discrimination task, indicating executive-functioning deficits, the participants' difficulties did not appear to be related to the ToM problems of this group.

Pickup concluded that second-order ToM problems did exist in patients with behavioral signs as well as in those with paranoid delusions. The difficulties were clearly circumscribed, being found only with mental-state material, and they did not seem to be related to coexisting executive-functioning problems in the behavioral-signs group.

ToM AND INTELLIGENCE LEVEL

Pickup's work indicated that the level of current functioning might be an important factor determining ToM performance in the paranoid group. Doody, Gotz, Johnstone, Frith, and Cunningham-Owens (1998) addressed the question of the role of IQ using a neat group methodology.

Five groups of patients were asked to perform two classic ToM tasks taken from the autism literature: the Sally-Anne task (Wimmer & Perner, 1983) and the ice cream van task (Perner & Wimmer, 1985).[1] The five groups consisted of people with schizophrenia, people with affective disorder with psychotic symptomatology, people with mild learning disability, people with schizophrenia and mild learning disability, and nonpsychiatric control individuals. The authors found that approximately 22% of the people with schizophrenia and mild learning disability showed evidence of first-order ToM problems. This figure was comparable to the 26% shown in the mild learning-disabled group. For the second-order tasks, both groups with schizophrenia and those with mild learning disabilities had difficulty with the task, but when patients who failed the "reality"/memory control question (indicating a more basic memory or comprehension problem) were excluded from the analysis, a specific problem with theory of mind was seen only in the schizophrenic groups. This difficulty was related to both negative and positive symptom clusters, as measured using the Positive and Negative Symptom Scale (Kay, Fiszbein, & Opler, 1987). The relationship to symptoms held only in the schizophrenic samples, however, even though the patients with affective disorders had the same type of symptoms. The study provides convincing evidence of a second-order ToM deficit that is related to symptomatology and which is specific to schizophrenia.

FALSE BELIEFS VERSUS INTENTIONS

Sarfati et al. (1997) were interested in exploring whether any difference existed in the understanding of false belief and intentions. They did so using a sample of patients with schizophrenia divided according to the *DSM–III–R* subtypes of paranoia, undifferentiated and residual; a clinical control sample with major depressive disorder; and a normal control group. Cartoon comic strips in which the participant is shown some incomplete scenes depicting intention or false belief scenarios were devised. The participants' task was to demonstrate their ToM strength by completing the cartoon sequence with the correct crucial last picture. Sarfati et al. showed, among other findings, that whereas a difficulty attributing false beliefs apparently was exclusive to the participants with schizophrenia, no difference was found between the schizophrenic and the depressed groups in their ability to infer intentions. Furthermore, the authors found no differences according to *DSM–III–R* subtype or according to the degree of negative signs or positive symptoms in the

---

[1]The Sally-Anne task involves one character removing a belonging of the other character, and taking it to a different place without her knowledge. It measures first-order false belief. The ice cream van task is a story in which one of two characters holds a false belief about another character's mental state. It measures second order false belief.

level of difficulty the schizophrenic participants encountered on the false-belief tasks. However, a tendency was reported for those patients scoring highest on a measure of thought and language disturbance to perform most poorly on the intention tasks. The authors concluded that although a deficit on false-belief appreciation characterized the whole group, a problem with inferring intentions was associated exclusively with formal thought disorder. Given that the data indicated that the false-belief items were the more difficult of the two types, the authors could not argue that the two types of attribution involve independent processes. Indeed, this difference in level of difficulty could explain why participants with thought disorder, who are easily distracted, performed more poorly on the easier intention tasks. This seems, for the moment, a more reasonable conclusion, given that the data from the hinting task (Corcoran et al., 1995), also a measure of intentional inference, indicated poor performance in other symptom and sign subgroups.

Sarfati et al. (1997) also considered the nature of the failures on the false-belief tasks. They pointed out that participants with schizophrenia tended to offer random responses to the tasks, as people with autism do, instead of attributing true beliefs. The conclusion that the authors drew was that "the schizophrenic subjects were unable to extract the relevant data which gave meaning and intention to the character's behavior" (p. 15). I return to this contextual-insensitivity hypothesis in the next section.

CHARACTERIZING THE GROUPS WITH ToM PROBLEMS

In the first of a series of investigations reported in Langdon et al. (1997), a four-card picture-sequencing task incorporating stories involving mechanical, social script, pretense, unrealized goal, intention, and false-belief information was used to subdivide a sample of schizophrenic participants into three groups. The first group comprised participants who correctly ordered all stories. The second was made up of patients who made errors only on the false-belief stories but who also took longer to complete those and the pretense stories. Patients in the second group were most likely to show the negative signs of alogia, social withdrawal, and flat affect. Finally, the third group of patients seemed to have general sequencing deficits; their prominent signs and symptoms here were of poverty and reality distortion.

The narratives given to the pictures were explored for mental-state language by a naive rater. Participants who had shown a selective meta-representational deficit used fewer intentional-cognitive terms than did the error-free group and the normal control participants, but they did not differ in their use of other forms of mental-state language. The group with general sequencing problems used less mental-state language across the board.

The authors next explored the relationship between awareness of one's own mental states and the ability to infer that of others. The ability to remember seen objects, past pretenses, finished goals, unrealized intentions, correct beliefs, and false beliefs was explored, and problems recalling past intentions and false beliefs were noted in the group with the selective ToM sequencing difficulties. The group with general sequencing problems had difficulty recalling all types of mental state but remembered seen objects normally. The data provided evidence of an interesting double dissociation: Some of the patients who had problems with the false-belief sequencing task did well on the recall of past intentions, whereas some who performed the false-belief sequencing task well could not remember their own past intentions. This double dissociation supports Frith's division of positive symptoms into those reflecting a deficit of self-monitoring and those arising from a ToM problem.

Langdon et al.'s (1997) findings differ from our own in failing to find a clear association between paranoia and ToM problems. They do, however, make the interesting speculation that patients with paranoia might fail because they use probabilistic reasoning instead of conditional reasoning to tackle social inferences. The next section presents an account of mentalizing that embodies conditional reasoning and which was devised to address the kind of problems seen in a schizophrenic sample.

The Achievement of Mentalizing

Following our initial studies, we went on to propose a neuropsychological model of ToM that was capable of explaining the dysfunctions we saw in schizophrenia; the characteristic disability in autism; normal, adult everyday ToM functioning; and the timing of the first appearance of the skill in normally developing youngsters. The model arose from ideas and evidence from several sources. A guiding principle of the model is that the entire human brain has evolved primarily as a social-information processor. Most information that we have to handle on a day-to-day basis is social in nature, and therefore it follows that the cognitive skills we have developed are suited best to dealing with precisely this type of information. The same skills may be hijacked to deal with more abstract, nonsocial material, but they do so less efficiently, just as the left hand in most right-handed people is less efficient when it comes to fine motor skills. This situation is possibly a result, in part, of insufficient experience, but it more likely results from the fact that the system is not being used at its optimum. I would argue, however, that this proposition is rather contrary to how most psychologists would view cognitive skills. More typical views rest on the idea that a certain part of the human brain is devoted to social information processing (Brothers, 1990) or that certain modular skills are used to achieve social cognition (e.g., Leslie, 1987). One highly robust finding that is consistent with the "whole brain as social brain" view comes from the literature on conditional reasoning. "If–then" reasoning, which can be investigated experimentally using versions of the Wason selection task (Wason, 1966), becomes much easier for most people if the conditional rule is embedded within a social context, even if that context is highly unfamiliar (see Cosmides, 1989). Extending this argument, it follows that the skills we use to infer the contents of others' minds have evolved precisely for that purpose. If they also can be used to perform various nonmentalizing tasks, so much the better.

One "lay" idea that influenced the model was that the most likely base from which to start the mentalizing process was one's knowledge of self. The knowledge of how we would react in similar circumstances to those in need of disambiguation would surely be of use to us in understanding the mental states of others. The same assumption underpins the simulation theory of mentalizing proposed by Harris (1990). However, we argue that this information about self—or, indeed, a familiar other—comes from a referral to social episodic or autobiographical memory. Instead of simulating a situation and pretending to be in the other's shoes, we argue that we try to recall a similar experience from our past to inform us about the current situation. If the current situation presents a real challenge to our powers of mentalizing, we will have had no previous experience of an exactly parallel situation. Therefore what we recall amounts to a "best-guess" base from which to begin the social inference process. What remains then to be done is to consider all the variables that differ in the present situation from one's recollection. These might be conditional upon, for example, the person involved, the precise contextual setting, and relevant information we already have. Thus, we must reason about the influence of conditional variables on the outcome of the present situation.

This, then, is the model: We achieve an understanding of another's mental states by harnessing the cognitive skills of autobiographical memory and conditional reasoning. To argue that a present challenge is achieved by reasoning from a base of knowledge derived from past experience is to argue that the achievement is accomplished using analogical reasoning. Sternberg (1977) argued that we reason analogically every time we refer to information derived from past experience to inform current reasoning. According to this model, theory of mind is a special form of analogical reasoning.

Several strands of evidence from the psychological literature on schizophrenia render this model credible. First is the increasing evidence indicating memory deficits in schizophrenia (Corcoran & Frith, 1993, 1994; Shallice et al., 1991; Tamlyn et al., 1992). For example, Baddeley, Thornton, Chua, and McKenna (1996) explored autobiographical memory in schizophrenia using the Autobiographical Memory Interview (Kopelman, Wilson, & Baddeley, 1993). They found that people with delusions were inclined to report markedly odd, often rather unpleasant episodes from their past when prompted to do so by the questions incorporated in the schedule. Whether the memories were true or delusional is an open question, but the significance of this finding to our model is clear. If patients with delusions do display a bias toward remembering odd, negative, or bizarre experiences from their past, it follows that the outcome of the social inference process will be unsuccessful and the ToM product itself will be odd, negative, or bizarre. The unusual and unpleasant autobiographical recollection is an inappropriate base from which to start the mentalizing process. A recollection of a more "normal" or everyday experience would be a better starting place because the aim is to infer someone else's mental state. Ideally, therefore, one would want to recall something personal yet with some degree of inherent commonality (Corcoran, 1999).

Although many studies point to executive skills deficits in schizophrenia, undoubtedly the most relevant to theory of mind are the studies that have explored reasoning, including studies of social reasoning (e.g., Dudley, John, Young, & Over, 1997; Young & Bentall, 1997) and inductive reasoning (e.g., John & Dodgson, 1994; Pishkin, Lovallo, Lenk, & Bourne, 1977), which have indicated clear difficulties in these areas in people with delusions (see chapter 4).

A link between autobiographical memory and theory of mind finds support in the developmental literature, where it is noted that the two skills emerge at about the same time in normal children (Howe & Courage, 1997; Nelson, 1992; Welch & Melissa, 1997). Furthermore, evidence of poor autobiographical memory functions in autism has been found. In 1981, Boucher examined event memory in autism and found it to be inferior to that of age-matched controls. More recently, Powell and Jordan (1993) looked at narrative ability and personal episodic memory in children with autism and noted that those children failed to produce narratives of personal events. Two alternative explanations were offered. First, they proposed that children with autism fail to develop an "experiencing self." Later, in a presentation to the British Psychological Society London Conference, they suggested that the findings might be explained by a failure to develop a social memory system.

THE MODEL AND ITS DYSFUNCTION IN RELATION TO THE SIGNS AND SYMPTOMS OF SCHIZOPHRENIA

Figure 5.1 illustrates the model as well as the locations of dysfunction that result in the ToM deficits associated with psychotic signs and symptoms. As shown, the ToM deficit can arise as a result of a failure or a bias in one or both of the cognitive skills that together make up the

---

FIGURE 5.1

Model of mentalizing, with malfunctions associated with signs and symptoms of schizophrenia.

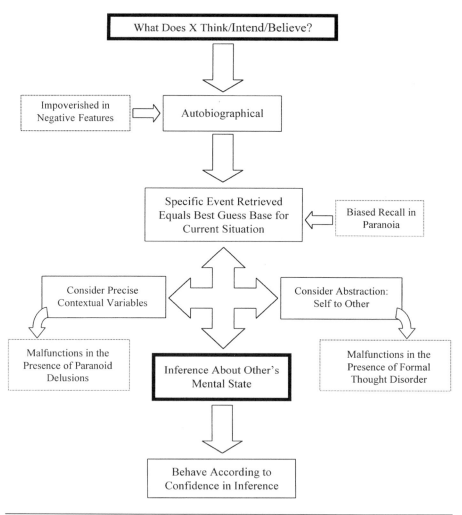

ToM skill. A dysfunctional autobiographical memory is implicated in chronic negative features and paranoid delusions, but different kinds of dysfunction are suggested.

We propose that people with chronic negative features have an impoverished autobiographical memory. Given the evidence of premorbid childhood social isolation in this subgroup of patients, the recollection of relevant event-specific information would be poor simply as a result of lack of exposure to social events. In people with paranoid delusions, we propose instead a bias in the retrieval of information from autobiographical memory. After Baddeley et al. (1996), we propose that those with paranoid symptoms will have a tendency to recall bizarre or unpleasant events from autobiographical memory. Thus, an inappropriate platform is used to initiate the mentalizing process.

It is almost tautological to state that conditional reasoning will be faulty if mentalizing progresses to a conclusion from a faulty initial starting point (i.e., an unusual or markedly unpleasant recollection); the first conditional variable that must be considered is whether a piece of personal information is likely to apply to another person. Consider what would happen if a person without paranoia were to recall a highly unusual personal event when prompted by a present-day ToM situation. It is probable that the person would realize that the recollection was inappropriate, reject it, and begin a new search for a more fitting recollection that has inherent commonality. It follows, therefore, that in our patients with paranoia (who do make inaccurate inferences about others' mental states), conditional reasoning must be faulty because they fail to reject the inappropriate recollection.

In patients with chronic negative feature schizophrenia, again we propose impaired conditional reasoning. This hypothesis is largely informed by previous psychological literature pointing to widespread cognitive deficits in this group. However, it is unlikely that an impairment of conditional reasoning has much effect on the ToM process in this subsample because their dearth of personal experiences already has rendered the ToM product unattainable. In other words, if they can recall nothing to inform the process, then mentalizing will not follow. Therefore, the autobiographical memory impairment is the core cognitive deficit affecting ToM skills in people with chronic negative features. In paranoia, however, the core deficit would be the conditional reasoning component. This poorly functioning skill allows use of the ill-fitting recollection; had the conditional reasoning component been working efficiently, it would have rejected the recollection.

In the case of formal thought disorder, it seems most parsimonious to argue for a core deficit in conditional reasoning if we accept the argument that the thought-disordered speaker recognizes no difference between one's own knowledge of a topic and that of the partner in communication. The reasoning of the thought-disordered speaker might be, "If I know, then he or she knows," instead of "If I know, then he or she may or may not know, depending on certain conditions."

For patients with schizophrenia who have other symptoms, one might assume that both conditional reasoning and ToM skills function adequately to produce an appropriate mentalizing skill. However, this may not be the case. The final inference of the mentalizing process could be fine, on the face of it, even if autobiographical memory is biased or somewhat weakened, as long as conditional reasoning is functional. The reasoning process in these cases will not allow the mentalizing process to begin from a markedly odd recollection. Therefore, the state of the autobiographical memory in these patients is not clear; however, one must assume that their powers of conditional reasoning are functioning at a level that enables the mentalizing process to progress. The same argument might be true of patients currently in remission.

A SUMMARY OF THE PRELIMINARY FINDINGS

Chris Frith and I have been exploring these hypotheses in people with schizophrenia using the Hinting Task and our ToM stories as measures of theory of mind. We are using thematic versions of the Wason selection task as measures of social and nonsocial conditional reasoning and the Autobiographical Memory Interview (Kopelman et al., 1993) to assess quantitative and qualitative aspects of autobiographical memory. The preliminary evidence from this work looks promising. There is evidence of parallel deficits in theory of mind, social conditional reasoning, and autobiographical memory impairment in patients with schizophrenia. In other words, our ongoing work is replicating our previous studies using a different sample and is providing evidence to enlighten us as to how an understanding of another's mental state is achieved by the mature brain and how it breaks down in patients with schizophrenia.

Conclusion

To have one's son, daughter, or partner suddenly declare, out of the blue, that you are some evil entity sent to do him or her harm must count among the most distressing of events. The origin of these extremely negative and hurtful false beliefs remains a mystery, yet they are held with deep conviction, and they always redefine family life. The idea that they arise as an understandable consequence of a brain dysfunction that disrupts the normal ability to understand and appreciate how others think must give some comfort. Furthermore, the thesis lends itself to psychological treatment techniques that could benefit patients with paranoia who do not comply with drug treatments. For these and other highly practical reasons, it is vital that we strive to achieve a more complete understanding of schizophrenia as an illness that originates from a core dysfunction of social cognition.

References

American Psychiatric Association. (1989). *Diagnostic and statistical manual of mental disorders* (3rd ed., rev.). Washington, DC: Author.

American Psychiatric Association. (1994). *Diagnostic and statistical manual of mental disorders* (4th ed.). Washington, DC: Author.

Ammons, R. B., & Ammons, C. H. (1962). *The Quick Test.* Missoula, MT: Psychological Test Specialists.

Baddeley, A., Thornton, A., Chua, S. E., & McKenna, P. (1996). Schizophrenic delusions and the construction of autobiographical memory. In D. C. Rubin (Ed.), *Remembering our past: Studies in autobiographical memory* (pp. 384–428). New York: Cambridge University Press.

Baron-Cohen, S. (1995). *Mindblindness: An essay on autism and theory of mind.* Cambridge, MA: MIT Press.

Baron-Cohen, S., Tager-Flusberg, H., & Cohen, D. J. (Eds.). (2000). *Understanding other minds. Perspectives from autism and developmental cognitive neuroscience* (2nd ed.). Oxford, England: Oxford University Press.

Bentall, R. P. (1990). The syndromes and symptoms of psychosis. In R. P. Bentall (Ed.), *Reconstructing schizophrenia* (pp. 23–60). London: Routledge.

Boucher, J. (1981). Memory for recent events in autistic children. *Journal of Autism and Developmental Disorders, 11,* 293–301.

Brothers, L. (1990). The social brain: A project for integrating primate behavior and neurophysiology in a new domain. *Concepts in Neuroscience, 1,* 27–51.

Corcoran, R. (1999). Autonoetic awareness, executive social skills and the appreciation of intention: Figurative reasoning in amnesia, confabulation and schizophrenia. *Cognitive Neuropsychiatry, 4,* 55–80.

Corcoran, R. (2000). Theory of Mind in other clinical samples: Is a selective theory of mind deficit exclusive to autism? In S. Baron-Cohen, H. Tager-Flusberg, & D. J. Cohen (Eds.), *Understanding other minds: Perspectives from autism and developmental cognitive neuroscience* (2nd ed., pp. 391–421). Oxford, England: Oxford University Press.

Corcoran, R., & Frith, C. D. (1993). Neuropsychology and neurophysiology in schizophrenia. *Current Opinion in Psychiatry, 6,* 74–79.

Corcoran, R., & Frith, C. D. (1994). Neuropsychology and neurophysiology in schizophrenia. *Current Opinion in Psychiatry, 7,* 47–50.

Corcoran, R., & Frith, C. D. (1996). Conversational conduct and the symptoms of schizophrenia. *Cognitive Neuropsychiatry, 1,* 305–318.

Corcoran, R., Cahill, C., & Frith, C. D. (1997). The appreciation of visual jokes in people with schizophrenia: A study of the "mentalizing" ability. *Schizophrenia Research, 24,* 319–327.

Corcoran, R., Mercer, G., & Frith, C. D. (1995). Schizophrenia, symptomatology and social inference: Investigating "theory of mind" in people with schizophrenia. *Schizophrenia Research, 17,* 5–13.

Cosmides, L. (1989). The logic of social exchange: Has natural selection shaped how humans reason? Studies with the Wason selection task. *Cognition, 31,* 187–276.

Doody, G. A., Gotz, M., Johnstone, E. C., Frith, C. D., & Cunningham-Owens, D. G. (1998). Theory of mind and psychoses. *Psychological Medicine, 28,* 397–405.

Dudley, R. E. J., John, C. H., Young, A. W., & Over, D. E. (1997). The effect of self-referent material on the reasoning of people with delusions. *British Journal of Clinical Psychology, 36,* 575–584.

Frith, C. D. (1987). The positive and negative symptoms of schizophrenia reflect impairments in the perception and initiation of action. *Psychological Medicine, 17,* 631–648.

Frith, C. D. (1992). *The cognitive neuropsychology of schizophrenia.* Hove, England: Lawrence Erlbaum.

Frith, C. D., & Corcoran, R. (1996). Exploring "theory of mind" in people with schizophrenia. *Psychological Medicine, 26,* 521–530.

Frith, C. D., & Done, D. J. (1989). Experiences of alien control in schizophrenia reflect a disorder in the central monitoring of action. *Psychological Medicine, 19,* 359–363.

Garety, P. A., & Freeman, D. (1999). Cognitive approaches to delusions: A critical review of theories and evidence. *British Journal of Clinical Psychology, 38,* 113–154.

Grice, H. P. (1975). Logic and conversation. In P. Cole & J. L. Morgan (Eds.), *Syntax and semantics: Vol. 3. Speech Acts.* New York: Academic Press.

Harris, P. L. (1990). The work of the imagination. In A. Whiten (Ed.), *The emergence of mindreading* (pp. 283–304). Oxford, England: Blackwell.

Howe, M. L., & Courage, M. L. (1997). The emergence and early development of autobiographical memory. *Psychological Review, 104,* 499–523.

John, C. H., & Dodgson, G. (1994). Inductive reasoning in delusional thought. *Journal of Mental Health, 3,* 31–49.

Jones, P. B., Bebbington, P., Foester, A., Lewis, S. W., Murray, R. M., Russell, A., Sham, P. C., Toone, B. K., & Wilkins, S. (1993). Premorbid social underachievement in schizophrenia. Results from the Camberwell Collaborative Psychosis Study. *British Journal of Psychiatry, 162,* 65–71.

Kay, S. R., Fiszbein, A., & Opler, L. A. (1987). The positive and negative symptom scale (PANNS) for schizophrenia. *Schizophrenia Bulletin, 13,* 261–276.

Kopelman, M., Wilson, B., & Baddeley, A. D. (1993). *The Autobiographical Memory Interview.* Bury St. Edmunds, England: Thames Valley Test Company.

Langdon, R., Michie, P. T., Ward, P. B., McConaghy, N., Catts, S. V., & Coltheart, M. (1997). Defective self and/or other mentalizing in schizophrenia: A cognitive neuropsychological approach. *Cognitive Neuropsychiatry, 2,* 167–193.

Leslie, A. M. (1987). Pretence and representation: The origins of "theory of mind." *Psychological Review, 94,* 412–426.

Mlakar, J., Jensterle, J., & Frith, C. D. (1994). Central monitoring deficiency and schizophrenic symptoms. *Psychological Medicine, 24,* 557–564.

Murray, R. M., & Lewis, S. W. (1987). Is schizophrenia a developmental disorder? *British Medical Journal, 295,* 681–682.

Nelson, K. (1992). The emergence of autobiographical memory at age 4. *Human Development, 35,* 172–177.

Ozonoff, S., Pennington, B. F., & Rogers, S. J. (1991). Executive function deficits in high functioning autistic children. Relationship to theory of mind. *Journal of Child Psychology and Psychiatry, 32,* 1081–1106.

Perner, J., & Wimmer, H. (1985). "John thinks that Mary thinks that. . . .": Attribution of second-order beliefs by 5–10 year old children. *Journal of Experimental Child Psychology, 39,* 437–471.

Persons, J. B. (1986). The advantages of studying psychological phenomena rather than psychiatric diagnosis. *American Psychologist, 41,* 1252–1260.

Pickup, G. (1997). *The prepresentation of mental states in schizophrenia.* Unpublished doctoral dissertation, University of London.

Pishkin, V., Lovallo, W. R., Lenk, R. G., & Bourne, L. E., Jr. (1977). Schizophrenic cognitive dysfunction: A deficit in rule transfer. *Journal of Clinical Psychology, 33,* 335–340.

Powell, S. D., & Jordan, R. R. (1993). Being subjective about autistic thinking and learning to learn. *Educational Psychology, 13,* 359–370.

Rochester, S., & Martin, J. R. (1979). *Crazy talk: A study of the discourse of schizophrenic speakers.* New York: Plenum Press.

Sarfati, Y., Hardy-Bayle, M.-C., Nadel, J., Chevalier, J.-F., & Widlocher, D. (1997). Attribution of mental states to others by schizophrenic patients. *Cognitive Neuropsychiatry, 2,* 1–17.

Shallice, T., Burgess, P. W., & Frith, C. D. (1991). Can the neuropsychological case study approach be applied to schizophrenia? *Psychological Medicine, 21,* 661–673.

Skuse, D. H., James, R. S., Bishop, D. V., Coppin, B., Dalton, P., Aamodt-Leeper, G., Bacarese-Hamilton, M., Creswell, C., McGurk, R., & Jacobs, P. A. (1997). Evidence from Turner's syndrome for an imprinted X-linked locus affecting cognitive function. *Nature, 387,* 705–708.

Sternberg, R. J. (1977). *Intelligence, information processing and analogical reasoning. The componential analysis of human abilities.* Hillsdale, NJ: Lawrence Erlbaum.

Tamlyn, D., McKenna, P. J., Mortimer, A. M., Lund, C., Hammond, S., & Baddeley, A. D. (1992). Memory impairment in schizophrenia: Its extent, affiliations and neuropsychological character. *Psychological Medicine, 22,* 101–115.

Wason, P. C. (1966). Reasoning. In B. M. Foss (Ed.), *New horizons in Psychology I.* Harmondsworth, England: Penguin.

Wechsler, D. (1955). *W. A. I. S. manual.* New York: The Psychological Corporation.

Welch, R., & Melissa, K. (1997). Mother-child participation in conversation about the past: Relationship to preschoolers theory of mind. *Developmental Psychology, 33,* 618–629.

Wellman, H. (1985). The child's theory of mind: The development of conceptions of cognition. In S. Yussen (Ed.), *The growth of reflection in children.* Academic Press.

Whiten, A., & Byrne, R. W. (1988). Tactical deception in primates. *Behavioral and Brain Sciences, 11,* 233–273.

Wimmer, H., & Perner, J. (1983). Beliefs about beliefs: Representation and constraining function of wrong beliefs in young children's understanding of deception. *Cognition, 13,* 103–128.

Wing, J. K., Cooper, J. E., & Sartorius, N. (1974). *Measurement and classification of psychiatric symptoms. An instruction manual for the PSE and Catego Program.* Cambridge, England: Cambridge University Press.

Young, H. F., & Bentall, R. P. (1997). Probabilistic reasoning in deluded, depressed and normal subjects: Effects of task difficulty and meaningful versus non-meaningful material. *Psychological Medicine, 27,* 455–465.

Do Stereotype Threats Influence Social Cognitive Deficits in Schizophrenia?

6

Patrick W. Corrigan and Kevin L. Holtzman

This book describes a variety of social cognitive deficits related to the disabilities of schizophrenia. Most authors attribute those deficits to the primary neurobiological dysfunctions of schizophrenia and assume that they are caused by neurophysiological or structural dysfunctions that arise developmentally and account for the primary symptoms and disabilities of the illness. Hence, models that explain the relationship between neurobiological constructs and social cognitive deficits are central in describing the etiology of schizophrenia. They also are important in developing psychopharmacological and rehabilitation strategies that may have a significant impact on social cognitive dysfunction.

This chapter argues that focusing on neurobiological causes of deficits in social cognition may provide an incomplete picture. We have maintained elsewhere that schizophrenia strikes with a two-edged sword: *biologically based disease,* which leads to symptoms and dysfunctions that interfere with quality of life, and *discrimination,* which further exacerbates handicaps and impedes opportunities (Corrigan & Penn, 1997). For example, a person with schizophrenia may not be able to obtain a job because of negative symptoms (resulting from the disease) that interfere with the social interactions and sense of industriousness needed to impress employers during a job interview. Alternatively, people labeled "mentally ill" may not be hired because of stereotypes held by the boss (e.g., "mental patients are incapable of productive work"). Hence, improving outcomes and opportunities requires remedying the symptoms and other primary dysfunctions of schizophrenia as well as the fallout from stigma and discrimination (Corrigan & Penn, 1999).

That social stereotypes have a deleterious effect on role functioning seems to make sense. People with schizophrenia may be less able to work, earn a reasonable income, live independently, or start a family because of societal stigma. This chapter examines whether social cognitive deficits are exacerbated as a result of stigma. In other words, are some of the social cognitive dysfunctions discussed in this book attributable to the impact of stigma on the person with schizophrenia? Social psychologists have shown that other victims of stereotype (e.g., African Americans and women) change the accuracy of their perceptions and cognitions as a result of stereotypes. This chapter considers whether this kind of effect in any way explains the social cognitive dysfunctions identified in schizophrenia. Before examining this issue further, it is necessary to define some important elements of stereotype and stigma.

STIGMA AND STEREOTYPE DEFINED

Social cognitive models of stigma include the concepts of stereotype, prejudice, and discrimination. Social psychologists view *stereotypes* as knowledge structures that are learned by most members of a social group (Augoustinos & Ahrens, 1994; Esses, Haddock, & Zanna, 1994; Hilton & von Hippel, 1996; Judd & Park, 1993; Krueger, 1996; Mullen, Rozell, & Johnson, 1996). Stereotypes are especially efficient means of categorizing information about social groups; they are considered "social" because they represent collectively agreed upon notions of groups of people. They are efficient because people can quickly generate impressions and expectations of members of a stereotyped group (Hamilton & Sherman, 1994).

Just because most people have knowledge of a set of stereotypes does not imply that they will endorse them, use them to generate negative judgments, or act on them in a discriminatory manner (Jussim, Nelson, Manis, & Soffin, 1995). For example, people can describe stereotypes about a racial group in America, but they do not necessarily agree that the stereotypes are valid. People who are prejudiced endorse negative stereotypes and act against minority groups in a discriminatory way (Devine, 1988, 1989, 1995; Hilton & von Hippel, 1996; Krueger, 1996); their behavior might include withholding jobs or housing because of a stereotype or robbing someone of their freedoms.

Cognitive Deficits and Stereotype Threat

Psychologists who study cognition have argued for more than three decades that cognitive processes in "normal" people are influenced by so-

FIGURE 6.1

An outline of stereotype threat and its effects on intellectual performance. (+) or (−) indicates increased or decreased consequences of causal variables. Adapted from C. M. Steele (1997).

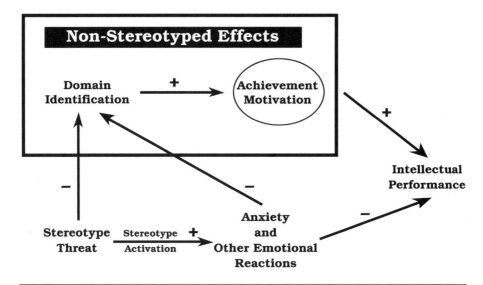

cial motivation and other interpersonal factors (Neuberg & Fiske, 1988). One social factor that influences cognitive functioning is a person's reaction to being the object of stereotype and prejudice (i.e., stereotype threat). In other words, does protecting oneself from stereotype and prejudice interfere with a person's intellectual abilities? Claude Steele (1997) of Stanford University outlined the impact of stereotype threat on the cognitive abilities of two groups victimized by prejudice in America: women and African Americans. Figure 6.1 summarizes Steele's model. Findings from research on the model may illustrate how social stereotypes influence the social cognitive deficits of schizophrenia.

IDENTIFICATION, STEREOTYPE THREAT, AND INTELLECTUAL PERFORMANCE

C. M. Steele (1997) argued that intellectual success in a specific setting depends on domain identification (i.e., one's self-regard depends on achievement in that domain). Many people in Western culture hold that success in the scholastic domain is important. Domain identification facilitates *achievement motivation,* or the need to be successful in pursuits related to that domain. In turn, people with high achievement motivation are likely to perform intellectual tasks related to that domain successfully. Hence, people with *school* identification show a significant association between their self-esteem and scholastic success. They report being highly motivated to achieve on school-related tasks such as educational tests, and their level of motivation is associated with actual performance on those tests.

As outlined in Figure 6.1, negative stereotypes may undermine a person's identification with a specific domain and reduce the resulting achievement motivation. C. M. Steele (1997) termed the phenomenon that causes this cascade *stereotype threat;* it is the social psychological threat that occurs when members of a stereotyped out-group (e.g., African Americans, women and, perhaps, people with schizophrenia) find themselves in a situation specific to a domain for which a negative stereotype applies. For example, a negative stereotype about African Americans is that they are intellectually inferior and not likely to do well scholastically (see Hernstein & Murray, 1994, for a discussion of this stereotype). African Americans experiencing stereotype threat may feel anxious when faced with an achievement exam in school. A negative stereotype about women related to school suggests that they have inferior mathematical and analytical abilities (see Eccles-Parsons et al., 1983). Women experiencing stereotype threat are likely to be concerned about taking an algebra test.

We hypothesize that negative stereotypes about mental illness might yield similar outcomes. Namely, some people with psychiatric disabilities are aware of the stereotype that mental patients are confused and intellectually dull. Hence, they may become anxious when placed in settings in which this stereotype could be confirmed (e.g., in test environments designed to uncover social cognitive deficits). Like people who are victimized by other stigma, this anxiety interferes with task performance.

C. M. Steele (1997) described several characteristics of stereotype threat:

1. Stereotype threat is not tied to the psychology of particular stigmatized groups, nor is it limited to minority ethnic groups and women. Stereotype threat affects the members of any group about whom there exists generally known negative stereotypes (e.g., that people with mental illness are confused and cannot understand the subtleties of interpersonal situations).

2. A concurrence between stereotypes and situations initiates stereotype threats. Rather than being an omnipresent phenomenon, stereotype threats are most acutely felt when people find themselves in situations about which stereotypes occur. Hence, stereotype threat related to African American intellectual achievement is most prominent in schools and may be absent in other settings

(S. Steele, 1990). Perhaps stereotype threat related to mental illness is most acute in clinical or research settings where deficits are being assessed. This mechanism suggests that stereotype threat is specific to certain situations depending on the stigmatized group in which a person is a member.

3. One need not believe a stereotype to experience stereotype threat (Aronson, Lustina, Good, Keough, Steele, & Brown, 1999). People with mental illness need not believe that everyone with schizophrenia is usually confused and intellectually incompetent in order to worry that the average citizen might believe this stereotype about them. Recognition of this belief can lead people into worrying about whether others will accept this notion (e.g., "my boss thinks I'm inept because I had a psychiatric relapse"), thereby experiencing the threat of this stereotype.

Steele and colleagues (Aronson et al., 1999; Spencer, Steele, & Quinn, 1999; Steele & Aronson, 1995) reported on a basic paradigm for researching stereotype threat. Research participants representing a stereotyped minority group (thus far, research in this area has focused on African Americans and women) and a control group (e.g., European Americans or men) are recruited to participate in a test of academic abilities. Participants are then told either that the task is or is not diagnostic of the poor performance that typically is associated with a minority group (e.g., "African Americans typically perform poorly on general intellectual tasks"; "women fail at mathematics tests"). Results from one study (Steele & Aronson, 1995) showed that African Americans who were told that an SAT verbal subtest "was diagnostic of poor ethnic performance" scored significantly lower than European Americans. However, African Americans who were not given those instructions scored no different from the control group. A similar effect was found with an even more subtle manipulation of stereotype threat: reporting one's ethnicity on a demographic form appended to the test. Those who reported that they were African American scored significantly lower than European Americans. African Americans who were not asked to report their racial group showed no difference in performance. Using this paradigm, similar results were found for women (Brown & Josephs, 1999; Shih, Pittinsky, & Ambady, 1999; Spencer, Steele, & Quinn, 1999) and people from lower socioeconomic groups (Croizet & Claire, 1998).

THE EFFECTS OF STEREOTYPE THREAT

Stereotype threat affects cognitive performance through several mediating processes, one of which is stereotype activation (see Figure 6.1). African Americans who were told that the research task was diagnostic of poor performance by African Americans showed elevated scores on measures of racial stereotype activation (Steele & Aronson, 1995). They were sensitized to the negative judgments that the majority makes about African American performance in those specific domains. Stereotype threat also causes negative emotional reactions to domain-specific tasks and can evoke what Cross (1991) called "spotlight anxiety": the belief that others, especially those in the majority, will discover that a person is incompetent in a manner similar to the predictions of a stereotype. The spotlight is particularly focused—that is, the stereotype is especially noticeable—in the domains or situations about which the stereotype applies. African Americans experience spotlight anxiety in school situations in which they risk doing poorly on educational exams, thereby confirming stereotypes that their race is less intelligent than the majority (Allport, 1954; Carter, 1991; Goffman, 1963; Steele, 1975).

Spotlight and general performance anxiety undermine the person's cognitive performance in these domains. For example, research has shown that the anxiety that resulted from knowing that a specific test measured stereotype-relevant abilities significantly predicted performances on measures of those abilities (Spencer, Steele, & Quinn, 1999; Steele & Aronson, 1995). According to Croizet and Claire (1998), this kind of anxiety may interfere with cognitive processing in several ways: distraction from the task (Easterbrook, 1959), evaluation apprehension (Green, 1985), and loss of motivation (Pyzcyznski & Greenberg, 1983).

Disengagement and Disidentification

People who occasionally experience the emotional distress that results from stereotype stress may *disengage* from the situations in which this stress occurs (Crocker, Major, & Steele, 1998; Major, Spencer, Schmader, Wolfe, & Crocker, 1998). African Americans, for example, may report that the kind of scholastic ability required in a specific situation that elicits stereotype threat is not important, and they might actually avoid those situations altogether. Alternatively, people who experience stereotype threat and emotional distress over a prolonged time may *disidentify* with the domain and task altogether (Steele, 1997). For example, minority group members who may have once believed that cognitive performance in a specific domain was an important part of their identity (e.g., "doing well in school is essential for my success") may no longer recognize performance in this domain as being part of their self-evaluative framework. As outlined in Figure 6.1, disidentifying with performance undermines achievement motivation for tasks in that domain and interferes with cognitive performance.

Disengagement and disidentification are domain-specific phenomena. Minority group members may believe scholastic performance is unimportant but still prize their competence in specific work settings. A person in this category would be expected to perform poorly on academic achievement tests but might excel on measures of mechanical aptitude. This finding may be one reason why many groups who are subject to negative stereotypes do not report low self-esteem (Crocker, 1999; Crocker & Major, 1989). Minority group members often dismiss the importance of domains on which poor performance is stereotyped. For example, women might respond that mathematics requires left-brain skills and is not as artful (or important) as the right-brain skills in which women typically shine.

Stereotype Threat in People With Schizophrenia

Steele's model of stereotype threat might suggest an environmentally based factor that exacerbates the social cognitive deficits that arise from biological precursors. Stereotypes about intellectual and cognitive inferiority in mental illness are activated in clinical and research settings where those abilities are tested. As a result, the person becomes anxious and undermines his or her performance on the task. After prolonged experiences, the person either disengages from those kinds of tasks or disidentifies with the goals of successful cognition.

Thus far, stereotype threat as applied to mental illness rests on parallels between this group and other stigmatized groups such as African Americans or women. However, the experiences of stereotypes related to schizophrenia differ markedly from those of other groups. Those differences need to be resolved if a model of stereotype threat is to be applied to the social cognitive deficits experienced by people with schizophrenia. The following sections examine three questions that might affect both a conceptual model and a research paradigm for examining the effects of stereotype threat on social cognitive deficits in schizophrenia:

1. Are the cognitive deficits of schizophrenia conceptually similar to the deficits that have been stereotyped in African Americans and women?
2. Is the experience of stigma from mental illness similar to the stigma experienced by ethnic minorities and women?
3. Many people with schizophrenia do not report awareness of their mental illness. Does this kind of awareness mitigate stereotype threat?

Before addressing those questions, we briefly summarize evidence that mental illness is stigmatized.

THE STEREOTYPES AND STIGMA OF MENTAL ILLNESS

Stereotypes about schizophrenia and other mental illness seem to be widely endorsed by the general public. Studies suggest that many citizens in the United States (Link, 1987; Rabkin, 1974; Roman & Floyd, 1981) and most Western nations (Bhugra, 1989; Brockington, Hall, Levings, & Murphy, 1993; Greenley, 1984; Hamre, Dahl, & Malt, 1994; Madianos, Madianou, Vlachonikolis, & Stefanis, 1987) agree with stigmatizing attitudes about mental illness, which can be categorized according to several themes. Media analyses of film and print representations of mental illness reveal three common misconceptions: that people with mental illness are homicidal maniacs who need to be feared; that they have childlike perceptions of the world that should be admired; and that they are rebellious, free spirits (Farina, 1998; Gabbard & Gabbard, 1992; Hyler, Gabbard, & Schneider, 1991; Mayer & Barry, 1992; Monahan, 1992; Wahl, 1995). Results of two independent factor analyses of the survey responses of more than 2,000 English and American citizens yielded three similar factors (Brockington et al., 1993; Taylor & Dear, 1980):

1. *Fear and exclusion:* People with severe mental illness should be feared and, therefore, kept out of most communities.
2. *Authoritarianism:* People with severe mental illness are irresponsible; life decisions should be made by others.
3. *Benevolence:* People with severe mental illness are childlike and need to be cared for.

Negative attitudes like those described above have a significant impact on the course of mental illness. One study found that 75% of family members believed stigma decreased their child's self-esteem, hindered their ability to make friends, and undermined their success in obtaining employment (Wahl & Harman, 1989). In more recent data, Wahl (1999) reported that up to 50% of a sample of people with mental illness reported negative impact from stigma. They believed that the public would be likely to exclude them from close friendships or competitive jobs because of their mental illness. Studies also have documented the behavioral impact (or discrimination) that results from stigma. People are less likely to hire applicants who are labeled mentally ill (Bordieri & Drehmer, 1986; Farina & Felner, 1973; Link, 1987; Olshansky, Grob, & Ekdahl, 1960), less likely to lease them apartments (Page, 1977, 1983, 1995), and more likely to falsely press charges for violent crimes (Sosowsky, 1980; Steadman, 1981).

The detrimental impact of stigma is not limited to discrimination by others. Some people with severe mental illness also endorse stigmatizing attitudes about psychiatric disability and, hence, about themselves. They may experience diminished self-esteem, which correlates with a lower quality of life (Markowitz, 1998; Mechanic, McAlpine, Rosenfield, & Davis, 1994). Moreover, people who self-stigmatize are less likely to be successful in work, housing, and interpersonal relationships (Link, Cullen, Struening, Shrout, & Dohrenwend, 1989); they seem to convince themselves that socially endorsed stigmas are correct and that they are incapable of independent living. In addition to those negative effects is the issue forming the central question of this paper: Does self-stigma negatively affect the cognitive functioning of people with schizophrenia?

COGNITIVE DEFICITS ATTRIBUTED TO SCHIZOPHRENIA VERSUS ETHNICITY AND GENDER

For Steele's (1997) model of stereotype threat to apply to the social cognitive deficits of schizophrenia, one must assume that those deficits parallel the *stereotyped* intellectual dysfunctions in African Americans, women, and other minority groups.[1] A conceptual and methodological problem arises when trying to reconcile the two literatures. Research on stereotype threat has focused mostly on *intellectual* deficits, whereas investigations into cognitive deficits of schizophrenia have been dominated by *information-processing* (IP) models. In some ways, this difference is significant in both theoretical framework and research design. Traditional models of intelligence focus on the content of learning and knowledge. Intelligence tests measure the body of information that a person has mastered over time. This view differs from IP theory, which explains the complex phenomena of human learning and understanding in terms of discrete cognitive functions that account for the perception, manipulation, storage, retrieval, and subsequent use of environmental inputs (Corrigan & Stephenson, 1994). Fortunately, recent perspectives of intelligence and information processing have been reconciled. Sternberg (1997), for example, proposed a triarchic model that includes intelligence and the internal world (i.e., metacognition, performance, and acquisition), intelligence and experience (i.e., dealing with novelty and automatizing information processing), and intelligence in the external world (i.e., adaptation, shaping, and selection). Intellectual and IP models are not so clearly distinct.

---

[1]Let us be clear here! We are NOT saying that persons of color or women are in any way intellectually inferior. Instead, we are repeating an old stereotype about these groups —that they are less cognitively competent—as a provocative attempt to ask whether this might *partially* be a stereotype that is also applied to persons with mental illness.

Even though this bridge suggests conceptual parallels between the stereotyped cognitive deficits of African Americans and women and the deficits of people with schizophrenia, the parallels are strained. No one maintains that any intellectual deficiencies of African Americans or women represent a disability. The cognitive deficits of psychiatric disorders represent a change from baseline and a significant impairment. Change from baseline is understood either within the individual (e.g., the person with schizophrenia showed a reduction in cognitive ability from premorbid states), or between individuals and their standard group (e.g., people with mental retardation have reduced cognitive ability compared to others of similar gender, ethnicity, and so forth).

The idea of stereotype threat would have more power if it were applied to the intellectual problems of people with psychiatric disabilities. Crocker, Major, and Steele (1998) mused how stereotype threat might appear in this kind of group:

> An elderly man trying to recall the name of an acquaintance may realize that he is at risk of confirming stereotypes about memory loss in the elderly, and may worry each time he forgets a name that Alzheimer's disease is setting in, or that his family will think it is. (p. 519)

One study, to our knowledge, has examined the impact of stereotype threat on a group that has a biologically based cognitive deficit. Levy (1996) showed that performance on memory tests diminished in older people who were exposed to negative stereotypes. Hence, stereotype threat seems to explain the exacerbation of what traditionally have been considered impaired cognitive deficits related to psychiatric etiologies.

STIGMA VISIBILITY

One's experience of stigma and stereotype also varies among people from ethnic and gender minorities and people with schizophrenia. Those subjected to racial and gender stereotypes exemplify what Goffman (1963) called a "discredited" stigma because the characteristics identifying the minority group (e.g., skin color) are readily visible to others. People with schizophrenia may include those who are both discredited (i.e., they may manifest psychotic symptoms in public) and "discreditable" (i.e., if in remission, they may be able to hide their mental illness from others). Does the relative visibility of stereotype markers affect the impact of stereotype threat on cognitive performance?

Research suggests that the visibility of a person's stigma can vary in impact (Frable, Wortman, & Joseph, 1997; Herman, Zanna, & Higgins, 1986). On the one hand, many people with concealable stigma report less discrimination and better self-evaluations because the public is unaware of their membership in a stigmatized group. Perhaps stereotype threat is muted in them because they are buffered from the judgment of others. On the other hand, people who choose to come out—who publicly declare they belong to a stigmatized group—benefit from visibility. They profit from the group identification and support they receive from peers (Garnets & Kimmel, 1993). Those most in peril from stereotype threat may be people whose group membership is obvious but who do not want to be visible. These different types of stereotype visibility need to be examined in future research.

THE ROLE OF AWARENESS

Steele (1997) noted that a minority group member does not have to agree with a stereotype to experience its threat or the resulting emotional distress and impairment on intellectual functioning. However, this model assumes that people are aware of whether threats that apply to a specific group, in turn, apply to them. For example, an African American woman can admit that a stereotype like "Black people are intellectually inferior" also applies to her because she is Black. Research shows that most members of ethnic (Casas, Ponterotto, & Sweeney, 1987; Rosenberg, 1979) and gender (Crosby, 1982) minority groups are aware of their membership in a group that is stigmatized by others. However, research suggests that a significant number of people with schizophrenia are unaware of their symptoms or other disabilities (Hayward & Bright, 1997); hence, it is conceivable that they do not experience stereotype threat because they are unaware the stereotype applies to them.

Lack of awareness or diminished insight about one's mental illness can be apparent in several ways: People may not believe they have a mental disorder; may be unaware of the consequences of the disorder; may have little insight into the effects of treatments; and may be unaware of experiences with symptoms like hallucinations, delusions, and formal thought disorder (Amador, Strauss, Yale, Gorman, & Endicott, 1993). Research has shown that lack of awareness is fairly prevalent; more than 50% of one large sample of people with schizophrenia exhibited moderate to severe lack of awareness of their illness and symptoms (Amador et al., 1994). Moreover, although present in many severe mental illnesses, lack of awareness seems most pronounced in schizophrenia.

Although most recent research has looked at biological models to explain this phenomenon (Amador, Strauss, Yale, & Gorman, 1991; McGlynn & Schachter, 1989; Young, Davila, & Scher, 1993), psychological defense mechanisms also have been posited as an explanation of poor awareness. Most such models are psychodynamic and have focused on the role that denial of illness plays in the person's self-esteem (Lally, 1989; Semrad, 1966). It seems reasonable that people might deny their disease to avoid the threat and other negative consequences of a stereotyping label. If this assumption were true, one might suspect that, in a parallel fashion, people of color reject their heritage to avoid stereotype threat. To our knowledge, however, social psychological research does not find this result. Hence, lack of disease awareness does not seem to arise as a protection against social pressures on the stereotyped person. Future research needs to examine this and other assumptions about stereotype threat and schizophrenia.

Changing Stereotype Threat to Improve Cognitive Performance

Research discussed in this chapter suggests that one way to improve cognitive performance in some minority groups is to diminish stereotype threat. Hence, strategies aimed at social factors may help members of a minority group cope with the emotional distress and lessen the disengagement or disidentification that occurs after stereotype threat. If a model of stereotype threat applies to the social cognitive deficits of schizophrenia, it suggests that another way to remediate those cognitive deficits is through changing the person's social environment. The strength of this effect was shown in several studies in which cognitive performance was improved after exposing out-group members to positive stereotypes (Levy, 1999; Shih, Pittinsky, & Ambady, 1999). For example, performance on memory tests actually increased after older people were exposed to positive stereotypes about the aged (Levy, 1999).

This general approach differs radically from remedial programs that reflect a prevailing stereotype; namely, that poor scholastic functioning represents *internal processes* ranging from genes to internalized deficits (Steele, 1997). Remedial programs, as a result, triage students to help them overcome weak identification, poor skills, and little confidence. As an alternative, Steele (1997) identified several strategies that undermined stereotype threat, promoted identification with the cognitive domain, and facilitated intellectual development. Research has shown that this kind of approach leads to significantly improved intellectual scores compared with standard remedial practices (Steele, 1997). Research needs to validate those findings on people with schizophrenia. If validated, however, this line of study has significant implications for redesigning rehabilitation programs for social cognitive deficits.

Conclusion

Almost all the assumptions in this chapter are conjectural; we know of no evidence testing them directly. We are guilty of leading the theory before the evidence and thus encourage the reader to consider our proposals with caution. Nevertheless, this chapter is intended to provoke the reader into considering other factors that may influence the social cognitive functions of people with schizophrenia. Contrary to popular notions about the neurophysiological and structural deficits that account for cognitive deficits (Green & Nuechterlein, 1999), some of the deficits of schizophrenia may be caused or exacerbated by environmental factors, which need to be considered as research progresses in this area.

References

Allport, G. (1954). *The nature of prejudice.* New York: Doubleday.

Amador, X. F., Flaun, M., Andreasen, N. C., Strauss, D. H., Yale, S. A., & Gorman, J. M. (1994). Awareness of illness in schizophrenia and schizoaffective and mood disorders. *Archives of General Psychiatry, 51,* 826–836.

Amador, X. F., Strauss, D. H., Yale, S. A., & Gorman, J. M. (1991). Awareness of illness in schizophrenia. *Schizophrenia Bulletin, 17,* 113–131.

Amador, X. F., Strauss, D. H., Yale, S. A., Gorman, J. M., & Endicott, J. (1993). The assessment of insight in psychosis. *American Journal of Psychiatry, 150,* 873–879.

Aronson, J., Lustina, M. J., Good, C., Keough, K., Steele, C. M., & Brown, J. (1999). When white men can't do math: Necessary and sufficient factors in stereotype threat. *Journal of Experimental Social Psychology, 35,* 29–46.

Augoustinos, M., & Ahrens, C. (1994). Stereotypes and prejudice: The Australian experience. *British Journal of Social Psychology, 33,* 125–141.

Bhugra, D. (1989). Attitudes toward mental illness: A review of the literature. *Acta Psychiatrica Scandinavica, 80,* 1–12.

Bordieri, J., & Drehmer, D. (1986). Hiring decisions for disabled workers: Looking at the cause. *Journal of Applied Social Psychology, 16,* 197–208.

Brockington, I., Hall, P., Levings, J., & Murphy, C. (1993). The community's tolerance of the mentally ill. *British Journal of Psychiatry, 162,* 93–99.

Brown, R. P., & Josephs, R. A. (1999). A burden of proofs: Stereotype relevance and gender differences in math performance. *Journal of Personality and Social Psychology, 76,* 246–257.

Carter, S. (1991). *Reflections of an affirmative action baby.* New York: Basic Books.

Casas, J. M., Ponterotto, J. G., & Sweeney, M. (1987). Stereotyping the stereotyper: A Mexican American perspective. *Journal of Cross Cultural Psychology, 18,* 45–57.

Corrigan, P. W., & Penn, D. L. (1997). Disease and discrimination: Two paradigms that describe severe mental illness. *Journal of Mental Health, 6,* 355–366.

Corrigan, P. W., & Penn, D. L. (1999). Lessons from social psychology on discrediting psychiatric stigma. *American Psychologist, 54,* 765–776.

Corrigan, P. W., & Stephenson, J. A. (1994). Information processing and clinical psychology. In V. S. Ramachandran (Ed.), *Encyclopedia of human behavior,* (Vol. 2, pp. 645–654). Orlando, FL: Academic Press.

Crocker, J. (1999). Social stigma and self-esteem: Situational construction of self-worth. *Journal of Experimental Social Psychology, 35,* 89–107.

Crocker, J., & Major, B. (1989). Social stigma and self-esteem: The self-protective properties of stigma. *Psychological Review, 96,* 608–630.

Crocker, J., Major, B., & Steele, C. M. (1998). Social stigma. In D. Gilbert, S. T. Fiske, & G. Lindzey (Eds.), *The handbook of social psychology* (4th ed., Vol. 2., pp. 504–553). New York: McGraw-Hill.

Croizet, J. C., & Claire, T. (1998). Extending the concept of stereotype threat to social class: The intellectual underperformance of students from low socioeconomic backgrounds. *Personality and Social Psychology Bulletin, 24,* 588–594.

Crosby, F. (1982). *Relative deprivation and working women.* New York: Oxford University Press.

Cross, W. E., Jr. (1991). *Shades of black: Diversity in African-American identity.* Philadelphia: Temple University Press.

Devine, P. G. (1988). *Stereotype assessment: Theoretical and methodological issues.* Unpublished manuscript, University of Wisconsin-Madison.

Devine, P. G. (1989). Stereotypes and prejudice: Their automatic and controlled components. *Journal of Personality and Social Psychology, 56,* 5–18.

Devine, P. G. (1995). Prejudice and out-group perception. In A. Tesser (Ed.), *Advanced social psychology* (pp. 467–524). New York: McGraw-Hill.

Easterbrook, J. A. (1959). The effects of emotion on cue utilization and the organization of behavior. *Psychological Review, 66,* 183–201.

Eccles-Parsons, J. S., Adler, T. F., Futterman, R., Goff, S. B., Kaczala, C. M., Meece, J. L., & Midgley, C. (1983). Expectations, values, and academic behaviors. In J. T. Spence (Ed.), *Achievement and achievement motivation* (pp. 75–146). New York: Freeman.

Esses, V. M., Haddock, G., & Zanna, M. P. (1994). The role of mood in the expression of intergroup stereotypes. In M. P. Zanna & J. M. Olson (Eds.), *The psychology of prejudice: The Ontario experience* (Vol. 7, pp. 77–101). Hillsdale, NJ: Erlbaum.

Farina, A. (1998). Stigma. In K. T. Mueser & N. Tarrier (Eds.), *Handbook of social functioning in schizophrenia* (pp. 247–279). Boston: Allyn & Bacon.

Farina, A., & Felner, R. D. (1973). Employment interviewer reactions to former mental patients. *Journal of Abnormal Psychology, 82,* 268–272.

Frable, D. E., Wortman, C., & Joseph, J. (1997). Predicting self-esteem, well being, and distress in a cohort of gay men: The importance of cultural stigma, personal visibility, community networks, and positive identity. *Journal of Personality, 65*(3), 599–624.

Gabbard, G. O., & Gabbard, K. (1992). Cinematic stereotypes contributing to the stigmatization of psychiatrists. In P. J. Fink & A. Tasman (Eds.), *Stigma and mental illness* (pp. 113–126). Washington, DC: American Psychiatric Association.

Garnets, L., & Kimmel, D. (1993). *Psychological perspectives on lesbian and gay male experiences.* New York: Columbia University Press.

Goffman, E. (1963). *Stigma: Notes on the management of spoiled identity.* New York: Touchstone.

Green, M. S., & Nuechterlein, K. (1999). Should schizophrenia be treated as a neurocognitive disorder? *Schizophrenia Bulletin, 25,* 309–320.

Green, R. G. (1985). Evaluation apprehension and response withholding in solution of anagrams. *Personality and Individual Differences, 6,* 293–298.

Greenley, J. (1984). Social factors, mental illness, and psychiatric care: Recent advances from a sociological perspective. *Hospital and Community Psychiatry, 35,* 813–820.

Hamilton, D. L., & Sherman, J. W. (1994). Stereotypes. In R. S. Wyer & T. K. Srull (Eds.), *Handbook of social cognition: Vol. 2. Applications* (2nd ed., pp. 1–68). Hillsdale, NJ: Erlbaum.

Hamre, P., Dahl, A., & Malt, U. (1994). Public attitudes to the quality of psychiatric treatment, psychiatric patients, and prevalence of mental disorders. *Nordic Journal of Psychiatry, 4,* 275–281.

Hayward, P., & Bright, J. A. (1997). Stigma and mental illness: A review and critique. *Journal of Mental Health, 6,* 345–354.

Herman, C., Zanna, M., & Higgins, E. (1986). *Physical appearance, stigma, and social behavior: The Ontario symposium.* Hillsdale, NJ: Erlbaum.

Hernstein, R. A., & Murray, C. (1994). *The bell curve.* New York: Grove Press.

Hilton, J. L., & von Hippel, W. (1996). Stereotypes. *Annual Review of Psychology, 47,* 237–271.

Hyler, S. E., Gabbard, G. O., & Schneider, I. (1991). Homicidal maniacs and narcissistic parasites: Stigmatization of mentally ill persons in the movies. *Hospital and Community Psychiatry, 42,* 1044–1048.

Judd, C. M., & Park, B. (1993). Definition and assessment of accuracy in social stereotypes. *Psychological Review, 100,* 109–128.

Jussim, L., Nelson, T. E., Manis, M., & Soffin, S. (1995). Prejudice, stereotypes, and labeling effects: Sources of bias in person perception. *Journal of Personality and Social Psychology, 68,* 228–246.

Krueger, J. (1996). Personal beliefs and cultural stereotypes about racial characteristics. *Journal of Personality and Social Psychology, 71,* 536–548.

Lally, S. J. (1989). Does being in here mean there is something wrong with me? *Schizophrenia Bulletin, 15,* 253–265.

Levy, B. (1996). Improving memory in old age through implicit self-stereotyping. *Journal of Personality and Social Psychology, 71,* 1092–1107.

Levy, B. (1999). The inner self of the Japanese elderly: A defense against negative stereotypes of aging. *International Journal of Aging and Human Development, 48,* 131–144.

Link, B. G. (1987). Understanding labeling effects in the area of mental disorders: An assessment of the effects of expectations of rejection. *American Sociological Review, 52,* 96–112.

Link, B. G., Cullen, F. T., Struening, E. L., Shrout, P. E., & Dohrenwend, B. P. (1989). A modified labeling theory approach to mental disorders: An empirical assessment. *American Sociological Review, 54,* 400–423.

Madianos, M. G., Madianou, D. G., Vlachonikolis, J., & Stefanis, C. N. (1987). Attitudes toward mental illness in the Athens area: Implications for community mental health intervention. *Acta Psychiatrica Scandinavica, 75,* 158–165.

Major, B., Spencer, S., Schmader, T., Wolfe, C., & Crocker, J. (1998). Coping with negative stereotypes about intellectual performance: The role of psychological disengagement. *Personality and Social Psychology Bulletin, 24,* 34–50.

Markowitz, F. E. (1998). The effects of stigma on the psychological well-being and life satisfaction of persons with mental illness. *Journal of Health and Social Behavior 39,* 335–347.

Mayer, A., & Barry, D. D. (1992). Working with the media to destigmatize mental illness. *Hospital and Community Psychiatry, 43,* 77–78.

McGlynn, S. M., & Schacter, D. L. (1989). Unawareness of deficits in neuropsychological syndromes. *Journal of Clinical and Experimental Neuropsychology, 11,* 143–205.

Mechanic, D., McAlpine, D., Rosenfield, S., & Davis, D. (1994). Effects of illness attribution and depression on the quality of life among persons with serious mental illness. *Social Science & Medicine, 39,* 155–164.

Monahan, J. (1992). Mental disorder and violent behavior: Perceptions and evidence. *American Psychologist, 47,* 511–521.

Mullen, B., Rozell, D., & Johnson, C. (1996). The phenomenology of being in a group: Complexity approaches to operationalizing cognitive representation. In J. L. Nye & A. M. Brower (Eds.), *What's social about social cognition?* (pp. 205–229). Thousand Oaks, CA: Sage.

Neuberg, S. L., & Fiske, S. T. (1988). Motivational influences on impression formation: Outcome dependency, accuracy-driven attention, and individuating processes. *Journal of Personality & Social Psychology, 53,* 431–444.

Olshansky, S., Grob, S., & Ekdahl, M. (1960). Survey of employment experience of patients discharged from three mental hospitals during the period 1951–1953. *Mental Hygiene, 44,* 510–521.

Page, S. (1977). Effects of the mental illness label in attempts to obtain accommodation. *Canadian Journal of Behavioral Sciences, 9,* 85–90.

Page, S. (1983). Psychiatric stigma: Two studies of behavior when the chips are down. *Canadian Journal of Community Mental Health, 2,* 13–19.

Page, S. (1995). Effects of the mental illness label in 1993: Acceptance and rejection in the community. *Journal of Health and Social Policy, 7,* 61–68.

Pyzcyznski, T., & Greenberg, J. (1983). Determinants of reduction in effort as a strategy for coping with anticipated failure. *Journal of Research in Personality, 17,* 412–422.

Rabkin, J. G. (1974). Public attitudes toward mental illness: A review of the literature. *Psychological Bulletin, 10,* 9–23.

Roman, P. M., & Floyd, H. H., Jr. (1981). Social acceptance of psychiatric illness and psychiatric treatment. *Social Psychiatry, 16,* 16–21.

Rosenberg, M. (1979). *Conceiving self.* New York: Basic Books.

Semrad, E. V. (1966). Longterm therapy of schizophrenia. In G. Usdin (Ed.), *Psychoneuroses and schizophrenia* (pp. 76–124). Philadelphia: J. B. Lippincott.

Shih, M., Pittinsky, T. L., & Ambady, N. (1999). Stereotype susceptibility: Identity salience and shifts in quantitative performance. *Psychological Science, 10,* 80–83.

Sosowsky, L. (1980). Explaining the increased arrest rate among mental patients: A cautionary note. *American Journal of Psychiatry, 137,* 1602–1604.

Spencer, S. J., Steele, C. M., & Quinn, D. (1999). Stereotype threat and women's math performance. *Journal of Experimental Social Psychology, 35,* 4–28.

Steadman, H. J. (1981). Critically reassessing the accuracy of public perceptions of the dangerousness of the mentally ill. *Journal of Health and Social Behavior, 22,* 310–316.

Steele, C. M. (1975). Name-calling and compliance. *Journal of Personality and Social Psychology, 31,* 361–369.

Steele, C. M. (1997). A threat in the air: How stereotypes shape intellectual identity and performance. *American Psychologist, 52,* 613–629.

Steele, C. M., & Aronson, J. (1995). Stereotype threat and the intellectual test performance of African Americans. *Journal of Personality and Social Psychology, 69,* 797–811.

Steele, S. (1990). *The content of our character.* New York: St. Martin's Press.

Sternberg, R. J. (1997). The triarchic theory of intelligence. In D. P. Flanigan & J. L. Genshaft (Eds.), *Contemporary intellectual assessment: Theories, tests, and issues* (pp. 92–104). New York: Guilford Press.

Taylor, S. M., & Dear, M. J. (1980). Scaling community attitudes toward the mentally ill. *Schizophrenia Bulletin, 7,* 225–240.

Wahl, O. F. (1995). *Media madness: Public images of mental illness.* New Brunswick, NJ: Rutgers University Press.

Wahl, O. F. (1999). Mental health consumers' experience of stigma. *Schizophrenia Bulletin, 25,* 467–478.

Wahl, O., & Harman, C. (1989). Family views of stigma. *Schizophrenia Bulletin, 15,* 131–139.

Young, D. A., Davila, R., & Scher, H. (1993). Unawareness of illness and neuropsychological performance in chronic schizophrenia. *Schizophrenia Research, 10,* 117–124.

II

Clinical Applications

Changing Causal Attributions | 7

Peter Kinderman

As outlined elsewhere in this book, the traditional Kraepelinian approach to the classification of psychiatric disorders is widely considered to have little validity (Bentall, 1990). It also is becoming more generally accepted that investigations of more specific psychological phenomena can be highly educational (Bentall, Jackson, & Pilgrim, 1988; Persons, 1986). A growing body of research based on those principles has investigated processes of self-representation and causal attribution in paranoia (see chapter 4).

This chapter develops those ideas by reviewing methods of altering causal attributions. It reviews evidence that is based on experiments examining factors that alter the explanations generated by experimental participants. It also reviews findings gleaned from psychotherapy research that examined changes in causal attributions that occur during therapy as well as direct attempts to address attributional abnormalities in therapy.

On the basis of this material, and in keeping with the more theoretical review in chapter 4, this chapter will develop a theoretical account of the mechanisms of causal attribution pertinent to therapy and provide suggestions for the cognitive therapy of people experiencing paranoid delusions.

Attributional Abnormalities in Paranoia

We previously have proposed and developed a model of paranoid ideation that is based principally on attributional abnormalities (Bentall &

Kinderman, 1999; Bentall, Kinderman, & Kaney, 1994). This model can be summarized as follows: People with paranoid delusions tend to show an attentional bias toward material that is both threat related (Bentall & Kaney, 1989) and related to negative self-representations (Kinderman, 1994). This bias appears to reflect a negative implicit self-schema, a theory supported by enhanced recall for negative and threat-related material (Bentall, Kaney, & Bowen-Jones, 1995; Kaney, Wolfenden, Dewey, & Bentall, 1992). The attributional model of paranoia notes that people experiencing persecutory delusions make abnormally internal attributions for positive events and abnormally external attributions for negative events (Candido & Romney, 1990; Fear, Sharp, & Healy, 1996; Kaney & Bentall, 1989, 1992; Sharp, Fear, & Healy, 1997). It is suggested that this pattern—which is only evident on explicit (as opposed to implicit) measures—serves as a mechanism for maintaining a positive self-image in the face of threats resulting from the attentional bias toward negative material (Lyon, Kaney, & Bentall, 1994).

Consistent with this model, Kinderman and Bentall (1996a) reported that people with paranoid delusions displayed small self-actual: self-ideal and self-actual:self-ought discrepancies, together with large discrepancies between self-perceptions and what they believed their parents' perceptions were about them. Examination of the content of the paranoid patients' responses indicated that they believed that their parents held exceptionally negative views about them. These findings are clearly consistent with the Bentall, Kinderman, and Kaney (1994) model.

CAUSAL ATTRIBUTIONS AND THEORY OF MIND

Research evidence appears to support the hypothesis that paranoia reflects an abnormal attributional strategy that maintains small self-actual: self-ideal discrepancies. A more recent development of this attributional model also suggests developments in the measurement of causal attributions. Attributions generally have been seen as falling along a unidimensional internality–externality axis (Reivich, 1995). Kinderman and Bentall (1996b) identified three loci of attributions: internal, external-personal and external-situational. Kinderman and Bentall (1997b) found that patients with paranoid delusions demonstrated not only an externalizing bias (attributing more positive events than negative events to internal loci) but also a personalizing bias (allocating most of their external attributions to personal as opposed to situational loci).

Bentall and Kinderman (Bentall & Kinderman, 1999; Kinderman, Dunbar, & Bentall, 1999) have suggested that this pattern of attributional abnormalities might be, in part, a consequence of failure of cognitive systems associated with social cognition. This hypothesis centers on theory of mind (ToM)—the ability to understand another person's perspective. Chris Frith and colleagues (Corcoran, Frith, & Mercer, 1995; Frith & Corcoran, 1996) have found that paranoid patients perform badly on ToM tasks. In a study of "normal" participants, Kinderman et al. (1999) found that those who performed worst on the ToM task made the least number of external-situational attributions and the greatest number of external-personal attributions. Because psychotic episodes are associated with dysfunctions of information-processing capacity (Green, 1992) and because ToM tasks appear to make considerable demands on cognitive resources, it is possible that the ToM deficits and attributional abnormalities that paranoid patients experience reflect these more general psychological impairments.

DEFICITS AND BIASES LEADING TO ATTRIBUTIONAL ABNORMALITIES

Despite the attractiveness of a simple attributional model of paranoid ideation, some difficulties remain, among the most significant of which are two findings that apparently run counter to the model. In its simple form, the attributional model of paranoia (Bentall & Kinderman, 1999) suggests that ToM deficits will lead to external-personal attributions and, hence, paranoid ideation. Blackshaw, Kinderman, Hare, and Hatton (in press), however, investigated cognitive processes and causal attributions in people with a diagnosis of Asperger's syndrome, a condition characterized by severe ToM deficits in people with preserved general intellectual and language skills. They found that despite the impairments in ToM ability, people with this diagnosis nevertheless failed to make excessive external-personal attributions for negative events. In fact their attributions for both positive and negative events were notable for being restricted in sophistication but made to a normal spread of loci. That is, the people with Asperger's syndrome tended to make little use of the possible mental states (wishes, thoughts, intentions, or desires) of other people and tended to be repetitive in their descriptions of social scenarios. Nevertheless, they did tend to use external-situational loci for negative event attributions as much as so-called normal people.

Another apparently inconsistent finding was reported by Kerr, Dunbar, and Bentall (submitted), who investigated ToM deficits in people with a diagnosis of bipolar disorder. They found that patients who were currently either depressed or in a manic state demonstrated deficits in ToM ability. This finding is consistent with the hypothesis that disruptions of cognitive capacity resulting from stress are associated with symptomatic psychological problems. It is not, however, consistent with the simpler model of attributional abnormalities in paranoia. If people with symptomatic bipolar disorder show ToM deficits, why do they not become paranoid? These findings suggest that although attributional models of psychopathology may be correct, attention needs to be paid to the processes by which causal attributions are made.

Search and Termination Strategies in Causal Attribution

Research from the social psychology field has suggested that the process of causal attribution can be thought of in terms of two relatively independent processes. First, people make effortful searches for possible explanations for social events. Second, people use heuristic and idiosyncratic rules for terminating this search.

SEARCH STRATEGY

Gilbert and colleagues (Gilbert, 1989; Gilbert, McNulty, Giuliano, & Benson, 1992) have argued that social attributions for the actions of other people proceed through three stages: categorization (What is the actor doing?), characterization (What trait does the action imply?), and correction (What situational constraints may have caused the action?). Clearly, this account suggests that the third stage of explanation—searching for situational factors—is chronologically later, more effortful, and more easily disrupted than the first two. Thus, when participants in research experiments were required to make judgments about an actor while performing an additional cognitive task, they tended to make more dispositional attributions for behavior than under no additional load (Gilbert, Krull, & Pelham, 1988). In a similar study, Webster, Richter, and Kruglanski (1996) also found that participants experiencing fatigue as a result of participation in a long final examination at a university showed greater primacy effects in impression formation than did nonfatigued participants. In the light of research into delusional reasoning (Huq, Garety, & Hemsley, 1988), it is significant that this tendency was entitled "jumping to conclusions."

It seems clear that people pursue a strategic search for material pertinent to making causal attributions. It also seems clear that, in keeping with the links between our attributional model of paranoia (Bentall & Kinderman, 1999) and ToM difficulties, the search for situational attributions may place a particular strain on this strategy. Fatigue, stress, depression, anxiety, and the presence of general or specific deficits in social cognition might limit the search strategy. The search strategy also might be biased as a result of affect-mediated motivational stances and influenced by experience. At present this framework has not been widely used to understand causal attributions, but we may speculate that all of these factors will influence attributional search strategies.

TERMINATION RULES

The social psychologist Arne Kruglanski and colleagues have extensively investigated impression formation and the generation of explanations in the social field (see DeGrada, Kruglanski, Mannetti, & Pierro, 1999; Dijksterhuis, van Knippenberg, Kruglanski, & Schaper, 1996). They have investigated people's apparently strong need to develop interpretative frameworks of their social world that satisfy a motivational need for "structure" or "closure." These have been defined as "the need to have some knowledge on a given topic, any knowledge as opposed to confusion and ambiguity" (Kruglanski & Freund, 1983, p. 450).

Reliable differences in the need for cognitive closure exist from person to person (Webster & Kruglanski, 1994). Some people appear to be motivated more strongly than others to have a model of their social universe that leaves little room for ambiguity. This motivational tendency has been seen as part of a wider issue of "motivated social cognition" (e.g., Kruglanski & Webster 1996), whereby information processing in the social arena is subject to biases and interpretations that serve personal functions.

This research implies that people possess idiosyncratic rules for the closure or termination of search strategies for causal attributions. That is, people seem to generate possible explanations for social events and then choose from the possible explanations generated. The search appears to terminate when an account is generated that is psychologically satisfactory. An enormous amount of research has established that causal attributions are extremely important in determining people's emotional and behavioral reactions to personally salient events (e.g., Buchanan & Seligman, 1995; Heider, 1958; Weiner, 1986). This research strongly suggests that the termination rules for attributional search strategies are not limited to closure but involve other motivational goals, including maintenance of affect and self-concept. When a person is not depressed, therefore, these rules are likely to include the basic rule not to terminate a search for explanations with an attribution that implies self-blame. If one is depressed, this self-serving rule will be absent.

If people do indeed use separate search strategies and specific, idiosyncratic termination strategies, examining the factors that influence the two processes may help us understand the nature of causal attributions in psychosis and elucidate the reasons for the apparently confusing findings.

The evidence from clinical and experimental studies pertinent to psychotic phenomena is consistent with the process described above. Our attributional model of paranoia suggests that failures in theory of mind lead to an increase of dispositional attributions (Kinderman, Dunbar, & Bentall, 1999). However, people who show deficits in theory of mind—that is, people with diagnoses of Asperger's syndrome (Blackshaw et al., in press) and bipolar disorder (Kerr, Dunbar, & Bentall, submitted)—have not been shown necessarily to demonstrate such a pattern. This finding can be explained in terms of the two aspects of attributional processes. ToM deficits may affect search strategies, resulting in difficulties appreciating the situational factors affecting the behavior of other people. There is no reason to believe that ToM deficits necessarily directly affect the termination rules.

Concerning Asperger's syndrome, considerable evidence indicates that people with preserved language and general intellectual skills learn to develop compensatory strategies. Typically, they develop logical techniques to deal with social challenges (Frith, 1991). These logical strategies may result in adaptive termination rules for what must inevitably be a restricted attributional search. At present, no research is available on attributional searches in Asperger's syndrome, but such an account is compatible with clinical impressions.

Similarly, in bipolar disorder, symptomatic episodes of illness are associated with ToM deficits (Kerr, Dunbar, & Bentall, submitted) but low levels of paranoid attributions (Bentall & Kinderman, 1999). This finding suggests that, again, benign termination rules govern the truncated attributional search. Almost certainly, specific rules both maintain a positive, proactive cognitive style redolent of self-serving processes and preserve the strong sense of social desirability present in bipolar disorder (Donnelly & Murphy, 1973).

The case of paranoia, or schizophrenia more generally, is somewhat different. In this case, one may hypothesize that there exist specific, biased termination rules as well as dysfunctional search strategies. The combination of biases and deficits is what leads to the particular pattern of attributions. In essence, people with paranoia appear to conclude, "That was not my fault. I can't understand what was going on in the head of that person, but it does seem reasonable to suggest that it was her fault."

Clearly, therapeutic strategies aimed at altering maladaptive attributional styles must address both the search for possible explanations and the choice of an appropriate conclusion.

Influences on Causal Attributions

It may be worthwhile to examine a range of possible influences on secret strategies and termination rules for casual attributions. Therapeutic influences on casual attributions are likely to be maximally successful if they use or mimic naturally occurring processes.

STABILITY OF ATTRIBUTIONAL STYLE

A great deal of research into clinical aspects of causal attribution has assumed that attributions are relatively traitlike—predictable and stable. In some ways the research by Kruglanski and Webster (1996) has taken this approach, viewing need for closure as a personality trait. Thus, using conventional methods of assessing causal attributions, a number of researchers have found stability of causal explanations over periods of 5 weeks (Peterson et al., 1982), months (Nolen-Hoeksema, Girgus, & Seligman, 1986), and even 5 decades (Burns & Seligman, 1989). Some debate exists over the nature of the relationship between depressive attributional styles and future depression (Robbins & Hayes, 1995), but evidence shows that those styles may act as traitlike diatheses in a stress–diathesis predictive model of later depression (Metalsky, Halberstadt, & Abramson, 1987). For people with psychotic disorders, abnormal attributional processes may be present some years before a psychiatric breakdown occurs (Frenkel, Kugelmass, Nathan, & Ingraham, 1995).

In children, the experience of trust may foster a positive (optimistic) attributional style, whereas experience of distrust may foster a negative style (Eisner, 1995). More generally, experiences of uncontrollable unhappiness, such as parental divorce (Nolen-Hoeksema, Girgus, & Seligman, 1991) or criticism by teachers (see Eisner, 1995, and Nolen-Hoeksema & Girgus, 1995) are likely to lead to pessimism or self-blame. It is not surprising that schematic patterns of cognition such as these have been targeted for psychological therapy.

COGNITIVE THERAPY AND CAUSAL ATTRIBUTIONS

Because patterns of causal attribution are thought to be risk factors for psychological problems, interacting with negative life events and leading to depression (Abramson, Metalsky, & Alloy, 1989; Hollon & Garber, 1980), many researchers have studied the effects of cognitive–behavioral therapy (CBT) on explanatory styles.

Hollon and colleagues (DeRubeis & Hollon, 1995) describe an experiment that investigated the impact of CBT and antidepressants on causal attributions. They reported that early change in attributional style, as measured by the Attributional Style Questionnaire (ASQ; Peterson et al., 1982), predicted symptomatic change in depression following CBT. Moreover, scores on the ASQ at the end of treatment were predictive of relapse: Self-blaming attributions for negative events were positively related to higher rates of relapse.

Several other psychotherapy researchers have concluded that changes in causal attribution are related to therapeutic outcome. Firth-Cozens and Brewin (1988), for example, found that causal attributions for negative events became significantly more unstable, specific, and controllable following CBT, and a positive relation existed between attributional change and change in depression symptoms. Although related to slightly different conditions, it is worth noting that Nixon and Singer (1993) found that successful CBT aimed at reducing the excessive self-blame and guilt in parents of children with severe disabilities, not unnaturally, resulted in fewer internal negative attributions. These findings suggest that shifts in attributional style may be an important factor in successful psychological therapies for depression and other related conditions (DeRubeis et al., 1990; Forsterling, 1985).

Three caveats must be noted, however. First, it is difficult to say that the shifts in causal attributions caused the therapeutic change; it is possible that both symptomatic improvement and changes in causal explanations follow from other changes. Many people (e.g., Beck, Rush, Shaw, & Emery, 1979) might claim that moderation of negative automatic thoughts is the important ingredient. Second, no specific therapeutic strategies exist for changing causal attributions. The benefits appear to follow from CBT per se, rather than from specific interventions for attributions themselves. Finally, even specific attributional therapies (e.g., Forsterling, 1985) have not been applied to psychotic problems.

Brewin (1994) found that successful CBT-based family therapy for relatives of patients with schizophrenia was associated with a shift toward making an increased number of universal attributions and attributions to illness for patients' negative behaviors. Of course, family therapy in this context is not necessarily related to therapy for positive symptoms themselves. Hudley and Graham (1993) attempted to modify peer-directed aggression in boys and found that following therapy, boys in the attributional intervention group were less likely to presume hostile intent by peers in hypothetical and laboratory simulations of ambiguous provocation. This finding may be relevant because aggression and paranoia may show similarities in terms of personal-external attributions for negative events. CBT appears to exert a powerful influence on causal attributions.

In the past few years, cognitive–behavioral interventions also have been shown to be effective in patients suffering from delusions (Chadwick & Lowe, 1990; Garety, Kuipers, Fowler, Chamberlain, & Dunn, 1994; Tarrier et al., 1993). The strategies developed by cognitive–behavioral therapists working with psychotic patients involve explicit attempts to modify patients' explanations for events and to address problems of self-esteem and hopelessness (Fowler, Garety, & Kuipers, 1995). Given the attributional abnormalities seen in schizophrenia, it would seem obvious to conclude that CBT is indicated. Future research into the cognitive abnormalities underlying psychotic symptomatology is likely to lead to increases in the effectiveness of this kind of treatment. However the processes that lead to attributional shifts are poorly understood. It remains unclear whether CBT alters search strategies, termination rules, or both. Specific indications of successful interventions for the attributional aspects of social cognition in schizophrenia also must come from other sources.

SELF-ESTEEM

Considerable evidence indicates a close relationship between causal attributions and self-esteem. People with low self-esteem display internal (i.e., self-blaming) attributions for negative events, whereas people with high self-esteem make external (i.e., self-serving) attributions for negative events. Indeed, some researchers have suggested that the attributional style seen in depressed patients may be related to low self-esteem rather than depression (Brewin & Furnham, 1996; Tennen & Herzenberger, 1987; Tennen, Herzenberger, & Nelson, 1987).

Both the helplessness and hopelessness models of depression (Abramson et al., 1989; Abramson, Seligman, & Teasdale, 1978) and our model of paranoia (Bentall et al., 1994) suggest a close relationship between causal attributions and self-esteem. Higgins and Bargh (1987) argued that when people's self-representations fall short of their ideals, they tend to make internal explanations for negative events because such causal representations are highly available to them ("I'm not as good as I would like to be; that is the reason for my failure").

The generation of internal attributions is therefore hypothesized to be governed by the availability of self-representations. Different groups of people have differing levels of availability of such self-representations. Ordinary people should have readily available positive self-representations and make more rapid internal explanations for positive than for negative events. This effect should be absent, or perhaps even reversed, in the case of depressed patients, whose available self-representations include both positive and negative elements (Williams, Watts, MacLeod, & Mathews, 1997). In the case of paranoid patients, our attributional model of paranoia suggests that internal explanations for negative events also should be made as least as quickly as for positive events because implicit negative self-representations should be highly accessible. Those predictions were recently tested experimentally.

Participants with depression, participants with paranoia, and ordinary, control participants were timed as they generated likely causes for hypothetical events. Consistent with our predictions, control participants generated internal explanations more rapidly for positive than for negative events. This bias was absent in the depressed and deluded patients, who, we hypothesized, had more negative self-representations. The findings support the view that explanatory style and self-representations are interrelated cognitive processes.

This relationship is, of course, likely to be circular, with self-esteem affecting causal attributions, and causal attributions affecting self-esteem. Kinderman and Bentall (2000) recently tested this prediction in two studies in which ordinary people reported their self-representations before and after generating explanations for hypothetical negative events. Students were asked to generate up to 10 self-descriptive words, 10 words that described their ideal selves, and 10 words that described how they believed they were seen by others; they then were asked to generate causal explanations for 16 negative social events (e.g., a friend talked about you behind your back). This measure was designed to prime self-referent schemata and assess the attributional style simultaneously. A clear relationship was observed between highly discrepant self-representations and self-ideals and subsequent internal explanations for negative events. The findings suggest that self-representations redolent of failure are associated with self-blame. When this effect was controlled for, explanations were highly predictive of future self-representations: Internal explanations predicted an increase in discrepancies between self-representations and self-ideals, whereas external explanations predicted a reduction in self-discrepancies. The data suggest that self-representations play a role in generating causal explanations but that causal explanations, in turn, influence future self-representations.

This discussion might be a little academic. However, it is not merely the case that self-esteem affects our pattern of causal attributions and that causal attributions affect our self-esteem. Delusions, it is argued, arise from a maladaptive strategy to maintain positive self-representations. It surely would be more sensible to address self-esteem directly. Many clinical researchers have discussed how different approaches to CBT may address self-esteem (Brewin, 1989). This effect is true in psychosis (Kuipers et al., 1997), where self-esteem may be improved by therapy, even though (consistent with the attributional model of paranoia) little correlation may exist between self-esteem and conviction in persecutory delusions (Freeman et al., 1998). Tim Strauman (1994) has discussed the possibility of developing specific self-discrepancy therapy, targeting directly the self-representations of patients.

Therapy, even relatively specific CBT, is a multifaceted and "dirty" intervention. Empirical research may provide considerable insight into the nature of possible influences on causal attributions. Undoubtedly, causal attributions determine the way in which salient events are interpreted. Experimental and quasi-experimental studies also provide clear evidence that events, usually failure and success experiences, affect causal explanations.

FAILURE AND SUCCESS

Forgas, Bower, and Moylan (1990) found that normal subjects given contrived failure experiences showed evidence of a more pessimistic attributional style after the experiences than beforehand. Forgas (1998) also reported that experimentally induced happy moods led to increases in the fundamental attributional error (i.e., the self-serving explanations for negative events). He concluded that these were linked through mood-induced differences in processing style. Finally, Alden (1987) examined attributions following four patterns of feedback: consistent success, improvement, deterioration, and consistent failure. Alden's findings revealed that for anxious participants, feedback of improvement led to the greatest internal attribution for positive outcomes. Nonanxious participants, in contrast, accepted greatest personal responsibility following consistent success.

We have argued (Bentall & Kinderman, 1999) that these effects reflect changes in the availability of self-representations. Following a success, it is likely that representations of the self as a successful person will be more available, making such attributions more likely.

Again, it remains unclear whether the experience of success or failure changes search strategies or termination rules. It would seem likely that both are affected. Following a success experience, people are likely to have a more positive mood and greater motivation. They also are likely to have fewer impediments to cognitive processing and are therefore likely to search for more flattering explanations and find positive self-representations more accessible. In addition, potential explanatory frameworks suggesting personal efficacy are likely to be seen as more acceptable (i.e., meeting termination criteria) when people have recently experienced success.

Again, the therapeutic relevance of these studies requires direct attention. Success experiences make healthy (or at least positive) explanations more likely, through increased accessibility of positive self-representations. The research strongly suggests that the social cognition of people with a diagnosis of schizophrenia can be ameliorated through occupational and social therapies. If people are helped to have a greater number of success experiences, they should develop more adaptive explanatory frameworks.

INFORMATION PROCESSING

People's causal explanations are, at least in part, influenced by the information available (Kelley, 1967; McArthur, 1972). Thus, if the data appear to suggest that an event covaries with a certain stimulus, people tend to conclude that the stimulus has caused the event. This pattern has two implications. First, it is possible that people with paranoid delusions have experienced a history of negative events consistently associated with the actions of other people. This is highly likely, given that Goff, Brotman, Kindlon, Waites, and Amico (1991) found that 43% of 61 chronically psychotic inpatients reported abuse in their childhood and Greenfield, Strakowski, Tohen, Batson, and Kolbrener (1994) reported that 20 out of 38 patients admitted for first-episode psychosis reported childhood abuse.

Altering the information available to people appears to alter their attributions for events (Kelley, 1967). In the case of paranoia, Young and Bentall (submitted) found a similar effect: Providing additional information leads to changes in the attributions selected for hypothetical events. This research is entirely consistent with Gilbert and colleagues' (1992) findings discussed earlier. In those studies, people failed, for circumstantial reasons, to incorporate situational factors into their search for possible explanations. Two potentially useful mechanisms are available for improving the accessibility of appropriate information into the attributional search.

Howlin, Baron-Cohen, and Hadwin (1999) describe a method for teaching children with autistic spectrum disorders to "mind-read" (i.e., an educational strategy for helping children with ToM deficits incorporate information pertaining to the mental states of others into their social cognitive information processing). At present, little empirical support exists for the efficacy of this approach. Nevertheless, Howlin et al. report preliminary investigations suggesting that children with autism can indeed learn to understand and use information related to other people's mental states. For children with autism, this teaching process is extremely labor-intensive and difficult. It relies (at least in Howlin and colleagues' approach) on the repeated use of examples involving social interactions as well as open-ended questions requiring the learner to generate and use mental-state representations of the actors. A simple example of basic understanding of emotions would be the presentation of clear photographs of actors expressing unambiguous emotions, requiring the learner to report the correct emotion. A more complex, belief-based example might involve the presentation of a clear and un-ambiguous belief (Mary wants an apple) and a situation (Mary's mommy has given her a banana) with the requirement that the student report the appropriate emotional response. It is inherent in such latter tasks that the expectations or beliefs of the actor are compared with reality and the consequence inferred. It is no accident that a large pro-portion of the learning vignettes used in that approach involve asking "why." Similar strategies could be used to help people with schizophre-nia incorporate previously unused information.

It also is possible that medication could help in this process. It is a little paradoxical that medication, with its generally dulling side effects (Day, Kinderman, & Bentall, 1997), has a beneficial effect on the thought processes of people with psychosis. It is possible that this ap-parent paradox may be explicable through the effects of medication on the attributional search process. Andrews, Parker, and Barrett (1998) speculated that the SSRIs (selective serotonin-reuptake inhibitors) may act as "antiworry" agents; they explicitly discussed the possibility that a reduction in anxious worrying may modify dysfunctional attributions. It seems entirely possible that reduced worry (or arousal or stress) could lead to an enhanced or facilitated attributional search. One could even understand how an inhibitory effect of antipsychotic medication might facilitate this search, reducing spurious or thought-disordered, "knight's-move" thinking.

A CASE STUDY

We have reported a case study of CBT directed at modifying the mala-daptive attributions of a man with persecutory delusions (Kinderman & Bentall, 1997a). In this case a patient suffering from persecutory delu-sions was helped to reattribute negative life experiences to situational causes rather than to a conspiracy directed toward himself. It was hy-pothesized that no resistance was encountered from the patient because no attempt was made to reattribute negative events to internal causes. A reduction in paranoid ideation, which was maintained at follow up, was accompanied by changes on formal measures of attributions.

The 33-year-old male patient had a systematized persecutory delu-sion held with full conviction. He had received a provisional diagnosis of paranoid schizophrenia and recorded a positive syndrome score of 33 (98th percentile compared with "medicated schizophrenics"; Kay, Opler, & Fiszbein, 1986) on the Positive and Negative Syndrome Scale (Kay & Opler, 1987). Using the Internal, Personal and Situational Attributions Questionnaire (IPSAQ; Kinderman & Bentall, 1996a), the patient demonstrated clearly dysfunctional causal attributions, disproportionally blaming other people for negative events.

The cognitive–behavioral intervention focused on the attributional model of paranoid ideation outlined earlier. A structured therapy based on attributional style was conducted during approximately weekly sessions. Using the IPSAQ data collected from the patient, discussions centered on the importance of explanation as a means of understanding and on the likely effects of different types of attribution. Using conventional diary sheets, the patient practiced generating multiple explanations for everyday events, paying special attention to the consideration of situational attributions. This therapeutic strategy was then brought to bear on the paranoid ideation by examining the events that triggered paranoid ideation. The patient was encouraged to generate possible situational attributions for these events.

The therapeutic strategy used in this case was entirely compatible with conventional CBT based on engagement, elicitation of cognitive schemata, and reality testing. Engagement and elicitation of cognitions were important elements of the therapy; however, the specific intervention was directed at eliciting the client's explanations for negative or ambiguous events and helping the client develop, through generating multiple possible alternatives, a pattern of attributions for such events that avoided the biases in attribution hypothesized to lie behind paranoid ideation.

At the final session of psychological therapy, formal assessment was repeated. The patient's mood was within normal limits, and his responses on the IPSAQ had changed so that they lay within the normal limits. Daily record sheets completed by the patient also reflected a substantial reduction in his paranoid ideation as measured by idiographic visual analog scales.

This case study illustrates the potential applicability of cognitive therapy specifically targeted at altering patterns of causal attributions. In particular, this therapy directly addressed both foreshortened attributional search strategies and maladaptive termination rules.

Conclusion

What does the future hold for therapy aimed at modifying causal attributions in psychosis? It seems clear that many strategies—therapeutic, experimental, and social—can have an influence. It is probably most appropriate for two developments to occur in parallel. Further work needs to occur in the area of cognitive therapy, because this therapeutic approach clearly changes patterns of causal attribution. In addition, work remains to be done on the nature and structure of attributional processes.

It seems reasonable to structure both clinical and therapeutic developments around the twin processes of truncated attributional searches and maladaptive termination rules. These processes also suggest that assessing deficits (stable and transient) might lead to inadequate searches for possible causal explanations. In addition, individual learning histories might provide clues as to the origin of maladaptive rules for the termination or conclusion of this search.

References

Abramson, L. Y., Metalsky, G. I., & Alloy, L. B. (1989). Hopelessness depression: A theory-based subtype of depression. *Psychological Review, 96*, 358–372.

Abramson, L. Y., Seligman, M. E. P., & Teasdale, J. D. (1978). Learned helplessness in humans: Critique and reformulation. *Journal of Abnormal Psychology, 78*, 40–74.

Alden, L. (1987). Attributional responses of anxious individuals to different patterns of social feedback: Nothing succeeds like improvement. *Journal of Personality and Social Psychology, 52*, 100–106.

Andrews, W., Parker, G., & Barrett, E. (1998). The SSRI antidepressants: Exploring their "other" possible properties. *Journal of Affective Disorders, 49*, 141–144.

Beck, A. T., Rush, A. J., Shaw, B. F., & Emery, G. (1979). *Cognitive therapy of depression.* New York: Guilford Press.

Bentall, R. P. (Ed.). (1990). *Reconstructing schizophrenia.* London: Routledge.

Bentall, R. P., Jackson, H. F., & Pilgrim, D. (1988). Abandoning the concept of schizophrenia: Some implications of validity arguments for psychological research into psychotic phenomena. *British Journal of Clinical Psychology, 27*, 303–324.

Bentall, R. P., & Kaney, S. (1989). Content-specific information processing and persecutory delusions: An investigation using the emotional Stroop test. *British Journal of Medical Psychology, 62*, 355–364.

Bentall, R. P., Kaney, S., & Bowen-Jones, K. (1995). Persecutory delusions and recall of threat-related, depression-related and neutral words. *Cognitive Therapy and Research, 19*, 331–343.

Bentall, R. P., & Kinderman, P. (1999). Self-regulation, affect and psychosis: The role of social cognition in paranoia and mania. In T. Dalgleish & M. Power (Eds.), *Handbook of cognition and emotion* (pp. 351–381). Chichester, England: Wiley.

Bentall, R. P., Kinderman, P., & Kaney, S. (1994). The self, attributional processes and abnormal beliefs: Towards a model of persecutory delusions. *Behaviour Research and Therapy, 32,* 331–341.

Blackshaw, A., Kinderman, P., Hare, D., & Hatton, C. (in press). *Theory-of-mind, causal attributions and paranoia in Asperger's Syndrome.* Manuscript submitted for publication.

Brewin, C. R. (1989). Cognitive change processes in psychotherapy. *Psychological Review, 96,* 379–394.

Brewin, C. R. (1994). Changes in attribution and expressed emotion among the relatives of patients with schizophrenia. *Psychological Medicine, 24,* 905–911.

Brewin, C. R., & Furnham, A. (1986). Attributional versus preattributional variables in self-esteem and depression: A comparison and test of learned helplessness theory. *Journal of Personality and Social Psychology, 40,* 1013–1020.

Buchanan, G. M., & Seligman, M. E. P. (Eds.). (1995). *Explanatory style.* Hillsdale, NJ: Erlbaum.

Burns, M. O., & Seligman, M. E. P. (1989). Explanatory style across the life span: Evidence for stability over 52 years. *Journal of Personality and Social Psychology, 56,* 471–477.

Candido, C. L., & Romney, D. M. (1990). Attributional style in paranoid vs depressed patients. *British Journal of Medical Psychology, 63,* 355–363.

Chadwick, P., & Lowe, C. F. (1990). The measurement and modification of delusional beliefs. *Journal of Consulting and Clinical Psychology, 58,* 225–232.

Corcoran, R., Frith, C. D., & Mercer, G. (1995). Schizophrenia, symptomatology and social inference: Investigating "theory of mind" in people with schizophrenia. *Schizophrenia Research, 17,* 5–13.

Day, J. C., Kinderman, P., & Bentall, R. P. (1997). A comparison of patients' and prescribers' beliefs about neuroleptic side-effects: Prevalence, distress and causation. *Acta Psychiatrica Scandinavica, 96,* 1–5.

DeGrada, E., Kruglanski, A. W., Mannetti, L., & Pierro, A. (1999). Motivated cognition and group interaction: Need for closure affects the contents and processes of collective negotiations. *Journal of Experimental Social Psychology, 35,* 346–365.

DeRubeis, R. J., Evans, M. D., Hollon, S. D., Garvey, M. J., Grove, W. M., & Tuason, V. B. (1990). How does cognitive therapy work? Cognitive change and symptom change in cognitive therapy and pharmacotherapy for depression. *Journal of Consulting and Clinical Psychology, 58,* 862–869.

DeRubeis, R. J., & Hollon, S. D. (1995). Explanatory style in the treatment of depression. In G. M. Buchanan & M. E. P. Seligman (Eds.), *Explanatory style* (pp. 99–111). Hillsdale, NJ: Erlbaum.

Dijksterhuis, A., van Knippenberg, A., Kruglanski, A. W., & Schaper, C. (1996). Motivated social cognition: Need for closure effects on memory and judgment. *Journal of Experimental Social Psychology, 32,* 254–270.

Donnelly, E. F., & Murphy, D. L. (1973). Social desirability and bipolar affective disorder. *Journal of Consulting and Clinical Psychology, 41,* 469.

Eisner, J. P. (1995). The origins of explanatory style: Trust as a determinant of optimism and pessimism. In G. M. Buchanan & M. E. P. Seligman (Eds.), *Explanatory style* (pp. 49–55). Hillsdale, NJ: Erlbaum.

Fear, C. F., Sharp, H., & Healy, D. (1996). Cognitive processes in delusional disorders. *British Journal of Psychiatry, 168,* 61–67.

Firth-Cozens, J., & Brewin, C. R. (1988). Attributional change during psychotherapy. *British Journal of Clinical Psychology, 27,* 47–54.

Forgas, J. P. (1998). On being happy and mistaken: Mood effects on the fundamental attribution error. *Journal of Personality and Social Psychology, 75,* 318–331.

Forgas, J. P., Bower, G. H., & Moylan, S. J. (1990). Praise or blame? Affective influences on attributions for achievement. *Journal of Personality and Social Psychology, 59,* 809–819.

Forsterling, F. (1985). Attributional retraining: A review. *Psychological Bulletin, 98,* 495–512.

Fowler, D., Garety, P., & Kuipers, E. (1995). *Cognitive-behaviour therapy for psychosis: Theory and practice.* Chichester, England: Wiley.

Freeman, D., Garety, P., Fowler, D., Kuipers, E., Dunn, G., Bebbington, P., & Hadley, G. (1998). The London-East Anglia randomized controlled trial of cognitive-behaviour therapy for psychosis. IV: Self-esteem and persecutory delusions. *British Journal of Clinical Psychology, 37,* 415–430.

Frenkel, E., Kugelmass, S., Nathan, M., & Ingraham, L. J. (1995). Locus of control and mental health in adolescence and adulthood. *Schizophrenia Bulletin, 21,* 219–226.

Frith, C. D., & Corcoran, R. (1996). Exploring "theory of mind" in people with schizophrenia. *Psychological Medicine, 26,* 521–530.

Frith, U. (Ed.). (1991). *Autism and Asperger syndrome.* Cambridge, England: Cambridge University Press.

Garety, P. A., Kuipers, L., Fowler, D., Chamberlain, F., & Dunn, G. (1994). Cognitive behavioural therapy for drug-resistant psychosis. *British Journal of Medical Psychology, 67,* 259–271.

Gilbert, D. T. (1989). Thinking lightly about others: Automatic components of the social inference process. In J. S. Uleman & J. A. Bargh (Eds.), *Unintended thought* (pp. 189–211). New York: Guilford.

Gilbert, D. T., Krull, D. S., & Pelham, B. W. (1988). Of thoughts unspoken: Social inference and the self-regulation of behaviour. *Journal of Personality and Social Psychology, 55,* 685–694.

Gilbert, D. T., McNulty, S. E., Giuliano, T. A., & Benson, J. E. (1992). Blurry words and fuzzy deeds: The attribution of obscure behavior. *Journal of Personality and Social Psychology, 62,* 18–25.

Goff, D. C., Brotman, A. W., Kindlon, D., Waites, M., & Amico, E. (1991). Self-reports of childhood abuse in chronically psychotic patients. *Psychiatry Research, 37,* 73–80.

Green, M. F. (1992). Information processing in schizophrenia. In D. J. Kavanagh (Ed.), *Schizophrenia: An overview and practical handbook* (pp. 45–58). London: Chapman & Hall.

Greenfield, S. F., Strakowski, S. M., Tohen, M., Batson, S. C., & Kolbrener, M. L. (1994). Childhood abuse in first episode psychosis. *British Journal of Psychiatry, 164,* 831–834.

Heider, F. (1958). *The psychology of interpersonal relations.* New York: Wiley.

Higgins, E. T., & Bargh, J. A. (1987). Social cognition and social perception. *Annual Review of Psychology, 38,* 369–425.

Hollon, S. D., & Garber, J. (1980). A cognitive-expectancy theory of therapy for helplessness and depression. In J. Garber & M. E. P. Seligman (Eds.), *Human helplessness: Theory and applications* (pp. 173–195). New York: Academic Press.

Howlin, P., Baron-Cohen, S., & Hadwin, J. (1999). *Teaching children with autism to mind-read.* Chichester, England: Wiley.

Hudley, C., & Graham, S. (1993). An attributional intervention to reduce peer-directed aggression among African-American boys. *Child Development, 64,* 124–138.

Huq, S. F., Garety, P. A., & Hemsley, D. R. (1988). Probabilistic judgements in deluded and nondeluded subjects. *Quarterly Journal of Experimental Psychology, 40A,* 801–812.

Kaney, S., & Bentall, R. P. (1989). Persecutory delusions and attributional style. *British Journal of Medical Psychology, 62,* 191–198.

Kaney, S., & Bentall, R. P. (1992). Persecutory delusions and the self-serving bias. *Journal of Nervous and Mental Disease, 180,* 773–780.

Kaney, S., Wolfenden, M., Dewey, M. E., & Bentall, R. P. (1992). Persecutory delusions and the recall of threatening and non-threatening propositions. *British Journal of Clinical Psychology, 31,* 85–87.

Kay, S. R., & Opler, L. A. (1987). The Positive and Negative Syndrome Scale (PANSS) for schizophrenia. *Schizophrenia Bulletin, 13,* 507–518.

Kay, S. R., Opler, L. A., & Fiszbein, A. (1986). *Positive and Negative Syndrome Scale (PANSS) Rating Manual.* San Rafael, CA: Social and Behavioural Sciences Documents.

Kelley, H. H. (1967). Attribution theory in social psychology. In D. Levine (Ed.), *Nebraska symposium on motivation* (Vol. 15, pp. 192–240). Lincoln: University of Nebraska Press.

Kerr, N., Dunbar, R. I. M., & Bentall, R. P. (submitted). *Theory of mind deficits in bipolar affective disorder.* Manuscript submitted for publication.

Kinderman, P. (1994). Attentional bias, persecutory delusions and the self concept. *British Journal of Medical Psychology, 67,* 53–66.

Kinderman, P., & Bentall, R. P. (1996a). A new measure of causal locus: The Internal, Personal and Situational Attributions Questionnaire. *Personality and Individual Differences, 20,* 261–264.

Kinderman, P., & Bentall, R. P. (1996b). Self-discrepancies and persecutory delusions: Evidence for a defensive model of paranoid ideation. *Journal of Abnormal Psychology, 106,* 106–114.

Kinderman, P., & Bentall, R. P. (1997a). Attributional therapy for paranoid delusions: A case study. *Behavioural and Cognitive Psychotherapy, 25,* 269–280.

Kinderman, P., & Bentall, R. P. (1997b). Causal attributions in paranoia and depression: Internal, personal and situational attributions for negative events. *Journal of Abnormal Psychology, 106,* 341–345.

Kinderman, P., & Bentall, R. P. (2000). Self-discrepancies and causal attributions: Analogue studies of hypothesised relationships. *British Journal of Clinical Psychology, 39,* 255–273.

Kinderman, P., Dunbar, R. I. M., & Bentall, R. P. (1998). Theory-of-mind deficits and causal attributions. *British Journal of Psychology, 89,* 191–204.

Kruglanski, A. W., & Freund, T. (1983). The freezing and unfreezing of lay-inferences: Effects on impressional primacy, ethnic stereotyping, and numerical anchoring. *Journal of Experimental Social Psychology, 19,* 448–468.

Kruglanski, A. W., & Webster, D. M. (1996). Motivated closing of the mind: "Seizing" and "freezing." *Psychology Review, 103,* 263–283.

Kuipers, E., Garety, P., Fowler, D., Dunn, G., Bebbington, P., Freeman, D., & Hadley, C. (1997). The London-East Anglia randomised controlled trial of cognitive-behavioural therapy for psychosis. I: Effects of the treatment phase. *British Journal of Psychiatry, 171,* 319–327.

Lyon, H. M., Kaney, S., & Bentall, R. P. (1994). The defensive function of persecutory delusions: Evidence from attribution tasks. *British Journal of Psychiatry, 164,* 637–646.

McArthur, L. A. (1972). The how and what of why: Some determinants and consequences of causal attributions. *Journal of Personality and Social Psychology, 22,* 171–193.

Metalsky, G. I., Halberstadt, L. J., & Abramson, L. Y. (1987). Vulnerability to depressive mood reactions: Towards a more powerful test of the diathesis/stress and causal mediation components of the reformulated theory of depression. *Journal of Personality and Social Psychology, 52,* 386–393.

Nixon, C. D., & Singer, G. H. (1993). Group cognitive-behavioral treatment for excessive parental self-blame and guilt. *American Journal of Mental Retardation, 97,* 665–672.

Nolen-Hoeksema, S., & Girgus, J. S. (1995). Explanatory style and achievement, depression, and gender differences in childhood and early adolescence. In G. M. Buchanan & M. E. P. Seligman (Eds.), *Explanatory style* (pp. 57–70). Hillsdale, NJ: Erlbaum.

Nolen-Hoeksema, S., Girgus, J. S., & Seligman, M. E. P. (1986). Learned helplessness in children: A longitudinal study of depression, achievement and explanatory style. *Journal of Personality and Social Psychology, 51,* 435–442.

Nolen-Hoeksema, S., Girgus, J. S., & Seligman, M. E. P. (1991). Sex differences in depression and explanatory style in children. *Journal of Youth and Adolescence, 20,* 233–245.

Persons, J. B. (1986). The advantages of studying psychological phenomena rather than psychiatric diagnoses. *American Psychologist, 41,* 1252–1260.

Peterson, C., Semmel, A., Von Baeyer, C., Abramson, L., Metalsky, G. I., & Seligman, M. E. P. (1982). The Attributional Style Questionnaire. *Cognitive Therapy and Research, 3,* 287–300.

Reivich, K. (1995). The measurement of explanatory style. In G. M. Buchanan & M. E. P. Seligman (Eds.), *Explanatory style* (pp. 21–48). Hillsdale, NJ: Erlbaum.

Robbins, C. J., & Hayes, A. M. (1995). The role of causal attributions in the prediction of depression. In G. M. Buchanan & M. E. P. Seligman (Eds.), *Explanatory style* (pp. 71–97). Hillsdale, NJ: Erlbaum.

Sharp, H. M., Fear, C. F., & Healy, D. (1997). Attributional style and delusions: An investigation based on delusional content. *European Psychiatry, 12,* 1–7.

Strauman, T. J. (1994). Self-representations and the nature of cognitive change in psychotherapy. *Journal of Psychotherapy Integration, 4,* 291–316.

Tarrier, N., Beckett, R., Harwood, S., Baker, A., Yusupoff, L., & Ugarteburu, I. (1993). A trial of two cognitive-behavioural methods of treating drug-resistant residual psychotic symptoms in schizophrenic patients I: Outcome. *British Journal of Psychiatry, 162,* 524–532.

Tennen, H., & Herzenberger, S. (1987). Depression, self-esteem and the absence of self-protective attributional biases. *Journal of Personality and Social Psychology, 52,* 72–80.

Tennen, H., Herzenberger, S., & Nelson, H. F. (1987). Depressive attributional style: The role of self-esteem. *Journal of Personality, 55,* 631–660.

Webster, D. M., & Kruglanski, A. W. (1994). Individual-differences in need for cognitive closure. *Journal of Personality and Social Psychology, 67,* 1049–1062.

Webster, D. M., Richter, L., & Kruglanski, A. W. (1996). On leaping to conclusions when feeling tired: Mental fatigue effects on impressional primacy. *Journal of Experimental Social Psychology, 32,* 181–195.

Weiner, B. (1986). Cognition, emotion and action. In R. M. Sorrentino & E. T. Higgins (Eds.), *Handbook of motivation and cognition: Foundations of social behaviour* (pp. 281–312). New York: Guilford Press.

Williams, J. M. G., Watts, F. N., MacLeod, C., & Mathews, A. (1997). *Cognitive psychology and emotional disorders* (2nd ed.). London: Wiley.

Young, H. F., & Bentall, R. P. (submitted). *Social reasoning in deluded, depressed and normal subjects: Attributional shift following the presentation of distinctiveness, consistency and consensus information.* Manuscript submitted for publication.

Cognitive Rehabilitation for Schizophrenia: Enhancing Social Cognition by Strengthening Neurocognitive Functioning

8

William D. Spaulding and Jeffrey S. Poland

An exciting recent development in treatment and rehabilitation of schizophrenia is the accumulation of evidence that the persistent cognitive impairments associated with the disorder are responsive to therapeutic psychological interventions (Corrigan, Hirschbeck, & Wolfe, 1995; Corrigan & Storzbach, 1993; Hogarty & Flesher, in press; Medalia, Aluma, Tyron, & Merriam, 1998; Spaulding, Reed, Sullivan, Richardson, & Weiler, 1999; Storzbach & Corrigan, 1996; Wykes, Reeder, Corner, Williams, & Everitt, 1999). It has been known for some time that among people with schizophrenia, impaired performance in laboratory tasks is affected by treatmentlike experimental manipulations. The most recent findings are beginning to show treatment effects in the domain of social functioning as well as in naturalistic settings. The advent of theories and models for *social* cognition in psychiatric disorders (Penn, Corrigan, Bentall, & Racenstein, 1997; see also the other chapters in this book) raises the question of whether and how social cognitive processes are involved in these treatment effects.

This chapter discusses the implications of cognitive treatment for the social competence impairments of schizophrenia. Before discussing those implications, however, it is necessary to first consider a number of prerequisite issues concerning the nature of schizophrenia, the general nature of cognition, and the types of changes that treatment is known to bring about.

Complications and Ambiguities Concerning Cognitive Impairment in Schizophrenia

First, as always, it is important to remember that schizophrenia is, after all, a somewhat arbitrary terminological convention, not a valid disease entity or any other "natural kind" (Boyd, 1991; Hacking, 1991). It would be a breakthrough indeed to find *anything* unique to schizophrenia, including cognitive impairments, social or otherwise, but a century of research indicates that this is not likely to happen. "Cognitive impairments" have more experimentally demonstrable validity as scientific constructs than does schizophrenia, which arguably is not even a construct but often is mistakenly treated as one. With respect to the etiological "origins" of cognitive impairment, the clinical heterogeneity of schizophrenia reflects experimental findings suggesting that key information is corrupted in different ways or at different points in the system in different patients. We stand to learn less by studying the role of cognitive impairments "in schizophrenia" than by studying the role of cognitive impairments in the specific developmental, biological, and psychological processes that the diagnostic label imperfectly connotes.

Second, although strong evidence exists that social cognition represents a distinct sector of human cognitive functioning (reviewed by Penn, Corrigan, Bentall, & Racenstein, 1997), some specifics of that distinction remain unclear. For example, the type of information processed in social cognitive subsystems is probably different from the type processed in other subsystems, but the processes themselves—the algorithms by which information is analyzed and transformed—may not always be different. Some subsystems may be highly specialized by evolution and exclusively dedicated to processing social information, whereas others are more general purpose, producing what we call *social cognition* when they process social information.

Similarly, "social" and "nonsocial" subsystems may be identical at one level of organization but different at another. For example, neurophysiological mechanisms such as those associated with neurotransmitters and their receptors may be identical across several subsystems, even though differences in anatomical organization across those subsystems produce different processing capabilities and characteristics. At molar levels of organization, anatomically similar subsystems may perform differently because they are processing different kinds of information or are regulated by different external subsystems.

Those ambiguities have important implications for theoretical models of schizophrenia as well as for clinical assessment and treatment. The "first fact" in the cognitive psychopathology of schizophrenia is that impairments are pervasively distributed throughout the system (for discussion of the methodological and clinical implications of this fact , see Chapman & Chapman, 1978, and Spaulding, 1986, respectively). Even though the disorder may involve impairments in distinctively social aspects of cognition, those impairments may be influenced by factors that also affect other cognitive subsystems. Some social cognitive subsystems may be impaired by factors indigenous to those subsystems, whereas others may be impaired because they rely on information from external, nonsocial subsystems that are impaired. The latter case reflects the familiar information-processing dictum, "garbage in–garbage out." Although the behavioral consequences of different impairments may be equivalent, whether a specific impairment is the source of dysfunction or simply a downstream victim of informational "garbage" has implications for etiology and for selection of treatment objectives.

Conversely, contemporary models of human cognition eschew such simplistic pathways of information processing. We understand cognition not as *linear,* but as *systemic,* wherein information is passed up, down, and across the system's organizational levels and subsystems (i.e., its *modules*) with such complex reciprocity that the "direction" of information flow has limited meaning (Figure 8.1). This process includes information that is exchanged between social and nonsocial subsystems in the course of planning and executing social behavior. There is thus some question as to whether such a thing as a "source" or "origin" of functional cognitive impairment actually exists. In human cognition, the garbage in–garbage out principle can be misleading. Information can be "corrupted" at multiple points in a systemic, reciprocal information exchange. In this sense, it may not be useful to try to determine whether social cognition is impaired by nonsocial cognition, or vice versa.

This problem predates the rise of social cognitive theories in psychopathology. When cognitive models of schizophrenia were based on simple models of human cognition, it made sense to attempt to identify the point in that linear organization where processing first shows impairments (Cromwell & Spaulding, 1978). Those attempts did not lead to breakthrough insights about schizophrenia, however, because cognition is systemic, not linear. The experimental findings quickly became complex and difficult to interpret, suggesting multiple origins of impairments, cognitive and otherwise, in a heterogeneous subject population. At one time, looking for the origin of cognitive impairment in schizophrenia had the romantic appeal of seeking the headwaters of the Nile. Now it seems more like chasing one's tail. (Cromwell, 1984, invoked more mythic imagery—the quest for the Holy Grail—but with

Old and new models of cognition. Older models of cognition conceptualized information as flowing through a linear sequence of registers (top); newer models conceptualize information as flowing in all directions between processing modules (bottom). The modules may include distinctively social or nonsocial information processing.

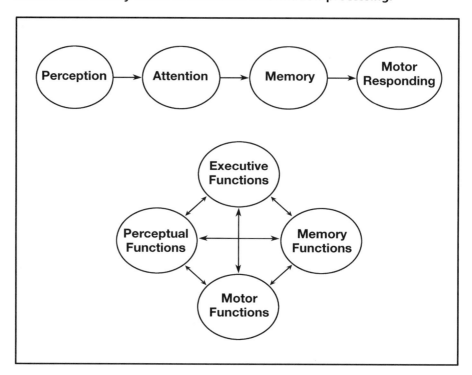

comparable implications about linear causality in schizophrenic cognition.)

The *course* of schizophrenia—with its vulnerability, prodromal, acute, postacute, and residual phases—complicates the relationships between cognitive subsystems. In the residual phase, impairments in social cognition probably reflect multiple causal factors, ranging from structural brain anomalies to a simple absence of information in declarative and procedural memory (normally acquired through developmental learning processes). In the acute phase, residual impairments and their substrates are eclipsed, to a significant degree, by neurophysiological events peculiar to the acute phase, by the cognitive sequelae of those events and, perhaps, by compensatory strategies the affected person uses to counteract the resulting impairments. Somewhere in the postacute phase a shift must occur, as cognitive impairments driven by acute-phase processes give way to those driven by vulnerability-linked and residual-phase processes (Figure 8.2). Little is known about this shift, and it is completely unknown how social cognition, as opposed to other kinds of cognition, is affected.

Any profile of specific neuropsychological measures generally is expected to show more severe and pervasive impairment during the acute episode, with more molecular processes (e.g., sensory-feature processing) showing less fluctuation than more molar processes (e.g., concept manipulation). However, the exact configurations in both acute and residual phases are influenced by many factors and are expected to vary

FIGURE 8.2

Hypothetical neuropsychological profiles of two people with a diagnosis of schizophrenia.

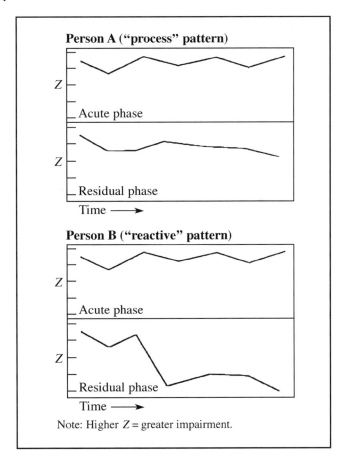

Person A ("process" pattern)

Z

Acute phase

Z

Residual phase

Time ⟶

Person B ("reactive" pattern)

Z

Acute phase

Z

Residual phase

Time ⟶

Note: Higher Z = greater impairment.

even among people with the same diagnosis. The profile during the residual phase generally is the more important limiting factor in rehabilitation, but in some people, the acute phase may be clinically indistinguishable from the residual phase. The traditional process-reactive distinction reflects individual differences, wherein process schizophrenia is associated with a smaller difference between acute and residual functioning. The neuropsychological measures themselves may be better indicators of phase-related functioning than are traditional indicators (i.e., positive and negative psychotic symptoms), at least in some cases.

Etiology of Impairments in Social Cognition and Implications for Treatment Strategy

The most enduring cognitive deficits in schizophrenia are those that appear prior to onset and which persist in the residual phase. Specific deficits appear at different stages of development, changing in severity and character. This process is thought to be at least partly a result of differential maturation of affected brain subsystems (Walker, 1994; Weinberger & Lipska, 1995). After onset, periods of psychosis may further modify preexisting impairments and produce new impairments.

The vulnerability-linked impairments that appear early in childhood are probably the more or less direct results of prenatal or perinatal CNS insults, whose origins may be genetic, viral, mechanical (e.g., mechanical injury during birth), or autotoxic (e.g., cell death from toxic levels of stress-related hormones). They appear primarily as abnormalities of attention (e.g., Erlenmeyer-Kimling & Cornblatt, 1992) and motor control (e.g., Walker, Savoie, & Davis, 1994). By adolescence, the impairments also are associated with abnormalities in social functioning (Cornblatt, Lenzenweger, Dworkin, & Erlenmeyer-Kimling, 1992; Dworkin et al., 1993) and may therefore play a role in impaired acquisition of social cognitive abilities, but little else is known about this process. Impairments in higher levels of the cognitive system (e.g., in processes that perform complex social valuations and judgments) may not become evident until the neurological substrates of those subsystems are activated in late adolescence and early adulthood. Adult social cognition presumably depends on the abilities that those subsystems provide, so the social cognitive deficits of schizophrenia probably are heavily influenced by the abnormal functioning of those processes and their substrates.

Presumably, then, enduring deficits in social cognition in stable, chronic, residual-phase schizophrenia result from two etiological factors: (a) the cumulative effects of cognitive impairments on the acquisition of normal adult social cognition through learning and related mechanisms, especially during critical developmental periods (hereafter, the *compromised acquisition* factor) and (b) the continuing direct effects of specific, ongoing, vulnerability-linked and residual cognitive impairments, both social and nonsocial, at all levels of the cognitive system (hereafter, the *active impairment* factor).

These putative etiological factors are associated with the evolution of two relatively distinct approaches to cognitive treatment. One approach, more relevant to the active impairment factor, is to identify specific impaired processes and "correct," "remediate," or "normalize" them. This approach evolved originally from laboratory paradigms in experimental psychopathology (Spaulding, Storms, Goodrich, & Sullivan, 1986), although it was influenced by Meichenbaum's work with self-instructional training in the 1970s (Meichenbaum & Cameron, 1973) and by clinical neuropsychology and rehabilitation of traumatic brain injury in the 1980s (e.g., Ben-Yishay et al., 1985; Goldberg & Weinberger, 1988; Goldstein, 1986; Goldstein & Ruthven, 1983; Levin, Yurgelun-Todd, & Craft, 1989). The specific processes targeted for treatment are drawn primarily from experimental psychopathology and neuropsychology paradigms. They generally lie within a domain of biosystemic organization that increasingly is called *neurocognitive* (see Green, 1998; Green & Nuechterlein, 1999). Our discussion will return later to variants of neurocognitively oriented treatment.

The second approach seeks to modify cognitive activity outside the neurocognitive domain. Beliefs, attributions, logical operations, and social problem solving are typical targets for treatment (Alford & Correia, 1994; Haddock et al., 1998). This approach evolved from schema-oriented cognitive–behavioral therapies, whose applications to depression and other nonpsychotic disorders are well known. The approach does not depend on any particular theory of the etiology of schizophrenic cognitive impairments or on any particular relationship between the processes it typically targets and the neurocognitive impairments of schizophrenia. However, the approach's focus on acquired informational structures and processes, reflecting its origins in social learning theory, is more complementary to the compromised acquisition factor than to the active impairment factor.

During the acute phase of schizophrenia, social cognition is further impaired by gross disruptions in many other domains of cognitive and behavioral functioning. The disruption is so pervasive that it is unclear whether a patient's cognitive functioning during the acute phase is of any relevance to clinical issues of the residual phase (although evidence indicates that cognitive assessment during the acute phase may provide clinically useful information; see Gilbertson, Yao, & Van Kammen, 1994; Spaulding et al., 1999). For that reason, one might expect that treatment strategy should be divided into two stages: (a) resolving the acute episode and (b) addressing specific impairments, social or otherwise, that remain in the residual phase. The boundaries between the acute, post-acute, and residual phases often are unclear, however, leading to major difficulty in interpreting the outcome of treatment that targets cognitive impairments. Especially in chronic populations, some people who are, for practical purposes, "stable" and "in the residual phase" have never responded well to any treatment and in that sense have never recovered from the "acute" phase. People who are less chronic or less severely affected may experience significant fluctuations that do not reach a clinical detection threshold. In a sense, "phase of illness" is defined in terms of observable treatment response; in that context, treatment-refractory impairments *are* residual deficits.

This difficulty applies to understanding biological as well as psychosocial treatment. For example, some evidence (reviewed by Meltzer & McGurk, 1999) indicates that certain atypical antipsychotic drugs are better than typical Neuroleptics in reducing certain cognitive impairments. The improvement may occur because the drugs actually affect residual cognitive impairments, or it may be because they affect episode-linked cognitive impairments (i.e., impairments specifically associated with acute psychosis, but not affected by typical antipsychotics). In other words, the atypical drugs simply may be better at resolving the acute psychosis. Also, it may be that the atypical drugs simply do not exert adverse side effects on cognition to the degree that typical drugs do. Much longitudinal research is required to sort out which treatment effects truly operate on residual impairments and which operate by enhancing recovery from the acute phase or by avoiding side effects.

Cultural trends and common clinical practice tend to lead us to think about treating the acute phase of schizophrenia with drugs and the residual phase with psychosocial approaches (if at all). This approach, however, ultimately is incompatible with a systemic view of human functioning, and research trends already are defying a simplistic dichotomy. As mentioned, interest is increasing in the potential of the newer drugs to improve residual impairments, and evidence shows that psychosocial factors can contribute to resolving acute psychosis (Drury, Birchwood, Cochrane, & MacMillan, 1996a, 1996b). Treatments of the future will most likely combine drug and psychosocial approaches at every point in the course of the disorder; as with the diagnostic label itself, imperfect constructs such as "acute phase" and "residual impairment" will be replaced by ones that more accurately reflect the disease process in individual patients and more directly indicate treatments.

In summary, although theories of schizophrenia have produced two distinct approaches to treatment of cognitive impairment (three, counting pharmacological approaches), it is unclear whether those approaches apply differently to the acute versus residual phase or to social versus nonsocial cognition. The treatment objectives of pharmacological and psychosocial approaches increasingly overlap. Although all the approaches have produced credible evidence of clinical benefit, it is unclear whether they do so through different mechanisms.

The remainder of this discussion focuses on the effects of *neurocognitive* treatment in the *residual phase* and related issues. Whether those effects differ from other treatment effects in other phases remains to be seen.

Two Approaches to Neurocognitive Treatment

At least two comprehensive, systematic approaches to treatment of neurocognitive impairments in schizophrenia have evolved over the past two decades: Integrated Psychological Therapy (IPT; Brenner et al., 1994) and Cognitive Enhancement Therapy (CET; Hogarty & Flesher, 1999, in press). In addition, a wealth of specific therapeutic techniques are available, any of which could be integrated into a more comprehensive modality (e.g., Corrigan, Hirschbeck, & Wolfe, 1995; Medalia et al., 1998; Reed, Sullivan, Penn, Stuve, & Spaulding, 1992; Spaulding et al., 1986). The two comprehensive approaches share the strategy of identifying, isolating, and exercising specific cognitive abilities that typically are impaired in chronic schizophrenia. They use somewhat similar procedures, including a variety of specific exercises—formatted as group activities—that target specific abilities. Both combine a primary focus on cognitive *process*es (i.e., an emphasis on strengthening information processing) with didactic provision of factual information (i.e., the *content* of cognition) pertinent to personal and social functioning.

Arguably, a theoretical difference exists between the two approaches. IPT was developed from classical ideas in experimental psychopathology that predate contemporary interest in distinctively social cognition. CET also draws heavily from experimental psychopathology and neuropsychology, but it is heavily influenced by developmental theories of social cognition. This theoretical difference implies two different types of treatment-effect mechanism. In IPT, treatment effects are thought to accrue in a stepwise fashion. Molecular cognitive processes are exercised first, so that those strengthened molecular processes later can enhance acquisition of molar abilities. Therefore, the rehabilitation process progresses from process-focused therapy to more conventional social skills and interpersonal problem-solving training.

CET is less linear and stepwise. It draws heavily on the theory that a crucial problem in schizophrenia is deficient apprehension of the "gist" of social problems and situations. "Gistful" social cognition is not a gradual compilation of information from more molecular processes (e.g., the gradual synthesis of "the big picture" from informational elements); it is a rapid and conceptual apprehension. The big picture is inferred from a relatively small amount of information about a situation, when that information correlates with specific social schemata (e.g., declarative relationships, social roles, and procedural scripts) stored in memory and acquired in the course of development. The CET approach is guided by the hypothesis (among others) that impairment of processes for identifying and using the "gist" of social situations and interactions is a fundamental limiting factor in schizophrenic social performance.

In controlled outcome studies, both IPT and CET have been shown to be effective in enhancing social competence and performance (Hogarty & Flesher, 1999; Spaulding, Reed, et al., 1999). So far, data is insufficient to conclude whether the mechanisms of their respective treatment effects are as different as their respective theoretical premises. Indeed, the actual procedural differences between the two approaches have yet to be systematically assessed. The subject samples in the two studies were quite different (the IPT participants were severely disabled and involuntarily institutionalized, whereas the CET participants were less severely disabled voluntary outpatients); any differences in outcome or treatment-effect mechanisms are potentially attributable to sample differences. In addition to sheer severity of impairment, the two samples could have been at different points in the continuum from acute to postacute to residual. Systematic comparative studies of the two approaches, across a range of subpopulations, will be necessary to sort this out.

Analyses of Neurocognitive Treatment Effects

In the initial analyses of the IPT outcome trial (Spaulding, Reed, et al., 1999), the participants showed significant improvement *whether they received IPT or not*, most notably on an elaborate measure of social competence, the Assessment of Interpersonal Problem Solving Skills (AIPSS; Donahoe, n.d.; Donahoe, Carter, Bloem, Hirsch, et al., 1990). They also showed improvements on measures of symptom expression and neurocognitive functioning. In addition, the participants who received IPT showed significantly *more* improvement on the AIPSS and on several symptom and neurocognitive measures. The size of the specific IPT treatment effect on AIPSS performance (i.e., the improvement of those who received IPT compared with those who did not) was comparable in size to the differential efficacy of the newer atypical antipsychotic medications over the older Neuroleptics. The symptom and neurocognitive measures that showed specific effects of IPT differed from those that showed nonspecific effects, attributable to psychiatric rehabilitation without IPT.

Taken together, the results of the IPT outcome trial were unequivocal in showing that psychiatric rehabilitation in general—and cognitive treatment in particular—produces significant improvements in social functioning as measured by the AIPSS. Further analyses of the IPT treatment effect were conducted to identify the neurocognitive factors most closely related to changing social competence, as the participants underwent comprehensive psychiatric rehabilitation either with or without IPT (Spaulding, Fleming, et al., 1999). If IPT enhances social competence by enhancing basic neurocognitive processes, then close relationships are expected between changes in the two domains. If, however, gains in social competence reflect gains in distinctively social cognition independent of nonsocial cognition, then correlations between social competence changes and changes in the nonsocial processes, as measured by traditional laboratory neurocognitive tests, are not expected.

The post hoc analyses did not support the hypothesis that the effects of IPT on social competence result from improvements in neurocognitive functioning. This finding energizes the hypothesis that other cognitive processes, perhaps distinctively social in character and not measured by traditional laboratory paradigms, mediate improvements in social competence. Conversely, the analyses also identified an important interaction between IPT and short-term memory, a nonsocial cognitive construct. Memory was one of the neurocognitive measures that showed a strong nonspecific treatment effect but not an IPT-specific effect. Nevertheless, memory improvement *in the presence of IPT* was significantly correlated with AIPSS improvement. In other words, the participants showed memory improvement independent of whether they received IPT, but the improvement helped their AIPSS performance only if they *did* receive IPT.

Several studies now have found relationships between short-term memory and social skills or social competence (Addington & Addington, 1999; Green, 1996; Kern & Green, 1994; Spaulding, Fleming, et al., 1999). This finding may occur simply because memory is a key prerequisite to adequate performance on the tasks used to measure social skills and competence. An additional and more stimulating possibility is that memory reflects certain nonsocial cognitive processes on which social cognition heavily relies. Such a finding would mean that in schizophrenia, memory impairments are a major source of informational garbage, impeding social competence in the residual phase even when the social cognitive processes themselves are intact. The Spaulding, Reed, et al. (1999) participants were medicated optimally and as clinically stable as possible throughout the study, indicating that such memory deficits may be found in the residual phase, or at least in a postacute phase so protracted that it is indistinguishable from the residual phase.

Learning-related processes of information acquisition and short-term memory storage and retrieval increasingly are associated with a group of neurocognitive processes related to *executive functioning* (e.g., Frith & Dolan, 1996; Gabrielli, 1995; Goldman-Rakic, 1990; Houk, 1995; Ito, 1990; Levine, Leven, & Prueitt, 1992). Those functions include problem analysis, planning of complex behavioral responses, working, memory, response monitoring, and concept manipulation. In the Spaulding, Reed, et al. (1999) study, measures of executive functions showed specific and nonspecific treatment effects. Previous studies (Penn et al., 1993; Spohn & Strauss, 1989; see also Spaulding et al., 1994) suggest that memory and executive processing improve in the course of recovery from the acute phase. Laboratory measures may be our best methodological window on an extensive phase-related process of loss and recovery of abilities that are centrally important to normal functioning, although they may not all lie squarely within the domain of social cognition.

Finally, the hypothesis that IPT exerts its effects on social functioning by interacting with other aspects of treatment is indirectly supported by another controlled study of neurocognitive treatment (Wykes et al., 1999). This study used a highly focused neurocognitive treatment approach, giving almost exclusive attention to the molecular levels of neurocognitive functioning. Although the treatment produced clear improvements on laboratory measures of neurocognition, the study found no evidence of generalization to ecologically important aspects of personal or social functioning. However, this study also revealed benefits of neurocognitive treatment in the subjective domain; in particular, participants reported more gains in self-esteem and self-efficacy than participants in the control condition. This finding is potentially important because subjective distress and poor self-esteem are common in schizophrenia and, in fact, often are the targets of schema-oriented CBT. It certainly is logical that improved neurocognitive performance would be associated with less subjective distress. Researchers' preoccupation with operationalizing social competence and performance could lead us to overlook another, completely separate benefit of neurocognitive treatment. The Wykes et al. (1999) finding should inspire further studies of neurocognitive treatment and subjective well-being.

The accumulating experimental findings on patients' response to psychiatric rehabilitation, particularly on neurocognitive treatment, call for development of explanatory theories. A theory explaining patients' response to treatment should incorporate (or at least not conflict with) what we already know about the neurophysiology, neuropsychology, and cognitive psychopathology of schizophrenia. In addition, the theory ideally would incorporate key insights about the nature and role of social cognition. The following section demonstrates that it already is possible to construct the outlines of such a theory.

COGNITIVE DISORGANIZATION AND SOCIAL COGNITION

First, it is necessary to postulate and describe a postacute state in which cognitive operations are disabled functionally but amenable to psychosocial treatment. Broen and Storms (1966) proposed a predecessor model of such a state; their idea was based on Hullian learning theory (see also Spaulding et al., 1986). In the Broen-Storms model, acute psychosis was hypothesized to represent a collapse of response hierarchies that is brought about by extreme levels of psychophysiological arousal. The elements of those hierarchies include "internal" responses (today they would be called "cognitive operations") that, under normal circumstances, direct attention, mediate memory storage and retrieval, and control motor behavior. The responses are organized into hierarchies of relative habit strength, as determined by differential reinforcement and punishment in specific environmental circumstances. For example, specific food getting behaviors most frequently reinforced have the strongest habit strength among related behaviors, and are therefore at the top of the hierarchy. This hierarchical organization optimizes behavioral response to the environment. Intrinsic structural characteristics of the nervous system cause the hierarchy to "collapse," or become functionally ineffective, during periods of extreme arousal associated with acute psychosis. After arousal returns to more moderate levels, the hierarchies may reorganize spontaneously, but they may not necessarily reorganize into the optimal configurations created by interactions with the environment. Optimal reorganization requires a *relearning* process, by which response hierarchies are again adjusted to match the demands of the environment.

An updated version of the Broen-Storms hierarchy-collapse model draws on recent developments in the neuropsychology of learning and behavioral organization (see Houk, 1995; Houk & Wise, 1993). Mechanisms that appear to be located in the basal ganglia and structures in the primitive frontal cortex continuously monitor environmental demands for particular responses and adjust the *activation thresholds* of those responses accordingly. The activation threshold of a particular response is the neurophysiological factor that determines the probability that the response will be elicited by a specific stimulus. The adjustment of activation thresholds in the course of interacting with the environment is a learning process. This adjustment process corresponds to construction and maintenance of Hullian response hierarchies in the Broen-Storms model. Failure of this mechanism corresponds to collapse of the response hierarchies.

The neurotransmitter dopamine appears to play a central role in the normal operation of the mechanisms that match response activation thresholds to environmental demand. Dopamine *dysregulation* appears to have an important role in acute psychosis. Among other consequences, dopamine dysregulation would be expected to disrupt normal maintenance and adjustment of activation thresholds, resulting in disorganized or dysfunctional response hierarchies. Thus, the "extreme psychophysiological arousal" factor in the Broen-Storms model is probably a dopamine dysregulation factor, but it leads to the same consequences for behavioral organization. The crucial idea remains that even a temporary condition of acute neurophysiological dysregulation creates a lingering consequence: functional disorganization of the person's response repertoire. The repertoire must be reorganized according to the same way in which it was originally constructed—through interaction with environmental demands.

Contemporary paradigms of cognitive psychology provide a much richer characterization of the nature of internal responses than was available to a Hullian theory. Today we can specify myriad cognitive operations, such as memory storage, deploying processing capacity, scanning, feature processing, concept formation, and accessing information in various memory stores, that must be used in specific ways to perform specific learned tasks. Any operation may be a fundamental element in the learned response hierarchies that are subject to disorganization in the wake of acute psychosis. It should be possible, through systematic experimentation, to identify specific cognitive operations, repertoires, and performance abilities that are particularly important in the disorganization and reorganization process of schizophrenia and related conditions. In fact, the analyses of cognitive and behavioral response to treatment described in this chapter have already begun this process.

A moment's reflection on the complexity of human behavior clarifies the meaning and importance of response-organization mechanisms. Humans are capable of acquiring and storing a much larger response repertoire than can be activated and performed at any one time. Different subsets of this repertoire are required for different activities and circumstances, even at the most molecular levels of cognition (including neurocognitive levels). For example, the perceptual, attentional, memory, conceptual, and analytical processes required for playing baseball are different from those required to negotiate an agreement with a marital partner. In this sense, it can be said that performance of different roles and scripts requires different subsets of molecular cognitive abilities. As people move from one role or script performance to the next, they must be able to rapidly activate different subsets of cognitive abilities.

Skilled role performance is a highly fluid process. Efficiency reflects *ongoing* environmental demand. When activation of specific elemental abilities is a crucial aspect of performance, performance can deteriorate noticeably after brief periods of disuse. To prevent this deterioration, it sometimes is necessary to create "artificial" environmental demands for particular responses. For example, even the most experienced musicians must rehearse daily to maintain their "performance edge." Rehearsal, in this context, is an artificial environmental demand for particular psychomotor responses. Some highly skilled abilities (or roles or responses) require no artificial rehearsal because daily life provides plenty of demand, a situation that generally is true for the skills associated with routine social interaction, although people who experience periods of social isolation may temporarily lose their interactive "edge" as well (e.g., attempting to converse in a second language after a period of disuse is a common experience of this phenomenon). Artificial or not, ongoing demand for particular elemental abilities lowers the neurophysiological activation threshold of those abilities, thus enhancing their accessibility to the performer.

Recent insights from models of social cognition suggest an especially important domain in which functioning is disrupted by response disorganization. Performance in complex (often social) situations relies heavily on the human capability to "chunk" large amounts of information for efficient processing. Multiple stimulus features of a complex situation are chunked into single *symbolic representations* of the situation. The chunking process enhances the efficiency of recognizing important but complex environmental demands and activating required responses accordingly. Just as activation thresholds for responses are tuned to configurations of environmental stimuli that signal a performance demand, symbolic situation representations also are tuned to be activated by those configurations. In turn, the responses are tuned to be activated by the symbolic representations. As a result, complex response patterns can be activated and made accessible when only part of the raw data in a stimulus configuration has been processed (i.e., the data necessary to activate the symbolic representation).

In a social context, people apprehend and act on the *gist* of a complex interpersonal situation according to this process. In the course of human development, people normally acquire and maintain an extensive repertoire of symbolic representations not only of situations but of complex response patterns, in the form of scripts and roles. Gistful social cognition is a process of rapidly matching situations to response scripts and roles before exhaustively processing all the attendant information. For example, interpersonal conflict is a generic human situation. People apprehend the gist of an interaction to be "I have a conflict with this other person" as soon as the stimulus features of the situation activate a symbolic representation of "interpersonal conflict situations." The key stimulus features activating the "conflict" gist representation usually would be evidence of specific incompatible goals, accompanied by evidence of distress in either or both people. When the "conflict" gist is apprehended, scripts and roles relevant to analyzing and resolving conflicts are activated and thus made accessible for performance. Performance of appropriate scripts and roles guides further information processing for managing the situation, gathering more data and, ultimately, resolving the conflict.

Faulty or inefficient apprehension of the gist of complex social situations has clear implications for the efficiency and competence of social behavior. "Gistful" processing of complex social situations clearly would be compromised by disruption of the mechanisms by which specific stimulus features activate specific situational gist representations, which in turn activate response roles, scripts, and so forth. In the response-disorganization model, the person in a postacute or residual phase of a psychotic disorder is experiencing reduced access to a broad range of cognitive operations and the symbolic representations that activate them, which are required for particular tasks. Even after re-regulation of dopaminergic behavioral organization mechanisms, the molecular cognitive abilities required for skilled interaction in a social situation (e.g., reading facial expressions, apprehending the gist of a situation, accessing scripts in memory, and analyzing conflicts) are less accessible in that situation than optimum performance demands. In the laboratory, the abilities needed to perform memory and executive tasks are comparably inaccessible.

Finally, the ubiquity of executive cognition in treatment response findings has stimulated one more elaboration of the response disorganization model, following a computer analogy (Spaulding et al., 1994). When a computer "crashes," it is because some intervening factor (e.g., line voltage fluctuations or software incompatibility) disrupts the functioning of the computer's "executive" software, its operating system. A computer's operating system consists of programs that perform the computer's "housekeeping" functions (e.g., managing memory resources and switching between external devices) and execute commands to run other programs. The operating system resides in core memory, for maximum efficiency and accessibility, but that is also what makes the computer vulnerable to a "crash." Some of the executive programs lost in a crash are the ones that are needed to load others into core memory, so the procedure for resuming computer operation after the crash must follow a particular sequence. The human biological "computer" doubtless contains corresponding "executive programs" whose operation is prerequisite to other cognitive operations. Those programs would be the ones that must "come back on line" first in the process of postacute reorganization. The data suggest that measures of executive functioning and short-term memory may be our best clinical indicators of prerequisite abilities. This theory makes especially good sense in the context of psychiatric rehabilitation because so much of the rehabilitation treatment effect is presumed to involve acquisition and retention of information (i.e., memory) and timely activation and performance of related behavioral skills (i.e., executive functioning).

The updated response-disorganization model thus accounts for

- the nonspecific effects of psychosocial treatment on cognitive impairments in the residual phase;
- the additional benefits of process-focused cognitive therapies such as IPT and CET; and
- the prognostic significance of measures of memory and executive functioning.

In addition, the model partially accounts for the pathways that the treatment effect appears to follow.

In the language of the original response-disorganization model, conventional psychiatric rehabilitation provides the environmental conditions needed to reestablish adaptive response hierarchies in the postacute phase. These conditions include consistent environmental demand for key cognitive operations, repetition, regularity, and reinforcement. The conditions follow from the priority that the rehabilitation approach puts on timely performance of basic, ecologically important behavior patterns, such as self-care, work, and socialization. Rehabilitation approaches most heavily influenced by social learning theory (see Glynn & Mueser, 1986) do this most focally, with different formal techniques to reinforce specific adaptive responses. This accounts for the superior clinical outcome that those approaches achieve (Paul & Menditto, 1992).

The additive benefits of process-focused cognitive treatments such as IPT or CET come from those treatments' ability to enhance activation of specific cognitive abilities particularly important to social competence, such as apprehension of the physical details of a social situation or gistful activation of roles and scripts. Cognitive therapy creates environmental demands for the key abilities that surpass the demands in the milieu in which rehabilitation occurs, much as intensive rehearsal creates a focused demand for performance-quality skills in a musician.

Patients whose performance on executive and memory tasks indicates a greater degree of reorganization of prerequisite cognitive abilities, regardless of the point in the rehabilitation process, are those who show the best response to subsequent rehabilitation tasks, such as social skills training (Spaulding, Fleming, et al., 1999). These patients have reorganized enough of their "operating system," with its attendant "housekeeping" functions, to effectively process the information involved in rehabilitation tasks.

The updated response-disorganization model also speaks to two more important issues: individual variability in schizophrenia and the distinction between social and nonsocial cognitive impairments as it relates to treatment strategy. With respect to the former, different people clearly have different resources in the struggle to reorganize response hierarchies in the wake of acute psychosis. Those differences are expected to affect the rate at which spontaneous or therapeutically induced reorganization occurs. All other factors being equal, a person with developmentally more advanced cognition and metacognition would show a postacute course different from a person with less advanced resources; the former person would more quickly regain functioning in critical cognitive domains. It long has been accepted that developmental variability affects the expression, course, and outcome of schizophrenia. This tenet is reflected in classical concepts of psychopathology such as *premorbid adjustment* and the *process-reactive* dimension of schizophrenia (e.g., Cromwell & Spaulding, 1978; Spaulding, 1986). The variability in schizophrenia suggests that some patients have such strong developmental resources that they can achieve substantial postacute cognitive reorganization without much help; others are so resource-poor that they never regain crucial cognitive abilities without help, and many fall somewhere between those extremes. Thus, the updated response-disorganization model points to a specific mechanism—the speed and efficiency of postacute cognitive reorganization—by which developmental factors affect the course of the disorder. This brings the model into conformity with the well-established relationships between course, prognosis, and developmental factors such as intelligence and premorbid adjustment.

A related source of individual variability is the *baseline* efficiency of response-organization mechanisms. Vulnerability to schizophrenia is associated with abnormalities in the same CNS structures and putative subsystems implicated in acute response disorganization. In addition to the attentional and psychomotor impairments observable in vulnerable children, the cognitive sequelae of those abnormalities would include inefficient response organization (in fact, the attentional and psychomotor impairments themselves may be the *result* of inefficient response organization). In the language of the original response-disorganization model, developmental abnormalities would result in inefficient construction of response hierarchies. In the updated model, it would correspond to inefficient informational chunking, adjustment of activation thresholds, and related processes. In both models, the result would be suboptimal response repertoires, impaired behavioral performance, more exposure to stress, and greater vulnerability to acute disorganization. The overall *severity* of baseline impairment in response organization efficiency would be influenced by a multiplicity of factors, both organismic (e.g., the extent of structural lesions) and environmental (e.g., education, learning opportunities, and social support associated with socioeconomic status) and would thus be highly variable, contributing to the heterogeneity of schizophrenia during all phases of the disorder. To the degree that the baseline impairments result from irreversible lesions, they represent a limiting factor in response to any treatment whose benefits accrue from enhancing response reorganization.

With respect to the distinction between social and nonsocial cognition, cognition that is most unequivocally social is that which involves social *content*, in the form of scripts, roles, and other schemata. It does not help to be able to efficiently access scripts and roles if the information in those structures is flawed or impoverished. Manipulation of the content of informational structures is a key tactic in schema-oriented cognitive–behavioral therapy, but it is less so in neurocognitive therapy. The updated response-disorganization model suggests that the focus of rehabilitation should shift from cognitive *process* to cognitive *content* as the individual patient regains the basic cognitive abilities to access information structures, and thus to enhance the content of those structures. This progression is more theoretically meaningful and potentially more measurable than those that traditionally dominate clinical assessment and decision making. An example of the latter is "resolving the acute episode," usually imperfectly operationalized as "suppressing the symptoms of acute psychosis," before proceeding with other aspects of rehabilitation.

How to Provide Neurocognitive Treatment for Schizophrenia

Demand is growing for provision of neurocognitive treatment in settings in which people with severe and disabling psychiatric conditions are served. At least one set of published guidelines for treatment of schizophrenia (American Psychiatric Association, 1997) mentions cognitive rehabilitation as a treatment of known efficacy showing promise for standard use. The demand predates appearance of large-scale controlled trials, so it most likely is inspired by the compelling logic of the approach, by the congruent experiences and observations of clinicians and people who have directly experienced schizophrenia, and by the urgent need for more and better services for this population. Concerns about undue optimism are being voiced (see Bellack, 1992; Jaeger, 1999; cf. Medalia, 1999). Developing neurocognitive treatment capability will be a significant investment and will compete with other priorities for limited fiscal resources. The burden of proof, however, is shifting, and soon providers may feel more pressed to explain why they are *not* providing a service of such promise. In that context, the situation justifies some discussion of how to actually provide neurocognitive treatment within the mental health systems that typically serve people with severe and disabling conditions.

The first resource requirement is a clinician with the training and background to assess cognitive and neuropsychological problems in people with severe and disabling disorders. Psychologists with substantial background in psychopathology, neuropsychology, and psychiatric rehabilitation are probably best suited to this role. Our understanding of the neuropsychological aspects of schizophrenia and related disorders is new enough that no universally accepted standards exist for assessment techniques (e.g., standard test batteries) or professional preparation and credentialing. Nevertheless, the ability to identify neurocognitive impairments and measure their changes over time is a prerequisite to responsibly providing any treatment (psychological or pharmacological) designed to address such impairments. The assessing clinician must be prepared to administer and interpret a range of neuropsychological instruments, especially measures of selective attention, vigilance, short-term and working memory, and executive functioning. Functional assessment of work, living, and social skills also is necessary, as is a formal functional analysis of behavior. Expertise in assessing the symptoms and related characteristics of schizophrenia is important in order to determine targets for treatment and distinguish between acute, postacute, and residual impairment. Because longitudinal assessment of change over time usually is necessary, expertise in experimental and quasi-experimental design applied to clinical assessment also is required.

Neurocognitive treatment can be provided in a variety of formats, which should be matched to the clientele, resources, and environmental characteristics of the specific service setting. The literature provides procedural descriptions of specific techniques easily adapted to a dyadic, psychotherapylike format (e.g., Corrigan & Storzbach, 1993; Reed et al., 1992; Spaulding et al., 1986). In this approach, exercises are constructed in an ad hoc manner, derived from the results of laboratory testing, direct observation, and functional assessment. Progress toward short-term treatment goals typically is assessed using laboratory tasks adapted to measure the specific impairments targeted for treatment. Generalization of treatment effects and progress toward long-term goals are assessed through measuring changes in performance of ecologically significant skills and in the abilities hypothesized to be affected by the targeted cognitive impairments. For example, when performance in a work setting is hypothesized to be compromised by distractibility and deficits in continuous attention, improvement on laboratory measures of attention and vigilance is expected following neurocognitive treatment, followed in turn by improvement on in vivo measures of work performance. Multiple-baseline, quasi-experimental designs capable of detecting the separate effects of medication, neurocognitive treatment, and other interventions are generally well suited to this purpose.

Individualized neurocognitive treatment usually is provided by including the specific exercises in a broad, dyadic rehabilitation counseling and psychotherapy context. The exercises are accompanied by collaborative formulation of relevant treatment and rehabilitation goals, discussion of how the abilities addressed by the exercises are important in natural situations, assignment and review of "homework" (i.e., in vivo applications of the exercises), and review and evaluation of rehabilitation progress. For example, "better interactions with people," evidenced by a lack of friends and frequent interpersonal altercations, may be identified as a treatment goal. Functional and laboratory assessment may indicate that the problem derives from social skill deficits, to which distractibility, poor interpersonal problem solving and a rigid, stereotypic way of analyzing complex social situations contribute (the assessment also would indicate that the deficits do not derive from a transient, acute psychotic state). Exercises demanding focused attention, resistance to distraction, and conceptual flexibility would be included in dyadic sessions, accompanied by interpersonal problem-solving and social skills training in group formats. In addition to the neurocognitive exercises, the dyadic sessions would include review of performance data in therapy and in vivo situations, discussion of the role of neurocognitive factors in ongoing experiences relevant to social competence and comfort, review of objective measures of social performance, and appraisal of progress toward the goal.

In addition to a dyadic, psychotherapy-like setting, individualized neurocognitive exercises can be integrated with occupational and recreational therapy, work, and other rehabilitative activities. The optimal setting varies with individual needs and rehabilitation goals.

For group-format treatment, both IPT and CET are potentially suitable. Both are highly manualized, and the IPT manual is commercially available (Brenner et al., 1994). No studies have been conducted on the skills or qualifications required to effectively provide these modalities. However, considerable clinical judgment is required to determine when to persist with a particular exercise, when to provide special assistance to group members, and when to move on. Extensive experience with neuropsychological assessment, functional assessment, and group skill training most likely are necessary.

The original developers of IPT recommend providing this modality separately to recipients with higher and lower cognitive functioning. The therapy procedures do not differ, but the rate of progress through the modality is expected to be slower with lower functioning groups. Comprehensive neuropsychological assessment is not required for group assignment, but a reliable evaluation of baseline cognitive and neuro-cognitive functioning, taking into account episodic psychosis, is necessary. Such assessment capability should be in the repertoire of any program or agency that serves people with severe and disabling psychiatric disorders.

The IPT subprograms proceed as a sequence of structured group activities, each demanding various combinations of cognitive abilities and operations. The therapist introduces each activity, guides the participation of the group members, and evaluates their responses. The therapist is given some flexibility to repeat specific activities when patients have difficulties that further practice may overcome. All the activities are designed to include social interaction between patients, and the therapist selectively facilitates social interaction relevant to completion of an activity. The Cognitive Differentiation subprogram includes activities designed to exercise concept manipulation and related operations. For example, a sorting task engages the group in alternative strategies for sorting objects of different color, size, and shape. The Social Perception subprogram includes activities designed to exercise the processing of social information (e.g., systematic examination and description of pictures of people involved in social situations). The Verbal Communication subprogram is designed to exercise the cognitive substrates of verbal interaction, including attention and short-term memory. In one such activity, patients carefully listen to each others' verbal statements, then repeat the statements verbatim, then paraphrase them. Across all the subprograms, the activities are graduated in complexity and amount of required social interaction.

To manage group dynamics, the therapist follows a set of interactional rules, which include maintaining a friendly but matter-of-fact social atmosphere; never telling patients they are wrong or factually incorrect, but rather eliciting group feedback and discussion; empathetically reflecting emotional expressions when they occur; clarifying patients' verbalizations; and encouraging participation by all group members. Bizarre behavior may be met with a brief reflection of its affective component (e.g., "Mr. Smith, it appears you find this topic distressing") but it is otherwise ignored. Disruptive behavior is met with a request to desist; if it continues, the patient is excused from the session. When participant populations include people who are involuntary recipients of treatment or who otherwise have difficulty engaging in treatment, a contingency management system may be a necessary adjunct to IPT (Spaulding, Reed, et al., 1999).

Conclusion and Future Directions

The updated response-disorganization model is a good start toward understanding cognitive treatment and rehabilitation effects in chronic schizophrenia and related disorders. It also sheds some light on the relationships between social and nonsocial cognition and how they may interact in the course of treatment. The elucidation of some gaps and vagaries in our knowledge could have a significant impact on development of treatment techniques.

One unresolved issue is whether "social versus nonsocial" is a dimension of cognition that lies more or less parallel to the "molecular versus molar" dimension. On the one hand, current views of social cognition hold that even molecular levels of cognition have become specialized for processing social information. For example, the feature processing used to read alphanumeric characters may be different from that used to read facial expressions. If this is the case, neurocognitive treatment intended to enhance social competence should probably focus on molecular *social* processes and avoid spending valuable time enhancing other molecular abilities that do not contribute to social competence. On the other hand, it often is argued that the essence of social cognition is the social situation and the personal relevance of the information being processed. This view suggests that it is not the specific process that is important but the context in which it is addressed. Despite their theoretical differences, both IPT and CET include tactics for creating a personal and social context for all the cognitive exercises those modalities include. For individualized neurocognitive treatment, rehabilitation counseling and the dyadic relationship provide important social context. Thus, as cognitive therapies are developed, researchers must carefully and systematically analyze the relative importance of the level of cognitive organization (molar vs. molecular) at which treatment is directed, whether the information processing involved is distinctively social in nature, and whether treatment is presented in a personally meaningful social context.

A related issue concerns the social effects of nonsocial cognitive treatment, and vice versa. It remains unclear whether treatment directed at nonsocial neurocognitive processes benefits social cognition and competence. The IPT trial certainly revealed a beneficial effect on social competence, as measured by the AIPSS, but this result did not come about as a direct consequence of therapeutic effects on neurocognitive functioning as measured in the laboratory. However, IPT does produce improvements in some molecular cognitive functions not produced by conventional treatment and rehabilitation. It is possible that the neurocognitive pathway by which response to conventional treatments is enhanced simply was not detected by the particular test battery Spaulding, Fleming, et al. (1999) used. Until a more direct pathway from cognitive treatment to cognitive improvement to sociobehavioral improvement can be demonstrated, this will be the "missing link" of the response disorganization model.

Part of the problem is lack of clarity about what constitutes a good measure of social cognition. Laboratory measures increasingly focus on processing information with social content, such as Corrigan's Social Cue Perception Task (Corrigan, 1993; Corrigan et al., 1995). Such measures, however, do not necessarily meet the requirement of personal relevance and meaning. A social cue or facial expression presented in the lab is still not the same as one that occurs naturally in the context of a person's life. The major methodological challenge to this field of study may be to develop measures of social cognition that combine personal relevance and meaning with laboratory reliability and precision.

Social competence assessment instruments such as the AIPSS use an artificial social context, created by the narrative quality of their primary stimulus materials (social vignettes) and by involving the person being assessed in role-play interactions. This approach may invoke genuine social cognition to a greater extent than socially sterile laboratory tasks do, but the quantitative parameters of that invocation are unknown. Indeed, people with schizophrenia may show abnormally weak activation of social cognition in response to artificial context, as yet another expression of more general neurocognitive and social cognitive impairments. This weakness would be difficult to demonstrate experimentally using current methodology because measures of AIPSS performance are derived from functional rather than neuropsychological analyses of social performance. Even the cognitive construct most often used in social skills training, problem solving, is derived from functional, not cognitive, analyses and has been pointedly criticized on those grounds (Bellack, Morrison, & Mueser, 1989). A truly cognitive understanding of AIPSS performance would require an entirely new analytic approach, which will probably come about as a synthesis of the many ideas about assessing social cognition, at both the molecular and molar levels of organization, that this book describes.

Should such an analysis become possible, familiar principles and constructs may gain new meaning. For example, although social problem-solving ability is not properly a cognitive paradigm and although social cognition probably does not work according to the accepted problem-solving model, the model probably does identify fundamental aspects of social performance that are supported by specifiable cognitive and neurocognitive functions. This model may ultimately bridge functional and cognitive analyses of important aspects of social skill performance. The specific attentional, perceptual, memory, and executive processes needed to recognize conflict, analyze its origins, and formulate and perform solutions *in a real or artificial social context* may prove to be measurable targets for assessment and treatment. For another example, if activation of distinctively social cognition by role playing or related manipulations could be quantitatively measured, the methods of affect- and attitude-induction familiar to experimental social psychologists may find new usefulness in clinical assessment of schizophrenia.

The measurement problem applies to treatment design as well. Without operational measures of social cognition, it is impossible to determine whether modalities such as IPT or CET really do have uniquely social cognitive components. Even schema-oriented cognitive therapy approaches, which more explicitly target cognition presumed to be uniquely social, have not been shown to produce changes in uniquely social cognition. It is possible that the effects of such treatments really accrue from unintended effects on *nonsocial* cognition!

Although the response-disorganization model partially clarifies the theoretical difference between social and nonsocial cognition, gray areas remain. Sometimes cognitive *content* is indistinguishable from cognitive *process*. The idea of gistful social cognition presents a particularly interesting example. Apprehension of the gist of an interaction depends on a good "library" of gist representations as well as on the processes of chunking incoming information and *recognizing* that a situation is symbolically represented by chunked information in memory. With current methods, it may be impossible to distinguish failures in gistful processing from failures stemming from a bad library of gist representations. Intensive research, including new measures of "gistful" social cognition, will be necessary to develop clinical techniques to reliably pinpoint a patient's problem and to decide whether to target the process or the content.

Meanwhile, current hypotheses about the nature of social cognition (see Penn et al., 1997, as well as the other chapters in this book) raise the possibility that the answer to current vagaries is "all of the above." Both social and nonsocial processes are probably distributed along the continuum from molecular to molar cognition. Different impairments probably play different etiological roles in different patients. In a reciprocally interactive information-processing system, the effects of treatment directed at *any* system component are expected to be distributed throughout the system. In the end, the most effective cognitive treatment approach for schizophrenia may be the one that provides the greatest number of avenues to all levels and divisions of the system.

Finally, other factors no doubt are involved in patients' response to psychiatric rehabilitation, beyond developmental resources and cognitive reorganization. For example, dysfunction of the hypothalamic-pituitary-adrenal (HPA) neuroendocrine axis is associated with cognitive impairment in chronic schizophrenia, and HPA dysfunction appears to normalize when people with chronic schizophrenia undergo comprehensive rehabilitation (see Spaulding, Fleming, et al., 1999). One of the hormones of the HPA axis, cortisol, is known to have a role in activation of frontal cortical neurons. A neuroendocrine mechanism could complement the effects of postacute cognitive reorganization. Much additional research is needed to articulate the relationships between social, cognitive, neuropsychological, and neuroendocrine functioning in rehabilitation of severe psychiatric conditions. The good news is that HPA models of cognitive impairment appear to be compatible with response-disorganization models; in fact, they may represent parallel mechanisms with complementary purposes, which simply operate in different time frames.

Meanwhile, research findings already provide a clear mandate to move forward. Both process-focused and content-focused cognitive treatment have been shown to benefit patients with severe, chronic, and disabling psychiatric conditions such as schizophrenia. As with the history of psychotherapy and psychopharmacotherapy research in previous decades, we have established the effectiveness of the treatment before fully understanding how the benefits accrue and for whom and under what conditions. Research on both process- and content-focused therapy needs to include thorough analyses of the mediating factors and mechanisms of treatment effects. Those analyses need to include measures of uniquely social cognition. As our understanding of the role of social cognition evolves, application of this understanding to treatment and rehabilitation should be expected to gradually clarify current ambiguities and lead to increasingly effective interventions.

References

Addington, J., & Addington, D. (1999). Neurocognitive and social functioning in schizophrenia. *Schizophrenia Bulletin, 25,* 173–182.

Alford, B., & Correia, C. (1994). Cognitive therapy of schizophrenia: Theory and empirical status. *Behavior Therapy, 25,* 17–33.

American Psychiatric Association. (1997). Practice guidelines for the treatment of patients with schizophrenia. *American Journal of Psychiatry, 154*(Suppl. 4), 1–63.

Bellack, A. S., Morrison, R. L., & Mueser, K. T. (1989). Social problem solving in schizophrenia. *Schizophrenia Bulletin, 15,* 101–116.

Bellack, A. S. (1992). Cognitive rehabilitation for schizophrenia: Is it possible? Is it necessary? *Schizophrenia Bulletin, 18,* 43–50.

Ben-Yishay, Y., Rattok, J., Lakin, P., Piasetsky, E., Ross, B., Silver, S., Zide, E., & Ezrachi, O. (1985). Neuropsychological rehabilitation: Quest for a holistic approach. *Seminars in Neurology, 5,* 252–299.

Boyd, R. (1991). Realism, anti-foundationalism, and the enthusiasm for natural kinds. *Philosophical Studies, 61,* 127–148.

Brenner, H., Roder, V., Hodel, B., Kienzle, N., Reed, D., & Liberman, R. (1994). *Integrated psychological therapy for schizophrenic patients.* Toronto, Ontario, Canada: Hogrefe & Huber.

Broen, W., & Storms, L. (1966). Lawful disorganization: The process underlying a schizophrenic syndrome. *Psychological Review, 73,* 265–279.

Chapman, L. J., & Chapman, J. P. (1978). The measurement of differential deficit. *Journal of Psychiatric Research, 14,* 303–311.

Cornblatt, B., Lenzenweger, M., Dworkin, R., & Erlenmeyer-Kimling, L. (1992). Childhood attentional dysfunctions predict social deficits in unaffected adults at risk for schizophrenia. *British Journal of Psychiatry, 161*(Suppl. 18), 59–64.

Corrigan, P. W. (1993, November). *Recognition of situational cues in schizophrenia: A limited capacity model.* Paper presented at the annual meeting of the Association for Advancement of Behavior Therapy, Atlanta.

Corrigan, P. W., Hirschbeck, J., & Wolfe, M. (1995). Memory and vigilance training to improve social perception in schizophrenia. *Schizophrenia Research, 17,* 257–265.

Corrigan, P. W., & Storzbach, D. (1993). The ecological validity of cognitive rehabilitation for schizophrenia. *Journal of Cognitive Rehabilitation, 11,* 14–21.

Cromwell, R. L. (1984). Preemptive thinking and schizophrenia research. In W. D. Spaulding & J. K. Cole (Eds.), *Nebraska Symposium on Motivation, Vol. 31: Theories of schizophrenia and psychosis* (pp. 1–46). Lincoln: University of Nebraska Press.

Cromwell, R. L., & Spaulding, W. (1978). How schizophrenics handle information. In W. E. Fann, I. Karacan, A. D. Pokorny, & R. L. Williams (Eds.), *The phenomenology and treatment of schizophrenia* (pp. 127–162). New York: Spectrum.

Donahoe, C. P., Carter, M. J., Bloem, W. D., Hirsch, G. L., Laasi, N., & Wallace, C. J. (1990). Assessment of interpersonal problem solving skills. *Psychiatry, 53*(4), 329–339.

Donahoe, C. P. (n.d.) *Assessment instrument for problem-solving skills.* Unpublished manuscript.

Drury, V., Birchwood, M., Cochrane, R., & MacMillan, F. (1996a). Cognitive therapy and recovery from acute psychosis: A controlled trial: I. Impact on psychotic symptoms. *British Journal of Psychiatry, 169,* 593–601.

Drury, V., Birchwood, M., Cochrane, R., & MacMillan, R. (1996b). Cognitive therapy and recovery from acute psychosis: A controlled trial: II. Impact on recovery time. *British Journal of Psychiatry, 169,* 602–607.

Dworkin, R., Cornblatt, B., Friedmann, R., Kaplanksy, L., Lewis, J., & Rinaldi, A. (1993). Precursors of affective vs. social deficits in adolescents at risk for schizophrenia. *Schizophrenia Bulletin, 19,* 563–577.

Erlenmeyer-Kimling, L., & Cornblatt, B. (1992). A summary of attentional findings in the New York High-Risk Project. *Journal of Psychiatric Research, 21,* 401–411.

Frith, C., & Dolan, R. (1996). The role of the prefrontal cortex in higher cognitive functions. *Cognitive-Brain-Research, 5*(1–2), 175–181.

Gabrielli, J. (1995). Contribution of the basal ganglia to skill learning and working memory in humans. In J. Houk, J. Davis, & D. Beiser (Eds.), *Models of information processing in the basal ganglia* (pp. 277–294). Cambridge, MA: MIT Press.

Gilbertson, M., Yao, J., & Van Kammen, D. (1994). Memory and plasma HVA changes in schizophrenia: Are they episode markers? *Biological Psychiatry, 35,* 203–206.

Glynn, S., & Mueser, K. T. (1986). Social learning for chronic mental inpatients. *Schizophrenia Bulletin, 12,* 648–668.

Goldberg, T. E., & Weinberger, D. R. (1988). Probing prefrontal function in schizophrenia with neuropsychological paradigms. *Schizophrenia Bulletin, 14,* 179–183.

Goldman-Rakic, P. S. (1990). The prefrontal contribution to working memory and conscious experience. In J. C. Eccles & J. Creutzfeldt (Eds.), *The principles of design and operation of the brain* (pp. 390–407). New York: Springer-Verlag.

Goldstein, G. (1986). The neuropsychology of schizophrenia. In I. Grant & K. Adams (Eds.), *Neuropsychological assessment of neuropsychiatric disorders.* New York: Oxford University Press.

Goldstein, G., & Ruthven, L. (1983). *Rehabilitation of the brain-damaged patient.* New York: Plenum Press.

Green, M. F. (1996). What are the functional consequences of neurocognitive deficits in schizophrenia? *American Journal of Psychiatry, 153,* 321–330.

Green, M. F. (1998). *Schizophrenia from a neurocognitive perspective: Probing the impenetrable darkness.* Boston: Allyn & Bacon.

Green, M. F., & Nuechterlein, K. (1999) Should schizophrenia be treated as a neurocognitive disorder? *Schizophrenia Bulletin, 25,* 309–320.

Haddock, G., Tarrier, N., Spaulding, W., Yusupoff, L., Kinney, C., & McCarthy, E. (1998). Individual cognitive-behavior therapy in the treatment of hallucinations and delusions: A review. *Clinical Psychology Review, 18,* 821–838.

Hacking, I. (1991). A tradition of natural kinds. *Philosophical Studies, 61,* 109–126.

Hogarty, G., & Flesher, S. (1999). A developmental theory for cognitive enhancement therapy of schizophrenia. *Schizophrenia Bulletin, 25,* 677–692.

Hogarty, G., & Flesher, S. (in press). Practice principles of Cognitive Enhancement Therapy for schizophrenia. *Schizophrenia Bulletin, 25,* 693–708.

Houk, J. (1995). Information processing in modular circuits linking basal ganglia and cerebral cortex. In J. Hauk, J. Davis, & D. Bieser (Eds.), *Models of information processing in the basal ganglia* (pp. 3–9). Cambridge, MA: MIT Press.

Houk, J., & Wise, S. (1993). Outline for a theory of motor behavior. In P. Rudomin, M. Arbib, & F. Cervantes-Perez (Eds.), *From neural networks to artificial intelligence* (pp. 452–470). Heidelberg, Germany: Springer-Verlag.

Ito, M. (1990). Neural control as a major aspect of high-order brain function. In J. C. Eccles & J. Creutzfeldt (Eds.), *The principles of design and operation of the brain* (pp. 281–301). New York: Springer-Verlag.

Jaeger, J. (1999). Studying the effectiveness of neurocognitive remediation in schizophrenia. *Schizophrenia Bulletin, 25,* 193–194.

Kern, R. S., & Green, M. F. (1994). Cognitive prerequisites of skill acquisition in schizophrenia: Bridging micro- and macro-levels of processing. In W. Spaulding (Eds.), *Cognitive technology in psychiatric rehabilitation* (pp. 49–66). Lincoln: University of Nebraska Press.

Levine, D. S., Leven, S. J., & Prueitt, P. S. (1992). Integration, disintegration, and the frontal lobes. In D. S. Levine & S. J. Leven (Eds.), *Motivation, emotion, and goal direction in neural networks* (pp. 301–335). Hillsdale, NJ: Erlbaum.

Levin, S., Yurgelun-Todd, D., & Craft, S. (1989). Contributions of clinical neuropsychology to the study of schizophrenia. *Journal of Abnormal Psychology, 98,* 341–356.

Medalia, A. (1999). Reply to "Studying the effectiveness of neurocognitive remediation in schizophrenia." *Schizophrenia Bulletin, 25,* 195–196.

Medalia, A., Aluma, M., Tyron, W., & Merriam, A. (1998). Effectiveness of attention training in schizophrenia. *Schizophrenia Bulletin, 24,* 147–152.

Meichenbaum, D. M., & Cameron, R. (1973). Training schizophrenics to talk to themselves: A means of developing attentional controls. *Behavior Therapy, 4,* 515–534.

Meltzer, H., & McGurk, S. (1999). The effects of clozapine, risperidone and olanzapine on cognitive functioning in schizophrenia. *Schizophrenia Bulletin, 25,* 233–255.

Paul, G., & Menditto, A. (1992). Effectiveness of inpatient treatment programs for mentally ill adults in public psychiatric facilities. *Applied and Preventive Psychology, 1,* 41–63.

Penn, D. L., Corrigan, P. W., Bentall, R. P., Racenstein, J. M., & Newman, L. S. (1997). Social cognition in schizophrenia. *Psychological Bulletin, 121,* 114–132.

Penn, D., van der Does, J., Spaulding, W., Garbin, C., Linzen, D., & Dingemans, P. (1993). Information processing and social-cognitive problem solving in schizophrenia. *Journal of Nervous and Mental Disease, 181,* 13–20.

Reed, D., Sullivan, M., Penn, D., Stuve, P., & Spaulding, W. (1992). Assessment and treatment of cognitive impairments. In R. P. Liberman (Eds.), *Effective psychiatric rehabilitation* (pp. 7–20). San Francisco, CA: Jossey-Bass.

Spaulding, W. (1986). Assessment of adult-onset pervasive behavior disorders. In H. Adams & K. Calhoun (Eds.), *Handbook of behavior assessment* (pp. 631–669). New York: Wiley.

Spaulding, W., Fleming, S., Reed, D. R., Sullivan, M., Storzbach, D., & Lam, M. (1999). Cognitive functioning in schizophrenia: Implications for psychiatric rehabilitation. *Schizophrenia Bulletin, 25,* 275–289.

Spaulding, W., Sullivan, M., Weiler, M., Reed, D., Richardson, C., & Storzbach, D. (1994). Changing cognitive functioning in rehabilitation of schizophrenia. *Acta Psychiatrica Scandinavica, 90*(Suppl. 384), 116–124.

Spaulding, W. D., Reed, D., Sullivan, M., Richardson, C., & Weiler, M. (1999). Effects of cognitive treatment in psychiatric rehabilitation. *Schizophrenia Bulletin, 25,* 657–676.

Spaulding, W. D., Storms, L., Goodrich, V., & Sullivan, M. (1986). Applications of experimental psychopathology in psychiatric rehabilitation. *Schizophrenia Bulletin, 12,* 560–577.

Spohn, H., & Strauss, M. (1989). Relation of neuroleptic and anticholinergic medication to cognitive functions in schizophrenia. *Journal of Abnormal Psychology, 98,* 367–380.

Storzbach, D., & Corrigan, P. (1996). Cognitive rehabilitation for schizophrenia. In P. Corrigan & S. Yudofsky (Eds.), *Cognitive rehabilitation for neuropsychiatric disorders* (pp. 299–328). Washington, DC: American Psychiatric Association.

Walker, E. (1994). Developmentally moderated expressions of the neuro-pathology underlying schizophrenia. *Schizophrenia Bulletin, 20,* 453–480.

Walker, E., Savoie, T., & Davis, D. (1994). Neuromotor precursors of schizophrenia. *Schizophrenia Bulletin, 20,* 441–451.

Weinberger, D., & Lipska, B. (1995). Cortical maldevelopment, anti-psychotic drugs and schizophrenia: A search for common ground. *Schizophrenia Research, 16,* 87–110.

Wykes, T., Reeder, C., Corner, J., Williams, C., & Everitt, B. (1999). The effects of neurocognitive remediation on executive processing in patients with schizophrenia. *Schizophrenia Bulletin, 25,* 291–307.

Cognitively Oriented Psychotherapy for Early Psychosis: Theory, Praxis, Outcomes, and Challenges

9

Henry J. Jackson, Patrick D. McGorry, and Jane Edwards

W e have characterized the history of psychotherapy in the psychoses as consisting of three phases (Jackson, Edwards, Hulbert, & McGorry, 1999). The first phase, best labeled as the *psychodynamic period*, arguably began in the second decade of the 20th century, and continued on until the late 1950s—perhaps even slightly later (see, e.g., Gunderson et al., 1984). The second phase—the *behavioral period*—began in the 1960s, and the third period—characterized as the *cognitive period*—began in the 1970s and has continued until the present day (Jackson et al., 1999).

The behavioral treatments that first emerged in the 1960s were interventions initially delivered within the context of experimental case methodologies. Essentially, they consisted of applications of approaches derived in part, if not wholly, from the principles of applied behavioral analysis, and they focused on target behaviors such as training social skills, managing inappropriate behaviors, and so forth. Later, psychoeducational family-therapy approaches emerged, which were tested in the context of randomized controlled studies. Increasingly, the same testing occurred with social skills training. The two approaches proved remarkably effective, durable, and attractive (Dixon & Lehman, 1995; Liberman, Kopelowicz, & Young, 1994; Scott & Dixon, 1995; Smith, Bellack, & Liberman, 1996). In fact, notwithstanding some apparent failures, both interventions should be firmly ensconced in the clinical practitioner's armamentarium (see Nathan & Gorman, 1998; Roth & Fonagy, 1996). Yet some researchers have expressed concern that such evidence-based approaches are grossly underutilized by clinical practitioners in the real world (Fadden, 1999; Lewis, 1999). Those approaches did not

249

challenge the emerging biological approaches (Andreasen, 1984; Robins & Guze, 1970; but for an archenthusiast's account of the ascendancy of the biological paradigm, see the recent book of the historian Edward Shorter, 1997); rather, they were viewed, quite appropriately, as complementary to biological interventions (i.e., neuroleptic medication).

The cognitive paradigm has emerged comparatively recently; it consists of three strands of activity. The first is cognitive remediation (e.g., Bellack, Gold, & Buchanan, 1999; Green, 1993; Green & Nuechterlein, 1999; Wykes, Reeder, Corner, Williams, & Everitt, 1999), which aims to assist in the improvement of nonsocial information-processing deficits. The second is the cognitive treatment of hallucinations and delusions (Bentall, Haddock, & Slade, 1994; Chadwick, Birchwood, & Trower, 1996; Fowler, Garety, & Kuipers, 1995; Kingdon & Turkington, 1994; Tarrier, 1992; Wykes, Tarrier, & Lewis, 1998; but for a recent critical review see Norman & Townsend, 1999). The third is the use of cognitive techniques to assist adaptation of the self in recovery from psychosis (Davidson & Strauss, 1992, 1995; Hogarty et al., 1995; Strauss, 1994). Although each cognitive strand is worthy of detailed commentary, this chapter focuses on our work with COPE (Cognitively Oriented Psychotherapy for Early Psychosis)—work firmly within the third strand of the cognitive paradigm (Jackson, McGorry, Edwards, & Hulbert, 1996; Jackson et al., 1998, 1999).

Objections to Traditional Conceptualizations of Psychosis

Despite the emergence of the new cognitive developments in treating psychosis, it must be acknowledged that the dominant paradigm within psychosis is quite clearly of a reductionistic biological nature (Jackson et al., 1996, 1998; McGorry, 1995; McGorry, Edwards, Mihalopoulis, Harrigan, & Jackson, 1996). The biological model often is referred to as the neo-Kraepelinian model (Robins & Guze, 1970) and is enshrined in successive editions of the *Diagnostic and Statistical Manual of Mental Disorders* (*DSM*; American Psychiatric Association, 1980, 1987, 1994). The model explicitly assumes that a diagnosis of schizophrenia prescribes course and outcome in that schizophrenia leads inevitably to both a deteriorating course and poor outcome, in the form of disabilities and handicaps.

The problems with the neo-Kraepelinian view are serious especially in relation to first-episode psychosis for the following reasons:

1. Schizophrenia is not isomorphic with psychosis. Not all first-episode patients have schizophrenia; other forms of psychosis occur. For example, among patients of the Early Psychosis Prevention and Intervention Centre (EPPIC; Edwards, Francey, McGorry, & Jackson, 1994; McGorry et al., 1996), published studies typically show that approximately 55% have either schizophrenia or schizophreniform disorder, 30% have affective psychosis (i.e., bipolar disorder, major depression, or schizoaffective disorder), and another 15% have other psychotic disorders (i.e., delusional disorder, brief reactive psychosis, or psychosis not otherwise specified; Jackson, McGorry, & Dudgeon, 1995; McGorry et al., 1996). The problem, of course, is that negative expectations are attached to people with nonaffective presentations. Nevertheless, these statistics are especially important in the sense that EPPIC is not a "boutique" tertiary referral service. Rather, it is an integrated, frontline clinical service (Edwards & McGorry, 1998) with primary responsibility for people aged 13 to 30 who present with a first episode of psychosis and are living in the Western geographic region of metropolitan Melbourne, Victoria, Australia. Note that this age group covers more than 200,000 of the roughly 820,000 people who live in that geographic region. (Melbourne has a total population of approximately 3.2 million.)

2. The treatment recovery figures for EPPIC patients show that 80% of a representative subsample of patients evinced a good response to antipsychotic medications, including most people with nonaffective psychosis. Sixty-three percent were in remission by the end of 3 months (Power et al., 1998). Note that in a U.S. site, Lieberman et al. (1992), focusing on first-episode schizophrenia-spectrum patients, found that 74% were considered fully remitted, 12% nonremitted, and 14% nonremitted following neuroleptic treatment.

3. Relatively few of our EPPIC patients have early-treatment-resistant psychotic symptoms: a total of 6.6%–8.9% in the 12-month period following initial treatment, depending on the range of psychotic diagnoses examined (Edwards, Maude, McGorry, Harrigan, & Cocks, 1998).

4. The specific diagnoses of schizophrenia, bipolar, and schizoaffective disorder are neither clear nor stable in the first episode (Fenning et al., 1994).

5. The meaning of the biological deficits evinced by first-episode patients is not clear at this stage. The problem is compounded by the fact that only certain proportions of first-episode patients evince such biological deficits and that the deficits may be manifold but not all be found in the same person. Also, it is not clear

that the deficits are progressive (for a comprehensive review of studies of biological variables in first-episode schizophrenia, see Chatterjee & Lieberman, 1999).

6. The long-term outcome for patients with chronic forms of schizophrenia is much better than would be predicted by advocates of the neo-Kraepelinian model (see, e.g., Birchwood, 1999; Harding, Zubin, & Strauss, 1987).

THE NEED FOR A NEW MODEL

We propose a new model. The first tenet of our model is that intervention needs to be delivered at the earliest opportunity (Birchwood, McGorry, & Jackson, 1997; McGlashan & Johannessen, 1996). In fact, Birchwood has proposed the existence of a critical period in the first 2 to 5 years, during which optimal treatment may produce powerful positive outcomes (Birchwood, 1999; Birchwood et al., 1997). For this reason, we believe first-presentation clients with psychosis offer the best opportunity for intervention and good outcomes.

The second tenet is that the psychotic person is instrumental in his or her own recovery, can effect positive change, and can come to be personally responsible for prophylactic treatment and his or her own quality of life. In this sense our overarching theoretical position is that of "critical constructivism" (Bruner, 1986; Kelly, 1955; Mahoney, 1991; Neimeyer & Mahoney, 1995; Perris, 1989). From this perspective the self—and mobilization of the self—should be the integral component of any new therapy for the treatment of the psychoses. Major theorists who have proposed such an approach include Perris (1989), Davidson and Strauss (1995) and, to a lesser extent, Hogarty et al. (1995). Perris (1989) emphasized the individual patient's ability to influence his or her adjustment by the therapist working with the healthy side of the person. Davidson and Strauss (1995) emphasized their life-context model, also construing the person as being able to positively affect his or her own continued development and adjustment. Finally, Hogarty et al. (1995) developed a phase-oriented psychotherapy for schizophrenia, which focuses on attempting to address the needs of the *whole person*. The therapy uses cognitive–behavioral techniques (e.g., modeling, rehearsal, practice, feedback, and homework) to establish skills, and it teaches coping techniques, with psychoeducation assuming an important part of the treatment package (for empirical outcomes with this approach, see Hogarty et al., 1997a, 1997b). All the researchers described in this section generally have dealt with clients with more established illnesses. In our view, a much greater need and opportunity exists at the early stages of the illness for "damage control" concerning the self.

The third tenet of our model is that first-presentation clients have different needs from those with chronic forms of the illness because of two interrelated factors: their developmental phase and their definition of self. Typically, psychosis occurs during the developmental stage of middle to late adolescence (Rey, 1992). This stage involves transitions from relative dependence to relative independence in a number of spheres. Although stage theories posit movement through developmental periods (Erikson, 1968; Levinson, 1986), we are not convinced that development should be considered as a "lump." Instead, we conceptualize it as consisting of a number of domains or spheres (e.g., physical-motor, cognitive, leisure or hobbies, family, social, and intimate-sexual). Examples would include moving from school to work or further study at tertiary institutions, from family to peer group, from generally asexual relationships to increasingly sexual and intimate relationships, and from the development of interests in hobbies and sports to demonstrating increasing competence and achievement in them. The person may not consistently develop at the same rate in all spheres in a "lock-step" fashion; development may be punctuated by plateaus and spurts. Despite differential rates of development within the same person, however, psychosis may engender traumatic effects, negatively interfering with the realization of the various developmental goals (e.g., leaving home, pursuing a career, or engaging in sports activities). This interference occurs because of the threat derived from the risk of self-stigmatization and the psychologically traumatic and self-deforming influence of the psychotic experience. Corrigan and Penn (1999) have provided a comprehensive review of stigmatization in serious mental illness, noting, for example, that "some people with severe mental illness also endorse stigmatizing attitudes about psychiatric disability and hence about themselves" (p. 767); they also say that "persons who self-stigmatize are less likely to be successful in work, housing, and relationships" (p. 767).

Of course, this same adolescent period is typically when the person is forming his or her identity, the key developmental task for young people in their teenage years (Erikson , 1968; Levinson, 1986). In discussing the self, we draw upon the social cognition literature pertaining to the concept of "possible selves" (Markus & Nurius, 1986; Ogilvie, 1987). The notion here is that there is no single self, but a network of connected selves (e.g., self as brother, self as partner, self as sportsperson, and so on). The selves may be of different importance to the person and may vary in terms of number, elaborateness, and "coreness." Accordingly, each self possess different motivational and emotional properties for the person. Consequently, psychosis may directly negatively affect the client's identity as revealed in the selves (for interesting discussions about the various roles played by the stories clients tell about them-*selves*, see Roberts, 1999a, 1999b). Penn, Corrigan, Bentall, Racenstein, and Newman (1997) noted that the self-structures of patients with schizophrenia tended to be less complex and elaborated, although the extent to which this effect resulted from chronicity is unclear; we simply do not know what the self-structures of people with psychosis are like before the first episode. We might assume (although it requires empirical testing) that the self-structures of adolescents prior to psychosis are less elaborate and fewer in number. The danger is that with advent of the psychosis, the self structures shrink further. Moreover, the illness may affect not only young people's present concept of themselves but also what they expect to become (*expected selves*) what they would like to become (*hoped-for selves* or *future positive possible selves*), and the self they fear they might become (*a feared or undesired self*; Ogilvie, 1987).[1] With psychosis the person may become engulfed (Lally, 1989) by the negative or undesired self (e.g., "a chronic mental patient"); he or she may give up on pursuing the aspirations, themes, and goals embodied in the positive possible selves. Self-efficacy may be severely reduced, and personality development may be compromised, with the psychosis and pre-existing personality style becoming inextricably and irrevocably entwined with one another (Hulbert, Jackson, & McGorry, 1996). In our collective view, much of this "implosion of self" occurs because of the unfavorable attributions the person makes about him- or herself in relation to other people or the negative attributions the person rightly or wrongly ascribes to other people in the social context. Penn et al. (1997) commented that people may withdraw from a variety of social situations in order to cope with stigmatization, whether that stigmatization is real or perceived. Birchwood (1999) stated that people with psychosis may evaluate themselves negatively, experience loss, and feel humiliated (i.e., lose social rank) and entrapped by the psychosis. The innovative work of Paul Gilbert, which concerns constructs such as defeat, entrapment, shame, humiliation, and guilt, mostly with reference to depression, is relevant here (Gilbert, 1997; Gilbert & Allan, 1998).

To summarize, we developed our COPE therapy on the basis of the tenets of the model described above, with the main goal of assisting the client in recovering from an initial episode of psychosis. By helping clients preserve a sense of self (i.e., identity) and by preserving or increasing their self-efficacy, COPE further aimed to help them cope with the experience of the psychosis (i.e., adaptation), its secondary effects (i.e.,

---

[1]We do not use a formal measure of possible selves in our routine clinical work. However, we did use one in a small study ($n = 56$) reported in the thesis of Filia (1996). This measure can be obtained by writing directly to H. J. Jackson. Filia comments that the self-descriptors used in such a formal measure may not have been relevant to the patients in the study. We have used the repertory grid (Fransella & Bannister, 1977; Kelly, 1955) more routinely in our work, mainly as a clinical assessment and therapy tool. Data are only now emerging (Harrigan, 1999).

alleviating or preventing the emergence of secondary morbidity), and the treatment experience itself (i.e., its potentially disempowering effects).

COPE Therapy

COPE therapy has five phases: engagement, assessment, adaptation, secondary morbidity, and termination. As indicated elsewhere (Jackson et al., 1999), the phases are not necessarily discrete, but they are presented as such in this chapter for the sake of clarity.

ENGAGEMENT

In this section we outline the need for establishing a relationship with clients, and describe the factors that may enhance the therapeutic relationship. We also outline the problems that the therapist may experience in engaging a person recovering from a first episode of psychosis.

Why We Need to Establish a Relationship With Clients

A working relationship with clients is absolutely pivotal to the success of COPE, as it is to any psychotherapeutic work involving collaboration between client and therapist (Beck, Freeman, & Associates, 1990; Frank & Gunderson, 1990). Within the general psychotherapy literature there is renewed interest in the therapeutic relationship, and therapist characteristics (e.g., warmth, empathy, tolerance, and the capacity to inspire trust) have received increasing interest, as has the patient–therapist fit (Binder & Strupp, 1997; Luborsky, McClellan, Diguer, Woody, & Seligman, 1997; Mohr, 1995; Weinberger, 1995). More specifically, within the COPE context, establishing such a collaborative relationship provides the necessary platform for subsequent work within the adaptation and secondary morbidity phases. An essential prerequisite for the therapist working with young first-presentation clients with psychosis is a solid knowledge of developmental and life-cycle issues. Engaging such clients may take a few sessions or last many months.

Factors That May Enhance the Therapeutic Relationship

It is difficult to disentangle the assessment phase from the engagement phase. On the basis of the information gathered by the therapist, an agenda for subsequent sessions can be established with the client. This process helps promote engagement with the client. Second, the therapist must discuss with the client the role of the therapist as well as the length and frequency of the sessions. Adherence to those guidelines provides the client with a clear structure and direction to future sessions and assists clients by allaying their anxiety; it communicates to the person that therapy is not "magical" but practical and nonthreatening.

Perhaps the most important initial step in engaging with the client, however, is that of the therapist attempting to gain an understanding of the client's explanatory model of the disorder. Showing respect for and working with the client's explanatory model assists in establishing some common ground between the therapist and client.

Listening, understanding, and clarifying are important factors in this phase of therapeutic work because they help establish client trust. They help communicate to the client that he or she is being taking seriously. In addition, as long as the questioning of the client is not perceived as too intrusive, it can help make the therapeutic "space" safe for the client. To further facilitate the working relationship, it behooves the therapist to be sensitive to the client's anxiety and general mental state.

Another method of promoting engagement with the client is through helping the client achieve immediate positive outcomes with issues that are currently important and distressing to them and are *not obviously related* to the psychotic disorder. An example might be the client who needs to find accommodation urgently. The assistance provided by the therapist may be of the utmost importance in establishing trust and fostering a working relationship, especially if the client is resistant and sees little benefit in continuing to come to therapy. A relationship also can be built if the therapist communicates interest in and works with the client's hobbies, as illustrated in the following case fragment:

> Priscilla is a 16-year-old with schizophreniform disorder who uses cannabis daily and heroin intermittently. The treating team had had difficulty engaging with Priscilla. The therapist first visited her at home with the treating doctor. The client displayed an interest in tigers and astrological charts, so the therapist suggested that she might be able to arrange for Priscilla to visit the zoo to view the tigers. Priscilla appreciated this offer, and after inquiring about the therapist's birth date, offered to construct the therapist's astrological chart and bring it to the clinic for their next session.

Perhaps a more prosaic but integral method of promoting engagement is for the therapist to demonstrate over the course of the therapy session a preparedness to renegotiate the length, timing, and geographic location of the sessions with the client (e.g., the sessions might take place in a café). In all interactions and at all times, the therapist should be tolerant, empathic, flexible and, above all, persistent!

Problems in Engaging the Client Recovering From a First Episode of Psychosis

Turning to potentially problematic factors specific to people with first-presentation psychosis, the therapist must take two sets of factors into account. The first set of factors pertains to the premorbid developmental and personality characteristics of the client, including the client's age, level of intelligence, educational attainment, and social competence (including the number and quality of their peer relationships). Because of these operative factors, the therapist should take his or her time in joining with the client; moreover, the therapist should be aware that because the clients are relatively young, they will have little experience with therapy and thus may not know what to expect from therapy and may have difficulty taking an objective stance to their illness. In fact, the young person with psychosis may find it unusual for someone to talk with them at all—not just about symptoms or the onset of their illness. The empathic therapist is sensitive to the client's mental state, phase of development, and degree of cognitive flexibility. It is important that the therapist be nonjudgmental and tolerant; he or she should not overreact but be prepared to set limits when necessary. Cautious optimism and humor from the therapist may be useful, especially in tempering difficult interactions or potentially emotional reactions.

The second set of factors are those directly pertinent to the client's illness, including the client's phase of illness (i.e., how acute they are), residual positive and negative symptomatology, and other morbidities (e.g., personality disorders, depression, social anxiety, or substance abuse—whether primary, coexistent, or secondary). It is important to consider whether the client is experiencing fluctuations in mental state. Obviously, illness characteristics such as grandiosity and paranoia—the latter manifested in overt distrust of the therapist—may inhibit, prevent, or generally slow the engagement process. It is also the case that the illness may directly impair the client's cognitive capacities (e.g., attention, concentration, memory, and abstraction or conceptual thinking) and the ability of the person to relate to the clinician. Denial of problems or illness also may affect the engagement process.

Clients already may have some experience of neuroleptic treatment and may believe that it has exacerbated their symptoms or inhibited their ability to function. Throughout therapy the therapist reviews medication, medication side effects, and medication compliance and conducts repeated mental-state examinations, especially if the client evinces fluctuations in his or her mental state. Excessive medication dosages, severe side effects of medication (e.g., akathisia), and poor medication compliance all can interfere with the building of a therapeutic alliance.

ASSESSMENT

The assessment phase goes hand in hand with the engagement phase and requires the therapist to gather data from the patient. The data cover a broad range of spheres or domains, including symptoms and onset; the client's explanatory model and level of insight; the client's level of functioning before, during, and after the psychotic episode; the client's descriptions of his or her possible selves (Markus & Nurius, 1986; Murray, 1938); the client's methods of coping and personality style; and the client's understanding and expectations of therapy. This assessment phase may take three or more sessions.

An initial step includes garnering data from the client about the client's symptoms. In questioning the client about the content of the primary positive psychotic symptoms, various parameters are documented, such as frequency, potency (omnipotence), and duration. Further questioning of the client determines the onset of the first signs and symptoms, internal and exogenous factors associated with the onset, and whether onset was gradual or rapid. The therapist is particularly interested in learning about what was going on in the client's life prior to the psychotic episode, any stressors that seemingly precipitated his or her admission or psychotic episode, and the nature and timing of the early warning signs and symptoms.

The assessment of symptoms continues with the therapist inquiring about negative symptoms and other morbidity, such as depression, social anxiety, panic attacks, substance abuse, personality disorder, and post-traumatic stress disorder (PTSD). Using timelines, an attempt is made to establish the relationship of the various symptoms or syndromes to one another and determine whether they are premorbid, comorbid, or secondarily morbid.

Another domain of inquiry pivots around the person's explanatory model—how the client explains the etiology and nature of his or her mental illness. In addition, the therapist is interested in determining why the client believes the illness developed during this period in his or her life, and how he or she believes the illness is maintained (e.g., does the client believe that he or she can exert some control over it?). Ascertaining how the client labels the illness—for example, "problems," "illness," or "terrifying thoughts"—also is important. The clinician must assess both the extent of the client's knowledge about mental illness and his or her level of judgment and insight (Amador, Strauss, Yale, & Gorman, 1991).

The clinician needs to ask the client about his or her level of functioning before, during, and after the onset of the episode in a number of domains, including social relationships; intimate relationships; educational and study activities; and work, family, and leisure pursuits. Following the garnering of this information, the therapist should be in a better position to make a determination about the quality of the client's recovery environment and level of available social support.

Related to the above are the clients' descriptions of their goals, values, and aspirations (the last item invokes the notion of possible selves; Markus & Nurius, 1986). Here, the clinician is interested in how the clients' perception of being psychotic has affected their past, present, and future selves. For example, consider the person intent on becoming a professional pianist and whose efforts (e.g., hours practicing at the piano, pursuit of a music degree, and so on) are directed toward the achievement of that goal. With the advent of psychosis, the person stops practicing, no longer attends classes, and relays to the therapist that he or she no longer believes that it is possible to achieve that goal. Of course, it may be difficult to fully elicit this information in the first sessions, when the focus is on emotional coping and support and the client feels easily threatened.

Another domain of inquiry focuses on the client's coping approaches. The therapist evaluates how the client has coped with the symptoms and related problems to date, what techniques or approaches he or she used, and whether the client found those techniques to be effective. It is useful for the clinician to learn whether the client has had to deal with past difficulties (e.g., loss of parents and friends or academic problems, the client's particular coping techniques for a given situation, and how successful the coping efforts were. Additionally, the therapist should carefully determine how the client's personality and intellectual level affect coping ability. How each client has manifested failed coping (e.g., with overdoses or substance abuse) is of obvious importance. In fact, it is our collective view that most clients are highly likely to fail— at least initially, and then at periodic intervals.

How the client describes his or her personality is important for a number of reasons. The therapist is interested in determining not only its current nature but also whether it has been changed in some way by the advent of the psychosis. Typical questions are, "How would you describe your usual self when you were well?"; "Are you different from how you were before you became unwell?"; "How do your family and friends describe your personality now? Is this different from how they would describe you before you became unwell?" Most critical is the assessment of personality traits or disorders (e.g., dependent, avoidant, or borderline)—especially how those personality traits might interfere with treatment. For example, severe obsessive personality traits can cause clients to be excessively "sticky" and pedantic in their interactions with the therapist and interfere with the formation or maintenance of everyday social relationships. Equally valuable is the ascertainment of "positive" personality traits that may be helpful in the therapeutic interaction as well as in daily social relationships, such as warmth, gregariousness, and openness to ideas (Costa & Widiger, 1994; Jackson, 1998). Although the primary source for assessment information is the client, it is our standard practice to collect informant and collateral data to supplement and "flesh out" our understanding of the client.

Obviously, the therapist needs to determine what clients want or expect from therapy, their perceptions of the therapist's role, and whether they understand the role of time-limited therapy. It also is useful to ask clients whether they have been seen previously by a therapist. If so, they can be asked about their experiences in therapy. In clinical interviews with the client, the clinician can use assessment devices other than direct questioning techniques, such as diaries, repertory grids, autobiographical methods, sheets to identify cognitive distortions, self-monitoring sheets, the writing of essays, the use of cassette recorders or video cameras, or "empty-chair" techniques.

ADAPTATION

With the advent of psychosis—and in its wake—the danger is that the person recovering from an initial psychotic episode will be reluctant to engage in previously undertaken activities, such as work and school. He or she also may not resume intimate and other relationships or take up new tasks.

Elsewhere, we have outlined the major goals of therapy for promoting adaptation (Jackson et al., 1996, 1999; McGorry, 1992, 1995; McGorry, Henry, Maude, & Phillips, 1998). Put briefly, the goals of adaptation in COPE are threefold. The first goal is to assist the person in searching for meaning in the experience of psychosis. The second is to promote a sense of mastery over the experience, so as to protect and enhance self-esteem. The third is to protect the viability of positive possible selves and to neutralize or detoxify negative possible selves that newly confront clients (see Jackson et al., 1996; Greenfeld, Strauss, Bowers, & Mandelkern, 1989; McGorry, Henry, et al., 1998).

Although COPE's origins were in the mid-1980s, we have found useful the work of Davidson and Strauss (1995). Accordingly, we follow their example in describing the adaptation phase of COPE as consisting of four subphases. In the first subphase, the therapist attempts to instill hope in the client by examining his or her goals and illness experiences. The therapist communicates to the client that others have undergone illness and have suffered similar experiences but have continued to pursue their goals and attempt to realize their ambitions, albeit in attenuated forms. In this regard, the therapist is attempting to help clients mobilize themselves and their resources, helping them prepare for change.

In our view, psychoeducation is integral to any treatment endeavor that attempts to change negative attributions about one's self, illness, and future (EPPIC, 1997; McGorry, 1992, 1995). It should be delivered on an individual basis, taking into account the client's developmental stage and phase of illness. A variety of delivery systems are useful in this regard, including EPPIC-developed videos (e.g., Ioannides & Hexter, 1994), pamphlets, semistructured interviews, and repertory grids (Fransella & Bannister, 1977). The latter is most useful in determining how the client sees him- or herself in relation to people with mental disorders (e.g., schizophrenia) and chronic physical conditions, such as diabetes.

The second subphase is concerned with collaboratively preparing the client for "action." A number of opportunities for intervention exist; Exhibit 9.1 outlines potential "targets" for assessment and intervention in the adaptation phase. The therapist should keep these targets in mind when assessing clients. The targets are based on a graphical model first introduced in Jackson et al. (1996, Figure 1, p. 140) and elaborated in Jackson et al. (1999, Figure 10.1, p. 278).

The first target includes specific appraisals about life events, the psychosis, or both. In this regard, cognitive interventions assume utmost importance for helping clients to both challenge their beliefs and develop "coping self-talk." Typically, clients' beliefs revolve around the idea that they can do nothing to alter the course of illness (thus overlapping with the first Adaptation subphase). Furthermore, clients usually believe that they will need to discontinue their schooling or their leisure pursuits and that having suffered a psychotic episode means that they will never be able to get back on track with their lives.

EXHIBIT 9.1

Targets for the Second Subphase of the Adaptation Phase of COPE

- Appraisals about psychosis itself—e.g., "This is the most terrible thing that has happened to me"—and about life events associated with or leading up to the onset of psychosis—e.g., losing one's place on the football team at school
- Attributional style—examination of globality, stability, and internality parameters
- Coping skills—examination of the range, type, and appropriateness of coping skills in client's repertoire
- Possible selves—examination of past, current, and future selves as well as undesired selves
- Core schemata/beliefs—examination of core beliefs, especially about self, e.g., "I am an incompetent person" or "I am an unlikeable person"
- Temperamental and personality characteristics—e.g., severe avoidance, perfectionism, excessive fantasy, or disagreeableness

---

The second potential target is attributional style (Seligman, 1991), which, of course, is linked with the first target of appraisal in that appraisals are channeled bidirectionally through the "deeper-level" attributional style. Attempting to help someone with a pessimistic attributional style is never easy; nevertheless, it is important to strive to help clients believe that they can effect change in themselves and in the environment. The therapist here can use psychoeducation—cognitive challenges to beliefs and distortions—together with "reality" experiments, graded tasks, and exposure treatments. (The latter behavioral approaches, however, strictly belong to the third subphase of adaptation.)

The third target is coping skills (see Lazarus & Folkman, 1984; Tarrier, 1992). The therapist needs to ascertain the type and appropriateness of the client's coping skills and resources, whether the client has used them in the past, and how effective they were. More often than not, the therapist may have to assist the client in increasing his or her coping repertoire by rehearsing newly acquired techniques within sessions using role plays and guided imagery. The compendium in Tarrier (1992) provides examples of coping skills for handling positive symptoms; those techniques can be adapted to the adaptation phase. Techniques include cognitive strategies, such as attention switching (e.g., distraction); behavioral activities, such as increasing activity levels (e.g., walking or exercise); and sensory and physiological strategies (e.g., relaxation).

The fourth target consists of the themes, goals, strivings, and aspirations encapsulated by the possible selves of the client. A major danger is that the client may be "swamped" by the psychosis, so that the psychosis becomes entangled with emerging possible selves and personality characteristics, thus affecting identity and attenuating the person's developmental trajectory. Put another way, the goal is to prevent the self from being engulfed by a feared or negative possible self (Markus & Nurius, 1986). Examination of the client's explanatory model and possible selves can determine the extent to which such engulfment has occurred. In an attempt to prevent engulfment (or denial), the therapist introduces psychoeducational material and complements it by gently challenging the client's cognitive appraisals of his or her stereotypes of mental illness and negative possible selves (e.g., failed partner or failed student). The therapist continues to examine the clients' goals, attempting to identify where the problems reside and the exact nature of the cognitive road blocks. Careful delineation of goals and intervention targets assumes the utmost importance. Behavioral analysis assists in breaking down tasks into small steps and establishing the sequence for the tasks. Here the therapist begins to deal with the responses of the client, who is typically highly invested in avoiding taking steps toward the achievement of his or her goals, usually because of stigma. A range of technologies selected from the cognitive–behavioral armamentarium may be critical to the enterprise. Diaries and self-monitoring sheets, role-plays, or guided imagery can assist in further detecting the cognitive distortions and beliefs that inhibit or prevent clients from tackling tasks.

Early on, it is a good idea for the client to identify and select a not-so-difficult goal, which the client and the therapist can tackle together, as shown in the following case fragment:

> John was a 17-year-old male recovering from a schizophreniform disorder. He was having difficulty contacting his homeroom teacher. John was frightened of doing this; he felt that the teacher was angry with him because of the way John had acted when he became ill. Apparently, John had behaved violently in class, overturning tables and screaming abuse at his fellow students. John was worried that his classmates and his class teacher would reject him when he attempted to make contact with them. It was important to precisely identify the problematic cognitions. John was fearful that his teacher (whom he perceived as high status and authoritarian) would think that John "was an idiot" because of the way he had acted when he was ill. John was convinced that his teacher would not want him back in his class and that the teacher would be further horrified to learn that he (John) was a "nut" who had spent time in a "nuthouse." Time was spent identifying the cognitions and the distortions that John evinced ("fortune-telling," "magnification," and "self-stigmatization") and collaboratively establishing each step involved in recontacting the teacher. Those steps included making a phone call to the teacher, arranging a time to see the teacher, going to school to see the teacher, and then informing the teacher that John had been ill when he had behaved in a disorganized way and that he had been hospitalized by his parents.
>
> In a sense this process is the same as establishing a hierarchy in systematic desensitization, with some important differences. The first is that beliefs and distortions about each of the steps in the hierarchy were elicited, examined, and challenged. Second, the patient learned coping techniques (e.g., breathing control to handle the physiological concomitants of anxiety) and wrote self-instructional coping statements on the back of cards. Covert rehearsal and role-plays were used to practice the steps involved in this plan. Time projection was used for both eliciting the cognitive roadblocks and practicing the adaptive behaviors to be used in the third subphase. The client later tackled these planned steps and ultimately returned to school.

Therapist and client may need to address the client's core schemata about self, as described in Beck, Freeman, and Associates (1990), Michael Mahoney (1991), and Jeffrey Young (1994); we do not as yet use formal measures of core schemata as published by Young (1994). Cognitive and behavioral strategies can be used to challenge core, long-standing, and stable assumptions about the person's sense of self. Those assumptions may have preexisted quite independently of the psychosis.

For example, a client might believe that he or she has no power to effect change in self or the world. Setting a series of achievable behavioral tasks would be a first step in tackling such a core issue. The accomplishment of each task would be followed up by gentle cognitive disputation, aimed at chipping away at this sense of powerlessness. More details are provided in Beck et al. (1990) and Young (1994).

Personality vulnerabilities may need to be addressed to a limited extent because they are considered to be risk factors for future episodes of psychosis. For example, perfectionism and "cognitive rigidity" may need to be given some attention (see Kyrios, 1998), as in the following case example:

> A 24-year-old client recovering from schizophreniform disorder but with marked obsessive–compulsive personality features had a nonexistent social network and a restricted and rigid series of "social" routines. The therapist construed this man's personality features as being a risk factor for future relapse. For instance, every day he went to the same coffee shop, sat at the same table, and ordered the same coffee and breakfast. He never spoke to the shop owner. A plan was determined collaboratively with the therapist to gradually change things. The client was asked to say "hello" and speak a few words to the café owner, eat at a different table, consume a different breakfast, read a different paper, and leave later than usual. The client's fears about tackling each step were addressed using psychoeducation and cognitive challenges. Eventually, the client was asked to visit different places for breakfast. This same approach was used to tackle more difficult tasks and issues for this man.

The third subphase of the adaptation phase is the actual implementation of the plans described in the second subphase (e.g., contacting friends, workmates, employers, teachers, and family; recommencing studies; and pursuing new goals). Most plans, however, will not involve planning a single discrete event, but rather planning, monitoring, and revising an ongoing series of events. Consider the following case fragment:

> A 25-year-old woman recovering from a first episode of psychosis has returned to undertake further study at university but is not coping with the daily tasks of her course of study. Within each therapy session, the therapist consistently reviews progress, identifying cognitive blocks to successful completion of academic tasks and constructing new plans that are then implemented. The therapist also provides encouragement and support and conducts mental-state examinations and medication reviews.

In this case, an ongoing feedback process exists between the second and third adaptation subphases.

The fourth subphase consists of reviewing the client's progress with the therapist. The therapist consistently points out gains the client is making and continues the work of the second and third subphases. Improving self-efficacy and self-directedness is the key goal of this subphase.

SECONDARY MORBIDITY

This section contains information on the diverse psychopathological conditions associated with psychosis and the various approaches to treating those same conditions.

Psychopathologies

Psychosis may be associated with manifold presentations of other morbidity, such as PTSD, agoraphobia, panic attacks, depression, social anxiety, obsessive–compulsive disorder (OCD), alcohol and drug abuse, and personality disorder (Bland, Newman, & Orn, 1987; Hulbert, Jackson, & McGorry, 1996; Jeffries, 1977; Labbate, Young, & Arana, 1999; McGorry et al., 1991; Mueser et al., 1990, 1998; Strakowski et al., 1993; Strakowski, Keck, McElroy, Lonczak, & West, 1995). Prevalence figures cited for secondary conditions in schizophrenia have varied widely; for depression, panic, or OCD, the rates have ranged from 7% to 75% (Argyle, 1990; Bermanzohn, Porto, & Siris, 1997; Boyd, 1986; Fenton & McGlashan, 1986; Siris, 1991). Prevalence rates of alcohol or drug use could be as high as 60% (Bland, Newman, & Orn, 1987). However, the exact prevalences of so-called "secondary" conditions in first-presentation psychosis are not reliably known. Some isolated studies are informative, such as the excellent study by Hambrecht and Häfner (1996) on alcohol and drug abuse in first-episode cases of schizophrenia, although the "secondary" nature of the conditions appeared questionable, at least for drug abuse; alcohol abuse tended to occur after the first symptoms of schizophrenia. Strakowski et al. (1995) also found that many of the so-called secondary disorders tended to be antecedent to the psychosis. Large-scale, representative epidemiological studies are needed to accurately document secondary conditions in first-episode clients.

In the context of the EPPIC program, social phobia, depression, and drug misuse are probably the most commonly occurring conditions (see Henry, McGorry, Jackson, Hulbert, & Edwards, 1997; Mooney & Pica, 1997). Naturally, those conditions may be exacerbations of preexisting Axis I conditions or of Axis II personality predispositions. Additionally, distinguishing between a comorbid disorder or a true secondary disorder is difficult; that is, two truly independent disorders may exist. Close questioning and the use of graphically drawn timelines may be invaluable aids in clarifying the situation.

We assert that true secondary morbidity arises as a failure of the person to adapt to the primary condition. So, for example, a client with "secondary" depression may be grieving over the loss of his or her job and the loss of meaning (e.g., "I no longer have any role in life"); PTSD may emerge following police involvement in the client's admission. To take a final example, social phobia is often a consequence of the person —embarrassed by actions that he or she may have undertaken when they were psychotic—experiencing or fearing rejection from community members and co-workers. That person now feels reluctant to go out, let alone return to work, because of the belief that he or she will be judged harshly by others.

Both alleviation of existing or emerging secondary morbidity and their prophylaxis are the legitimate foci of the therapeutic work of this secondary morbidity phase. Also, because they cause significant distress and disability, subthreshold forms of secondary morbidities are worthy of treatment (i.e., when the person's depressive symptoms are insufficient to meet the requirement for a full categorical diagnosis of depression).

Treatment

Most reports of the treatment of secondary conditions take the form of case reports (e.g., Sarron & Lelord, 1991). However, techniques used with people with so-called neurotic disorders may be apposite, although they may have to be modified and delivered in a slower fashion than the therapist might expect in dealing with clients with primary neurotic-type disorders. In addition, focal secondary conditions may be intertwined with residual psychotic symptoms, again interfering with the rate of therapeutic progress. The therapist should be prepared for disruptions and interruptions in the conduct of the therapy. Indeed, the agenda is unlikely to proceed in a straightforward and linear manner.

In treatment, although the therapist teaches cognitive disputation to clients (Beck, Rush, Shaw, & Emery, 1979), he or she relies far more on behavioral techniques than on cognitive approaches alone. The therapy emphasizes in vivo exposure, gradual approximations, graded task assignments, social skills training, behavioral rehearsal, problem solving, coping skills, and activity scheduling. Role plays and reverse role plays assume central importance. The material is presented simply and with multimodal media. Other useful adjunctive techniques include the empty-chair technique, imaginal exposure techniques, visualization, guided imagery, time projection, systematic desensitization, and self-instructions (see, e.g., Beck & Emery, 1985). Table 9.1 provides a list of secondary pathologies that may present in the wake of the first presentation of psychosis along with treatment techniques derived from

TABLE 9.1

Cognitive–Behavioral Treatments for Secondary Morbidity

Secondary Condition	Psychological Techniques
Depression	Cognitive therapy, including activity scheduling, increasing mastery and pleasure events, challenging beliefs and distortions, and graded tasks; social skills training
Social anxiety	Social skills (role plays), imaginal rehearsal, coping techniques, and breathing control (anxiety management), all as adjuncts to exposure treatment with cognitive restructuring
Posttraumatic stress disorder	Imaginal prolonged exposure, in vivo exposure, anxiety management, stress inoculation training (the latter two approaches include cognitive restructuring)
Obsessive–compulsive disorder	Response prevention and in vivo and imaginal exposure, with cognitive therapy as a possible adjunct
Generalized anxiety disorder	"Worry" treatment (relaxation and cognitive therapy)
Substance use disorder (especially alcohol)	Motivational interviewing; assertion skills, social skills, and refusal skills training; self-control training; stress management; cue exposure
Panic disorder with or without agoraphobia	In vivo exposure (and imaginal exposure, as needed), cognitive restructuring and coping skills, applied relaxation, breathing retraining as an adjunct
Simple phobia	In vivo exposure with or without modeling, systematic desensitization

Note. Adapted from Nathan & Gorman (1998) and Roth & Fonagy (1996).

evidence-based trials (Nathan & Gorman, 1998; Roth & Fonagy, 1996). For examples of our work in treating clients presenting with secondary conditions, see Jackson, Hulbert, and Henry (2000).

As previously emphasized, our view is that the techniques may have to be modified because of possible impediments to treatment, including clients' having lower IQs and less cognitive flexibility and clients' being young and unused to working within one-to-one therapeutic relationships. (Young clients mostly are used to interacting within a group- or classroom-based system.) Our young first-presentation clients are not especially introspective. Because they are not likely to undertake or complete their homework exercises, most therapy occurs in the therapeutic sessions. Clients are likely to drop out, be emotional, present only in crises, lack a long-range perspective, possess fewer coping skills, have compromised abstraction ability, and exhibit negative symptoms, meaning that clients often lack the energy and drive to accomplish tasks. They may possess personality vulnerabilities, such as dependency or perfectionism. Those vulnerabilities need to be addressed to some extent—if practical, in therapy. In view of these factors, it is imperative that clients are provided with clear and precise information about their diagnostic condition and the treatment proposed by the therapist (McGorry & Edwards, 1997).

TERMINATION

Broadly speaking, two closely related issues arise at termination. The first concerns the client's apprehensions that he or she will not be able to cope in the "real-world" without the therapist. The second involves the client's interpersonal attachment to the therapist.

In dealing with the first issue, we have found that collaboratively forming an agenda in the initial three sessions is essential to establishing the content, direction, frequency, length, and approximate number of sessions. The agenda communicates to the client at the outset that therapy is time-limited. The latter agenda may bear periodic repetition throughout the duration of the client's therapy, helping to prevent severe emotional issues at termination.

Second, it is imperative that throughout therapy, the therapist encourage independence and the attainment of goals in the client's daily life, so that therapy and the therapist do not become a substitute for life but rather assistance for dealing with day-to-day life. That is, the emphasis should be consistently on building and consolidating skills; reinforcement from the therapist is critical in that regard. In addition, periodically throughout therapy, and certainly near termination, the therapist should review the client's progress and ask the client to record his or her subjective therapeutic gains. Our approach is antiregressive and empowering, but it is conducted within the safety net of case management provided by EPPIC. That is to say, once the person completes COPE, he or she continues to have a case manager (Edwards, Cocks, & Bott, 1999).

Relapse prevention and ensuring that the patient is equipped with appropriate problem-solving and coping skills are important factors in preparing the patient for termination. High-risk situations from the client's past or hypothetical vignettes based on likely events can be used in therapy to rehearse client responses, as in the following case example:

> Robyn, a 23-year-old woman with schizophreniform disorder, is the mother of a 3-year-old child. She found access visits by the father of her child to be very stressful. She felt anxious both at

seeing her ex-partner and at "losing her child for the day." At these times, Jane feared that once therapy had terminated, she "would go crazy" without receiving regular support from her therapist. Strengthening Robyn's coping skills took priority. Responses to this situation were repeatedly rehearsed with the therapist, using techniques including behavior rehearsal, in vivo and imaginal exposure, muscle relaxation, coping self-statements, cognitive challenging, and distraction. The client also practiced contacting her friend and undertaking a pleasurable activity for the "access" day.

One way of gauging how clients may react at termination is from information gathered during therapy sessions, such as when the therapist is absent because of other work commitments, illness, or vacation. Another way of assessing how clients will deal with termination is to ask them how they have dealt with previous separations and "endings," such as leaving school, the deaths of people close to them in their life, the separation of parents, break-ups with friends, and moving schools. Generally, termination is not an unbearably *traumatic* time for most clients (although it may be a vulnerable time), perhaps because many of them are used to "moving on" in their lives. Nevertheless, clients may experience *some* degree of emotional turmoil during the termination phase. Attachment to the therapist is not uncommon, and the therapist should acknowledge that feeling *some* loss is appropriate for clients. With clients who may experience greater-than-expected emotional turmoil, it is important to be open in discussing the client's issues. Such discussion should begin in earnest at some lead-in time before the termination date, perhaps three to six sessions before therapy actually terminates. Besides allowing clients the opportunity to ventilate their grief and feelings of loss, clients can be asked, as noted previously, to describe how they have coped with losses in the past. If a client appears to be lacking in coping skills, the therapist can help him or her learn new approaches, as described in the previous case vignette. Note that our approach stands in contrast to the ethnocentric view of pure psychodynamic therapists.

Finally, as a general rule, the therapist should allow the client the opportunity to decide how he or she wishes to use the last session. This may take the form, for example, of having a "goodbye" coffee at a coffee shop. Before and during this session, the therapist should tactfully remind the client that it is the final session.

Research on COPE

To date, the research on COPE has consisted of a pilot study using a nonrandomized controlled group design and a randomized controlled group study. The data from the pilot study have been published (Jackson et al., 1998), and the report on the 1-year follow up of the pilot study has been completed (Jackson et al., in press). In the completed pilot study, 80 first-episode psychosis patients were placed in one of three groups. The first group consisted of patients who were attending EPPIC and were offered and accepted COPE ($n = 44$). The second group consisted of patients who also attended EPPIC and were offered but refused COPE ($n = 21$). The third group consisted of patients who were treated in EPPIC as inpatients, but because they belonged to geographic regions not served by EPPIC, were offered neither EPPIC outpatient services nor COPE once they were discharged from the EPPIC inpatient service ($n = 15$). All 80 patients were assessed on seven primary measures:

- Two psychological measures: the Integration/Sealing Over measure (I/SO; McGlashan, Wadeson, Carpenter, & Levy, 1977) and the Explanatory Model measure (EM; adapted from Kleinman, 1980)
- A measure of positive psychotic symptoms: the Brief Psychiatric Rating Scale (BPRS; Overall & Gorham, 1962, as modified by McGorry, Goodwin, & Stuart, 1988)
- A measure of negative symptoms: the Schedule for the Assessment of Negative Symptoms (SANS; Andreasen, 1983)
- Two measures of secondary morbidity: the 13-item Beck Depression Inventory (BDI; Beck & Beck, 1972) and the General Symptom Index (GSI) of the SCL–90–R (Symptom Checklist–90–Revised; Derogatis, 1977, 1983), which assesses a broad range of so-called neurotic symptoms
- A measure of psychosocial functioning: the Quality of Life Scale (QLS; Heinrichs, Hanlon, & Carpenter, 1984).

The seven measures were given at pretreatment, at 6 months, and at 12 months (end of treatment), but 6-month data were not analyzed. Treatment was delivered by one of six therapists who were trained and received ongoing weekly individual and group supervision in COPE. COPE patients received a mean number of 18 COPE sessions; the range was from 2 to 40, with the median number of COPE sessions being 19.

Results showed significant differences ($p < .05$) between COPE and the control group on the I/SO, EM, and QLS measures, favoring COPE; a trend ($p = .06$) on the SANS also favored COPE. The refusal group significantly outperformed the COPE group on the BDI, but this difference was not clinically meaningful, given that the mean BDI level recorded at the end of treatment for the COPE group was only 7.52, indicating mild levels of depression, compared with 2.70 and 4.21 for the refusal and control groups, respectively. Interestingly, on only one of the seven measures (i.e., the I/SO) did the COPE group outperform the refusal group, who received the range of services offered by EPPIC but refused COPE.

Effect sizes (ESs) favoring COPE relative to the control group varied from 1.04 and 0.80 for the I/SO and EM measures, respectively, to moderate ESs of 0.55 and 0.49 for the SANS and QLS, respectively. Apart from an ES of 0.71 for the I/SO measure, ESs favoring COPE over the refusal group were much smaller, varying from 0.10 to 0.25 for the BPRS, EM, QLS, and SANS. Both the control and the refusal groups outperformed COPE on the SCL–90–R GSI and BDI. ESs of 0.42 and 0.60 were reported for the COPE versus refusal group comparisons for the GSI and BDI, respectively; the ESs were 0.28 and 0.36 for the COPE versus control group comparisons for the same two measures. The poorer results for the COPE versus refusal comparisons might suggest that the intense and extensive range of services offered by EPPIC produce a ceiling effect, rendering it much harder for COPE to produce additional positive changes on the various measures. In summary, COPE tended to improve cognitive indicators of adjustment or adaptation, but not secondary morbidity. Functioning (as measured by the SANS and QLS) tended to be better in the COPE group, too. However, given the small obtained differences between the COPE and refusal groups, the enriched clinical service of EPPIC, which includes a group program and sophisticated case management programs, may contribute other factors (Edwards et al., 1999; Francey, 1999).

One must use caution in interpreting the above results because the pilot study used a nonrandomized design. Yet, it would seem that the positive results for the I/SO and EM measures reflect the relatively successful application of psychoeducation and cognitive–behavioral therapeutic techniques applied to the psychological targets (see Exhibit 9.1). In our subjective view, it is likely that improvement on the EM and I/SO measures reflects patients' developing some insight into their illness and developing a realistic yet nonpessimistic attitude toward the psychosis and their future. We also believe that COPE was most effective in changing negative appraisals about the psychosis itself, on improving coping skills, and on preventing engulfment of the self by the psychosis by cognitively mobilizing the person to reengage with their activities and pursue their goals. COPE was less effective in changing negative attributional style, negative core schemata/beliefs, and negative personality characteristics. We would argue that the positive results for the SANS and QLS represent successful behavioral activation of clients in tackling their activities and pursuing their goals. In our view, that successful activation followed from the positive changes effected in the psychological domain, as reflected by the positive results on the I/SO and EM.

The second empirical report recorded the 1-year follow-up data for the three groups (Jackson et al., in press). Only 51 of the 80 patients who completed assessments at the end of treatment attended the 1-year follow-up assessment. Significantly more patients from the COPE group (77%) returned to complete the follow-up assessment, whereas only 43% of the refusal group and 53% of the control group attended. (The superior attendance figure for the COPE participants at 1-year follow-up could be considered an outcome measure in itself.) No suicides occurred over the 1-year follow-up period; one accidental work-related death occurred in the refusal group. The three groups had no differences in the proportion of rehospitalizations or relapses.

For the 51 patients who actually completed the 1-year follow-up assessment, it was found that most within-group treatment gains were maintained over the follow-up period. The COPE group showed a 3-point deterioration in BPRS scores over follow-up, although positive symptoms were not a focus of the COPE treatment intervention. The refusal group showed trends for deterioration on the EM and QLS measures. The only significant between-group difference was between the COPE group and the refusal group on the I/SO measure, favoring the COPE group.

Subsidiary analyses (using 2×2 analyses of covariance) found a differential nonattender effect. Within the COPE group, patients with the poorer pretreatment and end-of-treatment scores were more likely to attend the follow-up assessment than higher scoring patients; the end-of-treatment within-group differences held, even though pretreatment scores were controlled for within the analysis of covariance model. In contrast, within the control group, patients with the better pretreatment and end-of-treatment scores were more likely to return for the 1-year follow-up assessment. The results reached statistical significance ($p < .05$) for the EM and SANS measures. On the whole, the results mean that between-group differences were reduced, especially between the COPE and the control group.

A second-generation study of COPE began in 1996. The between-group study is virtually completed, and analysis of the data will commence soon. This two-group design is a randomized control group design that uses the same seven primary measures as in the previous work. The two groups are a COPE group and a control group. The COPE group received the full range of EPPIC services as well as the COPE treatment; the control group received the full range of EPPIC services but was not offered COPE. This study is not a test of "standard treatment plus COPE" versus "standard treatment." Rather, it tests whether the provision of COPE contributes something over and above the services provided by EPPIC, which is a service delivery system offering far more enriched and comprehensive programs than those provided by standard psychiatric services (see Edwards & McGorry, 1998; Edwards et al., 1994; Francey, 1999; McGorry et al., 1996). The design has proved somewhat problematic, as it is open to the risk of leakage between therapy conditions; however, this appears to be a universal problem whenever studies are conducted in real-life services (S. Lewis, personal communication, September 1999).

Challenges

The EPPIC service has functioned as a clinical laboratory in the development of the COPE program. The data are still emerging. Although the COPE pilot data are somewhat encouraging, we are not convinced that we have established the optimal COPE treatment package. We view COPE as an evolving treatment and plan to test it over time in a series of studies. Specific challenges pertain to treatment delivery and applicability, the content of the treatment and the weighting given to the components of COPE, and the transportability (or generalizability) of treatment to other settings.

In dealing first with the delivery of COPE, we confront a series of issues pertaining to the timing of the treatment, the optimal number of sessions, the spacing of the sessions, and the length and duration of the sessions. In our studies, treatment sessions were held approximately every 2 weeks—in some cases, less often. We have contemplated whether more optimal results would follow if sessions were spaced weekly or twice weekly, rather than the most appropriate frequency being decided according to therapist discretion. Likewise, another issue involves whether sessions should be of a uniform length (e.g., 50 minutes or 15 or 30 minutes); those judgments also have been left to therapist discretion. The tension here is between scientific standards of rigor, on the one hand, and respect for the varying mental state of individual clients, on the other. Of course, this issue plagues many studies of effectiveness (Seligman, 1995).

The second vexing issue concerns the applicability of COPE. In our studies, clients were offered treatment if they were considered "settled" by the treating clinicians. Indeed, inspection of the mean BPRS scores confirms the low levels of positive symptoms acknowledged by clients (Jackson et al., 1998, 1999). We are considering whether the treatment should be offered to *all* first-episode clients on entry to the EPPIC service irrespective of their symptom severity, illness phase, and general mental state. Doing so may appear impractical, given the costliness in terms of therapist time; however, it may promote the importance of a psychological approach and its integration with biological treatment (i.e., the need for neuroleptic medication).

A related question is whether COPE treatment should be offered to first- or second-episode clients. The question is, Are first-episode psychotic clients more invulnerable in the sense that they feel that they will not suffer from a subsequent psychotic episode and so reject psychological treatments like COPE? Would clients be more ready to accept COPE if they had suffered a second or third episode? This question is empirical, of course; an equal concern pertains to the consequences of delaying treatment. The literature informs us that if we do not provide our optimal interventions as early as possible in the first episode, we may place people at risk of increased impairments, a negative course, and poor outcomes. In part, this outcome may be a result of biological kindling at the neurotransmitter level (Wyatt, 1991), but it also may stem from "psychological kindling" resulting from patient despondency, social withdrawal, and self- and other-stigmatization (Birchwood, 1999). All of those forces may lead to the client accruing disabilities, metaphorically being on a "moving train, unable to get off."

A third series of issues pertains to the content of the therapy. Should COPE treatment be more behaviorally oriented? Given the level of functioning of many clients, some members of our research group have asserted that we may have spent too much time working on client cognitions and that behavioral activities are more likely to produce positive effects and positive cognitive change. Another question concerns whether treatment is too diverse and unfocused. Rather than offering a smorgasbord of treatment targets and treatment techniques within COPE, would it be more sagacious (and effective) to focus more on one or two aspects of client adaptation? Although the two questions have been the focus of debate in our group, they are ultimately best settled by empirical methods. At the same time, from the clinical and ethical viewpoints, we are clearly of the view that COPE, however narrowly or broadly defined, can be but one of a number of treatments (e.g., case management, low-dose medication, and family interventions) offered routinely to clients with a psychotic disorder (McGorry & Jackson, 1999).

The final challenge is to find more appropriate psychological measures. We are dissatisfied with the I/SO and EM, although nearly a decade ago, we considered them to be reasonable measures of psychological functioning. The I/SO had a long history in the literature on schizophrenia, being authored by a leading researcher in the field, Thomas McGlashan. The I/SO is assessed by a 6-point scale measuring the client's recovery style and adaptation to the psychotic illness. Low scores represent integration of the illness, whereas high scores indicate "sealing over," or denial, of the illness. McGlashan himself has doubts about our use—or rather, our interpretation of the use—of the I/SO (T. Mc-Glashan, personal communication, June 2, 1997). Rather than viewing all high scores on sealing over as indicative of a poor "cognitive" attitude, with implications for a poor negative outcome, he views the I/SO as a descriptor of idiographic recovery styles.

The EM measure also is a source of dissatisfaction. The measure attempts to explain the client's understanding about five domains of an episode of illness by using a series of structured questions concerning the client's view of the etiology of the problem, time and mode of onset, pathology, course of illness, and treatment. The client's responses are compared with the treating clinician's model of illness, and the score represents the discrepancy between the client and clinician. Higher EM scores represent greater discrepancies. Consider the instance in which a case manager holds a stereotypic, neo-Kraepelinian view of schizophrenia and the patient does not: The patient may receive a poorer (i.e., higher) EM score, not because the patient's views are extreme or bizarre, but because they are at odds with his or her case manager's views. It may be that the best solution is to use a number of psychological instruments. Because one of the targets for adaptation involves restoring, improving, or increasing problem-solving and coping skills, measures of those two constructs should perhaps be included in new studies using COPE. In addition, new studies require a measure of self-efficacy (Bandura, 1977, 1986) because we are focusing on improving clients' sense of personal power. Finally, a measure of possible selves should be included to provide a shorthand method of accessing the client's goals, aspirations, and feared alternatives (see footnote, p. 254).

Summary and Conclusion

This chapter has reviewed the background and theoretical underpinning of COPE, emphasizing the protection of the self and continued positive life span development as important goals in the wake of the initial psychotic episode. The evaluation data on COPE are limited and emanate from one source, namely EPPIC. Our studies require replication elsewhere. As indicated, the virtually completed randomized controlled study tested the additive effects of COPE to EPPIC, an enriched program. However, COPE needs to be tested in combination with standard care and against standard care alone as well as in a diversity of settings.

Although COPE was developed quite specifically for a first-presentation psychosis group, aspects of it, such as the treatment of secondary morbidity, can be extrapolated to populations with chronic psychotic illnesses. Treating secondary morbidity in chronic patients might reduce their suffering and severity of disability. Again, this application would require evaluation. Finally, COPE offers a counter to the therapeutic nihilism still encountered in discussions about the nonorganic psychoses, especially schizophrenia, although ultimately, empirical outcomes will determine its viability and acceptability. For those of us trained and immersed in the scientist–practitioner model, this is as it should be.

References

Amador, X. F., Strauss, D. H., Yale, S. A., & Gorman, J. M. (1991). Awareness of illness. *Schizophrenia Bulletin, 17*, 113–132.

American Psychiatric Association. (1980). *Diagnostic and statistical manual of mental disorders* (3rd ed.). Washington, DC: Author.

American Psychiatric Association. (1987). *Diagnostic and statistical manual of mental disorders* (3rd ed., rev.). Washington, DC: Author.

American Psychiatric Association. (1994). *Diagnostic and statistical manual of mental disorders* (4th ed.). Washington, DC: Author.

Andreasen, N. C. (1983). *Schedule for the assessment of negative symptoms.* Iowa City: University of Iowa.

Andreasen, N. C. (1984). *The broken brain: The biological revolution in psychiatry.* New York: Harper & Row.

Argyle, N. (1990). Panic attacks in chronic schizophrenia. *British Journal of Psychiatry, 157*, 430–433.

Bandura, A. (1977). Self-efficacy: Toward a unifying theory of behavioral change. *Psychological Review, 84*, 191–215.

Bandura, A. (1986). *Social foundations of thought and action: A social cognitive theory.* Englewood Cliffs, NJ: Prentice-Hall.

Beck, A. T., & Beck, R. W. (1972). Screening depressed patients in family practice: A rapid technique. *Postgraduate Medicine, 52*, 81–85.

Beck, A. T., & Emery, G. (1985). *Anxiety disorders and phobias: A cognitive perspective.* New York: Basic Books.

Beck, A. T., Freeman, A., & Associates. (1990). *Cognitive therapy of personality disorders.* New York: Guilford Press.

Beck, A. T., Rush, A. J., Shaw, B. F., & Emery, G. (1979). *Cognitive therapy of depression.* New York: Guilford Press.

Bellack, A. S., Gold, J. M., & Buchanan, R. W. (1999). Cognitive rehabilitation for schizophrenia: Problems, prospects, and strategies. *Schizophrenia Bulletin, 25*, 257–274.

Bentall, R. P., Haddock, G., & Slade, P. D. (1994). Cognitive behavior therapy for persistent auditory hallucinations: From theory to therapy. *Behavior Therapy, 25*, 51–66.

Bermanzohn, P. C., Porto, L., & Siris, S. G. (1997, September). *Associated psychiatric syndromes (APS) in chronic schizophrenia: Possible clinical significance.* Paper presented at the XXVIII Congress of the European Association for the Behavioural and Cognitive Therapies, Venice, Italy.

Binder, J. L., & Strupp, H. H. (1997). "Negative process": A recurrently discovered and underestimated facet of therapeutic process and outcome in the individual psychotherapy of adults. *Clinical Psychology: Science and Practice, 4,* 121–139.

Birchwood, M. (1999). Early intervention in psychosis: The critical period. In P. D. McGorry & H. J. Jackson (Eds.), *The recognition and management of early psychosis: A preventive approach* (pp. 226–264). Cambridge, England: Cambridge University Press.

Birchwood, M., McGorry, P., & Jackson, H. (1997). Early intervention in schizophrenia. *British Journal of Psychiatry, 170,* 2–5.

Bland, R. C., Newman, S. C., & Orn, H. (1987). Schizophrenia: Lifetime co-morbidity in a community sample. *Acta Psychiatrica Scandinavica, 75,* 383–391.

Boyd, J. H. (1986). Use of mental health services for the treatment of panic disorder. *American Journal of Psychiatry, 143,* 1569–1574.

Bruner, J. (1986). *Actual minds, possible worlds.* Cambridge, MA: Harvard University Press.

Chadwick, P. J., Birchwood, M., & Trower, P. (1996). *Cognitive therapy for delusions, voices and paranoia.* Chichester, England: Wiley.

Chatterjee, A., & Lieberman, J. A. (1999). Studies of biological variables in first-episode schizophrenia: A comprehensive review. In P. D. McGorry & H. J. Jackson (Eds.), *The recognition and management of early psychosis: A preventive approach* (pp. 115–152). Cambridge, England: Cambridge University Press.

Corrigan, P. W., & Penn, D. L. (1999). Lessons from social psychology on discrediting psychiatric stigma. *American Psychologist, 54,* 765–776.

Costa, P. T., Jr., & Widiger, T. A. (Eds.). (1994). *Personality disorders and the five-factor model of personality.* Washington, DC: American Psychological Association.

Davidson, L., & Strauss, J. S. (1992). Sense of self in recovery from severe mental illness. *British Journal of Medical Psychology, 65,* 131–145.

Davidson, L., & Strauss, J. S. (1995). Beyond the biopsychosocial model: Integrating disorder, health, and recovery. *Psychiatry, 58,* 44–55.

Derogatis, L. R. (1977). *SCL-90-R: Administration, scoring & procedures manual.* Towson, MD: Clinical Psychometric Research.

Derogatis, L. R. (1983). *SCL-90-R: Administration, scoring & procedures manual-II for the revised version.* Towson, MD: Clinical Psychometric Research.

Dixon, L. B., & Lehman, A. F. (1995). Family interventions for schizo-phrenia. *Schizophrenia Bulletin, 21*, 631–643.

Early Psychosis Prevention and Intervention Centre. (1997). *Psycho-education in early psychosis: Manual 1 in a series of early psychosis manuals.* Melbourne, Australia: Victoria Department of Human Services, EPPIC Statewide Services and the Mental Health Branch.

Edwards, J., Cocks, J., & Bott, J. (1999). Preventive case management in first-episode psychosis. In P. D. McGorry & H. J. Jackson (Eds.), *The recognition and management of early psychosis: A preventive approach* (pp. 308–337). Cambridge, England: Cambridge University Press.

Edwards, J., Francey, S. M., McGorry, P. D., & Jackson, H. J. (1994). Early Psychosis Prevention and Intervention: Evolution of a compre-hensive community-based service. *Behaviour Change, 11*, 223–233.

Edwards, J., Maude, D., McGorry, P. D., Harrigan, S. M., & Cocks, J. T. (1998). Prolonged recovery in first-episode psychosis. *British Journal of Psychiatry, 172*(Suppl. 33), 107–116.

Edwards, J., & McGorry, P. D. (1998). Early intervention in psychotic disorders: A critical step in the prevention of psychological morbidity. In C. Perris & P. D. McGorry (Eds.), *Cognitive psychotherapy of psychotic and personality disorders: Handbook of theory and practice* (pp. 167–195). Chichester, England: Wiley.

Erikson, E. H. (1968). *Identity: Youth and crisis.* New York: Norton.

Fadden, G. (1999, September). *The implementation of therapies into the health services.* Paper presented at the Third International Conference on Psychological Treatments for Schizophrenia, Oxford, England.

Fenning, S., Kovasznay, B., Rich, C., Ram, R., Pato, C., Miller, A., Ru-binstein, J., Carlson, G., Schwartz, J. E., Phelan, J., Lavelle, J., Craig, T., & Bromet, E. (1994). Six-month stability of psychiatric diagnoses in first-admission patients with psychosis. *American Journal of Psychi-atry, 151*, 1200–1208.

Fenton, W., & McGlashan, T. (1986). The prognostic significance of obsessive-compulsive symptoms in schizophrenia. *American Journal of Psychiatry, 143*, 437–441.

Filia, S. L. (1996). *Possible selves in a clinical sample of first episode psychotic patients.* Unpublished thesis, University of Melbourne, Melbourne, Australia.

Fowler, D., Garety, P., & Kuipers, E. (1995). *Cognitive behaviour therapy for psychosis: Theory and practice.* Chichester, England: Wiley.

Francey, S. M. (1999). The role of day programmes in recovery in early psychosis. In P. D. McGorry & H. J. Jackson (Eds.), *The recognition and management of early psychosis: A preventive approach* (pp. 407–437). Cambridge, England: Cambridge University Press.

Frank, A. F., & Gunderson, J. G. (1990). The role of the therapeutic alliance in the treatment of schizophrenia. *Archives of General Psychiatry, 47,* 228–236.

Fransella, F., & Bannister, D. (1977). *A manual for repertory grid techniques.* London: Academic Press.

Gilbert, P. (1997). The evolution of social attractiveness and its role in shame, humiliation, guilt and therapy. *British Journal of Medical Psychology, 70,* 113–147.

Gilbert, P., & Allan, S. (1998). The role of defeat and entrapment (arrested flight) in depression: An exploration of an exploratory view. *Psychological Medicine, 28,* 585–598.

Green, M. F. (1993). Cognitive remediation in schizophrenia: Is it time yet? *American Journal of Psychiatry, 150,* 178–187.

Green, M. S., & Nuechterlein, K. H. (1999). Should schizophrenia be treated as a neurocognitive disorder? *Schizophrenia Bulletin, 25,* 309–319.

Greenfeld, D., Strauss, J. S., Bowers, M. B., & Mandelkern, M. (1989). Insight and interpretation of illness in recovery from psychosis. *Schizophrenia Bulletin, 15,* 245–252.

Gunderson, J. G., Frank, A. F., Katz, H. M., Vannicelli, M. L., Frosch, J. P., & Knapp, P. H. (1984). Effects of psychotherapy in schizophrenia. II. Comparative outcome of two forms of treatment. *Schizophrenia Bulletin, 10,* 564–598.

Hambrecht, M., & Häfner, H. (1996). Substance abuse and the onset of schizophrenia. *Biological Psychiatry, 5,* 56–62.

Harding, C. M., Zubin, J., & Strauss, J. S. (1987). Chronicity in schizophrenia: Fact, partial fact, or artifact? *Hospital and Community Psychiatry, 38,* 477–486.

Harrigan, S. (1999). *Repertory grid technique: An application in first-episode psychosis.* Melbourne, Australia: Swinburne University of Technology.

Heinrichs, D. W., Hanlon, T. E., & Carpenter, W. T., Jr. (1984). The quality of life scale: An instrument for rating the schizophrenic deficit syndrome. *Schizophrenia Bulletin, 10,* 388–398.

Henry, L., McGorry, P. D., Jackson, H. J., Hulbert, C. A., & Edwards, J. (1997, September). *Cognitive psychotherapy and the prevention of secondary morbidity in first episode psychosis.* Paper presented at the XXVIII Congress of the European Association for the Behavioural and Cognitive Therapies, Venice, Italy.

Hogarty, G. E., Kornblith, S. J., Greenwald, D., DiBarry, A. L., Cooley, S., Flesher, S., Reiss, D., Carter, M., & Ulrich, R. (1995). Personal therapy: A disorder-relevant psychotherapy for schizophrenia. *Schizophrenia Bulletin, 21,* 379–393.

Hogarty, G. E., Kornblith, S. J., Greenwald, D., DiBarry, A. L., Cooley, S., Ulrich, R. F., & Carter, M. (1997a). Three-year trials of personal therapy among schizophrenic patients living with or independent of family: I. Description of study and effects on relapse rates. *American Journal of Psychiatry, 154,* 1504–1513.

Hogarty, G. E., Greenwald, D., Ulrich, R. F., Kornblith, S. J., DiBarry, A. L., Cooley, S., Carter, M., & Flesher, S. (1997b). Three-year trials of personal therapy among schizophrenic patients living with or independent of family: II. Effects on adjustment of patients. *American Journal of Psychiatry, 154,* 1514–1524.

Hulbert, C. A., Jackson, H. J., & McGorry, P. D. (1996). Relationship between personality and course and outcome in early psychosis: A review of the literature. *Clinical Psychology Review, 16,* 707–727.

Ioannides, T. (Producer), & Hexter, I. (Director). (1994). *A stitch in time* [Video]. Melbourne, Australia: Early Psychosis Prevention and Intervention Centre (EPPIC) for Psychiatric Services Branch, and the Victorian Government Department of Health and Community Services.

Jackson, H. J. (1998). The assessment of personality disorder: Selected issues and directions. In C. Perris & P. D. McGorry (Eds.), *Cognitive psychotherapy of psychotic and personality disorders* (pp. 293–314). Chichester, England: Wiley.

Jackson, H. J., Edwards, J., Hulbert, C., & McGorry, P. D. (1999). Recovery from psychosis: Psychological treatments. In P. D. McGorry & H. J. Jackson (Eds.), *The recognition and management of early psychosis: A preventive approach* (pp. 265–307). Cambridge, England: Cambridge University Press.

Jackson, H. J., Hulbert, C. A., & Henry, L. P. (2000). The treatment of secondary morbidity in first episode psychosis. In M. Birchwood, D. Fowler, & C. Jackson (Eds.), *Early intervention in psychosis: Guide to concepts, evidence and intervention* (pp. 213–235). Chichester, England: Wiley.

Jackson, H. J., McGorry, P. D., & Dudgeon P. (1995). Prodromal symptoms of schizophrenia in first episode psychosis: Prevalence and specificity. *Comprehensive Psychiatry, 36,* 241–250.

Jackson, H. J., McGorry, P. D., Edwards, J., & Hulbert, C. (1996). Cognitively oriented psychotherapy for early psychosis (COPE). In P. Cotton & H. J. Jackson (Eds.), *Early intervention and prevention in mental health* (pp. 131–154). Melbourne: Australian Psychological Society.

Jackson, H. J., McGorry, P. D., Edwards, J., Hulbert, C., Henry, L., Francey, S., Maude, D., Cocks, J., Power, P., Harrigan, S., & Dudgeon, P. (1998). Cognitively-oriented psychotherapy for early psychosis (COPE): Preliminary results. *British Journal of Psychiatry, 172*(Suppl. 33), 93–100.

Jackson, H., McGorry, P., Henry, L., Edwards, J., Hulbert, C., Harrigan, S., Dudgeon, P., Francey, S., Maude, D., Cocks, J., & Power, P. (in press). Cognitively-oriented psychotherapy for early psychosis (COPE): A one-year follow-up. *British Journal of Clinical Psychology.*

Jeffries, J. J. (1977). The trauma of being psychotic: A neglected element in the management of chronic schizophrenia. *Canadian Psychiatric Association Journal, 22,* 199–206.

Kelly, G. A. (1955). *The psychology of personal constructs.* New York: Norton.

Kingdon, D. G., & Turkington, D. (1994). *Cognitive-behavioral therapy of schizophrenia.* New York: Guilford Press.

Kleinman, A. (1980). *Patients and healers in the context of culture. An exploration of the borderline between anthropology, medicine, and psychiatry.* Berkeley: University of California Press.

Kyrios, M. (1998). A cognitive-behavioural approach to the understanding and management of obsessive-compulsive personality disorder. In C. Perris & P. D. McGorry (Eds.), *Cognitive psychotherapy of psychotic and personality disorders* (pp. 352–378). Chichester, England: Wiley.

Labbate, L. A., Young, P. C., & Arana, G. W. (1999). Panic disorder in schizophrenia. *Canadian Journal of Psychiatry, 44,* 488–490.

Lally, S. J. (1989). "Does being in here mean there is something wrong with me?" *Schizophrenia Bulletin, 15,* 253–265.

Lazarus, R. S., & Folkman, S. (1984). *Stress, appraisal, and coping.* New York: Springer.

Levinson, D. J. (1986). A conception of adult development. *American Psychologist, 41,* 3–13.

Lewis, S. (1999, September). *Integrating drug and non-drug treatments in schizophrenia.* Paper presented at the Third International Conference on Psychological Treatments for Schizophrenia, Oxford, England.

Liberman, R. P., Kopelowicz, A., & Young, A. S. (1994). Biobehavioral treatment and rehabilitation of schizophrenia. *Behavior Therapy, 25,* 89–107.

Lieberman, J. A., Alvir, J., Woerner, M., Degreef, G., Bilder, R. M., Ashtari, M., Bogerts, B., Mayerhoff, D. I., Geisler, S. H., Loebel, A., Levy, D. J., Hinrichsen, G., Szymanski, S., Chakos, M., Koreen, A., Borenstein, M., & Kane, J. M. (1992). Prospective study of psychobiology in first episode schizophrenia at Hillside Hospital. *Schizophrenia Bulletin, 18,* 351–371.

Luborsky, L., McLellan, A. T., Diguer, L., Woody, G., & Seligman, D. A. (1997). The psychotherapist matters: Comparison of outcomes across twenty-two therapists and seven patient samples. *Clinical Psychology: Science and Practice, 4,* 53–65.

Mahoney, M. J. (1991). *Human change processes: The scientific foundations of psychotherapy.* New York: Guilford Press.

Markus, H., & Nurius, P. (1986). Possible selves. *American Psychologist, 41,* 954–969.

McGlashan, T. H., & Johannessen, J. O. (1996). Early detection and intervention with schizophrenia: Rationale. *Schizophrenia Bulletin, 22,* 201–222.

McGlashan, T. H., Wadeson, H. S., Carpenter, W. T., & Levy, S. T. (1977). Art and recovery style from psychosis. *Journal of Nervous and Mental Disease, 164*, 182–190.

McGorry, P. D. (1992). The concept of recovery and secondary prevention in psychotic disorders. *Australian and New Zealand Journal of Psychiatry, 26*, 3–17.

McGorry, P. D. (1995). Psychoeducation in first-episode psychosis: A therapeutic process. *Psychiatry, 58*, 329–344.

McGorry, P. D., & Edwards, J. (1997). *Early psychosis training pack*. Cheshire, England: Gardiner-Caldwell Communications.

McGorry, P. D., Chanen, A., McCarthy, E., van Riel, R., McKenzie, D., & Singh, B. S. (1991). Posttraumatic stress disorder following recent-onset psychosis. An unrecognized postpsychotic syndrome. *Journal of Nervous and Mental Disease, 179*, 253–258.

McGorry, P. D., Edwards, J., Mihalopoulis, C., Harrigan, S. M., & Jackson, H. J. (1996). EPPIC: An evolving system of early detection and optimal management. *Schizophrenia Bulletin, 22*, 305–326.

McGorry, P. D., Goodwin, R. J., & Stuart, G. W. (1988). The development, use, and reliability of the BPRS (Nursing Modification): An assessment procedure for the nursing team in clinical and research settings. *Comprehensive Psychiatry, 29*, 575–587.

McGorry, P. D., Henry, L., Maude, D., & Phillips, L. (1998). Preventively-oriented psychological interventions in early psychosis. In C. Perris & P. D. McGorry (Eds.), *Cognitive psychotherapy of psychotic and personality disorders: Handbook of theory and practice* (pp. 213–236). Chichester, England: Wiley.

McGorry, P. D., & Jackson, H. J. (Eds.). (1999). *The recognition and management of early psychosis: A preventive approach*. Cambridge, England: Cambridge University Press.

Mohr, D. C. (1995). Negative outcome in psychotherapy: A critical review. *Clinical Psychology: Science and Practice, 2*, 1–27.

Mooney, M., & Pica, S. (1997, September). *Social phobia in psychosis. Detection and treatment*. Paper presented at the XXVIII Congress of the European Association for the Behavioural and Cognitive Therapies, Venice, Italy.

Mueser, K. T., Yarnold, P. R., Levinson, D. F., Singh, H., Bellack, A. S., Kee, K., Morrison, R. L., & Yadalam, K. G. (1990). Prevalence of substance abuse in schizophrenia: Demographic and clinical correlates. *Schizophrenia Bulletin, 16*, 31–56.

Mueser, K. T., Goodman, L. B., Trumbetta, S. L., Rosenberg, S. D., Osher, F. C., Vidaver, R., Auciello, P., & Foy, D. W. (1998). Trauma and post-traumatic stress disorder in severe mental illness. *Journal of Consulting and Clinical Psychology, 66*, 493–499.

Murray, H. A. (1938). *Explorations in personality.* New York: Oxford University Press.

Nathan, P. E., & Gorman, J. M. (Eds.). (1998). *A guide to treatments that work.* Oxford, England: Oxford University Press.

Neimeyer, R. A., & Mahoney, M. J. (Eds.). (1995). *Constructivism in psychotherapy.* Washington, DC: American Psychological Association.

Norman, R. M. G., & Townsend, L. A. (1999). Cognitive-behavioural therapy for psychosis: A status report. *Canadian Journal of Psychiatry,* 44, 245–252.

Ogilvie, D. M. (1987). The undesired self: A neglected variable in personality research. *Journal of Personality and Social Psychology, 52,* 379–385.

Overall, J. E., & Gorham, D. R. (1962). The brief psychiatric rating scale. *Psychological Reports, 10,* 799–812.

Penn, D. L., Corrigan, P. W., Bentall, R. P., Racenstein, J. M., & Newman, L. S. (1997). Social cognition in schizophrenia. *Psychological Bulletin, 121,* 114–132.

Perris, C. (1989). *Cognitive therapy with schizophrenic patients.* New York: Guilford Press.

Power, P., Elkins, K., Adlard, S., Curry, C., McGorry, P., & Harrigan, S. (1998). Analysis of the initial treatment phase in first-episode psychosis. *British Journal of Psychiatry, 172*(Suppl. 33), 71–76.

Rey, J. M. (1992). The Epidemiological Catchment Area (ECA) study: Implications for Australia. *Medical Journal of Australia, 156,* 200–203.

Roberts, G. (1999a). Introduction: A story of stories. In G. Roberts & J. Holmes (Eds.), *Healing stories: Narrative in psychiatry and psychotherapy* (pp. 3–26). Oxford, England: Oxford University Press.

Roberts, G. (1999b). The rehabilitation of rehabilitation: A narrative approach to psychosis. In G. Roberts & J. Holmes (Eds.), *Healing stories: Narrative in psychiatry and psychotherapy* (pp. 152–180). Oxford, England: Oxford University Press.

Robins, E., & Guze, S. B. (1970). Establishment of diagnostic validity in psychiatric illness: Its application to schizophrenia. *American Journal of Psychiatry, 126,* 983–987.

Roth, A., & Fonagy, P. (1996). *What works for whom? A critical review of psychotherapy research.* New York: Guilford Press.

Sarron, C., & Lelord, F. (1991). In vivo exposure of a schizophrenic patient with agoraphobic symptoms. *European Psychiatry, 6,* 107.

Scott, J. E., & Dixon, L. B. (1995). Psychological interventions for schizophrenia. *Schizophrenia Bulletin, 21,* 621–630.

Seligman, M. E. P. (1991). *Learned optimism.* Sydney: Random House.

Seligman, M. E. P. (1995). The effectiveness of psychotherapy: The *Consumer Reports* study. *American Psychologist, 50,* 965–974.

Shorter, E. (1997). *A history of psychiatry: From the era of the asylum to the age of Prozac.* New York: Wiley.

Siris, S. G. (1991). Diagnosis of secondary depression in schizophrenia: Implications for DSM-IV. *Schizophrenia Bulletin, 17,* 75–98.

Smith, T. E., Bellack, A. S., & Liberman, R. P. (1996). Social skills training for schizophrenia: Review and future directions. *Clinical Psychology Review, 16,* 599–617.

Strakowski, S. M., Tohen, M., Stoll, A. L., Faedda, G. L., Mayer, P. V., Kolbrener, M. L., & Goodwin, D.C. (1993). Comorbidity in psychosis at first hospitalisation. *American Journal of Psychiatry, 150,* 752–757.

Strakowski, S. M., Keck, P. E., Jr., McElroy, S. L., Lonczak, H. S., & West, S. A. (1995). Chronology of comorbid and principal syndromes in first-episode psychosis. *Comprehensive Psychiatry, 36,* 106–112.

Strauss, J. S. (1994). The person with schizophrenia. II. Approaches to the subjective and complex. *British Journal of Psychiatry, 164*(Suppl. 23), 103–107.

Tarrier, N. (1992). Management and modification of residual positive psychotic symptoms. In M. J. Birchwood & N. Tarrier (Eds.), *Innovations in the psychological management of schizophrenia: Assessment, treatment and services* (pp. 147–169). Chichester, England: Wiley.

Weinberger, J. (1995). Common factors aren't so common: The common factors dilemma. *Clinical Psychology: Science and Practice, 2,* 45–69.

Wyatt, R. J. (1991). Neuroleptics and the natural course of schizophrenia. *Schizophrenia Bulletin, 17,* 325–351.

Wykes, T., Tarrier, N., & Lewis, S. W. (Eds.). (1998). *Outcome and innovation in psychological treatment of schizophrenia.* Chichester, England: Wiley.

Wykes, T., Reeder, C., Corner, J., Williams, C., & Everitt, B. (1999). The effects of neurocognitive remediation on executive processing in patients with schizophrenia. *Schizophrenia Bulletin, 25,* 291–307.

Young, J. E. (1994). *Cognitive therapy for personality disorders: A schema-focused approach* (Rev. ed.). Sarasota, FL: Professional Resource Press.

Object-Relations and Reality-Testing Deficits in Schizophrenia | 10

Morris D. Bell

Diana[1] was angry, on edge, and speaking rapidly: "I know I have to stop losing it. I don't want my kids to grow up with this. I'm screaming way too much. I mean it's sort of cute, he'll say, 'Daddy's been a bad boy, so mommy's yelling at him,' but I know that it's not good for him." Diana's son is 2½, and her daughter is 7 months old. Her husband has been on worker's compensation because of a hand injury for more than a year and does not do nearly enough of the daily chores. She has been working full-time as a delivery driver and has been taking overtime whenever she can get it. They own their own suburban home, and she gets up at 5:30 a.m. to run with her dogs through the land-trust woods that abut her property. The city is considering building an incinerator on the site, and she has been leading a citizens' action committee to prevent this. "I'm exhausted, I don't come home some days till 2:00 a.m., and I'm up at 5:30 a.m. I like being busy, I need to be busy, but I'm losing it half the time." Diana has another problem: She has a diagnosis of paranoid schizophrenia.

I first met Diana 12 years ago when she was in her early 20s. She had had her first psychotic episode while in the U.S. military. She had been transferred overseas, where she developed paranoid delusions about her new companions and officers; she heard voices threatening her, and she thought her food was poisoned. She was given a medical

---

[1]Diana is not her real name. Otherwise this is a faithful account of what occurred. She was pleased to sign a release for its use in this chapter.

retirement from the military and had been hospitalized almost continuously for 2 years when she entered a residential rehabilitation program where I worked. She appeared stiff, suspicious, and aloof during most of her stay, although she was cooperative and developed emotional connections with some of the staff. I saw her a few times after her discharge, when she would come to "alumnae" picnics, usually with the small children of her sister, whom she cared for while her sister was at work.

Diana maintained treatment with a psychiatrist in our mental hygiene clinic, but 3 years ago she had stopped taking medication because she was married and wanted to become pregnant. Except for occasional telephone contact, she had received no formal treatment. Her psychiatrist was on maternity leave, and when Diana came in, I offered to see her. She was glad for a familiar face but said that she hated being reminded of all the things doctors had put her through. "That medicine they gave me was poison. It made me stiff, and I was so scared. Just coming here reminds me of it. Restraints, seclusion—a nightmare." When I gently asked about psychotic symptoms, she wanted to deny them. "I just block it out. I don't have time for it, I try to block it out!" Tears shot from her eyes. "The voices in the woods are bothering me and sometimes the radio starts talking to me again, and the license numbers on the cars I pass, I think they're following me. I think my house is being videotaped, but maybe that's because of those city politicians who know I'd kill them if I could." Like a woman who knows that the lump she's been trying to ignore is a sign of recurring disease, Diana was caught between her wish to get better and her fear of acknowledging the truth of her condition.

I persuaded her that new medications might give her relief without the side effects she dreaded and that a psychiatrist I trusted would work with us slowly to reduce the symptoms. "I can't drive if I get blurry vision, and I don't want to walk around all the time with a water bottle 'cause my mouth is dry. But I know I've got to do something!"

Diana arrived late to her next appointment, but by the end, she had agreed to a subclinical dose of risperidone, one of a new generation of antipsychotic medications. The next week she was much calmer and less pressured, and she reported that she had had no side effects. She was not sure whether it was working or not. The dose was increased to a minimal therapeutic level, and the following week she again reported no side effects and no symptoms. She later commented, "My grandmother died in a mental institution. I think my mother's got this disease, although she'll never admit it. But I think it's not such a big deal. If my kids start showing signs of schizophrenia, I'll get them help right away, 'cause there's no reason to let it get bad before you do something about it."

Four weeks later, there had been no recurrence of symptoms, her husband and she were getting along much better, and she had rearranged her work hours to a more sensible schedule. She said that she'd like to keep coming for a while, just to talk, because "my husband has selective listening. He listens to what he thinks is important. I know he cares, but it helps to have someone else to talk to."

I begin this chapter with Diana because she represents many people with schizophrenia who recover sufficiently to lead productive and meaningful lives. She demonstrates no serious object-relations deficits, although her relationships are becoming adversely affected by her illness and she has enough observing ego to be aware of her reality-testing deficits. In fact, she called upon her good object relations and other features of good ego functioning to cope with paranoid symptoms. But the drain on her psychological resources was becoming too great. Combined with other stresses, her symptoms were worsening. In the end, she sought treatment out of fear of relapse and because of her deep commitment to her family. They were counting on her, and she needed to be well for them.

Ego Functions: The Highest Level of Organization for Human Thought and Behavior

Human behavior is organized hierarchically. Although neuroscience may reveal the molecular mechanisms of neuronal functions, distinguish elemental features of cognition, and map complex neural networks that link those features together, people are not necessarily best or most completely understood by tracing their behavior to those fundamental processes. Even higher cortical functions, such as problem solving, decision making, and conation, do not themselves represent the highest level of psychological organization. I argue that the ego and its functions have a useful place in our conception of how the human organism is psychologically constructed, particularly as a metaphor for irreducible characteristics of human capacity.

Definitions of ego functions have been refined by ego psychologists and other psychoanalytic thinkers and were most clearly and concretely articulated by Bellak, Hurvich, and Gediman (1973) in *Ego Function in Schizophrenics, Neurotics and Normals*. They identified 12 distinct ego functions, offered a semistructured interview for their assessment, and developed rating scales for each. Recognizing the variability of ego functions, they recommended rating a subject's highest, lowest, and typical level of function. Their method operationalized the construct of a "bracket of functioning," the range along a continuum of ego functioning within which a person was likely to behave. By defining the ego in terms of its functions, Bellak et al. avoided the contentious and irresolvable conflicts among schools of psychoanalysis regarding etiology and metapsychology (cf. Greenberg & Mitchell, 1983, for the diversity of theories). Object relations was defined in terms of the degree and kind of relatedness to others (e.g., symbiotic, narcissistic, mutual, or empathic), primitivity or maturity, extent to which others are perceived as independent entities, and the extent to which object constancy is maintained. Reality testing was defined in terms of accuracy of perception and interpretation of external events, internal events, and the ability to distinguish between them.

Following their method, Diana can be described as having possessed a well-developed capacity for empathy (e.g., with her children); a moderately effective achievement of ambivalence (e.g., being able to tolerate loving and angry feelings toward the same person, such as her husband); a sense of basic trust and the belief that relationships are worthwhile; and a moderately stable sense of self. It also appears that this level of object relations was threatened by the increased pressure of her reality-testing impairments. She was becoming more suspicious, viewing her husband more in terms of her own needs (e.g., not doing enough around the house) rather than as a separate entity (i.e., man with an injury), and viewing the world in more black-and-white terms with less ability to metabolize dangerous, negative affects (e.g., politicians are bad, trying to get me, I'd like to kill them). Thus, she was displaying a wider bracket of object-relations functioning than would be normally expected. Reality-testing deficits were in evidence in the recrudescence of paranoid symptoms, which included reality distortions such as ideas of reference (license plates on passing cars having personal meaning, radio sending her special messages), suspiciousness (house under surveillance), and hallucinatory experiences (hearing whispering in the woods). The experiences were not continuous, and she could argue with herself to maintain a more realistic perspective, but it appeared that she was rapidly losing her ability to do so. Once on appropriate medication, her reality testing was restored and her object relations returned to a higher level.

SOCIAL COGNITION AND OBJECT RELATIONS

Does a chapter on object relations have a place in a volume devoted to social cognition in schizophrenia? I believe it does. Penn, Corrigan, Bentall, Racenstein, and Newman (1997) underscored the contribution that cognitive psychology may make to understanding people with schizophrenia, particularly in regard to their processing of social information about themselves, other people, and social situations and how they interact. To acquire, process, evaluate, and respond to social information and to perceive others as distinct from one's own biases are social cognitive abilities that are fundamental to object relations.

Because cognitive psychology and ego psychology come from separate historical roots and scientific foundations, they seldom meet in the same intellectual endeavor. Yet, they both may contribute to our understanding of the human experience. A painting may be analyzed by examining the artist's skills—his sensitivity to color, his brush technique, his sense of composition—or it may be analyzed in terms of its emotional impact—its artistic allusions, its expression of ineffable human experience, its artistic merit. Just as both approaches illuminate important features of artistic creation, social cognition and object relations are approaches that highlight important but different elements of the human creation called relatedness. Furthermore, it seems likely that a certain amount of social cognitive processing skill is necessary to establish and sustain good object relations, and it will be of great significance to learn which components (e.g., theory of mind, affect recognition, and working memory) contribute most to relatedness. However, superior social cognition may not be sufficient to produce good object relations. Indeed, many people excel at processing social information for the purpose of serving narcissistic aims. They have the artist's skills, but their creations are frightful. Therefore, the assessment of object-relations functioning in schizophrenia supplies the student of social cognition with a method of description that captures essential features of human relatedness and may serve a complementary role in its exploration and exposition.

OBJECT-RELATIONS DEVELOPMENT AND SCHIZOPHRENIA

Formal developmental studies have at last liberated the investigation of object relations from the guesswork and freewheeling theorizing of early psychoanalysts, whose principal sources of data were their patients' recollection of childhood events. Bowlby (1969), Mahler (1979), Stern (1985), and Schore (1994) are examples of synthetic thinkers who have used direct observation of children, mother–child, and child–caregiver interactions as well as ethological reports, animal research, and neurobiological studies to explicate the development of human relatedness from infancy into adulthood. Their theories recognize the critical importance of early attachment experiences in the development of basic trust, the self-regulation of affect, and the capacity for social processing. Just as basic nutrition is required for normal physical growth, appropriate levels of stimulation, affection, and freedom of exploration are required for normal relatedness. Stages of psychological growth can be defined through the life span, with the achievement in adulthood of good levels of object-relations functioning as characterized by Bellak et al. (1973).

This normal progression of object-relations development can be arrested in many ways. Pervasive developmental delay and autism, in particular, are examples of disorders in which necessary cognitive processes for relatedness are impaired during fetal development (Volkmar, 1998). Maternal deprivation (Spitz, 1965), childhood trauma (Haviland, Sonne, & Woods, 1996), severe social disruption (Krystal, 1988) or acquired brain disease (Damasio, 1994) also may profoundly affect a person's capacity for object relations.

Schizophrenia may be regarded best as a neurodevelopmental disorder that results from a combination of genetic predisposition, a biologically acquired diathesis (e.g., from influenza infection in second trimester, starvation during pregnancy, or perinatal complications), and environmental or interpersonal stresses (e.g., poverty, maternal deprivation, or social disruption). Schizophrenia may profoundly alter object relations, but because schizophrenia is a heterogeneous disorder, it is likely that its effect on object-relations functioning also may vary. For people with the most severe form of "deficit syndrome" schizophrenia (Kirkpatrick, Buchanan, McKenney, Alphs, & Carpenter, 1989), it is likely that the disorder may include ventricular enlargements (suggesting cortical atrophy) and a compromise of elemental cognitive processes that underlie object-relations functioning. For some, an early onset of the illness profoundly disrupts the normal acquisition of experiences that would have allowed their object relations to mature, so their object relations appear arrested in development. For some, the negative symptoms of alogia, avolition, and anergia or the positive symptoms of hallucinations and delusions so disrupt normal functioning that their latent capacity for relatedness is veiled and distorted by these extreme experiences. Finally, for some people, like Diana, the development of object relations is not impaired, despite a likely genetic predisposition to the illness, and the capacity for good object relations is restored when symptoms are properly treated.

My description of the connection between object-relations impairment and schizophrenia differs sharply from traditional psychoanalytic writings, which identified failures of maternal attachment as the causal factor in psychosis (e.g., the schizophrenogenic mother). In the neurodevelopmental model of schizophrenia that I have offered, it should be clear that the question, "Which came first: poor object relations or schizophrenia?" cannot be answered easily and that bad parenting is not to blame. It may be that neurodevelopmental impairments that affect attachment do play some role. The evidence so far suggests that people often display early cognitive manifestations of what later becomes schizophrenia (although many children with these cognitive problems do not develop schizophrenia) and that those cognitive impairments may affect attachment (and, by inference, internalized object relations). Poorly developed object relations may make a person more vulnerable to confused and stressful interpersonal experiences and less able to benefit from the support of family or friends. As confusion and isolation increases, so does the likelihood of overt psychosis. Symptoms of schizophrenia, in turn, may have profound effects on object relations, as I have already suggested.

The research described in the sections that follow provides empirical evidence for the diversity of object-relational capacity and the reality-testing deficits that relate to it. The research shows that good object-relations and reality-testing functioning are more likely to be preserved in people whose onset of illness comes after adolescence and young adulthood, that a variety of distinct patterns of object-relations and reality-testing impairment are found within schizophrenia, and that those patterns are associated with particular symptoms and personality features.

Assessment of Object-Relations and Reality-Testing Ego Functioning: The Bell Object Relations Reality Testing Inventory

A Gary Larson cartoon shows a caveman mounted atop a mammoth. He is examining the creature with a magnifying glass. The caption reads "It's a mammoth!" The humor derives from the incongruity between the refined method of assessment and the size of the phenomenon being examined. Although object relations and reality testing are significant functions that profoundly affect behavior, they are not necessarily detectable without the proper approach to assessment. Bizarre behavior, poor hygiene, excitability, or aggression are mammoth-size clinical features that do not require magnification for appraisal, but the internal experience of a person in relation to others or the private fears, reality distortions, and hallucinations of impaired reality testing are not directly observable. They can be discovered only with proper tools. The semistructured interview for assessing ego functioning recommended by Bellak et al. (1973) asked probing questions that were based on the assumption that reliable ratings of levels of ego functioning could be inferred from people's descriptions of their inner life and experiences with others. Because of the clinical sensitivity and theoretical sophistication of Bellak et al.'s definition of object-relations and reality-testing ego functions, I initially used their methods in assessing people with schizophrenia. It also is why I later chose their scales as the theoretical foundation for constructing a self-report instrument that eventually became the Bell Object Relations and Reality Testing Inventory (BORRTI; Bell, 1995). I selected these two ego functions for special study because I believed that they would be highly important in schizophrenia and because they were amenable to self-report.

The main reasons for creating a self-report instrument were the length of the Bellak interviews, the effort involved in transcription and scoring, and difficulties in maintaining interrater reliability. The BORRTI was developed to solve those problems by providing a set of 90 true–false statements that offer descriptions of experiences common to people at various levels of object-relations (OR) or reality-testing (RT) functioning. Many of the statements came directly from responses people made in Bellak interviews that I conducted (e.g., "It is my fate to lead a lonely life" and "It is hard for me to get close to anyone").

After much refinement and testing of items (see Bell, 1995, for description of instrument development), factor analyses and their replications revealed that four OR subscales and three RT subscales had a high degree of factorial invariance (Bell, Billington, & Becker, 1985, 1986; See Exhibit 10.1 for subscale descriptions). Tests of the subscales' psychometric properties demonstrated internal consistency; split-half reliability; test–retest reliability; and relative freedom from gender, age, or social desirability bias. In a schizophrenia sample, test–retest reliability over 6 months showed remarkable stability with six of the seven subscales having correlations in the good to excellent range. Because no "gold standard" exists for ego-function assessment to which the BORRTI could be compared, external validity of the subscales depended on the convergence of experience in a wide variety of relevant research. Evidence for the BORRTI's utility has come from correlating individual differences on its subscales with other tests, with group membership, and with other appropriate criteria. Accumulated experience over the past 15 years by more than 100 researchers in more than a dozen countries has demonstrated that the BORRTI subscales exhibit lawful relationships to diagnostically defined psychiatric samples, other psychological testing instruments, and many specific research questions. The BORRTI has found wide application in studies outside of psychopathology, including organizational management, health-related issues, psychology of religion, and normal personality and development (see Bell, 1995, for summary of validity studies and bibliography).

BORRTI AND SCHIZOPHRENIA

The BORRTI's original purpose was to understand OR and RT functioning in schizophrenia. Studies within this population have revealed that

EXHIBIT 10.1

BORRTI Subscales: Characteristics of High Scores and Item Examples

Object Relations

Alienation (ALN): Lack of basic trust. Serious difficulties with intimacy. Lacks sense of connection or belonging.
- "I have at least one stable and satisfying relationship." (F)
- "It is hard for me to get close to anyone." (T)
- "It is my fate to lead a lonely life." (T)

Insecure Attachment (IA): Rejection sensitive. Fears separation and abandonment. Easily hurt by others.
- "I feel I have to please everyone or else they may reject me." (T)
- "I am extremely sensitive to criticism." (T)
- "I often worry that I will be left out of things." (T)

Egocentricity (EGC): Lack of empathy. Self-protective. Exploitative. Controlling.
- "People are never honest with each other." (T)
- "I am usually sorry that I trusted someone." (T)
- "I believe a good mother should always please her children." (T)

Social Incompetence (SI): Social discomfort. Shy. Avoidant. Difficulty making friends.
- "Making friends is not a problem for me." (F)
- "I feel shy about meeting or talking with members of the opposite sex." (T)
- "I generally rely on others to make my decisions for me." (T)

Reality Testing

Reality Distortion (RD): Distorts internal and external reality. Ideas of reference.
- "I feel that my thoughts are being taken away from me by an external force." (T)
- "People are often angry at me whether they admit it or not." (T)
- "I possess mystical powers." (T)

Uncertainty of Perception (UP): Doubts own perceptions. Confused by own feelings.
- "I know my own feelings." (F)
- "I feel out of touch with reality for days at a time." (T)
- "I am usually able to size up a new situation quickly." (F)

Hallucinations and Delusions (HD): Hallucinations. Delusions. Paranoia. Grandiosity.
- "I hear voices that others do not hear which keep up a running commentary on my behavior and thoughts." (T)
- "I am being followed." (T)
- "I experience strange feelings in various parts of my body which I can't explain." (T)

Positive and Negative Syndrome Scale (PANSS; Kay, Fiszbein, & Opler, 1987; Bell, Lysaker, Beam-Goulet, & Milstein, 1994) positive symptom totals correlate significantly with RT subscales but have much weaker correlations with OR subscales. Negative symptoms correlate significantly only with the OR Social Incompetence subscale, and cognitive symptoms do not relate to either RT or OR scales (Bell, 1995). The results supported the validity of RT scales while demonstrating the divergent validity of the OR subscales. OR subscales were measuring a feature of psychological functioning that was not closely related to psychotic symptoms.

In our first effort to examine whether OR scores differentiated subtypes of schizophrenia, we assessed 45 men and 3 women who were U.S. military veterans and diagnosed with schizophrenia or schizoaffective disorder (Bell, Lysaker, & Milstein, 1992). They were inpatients, and most were in early stages of recovery from an acute exacerbation. We found that more than 90% had at least one pathological elevation on OR subscales (a pathological elevation is defined as a t score of greater than or equal to 60, which is one standard deviation above the mean). OR scores did not differentiate schizoaffective from other schizophrenia diagnoses, paranoid from nonparanoid schizophrenia, or good premorbid adjustment from poor premorbid adjustment (based on self-report using methods of Cannon-Spohr, Potkin, & Wyatt, 1986), but patients with prominent negative symptoms had much lower scores on the Insecure Attachment subscale. This low score suggested that they had withdrawn from interpersonal engagement to the point where their fears of abandonment and anxious attachment had been dulled and blunted. Thus, they suffered the alienation of schizophrenia but lacked the self-experience of anguished yearnings for relatedness.

Limitations From Sample Selection: The Blind Men and the Elephant

The limitations of the study described above are a relatively small sample size and the selective circumstances under which the sample was obtained. Like blind men examining an elephant, one by feeling its long, flexible nose; another by reaching around its tree trunk–like leg; and a third groping along the walls of its flanks, schizophrenia researchers often are describing different kinds of schizophrenia at different points in the course of the illness. Hence research reports continually remind us of the limitations imposed on conclusions by virtue of the sample selected for study. One advantage of using a self-report instrument like the BORRTI is that it makes it practical to obtain relatively large samples of research participants who can be assessed in the same way each time. Although sample size does not guarantee that all manifestations of the disorder will be included, it increases the likelihood that more variation will be represented.

In the following study, the sample comprised 157 outpatient participants in my work-rehabilitation research program for schizophrenia. Funded by the Rehabilitation Research and Development Service of the Department of Veterans Affairs, this research program examines occupational dysfunction in schizophrenia and the variables that most affect rehabilitation. Participants in work research were eligible for inclusion if they met *DSM–III–R* diagnostic criteria for schizophrenia (American Psychiatric Association, 1987) and were stabilized in treatment (i.e., without housing or medication changes in the past 30 days). They were administered the BORRTI, the PANSS, and various neuropsychological tests at intake, at 5 months, and at 1-year follow-up intervals. Because the sample consisted of a veteran population, it was 95% male and 57.8% White, and it had an average age of 42.9 years and average education of 12.5 years. On average, participants had been hospitalized for the first time at 25.4 years, and their illness had an average duration of 17.57 years. Most (57%) had never been married. They displayed a wide range of severity and variety of symptoms, and although some had an episodic course of illness, many had had an unremitting course since onset. Diagnoses included paranoid (67.2%), undifferentiated (21.9%), disorganized (6.3%), and residual (4.7%). Missing from this sample were people with schizophrenia who did not have occupational impairments and those who were too acutely ill to participate in rehabilitation. Also excluded from our sample were people with schizoaffective disorder because research on onset of illness has exclusively focused on schizophrenia. With data from this sample, it was possible to test the hypothesis that early onset of schizophrenia disrupts object-relations development, leading to more severe impairments.

Hypothesis: Late-Onset Schizophrenia Allows Better Object-Relations and Reality-Testing Functioning

We began our report on this study (Greig, Bell, Kaplan, & Bryson, 2000) by noting that previous research on age of onset (Gupta, Rajaprabhakaran, Ardnt, Flaum, & Andreasen, 1995; Harris & Jeste, 1988; Jeste et al., 1995) had found consistently that people with later onset typically had better premorbid function, were more likely to be women, and were more likely to have a diagnosis of paranoia. However, the researchers failed to identify any contemporaneous clinical characteristics that distinguished people with early- and late-onset schizophrenia, including symptoms and neuropsychological test variables. Indeed, their findings supported the *DSM-IV* (American Psychiatric Association, 1994) conclusion that early- and late-onset schizophrenia did not require separate clinical categories. We decided to compare age-of-onset groups on symptoms, neuropsychological testing, and BORRTI scores, expecting that object relations alone would demonstrate group differences. We hypothesized that early- and late-onset groups would differ in ego functioning on the BORRTI.

We created two discontinuous age groups, defining those whose illness began before age 20 as early onset (*n* = 36) and those whose illness began after age 30 as late onset (*n* = 28). Those whose onset occurred between ages 21 and 30 (*n* = 93) were retained for later analysis. Those in our early-onset group typically received psychiatric care while in the military and were discharged. Members of the late-onset group typically completed their military service. Given that those in our late-onset group were under scrutiny throughout military service, it is unlikely that they could have been grossly psychotic without symptoms being observed. Therefore, military history provides a valid basis for judging when onset of symptoms occurred.

We reasoned that those who did not become symptomatic until their 30s would have had more opportunity to develop ego strength through the mastery of living skills, vocational achievements, and more complex social relationships and would therefore have better ego functioning than those whose illness began in adolescence. The benefit of the years of maturity should still be detectable through less impaired object relations, despite symptom severity and cognitive impairments equivalent to those of people with an early onset.

As hypothesized, a comparison of the two onset groups showed that the early-onset group was significantly more impaired on three of four OR subscales (Alienation, Insecure Attachment, and Social Incompetence). The early-onset group also showed significantly greater impairment on all three RT subscales (Reality Distortion, Uncertainty of Perception, and Hallucinations and Delusions).

We also compared early- and late-onset groups on the frequency of elevated subscale scores. Analysis revealed that more than two thirds of people in the early-onset group had two or more significant subscale elevations; in contrast, fewer than one third of those in the late-onset group had two or more clinically significant elevations.

Having found these striking differences between early- and late-onset groups, we repeated the analyses with the middle-onset group. Results indicated that the middle-onset group had scores on all subscales that fell between the early- and late-onset groups, although a clear pattern did not emerge. On some subscales (i.e., Social Incompetence and Reality Distortion), the middle- and early-onset groups were significantly different from the late-onset group, whereas on other subscales (i.e., Alienation, Insecure Attachment, and Uncertainty of Perception) the middle and late groups were significantly different from the early-onset group.

When onset groups were compared on symptoms, the five PANSS components (Positive, Negative, Cognitive, Emotional Discomfort, and Hostility) did not differ, nor did the groups differ on IQ (Slosson, 1963; Wechsler, 1982), Wisconsin Card Sorting Task (Heaton, Chelune, Talley, Kay, & Curtis, 1993), or Continuous Performance Task (Loong, 1991) variables.

Examination of BORRTI profiles using frequency of elevations revealed that the most common profile types for the early onset group included elevations on Alienation, Egocentricity, and Social Incompetence in various combinations. This pattern of scores indicates difficulties in establishing trust, forming satisfying relationships, and interacting socially; people with this pattern tend to perceive others as existing only to meet one's own needs. Patients in the late-onset group tended to have a single elevation on Alienation, indicating difficulties in basic trust, but they did not tend to have concurrent elevations on other subscales. Social Incompetence was seldom elevated. This finding particularly supports the contention that those with later onset have retained a sense of mastery in relation to social demands that people with early-onset schizophrenia lack.

Important group differences also were found on the reality-testing subscales. Specifically, the early-onset group demonstrated significantly higher mean scores on all three RT subscales than did people in the late-onset group, indicating a greater level of impairment for the early-onset group. Frequencies revealed that more than four fifths of those in the early-onset group had one or more pathological elevations on reality-testing subscales; in contrast, a little more than half of the people in the late-onset group had one or more such elevations. In particular, about 67% of the early-onset group had elevations on Hallucinations and Delusions, compared with 40% for the late-onset group. Furthermore, the most common types of profile for the early-onset group were for all three subscales to be elevated or for Reality Distortion and Hallucinations and Delusions to be elevated. The late-onset group had more profiles with Reality Distortion alone, although Reality Distortion often was combined with the other two subscales.

The results of this study were important for several reasons. First, they supported the hypothesis that late onset is more favorable for ego functioning than is early onset. Second, it demonstrated that in this application, the constructs of ego functioning had greater discriminative power than did symptom and neuropsychological variables. Whereas symptoms and cognitive performance were accurate depictions of contemporary functioning, object relations and reality testing, as measured by the BORRTI, captured the self-experience of the person coping with his or her external and internal environment. Therefore, a later onset may favorably affect the ability of people with schizophrenia to sustain a view of themselves and their world, which in turn protects them from the fears and distortion that accompany their illness. Thus, they are somewhat more likely to be able to maintain basic trust, tolerate the painfulness of relationships, have empathy for others, and feel less socially incompetent. Similarly, they may be more likely to maintain an observing ego, which reduces vulnerability to experiences of hallucinations and delusions.

Finally, the results were important because they suggested that discernible BORRTI profile types might exist within schizophrenia. Rather than comparing schizophrenia subgroups on BORRTI scores, another strategy was implied: We could search for unique and reliable patterns of OR and RT subscale scores by a method called cluster analysis. If we found meaningful patterns into which most people with schizophrenia could be classified, we could provide a fresh and heuristically valuable way of conceptualizing the heterogeneity of schizophrenia that would be based on ego functioning rather than on traditional methods such as signs, symptoms, and course of illness. These ego-function types would be expected to have distinct clinical correlates and be related to other aspects of personality as well. We therefore hypothesized that responses to the BORRTI by a sample of people with schizophrenia would yield meaningful clusters, that the clusters could be replicated, and that the replicated clusters would possess distinctive clinical and personality correlates.

BORRTI Profiles From a Large Sample of People With Schizophrenia

As in the previous study, our BORRTI respondents were from the work-rehabilitation studies program. However, we included people with schizoaffective disorder as well as additional people who had entered the program since the analysis regarding onset of illness. In all, 224 outpatient participants with *DSM–IV* diagnoses of schizophrenia (*n* = 162) or schizoaffective disorder (*n* = 60) were administered the BORRTI, the Eysenck Personality Questionnaire (EPQ; Eysenck & Eysenck, 1975), the PANSS symptom interview, neuropsychological testing, and a psychosocial interview. As with the sample in the previous study, women were underrepresented; also missing were people with schizophrenia without occupational impairment and those so acutely ill as to be unable to participate in rehabilitation. Also absent were people whose illness was so apparent before age 18 that they were ineligible for military service. Even with these limitations, this sample represents the largest ever reported for the study of ego functioning in schizophrenia (see Bell, Greig, Kaplan, & Bryson, 2001).

HYPOTHESIS: MOST PEOPLE WITH SCHIZOPHRENIA CAN BE CLASSIFIED INTO A FEW RELIABLE BORRTI PROFILES

The first step in finding reliable BORRTI profile types was to use a hierarchical clustering procedure called the Ward method, which determined whether the pool of participants could be classified into a small number of homogeneous groups based on BORRTI profiles. We then used the cubic clustering criterion, providing the maximum value across hierarchy levels (Sarle, 1983) to find the most appropriate and accurate clustering solution. This method indicated an 8-cluster solution.

We conducted a replication analysis (McIntyre & Blashfield, 1980) in an effort to provide internal validity for the eight-cluster solution. Samples were obtained for comparison by randomly dividing the larger data set into two smaller samples. The first sample was clustered using a disjoint cluster analysis that computed the distance between centroids for each cluster. Cluster means were generated for each cluster. The second sample was cluster-analyzed using the cluster means generated from the first sample as cluster seeds, producing a cluster solution of the second sample based on the characteristics of the first sample. The second sample was then cluster-analyzed using its own data. Cluster membership was compared between the two analyses of the second sample, and the kappa (κ) statistic was used as a measure of agreement. Six of the eight clusters proved to be stable and replicable with a high degree of agreement $\kappa = .78$). All but 38 participants (17%) were identified with a specific cluster. Figure 10.1 displays the BORRTI profiles for the six clusters paired according to their similarity. The names given for each of the clusters are explained in the discussion to follow. Thus, six distinctive BORRTI profile types (or clusters) had been discovered, proven replicable, and their membership determined. We could now go on to look at how these six types differed on symptom and personality measures.

HYPOTHESIS: BORRTI CLUSTERS DIFFER IN SYMPTOM AND PERSONALITY CHARACTERISTICS

All participants had been administered the PANSS symptom interview and the EPQ at the same time as the BORRTI. Multivariate analyses of

Three pairs of cluster profiles for the BORRTI from a schizophrenia sample. The *t* scores are based on norms published in the BORRTI manual. The object-relations subscales are Alienation (ALN), Insecure Attachment (IA), Egocentricity (EGC), and Social Incompetence (SI). The reality-testing subscales are Reality Distortion (RD), Uncertainty of Perception (UP), and Hallucinations and Delusions (HD).

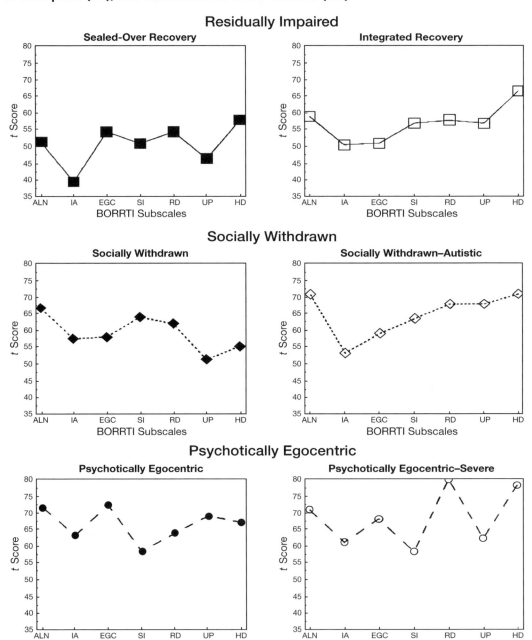

variance (MANOVA) between the six clusters on PANSS component scores (see Exhibit 10.2 for descriptions of the PANSS components) demonstrated a significant difference ($p < .001$). In post hoc comparisons (Scheffe's test), patients with Psychotically Egocentric–Severe (PES) profiles demonstrated significantly higher positive component scores than did those in the other clusters, except for Socially Withdrawn–Autistic (SWA). In addition, Sealed-Over Recovery (SOR) demonstrated significantly lower emotional discomfort scores than did SWA and PES. Scheffe's test failed to reveal further significant differences between clusters on PANSS components. Comparisons of the clusters on PANSS components are displayed in Figure 10.2.

The EPQ is a self-report inventory that generates three subscale scores: Extraversion (with introversion at one end and extraversion at the other), Neuroticism, and Psychoticism (see Exhibit 10.2). The EPQ

EXHIBIT 10.2

PANSS Components (Bell et al., 1994) and Characteristics of High Scores on the EPQ Subscales (Eysenck & Eysenck, 1975)

PANSS	EPQ
Positive	*Extraversion*
Hallucinations,	Sociable
Delusions, Paranoia	Craves excitement, Takes chances
Grandiosity, Unusual	Impulsive
Thoughts	Aggressive
Negative	*Neuroticism*
Passive withdrawal	Anxious
Blunted Affect	Worried
Motor Retardation	Moody
Cognitive	Overemotional
Conceptual Disorganization	Somatic
Poor attention	*Psychoticism*
Difficulty in abstract thinking	Tough-mindedness
Emotional Discomfort	Insensitive
Anxiety, Depression	Hostile
Guilt	Lacks empathy
Hostility	Solitary
Hostility, Poor impulse	*Lie*
control, Uncooperativeness	Denial of common human weakness
Excitement	Tendency to endorse only socially desirable items
	Faking "good"

Positive and Negative Syndrome Scale (PANSS; Kay, Fiszbein, & Opler, 1987; Bell, et al., 1994) component *t* scores for the three pairs of schizophrenia BORRTI types. The *t* scores are based on sample distribution. PANSS components are Positive Symptoms (Pos), Negative Symptoms (Neg), Cognitive Disorganization (Cog), Emotional Discomfort (Emo), and Hostility (Hos). The types are Sealed-Over Recovery (SOR), Integrated Recovery (IR), Psychotically Egocentric (PE), Psychotically Egocentric–Severe (PES), Socially Withdrawn (SW), and Socially Withdrawn–Autistic (SWA).

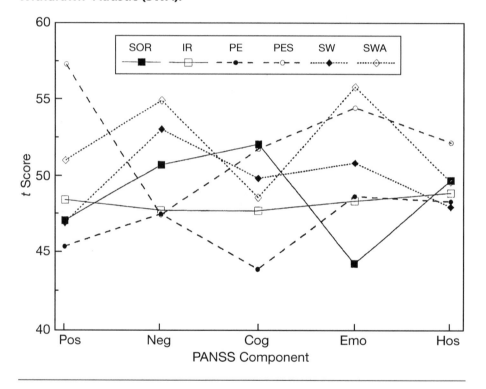

also contains a Lie scale, which measures the respondent's attempt to "fake good." The EPQ has been reported to be reliable and valid (Eysenck & Eysenck, 1975) and has been used in other studies on schizophrenia. On EPQ, multiple analysis of covariance (Lie scale was the covariate) across clusters demonstrated significance ($p < .001$). In post hoc comparisons, individual clusters showed significant differences from each other in a variety of complex patterns, as shown in Figure 10.3. The findings provided interpretable associations between each cluster and PANSS and EPQ variables.

FIGURE 10.3

Eysenck Personality Questionnaire (Eysenck & Eysenck, 1975) subscale *z* score profiles for the three pairs of schizophrenia BORRTI types. The *z* scores were derived from standardized norms published in the manual. The types are Sealed-Over Recovery (SOR), Integrated Recovery (IR), Psychotically Egocentric (PE), Psychotically Egocentric–Severe (PES), Socially Withdrawn (SW), and Socially Withdrawn–Autistic (SWA).

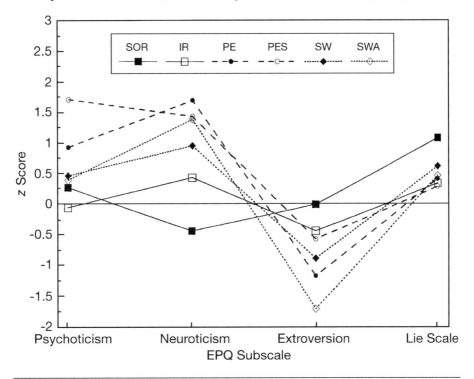

INTERPRETATION OF 6 BORRTI PROFILE TYPES

Six clusters were identified and replicated. We grouped the clusters into three pairs: Residually Impaired, Socially Withdrawn, and Psychotically Egocentric.

Residually Impaired

As Figure 10.1 shows, the first cluster presents a profile distinctive for having no clinical elevations and for having a clinically significant *low* score on Insecure Attachment. We have labeled this profile *Sealed-Over Recovery* (SOR) to indicate that return of good ego functioning has been achieved by erecting rigid defenses. The abnormally low Insecure At-tachment score suggests that people in this group avoid or deny any pain and longing in interpersonal relationships. Furthermore, their av-erage Social Incompetence score indicates that they are relatively suc-cessful in interacting socially and can maintain superficial relationships. They are not overly suspicious or mistrustful and may have sufficient basic trust to be able to gain some gratification from their relationships with others. Yet, those relationships may lack depth, and more intimate involvement may be destabilizing. Such people may live comfortably with their family and participate in social activities at a psychosocial clubhouse, but they avoid any deeper involvement that might upset their psychological equilibrium. They have only residual features of reality-testing impairment and endorse few items suggesting first-rank symptoms of schizophrenia. As might be expected, the other psycholog-ical features associated with this cluster include lower scores than mem-bers of other clusters on the EPQ Neuroticism scale and relatively higher scores on EPQ Extraversion (see Figure 10.3). The elevated Lie scale further indicates rigid defenses, revealed by an unwillingness to ac-knowledge common human failings. The PANSS profile (see Figure 10.2) is notable for relatively low positive symptoms, higher cognitive disorganization (commonly observed in association with poorer insight), and the lowest level of emotional discomfort. Thus, it appears that peo-ple with this cluster are in a residual phase of recovery of ego function-ing, in which their defenses are relatively rigid but effective in warding off emotional distress, even if it is at the cost of avoiding more intimate relationships.

The second cluster in the pair has a similar profile shape. We call this cluster *Integrated Recovery* (IR) because the profile indicates more interest in relationships and acknowledgement of symptoms. The BORRTI profile shows Alienation and Reality Distortion at the border of clinical elevation, and the Hallucinations and Delusions subscale is clinically elevated. All other scales are within the normal range. People with this profile are likely to be interested in more intimate relationships and experience more emotional pain as a result. They have some mild psychotic symptoms, which may include hallucinations or delusional beliefs, but these experiences are likely to be understood and accepted as symptoms of their illness. At the same time, they are likely to have the capacity to engage in social interactions, despite their symptoms, and to experience some gratification from relationships. Associated fea-tures on the EPQ (Figure 10.3) are similar to those of the SOR cluster with which they are paired. They have low Psychoticism and relatively low Neuroticism, and they are the second most extraverted of the clus-ters. What distinguishes this cluster from SOR on the EPQ is its relatively low score on the Lie scale, reflecting a willingness to acknowledge common difficulties. PANSS scores (Figure 10.2) are similar to those of SOR, although the cognitive disorganization score is somewhat lower and the emotional discomfort score is somewhat higher. Despite the elevated Hallucinations and Delusions subscale score, the level of positive symptoms does not differ significantly from those of SOR.

Socially Withdrawn

The second pair of cluster profiles share similar OR scores, marked by clinical elevations on Alienation and Social Incompetence. People with these elevations are likely to lack basic trust in relationships, experience themselves as socially inept, are unable to relate to members of the opposite sex, and avoid even superficial interactions with others. Although they may have some interest in relationships, they may not believe that relationships can be emotionally gratifying. They tend to be shy and isolative and maintain stability only by carefully modulating their amount of involvement. The two clusters differ dramatically in their reality-testing impairment. We call the first cluster *Socially Withdrawn* (SW), because of the OR profile, but people in this cluster report only residual paranoid beliefs and reality distortions and do not endorse items suggesting widespread delusions or hallucinations. We call the second cluster in the pair *Socially Withdrawn–Autistic* (SWA) to reflect the clinically significant elevations on all three reality-testing subscales. This profile suggests that people in this cluster may be preoccupied by psychotic experiences such as auditory hallucinations and paranoid delusions, which substitute an autistic pseudocommunity of spirits, voices, or pursuing forces for any real involvement with people. Such a profile may indicate social isolation as a direct response to paranoid experiences or hallucinations, rather than a more benign avoidance of stimulation, which might be the case for SW.

Whereas people in the SW cluster have moderate scores on all the associated features from EPQ and PANSS, those in the SWA cluster are distinctive for their high scores on Neuroticism and lowest scores on Extraversion (Figure 10.3). The SWA PANSS profile (Figure 10.2) is notable for highest scores on negative symptoms in the presence of high positive symptoms as well as having the highest scores on emotional discomfort. These findings portray people who are highly introverted, have severe negative and positive symptoms, and experience considerable emotional distress.

Psychotically Egocentric

The third pair possesses nearly identical OR profiles and has elevations on all RT scales, although the pair differs in the severity of reality-testing impairment. The OR profiles have high Alienation and Egocentricity scores with a lesser, though clinically elevated, Insecure Attachment and a marginally elevated score on Social Incompetence. People with this type of OR profile lack basic trust and view relationships principally in terms of whether they are need frustrating or need gratifying. When they do get involved with others, the relationships usually are described as painful, and they respond to their distress by being controlling, manipulative, demanding, rejecting, or sadistic. Although they experience object hunger and may yearn for closeness, they feel suspicious and may turn against others when their emotional needs are frustrated. The relatively lower Social Incompetence scale indicates that they may engage in relationships with the opposite sex and can tolerate superficial social involvement.

Those in the *Psychotically Egocentric* (PE) cluster have moderately elevated reality-testing subscale scores. This profile of RT subscales suggests that they have psychotic experiences that may include hallucinations, delusions, and various forms of reality distortion. However, their Uncertainty of Perception score indicates that they have the self-awareness to recognize that something is wrong with their minds and regard their hallucinations and reality distortions as ego-dystonic. They have impaired reality testing, but they also have some observing ego. Their distortions of reality create unease, but they may be less likely to act on their psychotic beliefs or hallucinated voices.

On the EPQ, the PE cluster had the highest score on Neuroticism and the second-highest score on Psychoticism (Figure 10.3), reflecting the high degree of symptoms and discomfort that they experience. They differed significantly from their paired cluster, *Psychotically Egocentric–Severe* (PES), by scoring much lower on Extraversion. They also differed significantly from PES on the PANSS (Figure 10.2) in that they had fewer positive symptoms. They had nonsignificant but lower scores on the cognitive, emotional discomfort, and hostility components as well.

The PES cluster has the most disturbing set of ego impairments because in addition to severe scores, they may lack awareness of their reality-testing impairments. People in this cluster had the highest elevations ($t > 80$) on Reality Distortion and Hallucinations and Delusions, meaning that they are reporting severe primary symptoms in multiple domains (e.g., delusions, paranoia, hallucinations, magical thinking). At the same time, they have only a limited awareness of their illness, as suggested by their marginally elevated score on Uncertainty of Perception. This profile suggests that people in this cluster may lack the ego strength to resist acting on their misperceptions. Because they may view people as trying to hurt them, they may be more likely to turn against others in retaliation for perceived slights. This pattern of severe OR and RT impairments may predict a greater likelihood of violent or disruptive behavior. As might be expected, people in this cluster score high on the EPQ Psychoticism scale (Figure 10.3), indicating that they are likely to be controlling, to lack empathy, and to be more rigid in their thinking. They are not particularly socially isolated and scored in the average range of the sample on the Extraversion scale. Our concern for the potential dangerousness of PES members finds some support in their PANSS profile (Figure 10.2), which revealed that they had the highest ratings on positive symptoms, lowest on negative symptoms, and among the highest on cognitive disorganization, emotional discomfort, and hostility.

These three pairs of profiles account for most people in our schizophrenia sample. The six BORRTI patterns can be used to identify a person according to his or her BORRTI responses. Relating a person to one of the BORRTI types may increase the interpretative value of the assessment.

Diana's BORRTI

Figure 10.4 presents Diana's BORRTI profile along with the IR profile type. Her scores closely match the IR type and indicate that her responses are most like those of people who are recovering from schizophrenia, have the capacity to acknowledge their lapses in reality testing, and are able to sustain good object-relations ego function. In particular, her average score on Insecure Attachment in the presence of low Alienation suggests that relationships can be gratifying to her and that she values them. She can participate in interpersonally meaningful interactions without becoming overwhelmed by fears of abandonment and loss. Her low score on Social Incompetence also speaks to her comfort in social interactions and ability to be effective in relating to a wide range of people. These object-relational qualities make it likely that she can be a good collaborator in her psychopharmacotherapy and make good use of her psychotherapy.

Implications and Future Research

The three pairs of profiles account for most of the people in our large sample. Our findings indicate that people with schizophrenia differ considerably in their ego functioning. We have found reliable patterns that

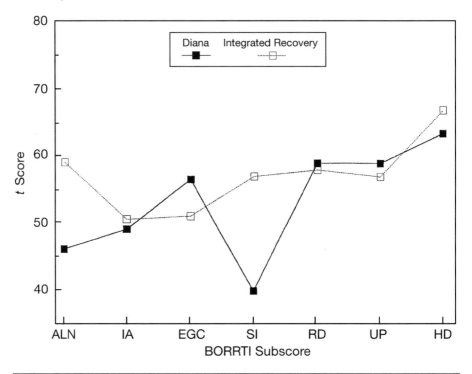

FIGURE 10.4

Diana's BORRTI profile compared with the BORRTI profile for the Integrated Recovery type. The *t* scores are based on norms provided in the BORRTI manual. The object-relations subscales are Alienation (ALN), Insecure Attachment (IA), Egocentricity (EGC), and Social Incompetence (SI). The reality-testing subscales are Reality Distortion (RD), Uncertainty of Perception (UP), and Hallucinations and Delusions (HD).

reflect important distinctions in how people have been affected by their illness. Although schizophrenia may be devastating to interpersonal functioning, particularly when it occurs early in life, some people are able to retain relatively good object relations. Among those in our sample who are involved in rehabilitation, we found many who reported only residual ego-functioning impairment, whereas others remained significantly impaired. The six replicated clusters in this study can be used to identify other patients according to their BORRTI responses. Relating patients to one of the BORRTI types may increase the interpretative value of their assessment.

Our next step will be to examine the predictive power of cluster membership in determining response to our work-rehabilitation program. For example, it seems reasonable to expect that those in the IR cluster will have the most favorable outcomes, whereas those in the SOR may do well only as long as their defenses are not too challenged in work situations. Those in the SW cluster may demonstrate the greatest improvement in quality of life as a result of rehabilitation, whereas those in the PE cluster may show the most improvement in positive symptoms as a result of the reality-based activity of rehabilitation. Cluster membership also may be used to plan rehabilitation strategies better so that counseling, accommodations, and remediation efforts can be shaped according to vulnerabilities suggested by the profile.

The generalizability of the clusters also is unknown. It may be that some of the cluster patterns are relevant to other psychiatric disorders and can contribute to treatment planning and outcome. Also, as treatments for schizophrenia continue to improve and more people experience the "awakening" that has been described in some recent clinical papers (Duckworth, 1998), we may come to see the restoration of object-relations and reality-testing ego functioning for more and more people. The BORRTI can be used to track those changes as people with schizophrenia reestablish their sense of relatedness.

Finally, the clusters may be associated with impairments in specific types of social information processing. It may be that poor executive functioning and cognitive perseveration is related to SOR, whereas cognitive flexibility is necessary for IR. Poor affect recognition and failure of theory of mind may play a prominent role in the object-relations deficits of the PE clusters, playing a lesser role in the problems of the SW clusters. The availability of clusters will make it possible to test these and other hypotheses about social cognition and its impact on object relations. In so doing, we will be able to bridge the intellectual canyon that has for too long separated object relations from social cognition.

References

American Psychiatric Association. (1987). *Diagnostic and statistical manual of mental disorders* (3rd ed. revised). Washington, DC: Author.

American Psychiatric Association. (1994). *The diagnostic and statistical manual of mental disorders* (4th ed.). Washington, DC: Author.

Bell, M. D. (1995). *Bell object relations and reality testing inventory (BORRTI) manual.* Los Angeles: Western Psychological Services.

Bell, M. D., Billington, R., & Becker, B. (1985). A scale for the assessment of object relations: Reliability, validity, and factorial invariance. *Journal of Clinical Psychology, 42,* 733–741.

Bell, M. D., Billington, R., & Becker, B. (1986). A scale for the assessment of reality testing: Reliability, validity, and factorial invariance. *Journal of Consulting and Clinical Psychology, 53,* 506–511.

Bell, M. D., Greig, T. C., Kaplan, E., & Bryson, G. (2001). Patterns of object relations and reality testing impairment in schizophrenia. *Journal of Clinical Psychology*.

Bell, M. D., Lysaker, P. H., Beam-Goulet, J. L., & Milstein, R. M. (1994). Five-component model of schizophrenia: Assessing the factorial invariance of the positive and negative syndrome scale. *Psychiatry Research, 59*, 295–303.

Bell, M. D., Lysaker, P., & Milstein, R. (1992). Object relations deficits in subtypes of schizophrenia. *Journal of Clinical Psychology, 48*, 433–444.

Bellak, L., Hurvich, M., & Gediman, H. (1973). *Ego functions in schizophrenics, neurotics, and normals.* New York: Wiley.

Bowlby, J. (1969). *Attachment and loss. Vol. 1: Attachment.* New York: Basic Books.

Cannon-Spohr, H. E., Potkin, S. G., & Wyatt, R. J. (1986). Measurement of premorbid adjustment in chronic schizophrenia. *Schizophrenia Bulletin, 8*, 470–484.

Damasio, A. R. (1994). *Descartes' error: Emotion, reason and the human brain.* New York: Avon Books.

Duckworth, K. (1998, December). Awakenings with the new antipsychotics. *Psychiatric Times Monograph*, 26–27.

Eysenck, H. J., & Eysenck, S. B. G. (1975). *Eysenck Personality Questionnaire manual.* San Diego, CA: EdITS/Educational and Industrial Testing Service.

Greenberg, J. R., & Mitchell, S. A. (1983). *Object relations in psychoanalytic theory.* Cambridge, MA: Harvard University Press.

Greig, T. C., Bell, M. D., Kaplan, E., & Bryson, G. (2000). Object Relations and Reality Testing in early and late onset schizophrenia. *Journal of Clinical Psychology, 56*, 505–517.

Gupta, S., Rajaprabhakaran, R., Ardnt, S., Flaum, M., & Andreasen, N. N. (1995). Premorbid adjustment as a predictor of phenomenological and neurobiological indices in schizophrenia. *Schizophrenia Research, 16*, 189–197.

Harris, M. J., & Jeste, D. V. (1988). Late-onset schizophrenia: An overview. *Schizophrenia Bulletin, 14*, 39–55.

Haviland, M. G., Sonne, J. L., & Woods, L. R. (1996). Beyond posttraumatic stress disorder: Object relations and reality testing disturbances in physically and sexually abused adolescents. *Journal of the American Academy of Child and Adolescent Psychiatry, 34*, 1054–1059.

Heaton, R. K., Chelune, G. J., Talley, J. L., Kay, G. G., & Curtis, C. (1993). *Wisconsin card sorting test manual: Revised and expanded.* Los Angeles: Western Psychological Services.

Jeste, D. V., Harris, M. J., Krull, A., Kick, J., McAdams, L. A., & Heaton, R. (1995). Clinical and neuropsychological characteristics of patients with late-onset schizophrenia. *American Journal of Psychiatry, 152,* 722–730.

Kay, S. R., Fiszbein, A., & Opler, L. A. (1987). The Positive and Negative Syndrome Scale for schizophrenia. *Schizophrenia Bulletin, 13,* 261–276.

Kirkpatrick, B., Buchanan, R. W., McKenney, P. D., Alphs, L. D., & Carpenter, W. T. (1989). The schedule for deficit syndrome: An instrument for research in schizophrenia. *Psychiatry Research, 30,* 119–123.

Krystal, H. (1988). *Integration and self-healing: Affect, trauma, and alexithymia.* Hillside, NJ: Analytic Press.

Loong, J. (1991). *The manual for the Continuous Performance Test.* San Louis Obispo, CA: Wang Neuropsychological Laboratory.

Mahler, M. S. (1979). *The selected papers of Margaret S. Mahler. Vols. I & II.* New York: Jason Aronson.

McIntyre, R. M., & Blashfield, R. K. (1980). A nearest-centroid technique for evaluating the minimum-variance clustering procedure. *Multivariate Behavioral Research, 15,* 225–238.

Penn, D. L., Corrigan, P. W., Bentall, R. P., Racenstein, J. M., & Newman, L. S. (1997). Social cognition in schizophrenia. *Psychological Bulletin, 121,* 114–132.

Sarle, W. S. (1983). *Cubic clustering criterion* (Tech. Rep. A-108). Cary, NC: SAS Institute.

Schore, A. N. (1994). *Affect regulation and the origin of the self: The neurobiology of emotional development.* Hillsdale, NJ: Erlbaum.

Slosson, R. L. (1963). *Slosson Intelligence Test for Children and Adults.* East Aurora, NY: Slosson Educational Publications.

Spitz, R. (1965). *The first year of life.* New York: International Universities Press.

Stern, D. N. (1985). *The interpersonal world of the infant.* New York: Basic Books.

Volkmar, F. R. (Ed.). (1998). *Autism and pervasive developmental disorders.* New York: Cambridge University Press.

Wechsler, D. (1982). *WAIS-R Manual: Wechsler Adult Intelligence Scale— Revised.* New York: Psychological Corporation.

III

Future Directions

Social Cognition in Schizophrenia: Answered and Unanswered Questions

11

David L. Penn and Patrick W. Corrigan

This book set out to provide an overview of social cognition and schizophrenia. To achieve this goal, we asked prominent experts in the field to describe their work and speculate on the current and future state of the field. This final chapter summarizes some "take-home" points comprising what we know and do not know about social cognition and schizophrenia. We hope that books such as this will have heuristic value for the field and inspire researchers and clinicians to develop better methods and theories for examining this important construct in people with schizophrenia.

Answered Questions

Clearly, no one theory of social cognition in schizophrenia or single conceptual framework guides the field. This state likely reflects the nebulous definition of social cognition as applied to schizophrenia research. Multiple theories describe how social cognitive difficulties contribute to and underlie the symptoms and behavioral deficits of schizophrenia. One theoretical approach appears to be based on the performance-deficit models found in the neurocognitive literature (Penn, in press; Spaulding & Poland, this book). This approach is dominated more by biologically oriented, reductionistic models that seek to identify the neural mechanisms underlying the disorder. Thus, research on deficits may start with the question, "What is the impact of neuropathology on social cogni-

315

tion?" (e.g., Frith & Frith, 1999) rather than "What psychological and/ or behavioral function do these social cognitive processes serve?"

Studies based on the deficit model tend to use "differential-deficit" design; that is, they compare a group with schizophrenia with a matched group on two tasks; impaired performance on one task is thought to reflect deficits on the underlying construct. Because task performance is compared across various measures, researchers using this approach tend to be concerned with psychometrically matching tasks to ensure that group differences are not merely an artifact of differential task difficulty or reliability (Chapman & Chapman, 1973, 1978). This concern has been especially the case in the work on emotion perception, which has carefully examined whether deficits in emotion perception reflect specific impairments or generalized poor performance (for reviews, see Edwards, Jackson, & Pattison, 1999; Hellewell & Whittaker, 1998; Mandal, Pandey, & Prasad, 1998; Morrison, Bellack, & Mueser, 1988; Penn, Corrigan, Bentall, Racenstein, & Newman, 1997).

The theory underlying the deficit approach to understanding social cognition in schizophrenia still relies significantly on models drawn from nonsocial cognition. Efforts to differentiate social from nonsocial cognition in schizophrenia typically have come in the form of two strategies. The first draws on work from basic science that attempts to identify different neural substrates for social and nonsocial cognition (Brothers, 1990a, 1990b; Frith & Frith, 1999). The second strategy is to determine whether measures of social cognition contribute independent variance to social functioning beyond the contribution of nonsocial cognition (e.g., Corrigan & Toomey, 1995; Penn, Spaulding, Reed, & Sullivan, 1996). In both cases, one could argue that the deficit model of social cognition is largely atheoretical, based more on what nonsocial cognition is not or does not do, rather than on what social cognition is or does. Consequently, a more useful strategy, at least for developing psychological models of social cognition in schizophrenia, may be to look toward social cognition work in nonclinical samples (see chapters in this book by Newman and by Corrigan and Holtzman, for examples).

Fortunately, we have learned much from the deficit models of social cognition. As summarized in some of the other chapters of this book (i.e., Leonhard & Corrigan and Penn et al.), we now know that people with schizophrenia have impairments in emotion perception, particularly for negative emotions. Interestingly, a social cognitive model of emotion perception might help reconcile those findings with those from the expressed emotion (EE) literature (reviewed by Bebbington & Kuipers, 1994). In other words, if people with schizophrenia have impairments in perceiving negative emotions, why are they sensitive to high levels of EE? We also have learned that people with schizophrenia have difficulties in perceiving abstract features and cues in social situations, a finding that seems to tie together work on social perception (Leonhard & Corrigan, this book), theory of mind (ToM; Corcoran, this book), and the clinical observations of Spaulding and Poland (this book). Finally, people with schizophrenia have less "social knowledge" than do control subjects (reviewed in Penn, Combs, & Mohamed, this book). This lack of social knowledge is manifest in their unfamiliarity with a number of social situations, including what is and is not appropriate to do, and an oversimplified view of the self. In the chapter on theory of mind, Corcoran implicates a lack of knowledge about the self, biased recollections about the self (i.e., autobiographical memory), or both as underlying performance deficits on ToM tasks. Thus, an inability to recall how one handled certain past social situations or a tendency to remember them in a distorted manner should influence one's current social cognitive and behavioral activities. Corcoran's model is an excellent example of how a construct often associated with a deficit model (Frith & Frith, 1999) can be incorporated into a theoretical psychological model.

A second approach to understanding social cognition in schizophrenia is based more on "bias" models. As noted in Leonhard and Corrigan's chapter, *performance bias* refers to a response style that is not necessarily indicative of poor performance. Rather, a performance bias reflects a response pattern as a function of condition and context. In addition, the bias approach tends to be more content oriented and symptom focused than the deficit approach. Therefore, the researcher of social cognitive bias will likely group subjects by symptoms—typically, persecutory delusions—and assess how delusional content influences social information processing. This approach also assumes continuity between the social cognition of "normal" and "schizophrenia," such that the pattern of responses in people with schizophrenia is thought to represent extremes of normative performance.

We also have learned much from this approach to social cognition. In particular, people with persecutory delusions, relative to those without such delusions, tend to make decisions based on less information (i.e., "jump to conclusions"), preferentially process and recall threatening information, and tend to blame others for negative outcomes (i.e., an externalizing bias; see Bentall, this book, and Garety & Freeman, 1999). Furthermore, evidence of a "self-serving" bias (i.e., taking credit for success and denying responsibility for failure) tends to be strongest when those with persecutory delusions are compared with people with depression (Garety & Freeman, 1999). Unlike deficit models of social cognition, those espousing a bias approach, particularly research on attributional style, have recruited psychological explanations for performance patterns. Bentall and Kinderman's work, in particular, has been ambitious in trying to incorporate how attributional style may be linked to self-esteem and impairments in ToM (Bentall, this book).

Clearly, a need exists to better integrate the deficit and bias approaches to social cognitive research in schizophrenia. As a first step, studies need to incorporate multiple social cognitive constructs and measures in their design, so that the relationship between bias and deficit tasks can be assessed (e.g., Kinderman, Dunbar, & Bentall, 1998). Furthermore, the tendency for researchers using bias approaches to subclassify according to symptoms needs to be reconciled with the tendency for those using the deficit approach to focus on broad group performance. Of course, both approaches have their merits, but they also suffer from limitations. The bias approach risks forming groups that may change over a short time period (Bentall, 1999); group performance biases therefore may reflect state rather than trait subject characteristics. The deficit approach runs the risk of obscuring important information by collapsing across symptom subgroups and by focusing on summary measures of performance rather than fine-grained performance indices (as often has been the case in research on emotion and social perception in schizophrenia, but not in the case of ToM work; Corcoran, this book). It would appear that by reconciling the two approaches to social cognition, a truly comprehensive social cognitive model of schizophrenia could emerge.

Unanswered Questions

A number of questions regarding social cognition in general remain unanswered. First, the fairly consistent pattern of impairments in social cognition found in people with schizophrenia raises the question of how functioning could be improved in this area. One possibility is to apply technology used to remediate cognitive impairments, such as reinforcement and enhanced instructions (e.g., Hellman, Kern, Neilson, & Green, 1998; Kern, Green, & Goldstein, 1995). In fact, preliminary findings from our laboratory show that both contingent monetary reinforcement and promoting proprioceptive feedback (i.e., by asking research participants to imitate the affective expressions of others) were associated with improvements in facial emotion identification (Penn & Combs, in press). An alternative, although certainly not exclusive, approach to social cognitive treatment is use of atypical medication. In particular, a recent report has shown that Risperidone improved emotion perception to a greater extent than Haloperidol in a sample of treatment-resistant inpatients with schizophrenia (Kee, Kern, Marshall, & Green, 1998). The new wave of atypical neuroleptics should be investigated for their effectiveness in improving social cognition in schizophrenia.

Of course, it is possible that current psychosocial interventions that target aspects of the self, such as Personal Therapy (Hogarty et al., 1997a, 1997b), cognitive–behavioral therapy (CBT; reviewed by Garety, Fowler, & Kuipers, 1999; Kinderman, this book), and cognitively oriented psychotherapy for early psychosis (COPE; Jackson et al., this book) also may improve social cognitive functioning. All of these approaches share the goal of addressing individual beliefs and perceptions of the self as a basis for changing how people with schizophrenia relate to their social environment. Cognitive rehabilitation tends to take a different approach by attempting to strengthen the basic cognitive processes that are presumed to underlie and support social cognition (Spaulding & Poland, this book). The hope is that remediation of basic cognitive processes will have a "springboard" effect on social cognition (Penn, 1991). Spaulding and Poland report, however, that improvement in social functioning was not related to improvements in nonsocial processes, suggesting that Integrated Psychological Therapy (IPT) did not have a springboard effect but may have indirectly affected social cognitive processes.

An indirect way of examining the effect of psychosocial intervention on social cognition is to investigate the mechanisms underlying the apparent efficacy of supportive counseling treatments. Of course, such interventions are not always effective, but evidence indicates that their effects are not trivial and, in some cases, are comparable to the effects of CBT (Tarrier et al., 1999). This information raises the question of how supportive therapy works. In particular, what is it about friendship and interpersonal contact that motivates a person with schizophrenia to improve? One could explain such effects in terms of learning theory: The therapist models appropriate social behavior that the client with schizophrenia incorporates into his or her social repertoire. An alternative explanation is that the client's view of self, including his or her self-esteem and possible selves (see Jackson et al.'s chapter in this book), is bolstered by the development of an important interpersonal relationship. Thus, the self is indirectly strengthened through the relationship with the therapist. This is consistent with Mead's (1934) theory of the self as developing from the "outside in"; that is, our view of ourselves is shaped by our relationships with others and how we believe others view us (see Newman's chapter, this book, for a more extensive discussion of this issue). This assertion suggests that a therapeutic approach based on interpersonal relationships, comparable to interpersonal therapy (Klerman & Weissman, 1993), may be beneficial for people with schizophrenia.

A more interpersonal approach to psychosocial treatment in schizophrenia is consistent with CBT interventions that attempt to "interpersonalize" auditory hallucinations as a first step in ameliorating them

(Chadwick, Birchwood, & Trower, 1996). In this context, a therapeutic model that focuses on relationships would serve two primary purposes. First, it would help the client with schizophrenia replace the voices (or deluded beliefs) with actual, rather than imagined, relationships. Such an approach also might affect indirectly how the client mentally represents social relationships, which, as summarized in Morris Bell's chapter, have potentially important implications for social functioning. Second, it would help give meaning to the client's life. We know from reading personal accounts of people with schizophrenia (e.g., *Schizophrenia Bulletin*; Davidson, Stayner, & Haglund, 1998) that this illness can rob them of their hopes and dreams. Sometimes the person's sense of self is blurred, and what remains is a person whose identity is confused with the disorder itself. Thus, an intervention that places *relationships* at its core is one that will help the person with schizophrenia achieve one of the central goals of life, namely enhancing connections with others (Ryff & Singer, 1998).

A second issue concerns the developmental and biological etiology of social cognitive impairment in schizophrenia. Without question, behavioral problems often are manifest in childhood for at least a subgroup of people with schizophrenia (Bearden et al., 2000; Neumann & Walker, 1998). In fact, Cornblatt and Keilp (1994) hypothesized that impairments in social information processing may predict later social deficits in at-risk subjects. Furthermore, an external locus of control in adolescence was predictive of poor mental health in adulthood in the Israeli high-risk project (Frenkel, Kugelmass, Nathan, & Ingraham, 1995). Finally, preliminary evidence shows that the healthy relatives of people with schizophrenia have some social perceptual deficits (Toomey, Seidman, Lyons, Faraone, & Tsuang, 1999). The findings suggest that impairments in social cognition may predate the onset of the disorder and that a genetic component to this impairment may be present. At this time, however, the disparate findings are merely speculative; they need replication and considerable expansion before more confident conclusions can be drawn.

The etiology of social cognitive impairment in schizophrenia also can be understood within a neuropathological context. Specifically, many scholars hypothesize that disruptions in the fronto-temporo/limbic circuitry underlie deficits in social cognition (Brothers, 1990a, 1990b; Frith, 1992, 1994; Frith & Frith, 1999; Kirkpatrick & Buchanan, 1990; Silverstein, 1997; Taylor & Cadet, 1989). Dysfunction of the right hemisphere and interhemispheric transfer of information also have been raised as a model to explain deficits in emotion perception (Mandal et al., 1998; Morrison et al., 1988). Interestingly, people with right-hemisphere damage also tend to do worse on ToM-type tasks (reviewed in Brownell, Griffin, Winner, Friedman, & Happe, in press), suggesting a common neuropathology underlying emotion perception and ToM skills. A first step in exploring the neuropathology of social cognition may be to assess the underlying structure of the social cognition construct itself, as has been done for the dimensions of symptomatology (Grube, Bilder, & Goldman, 1998). In other words, are deficits in social cognition explained by single or multiple factors? If we can determine the structure of social cognition in schizophrenia—for example, by assessing the relationship among various social cognitive measures (Kinderman, Dunbar, & Bentall, 1998) the next step would be to identify the neural mechanisms underlying each of its components.

A final issue to address concerns the internal and ecological validity of current social cognition measures. In particular, the psychometric properties of many social cognitive instruments used in schizophrenia research often have suffered from poor reliability (e.g., internal consistency). This has been the case for measures of attributional style (Bentall, 1999; Martin & Penn, in press) and emotion perception (Penn et al., 2000). Furthermore, the psychometric properties of some measures, such as those used in ToM research, are rarely examined (discussed in Bentall, 1999). This situation raises the uncomfortable possibility that models of social cognition in schizophrenia rest on a shaky psychometric foundation, leading one to ask how such models would change if different, more reliable measures were used.

Researchers also should exercise caution before assuming that measures of social cognition with face validity automatically have ecological validity. Just because an emotion perception test *seems* to tap into the processes underlying social behavior does not mean that it actually does. For example, tests of facial-affect perception are presented without context, a situation that rarely occurs in daily interactions. In fact, contextual information does influence our perceptions of others' affect (Trope, 1986; Trope, Cohen, & Maoz, 1988), suggesting that omitting contextual information from affect-perception tasks may seriously compromise the value of these tests. Results of tests of attributional style that involve hypothetical situations (e.g., "Someone compliments you") are likely to be a function of at least two processes: (a) imagining the scenario happening to oneself and (b) making the attributional judgment. It thus is possible that attributional biases associated with paranoia may result from processing difficulties at either stage. In other words, people with paranoid delusions may show a self-serving attributional bias not because of attributional problems but because they remembered an event in which they were truly *not* at fault or because they imagined it differently from how it occurred. "On-line" attributional judgments may differ from those made when trying to imagine a hypothetical event. Therefore, a challenge to attributional research in schizophrenia will be to develop tasks that assess attributions for actual, rather than imagined, events. Methodologies drawn from social psychology, which involve providing research participants with bogus feedback concerning their success or failure on a given task, followed by soliciting subject attributions about the outcome (e.g., Alden, 1987; Forgas, Bower, & Moylan, 1990), might prove useful for people with schizophrenia.

A related approach has been undertaken in the autism literature, where researchers have attempted to behaviorally assess ToM-type impairments by evaluating the reaction of children with autism to staged interpersonal scenarios (Sigman & Ruskin, 1999). For example, one scenario involved an experimenter approaching a table (where a child was seated) with a tray of refreshments and snacks. However, the table was completely covered with objects, so the primary dependent variable was whether and how quickly the child spontaneously removed the objects from the table (Sigman & Ruskin, 1999). Similar scenarios were constructed that involved responses to distress (e.g., the experimenter pretends to bump his or her knee and the child's reactions are videotaped). These types of tasks afford the opportunity to assess the convergence of performance on paper-and-pencil ToM tasks with more behavioral ToM skills. In this sense, one can view ToM skills "in action" rather than relying on hypothetical scenarios.

Conclusion

We hope this book has stimulated your thinking about social cognition in schizophrenia. We are confident that social cognition will prove to be a fruitful domain for researchers and clinicians alike. Ultimately, through the efforts of researchers in this book and you, the reader, more comprehensive and effective approaches to the prevention and treatment of schizophrenia will be developed.

References

Alden, L. (1987). Attributional responses of anxious individuals to different patterns of social feedback: Nothing succeeds like improvement. *Journal of Personality and Social Psychology, 52,* 100–106.

Bearden, C. E., Rosso, I. M., Hollister, J. M., Sanchez, L. E., Hadley, T., & Cannon, T. D. (2000). A prospective cohort study of childhood behavioral deviance and language abnormalities as predictors of adult schizophrenia. *Schizophrenia Bulletin, 26,* 395–410.

Bebbington, P., & Kuipers, L. (1994). The predictive utility of expressed emotion in schizophrenia: An aggregate analysis. *Psychological Medicine, 24,* 707–718.

Bentall, R. P. (1999). Commentary on Garety & Freeman III: Three psychological investigators and an elephant. *British Journal of Clinical Psychology, 38,* 323–327.

Brothers, L. (1990a). The neural basis of primate social communication. *Motivation and Emotion, 14,* 81–91.

Brothers, L. (1990b). The social brain: A project for integrating primate behavior and neurophysiology in a new domain. *Concepts in Neuroscience, 1,* 27–61.

Brownell, H., Griffin, R., Winner, E., Friedman, O., & Happe, F. (in press). Cerebral lateralization and theory of mind. In S. Baron-Cohen, H. Tager-Flusberg, & D. Cohen (Eds.), *Understanding other minds: Perspectives from autism and cognitive neuroscience* (2nd ed.). Oxford, U.K.: Oxford University Press.

Chadwick, P. D. J., Birchwood, M., & Trower, P. (1996). *Cognitive therapy for delusions, voices, and paranoia.* Chichester, England: Wiley.

Chapman, L. J., & Chapman, J. P. (1973). Problems in the measurement of cognitive deficit. *Psychological Bulletin, 79,* 380–383.

Chapman, L. J., & Chapman, J. P. (1978). The measurement of differential deficit. *Journal of Psychiatric Research, 14,* 303–311.

Cornblatt, B. A., & Keilp, J. G. (1994). Impaired attention, genetics, and the pathophysiology of schizophrenia. *Schizophrenia Bulletin, 20,* 31–46.

Corrigan, P. W., & Toomey, R. (1995). Interpersonal problem solving and information processing in schizophrenia. *Schizophrenia Bulletin, 21,* 395–403.

Davidson, L., Stayner, D., & Haglund, K. E. (1998). Phenomenological perspectives on the social functioning of people with schizophrenia. In K. T. Mueser & N. Tarrier (Eds.), *Handbook of social functioning in schizophrenia* (pp. 97–120). Boston: Allyn & Bacon.

Edwards, J., Jackson, H. J., & Pattison, P. (1999). *Emotion recognition via facial expression and affective prosody in schizophrenia: A methodological review.* Manuscript submitted for publication.

Forgas, J. P., Bower, G. H., & Moylan, S. J. (1990). Praise or blame? Affective influences on attributions for achievement. *Journal of Personality and Social Psychology, 59,* 809–819.

Frenkel, E., Kugelmass, S., Nathan, M., & Ingraham, L. J. (1995). Locus of control and mental health in adolescence and adulthood. *Schizophrenia Bulletin, 21,* 219–226.

Frith, C. D. (1992). *The cognitive neuropsychology of schizophrenia.* Hillsdale, NJ: Erlbaum.

Frith, C. D. (1994). Theory of mind. In A. S. David & J. C. Cutting (Eds.), *The neuropsychology of schizophrenia* (pp. 147–161). East Sussex, England: Erlbaum.

Frith, C. D., & Frith, U. (1999). Interacting minds—A biological basis. *Science, 286,* 1692–1695.

Garety, P. A., Fowler, D., & Kuipers, E. (1999). Cognitive-behavioral therapy for medication-resistant symptoms. *Schizophrenia Bulletin, 26,* 73–86.

Garety, P. A., & Freeman, D. (1999). Cognitive approaches to delusions: A critical review of theories and evidence. *British Journal of Clinical Psychology, 38,* 113–154.

Grube, B. S., Bilder, R. M., & Goldman, R. S. (1998). Meta-analysis of symptom factors in schizophrenia. *Schizophrenia Research, 31,* 113–120.

Hellewell, J. S. E., & Whittaker, J. F. (1998). Affect perception and social knowledge in schizophrenia. In K. T. Mueser & N. Tarrier (Eds.), *Handbook of social functioning in schizophrenia* (pp. 197–212). Boston: Allyn & Bacon.

Hellman, S. G., Kern, R. S., Neilson, L. M., & Green, M. F. (1998). Monetary reinforcement and Wisconsin Card Sorting performance in schizophrenia: Why show me the money? *Schizophrenia Research, 34,* 67–75.

Hogarty, G. E., Kornblith, S. J., Greenwald, D., DiBarry, A. L., Cooley, S., Ulrich, R. F., Carter, M., & Flesher, S. (1997a). Three year trials of Personal Therapy among schizophrenic patients living with or independent of family: I. Description of study and effects on relapse rates. *Archives of General Psychiatry, 154,* 1504–1513.

Hogarty, G. E., Greenwald, D., Ulrich, R. F., Kornblith, S. J., DiBarry, A. L., Cooley, S., Carter, M., & Flesher, S. (1997b). Three year trials of Personal Therapy among schizophrenic patients living with or independent of family: II. Effects on adjustment of patients. *American Journal of Psychiatry, 154,* 1514–1524.

Kee, K. S., Kern, R. S., Marshall, B. D., & Green, M. F. (1998). Risperidone versus haloperidol for perception of emotion in treatment-resistant schizophrenia: Preliminary findings. *Schizophrenia Research, 31,* 159–165.

Kern, R. S., Green, M. F., & Goldstein, M. J. (1995). Modification of performance on the span of apprehension, a putative marker of vulnerability to schizophrenia. *Journal of Abnormal Psychology, 104,* 385–389.

Kinderman, P., Dunbar, R. I. M., & Bentall, R. P. (1998). Theory-of-mind deficits and causal attributions. *British Journal of Psychology, 71,* 339–349.

Kirkpatrick, B., & Buchanan, R. W. (1990). The neural basis of the deficit syndrome of schizophrenia. *Journal of Nervous and Mental Disease, 178,* 545–555.

Klerman, G. L., & Weissman, M. M. (Eds.). (1993). *New applications of interpersonal therapy*. Washington, DC: American Psychiatric Press, Inc.

Mandal, M. K., Pandey, R., & Prasad, A. B. (1998). Facial expressions of emotions and schizophrenia: A review. *Schizophrenia Bulletin, 24*, 399–412.

Martin, J., & Penn, D. L. (in press). Attributional style in schizophrenia: An investigation in outpatients with and without persecutory delusions. *Schizophrenia Bulletin*.

Mead, G. H. (1934). *Mind, self, and society*. Chicago: University of Chicago Press.

Morrison, R. L., Bellack, A. S., & Mueser, K. T. (1988). Deficits in facial-affect recognition and schizophrenia. *Schizophrenia Bulletin, 14*, 67–83.

Neumann, C. S., & Walker, E. (1998). Developmental origins of interpersonal deficits in schizophrenia. In K. T. Mueser & N. Tarrier (Eds.), *Handbook of social functioning in schizophrenia* (pp. 121–133). Boston: Allyn & Bacon.

Penn, D. L. (1991). Cognitive rehabilitation of social deficits in schizophrenia: A direction of promise or following a primrose path? *Psychosocial Rehabilitation Journal, 15*, 27–41.

Penn, D. L. (in press). Some reflections on social-cognitive research in schizophrenia: Commentary on Hooker, Roese, and Park "Impaired counterfactual thinking is associated with schizophrenia." *Psychiatry*.

Penn, D. L., & Combs, D. (in press). Modification of facial affect perception in schizophrenia. *Schizophrenia Research*.

Penn, D. L., Combs, D., Ritchie, M., Francis, J., Cassisi, J., Morris, S., & Townsend, M. (2000). Emotion recognition in schizophrenia: Further investigation of generalized versus specific deficit models. *Journal of Abnormal Psychology, 109*, 512–516.

Penn, D. L., Corrigan, P. W., Bentall, R. P., Racenstein, J. M., & Newman, L. S. (1997). Social cognition in schizophrenia. *Psychological Bulletin, 121*, 114–132.

Penn, D. L., Spaulding, W. D., Reed, D., & Sullivan, M. (1996). The relationship of social cognition to ward behavior in chronic schizophrenia. *Schizophrenia Research, 20*, 327–335.

Ryff, C. D., & Singer, B. (1998). The contours of positive human health. *Psychological Inquiry, 9*, 1–28.

Sigman, M., & Ruskin, E. (1999). Continuity and change in the social competence of children with autism, Down syndrome, and developmental delays. *Monographs of the Society for Research in Child Development, 64*, 1–142.

Silverstein, S. M. (1997). Information processing, social cognition, and psychiatric rehabilitation in schizophrenia. *Psychiatry, 60*, 327–340.

Tarrier, N., Wittkowski, A., Kinney, C., McCarthy, E., Morris, J., & Humphreys, L. (1999). The durability of the effects of cognitive–behavior therapy in the treatment of chronic schizophrenia: Twelve months follow-up. *British Journal of Psychiatry, 174,* 500–504.

Taylor, E. H., & Cadet, J. L. (1989). Social intelligence: A neurological system. *Psychological Reports, 64,* 423–444.

Toomey, R., Seidman, L. J., Lyons, M. J., Faraone, S. V., & Tsuang, M. (1999). Poor perception of nonverbal social-emotional cues in relatives of schizophrenic patients. *Schizophrenia Research, 40,* 121–130.

Trope, Y. (1986). Identification and inference processes in dispositional attribution. *Psychological Review, 93,* 239–257.

Trope, Y., Cohen, O., & Maoz, Y. (1988). The perceptual and inferential effects of situational inducements on dispositional attribution. *Journal of Personality and Social Psychology, 55,* 165–177.

Author Index

Numbers in italics refer to listings in reference sections.

Subject Index

About the Editors

Patrick W. Corrigan, PsyD, is associate professor of psychiatry at the University of Chicago, where he directs the Center for Psychiatric Rehabilitation, a clinical, research, and training program for people with severe mental illness and their families. Dr. Corrigan is also principal investigator and director of the Illinois Staff Training Institute for Psychiatric Rehabilitation, a program that examines organizational and educational issues related to the implementation and maintenance of effective rehabilitation programs in real-world settings. He has published more than 100 articles as well as 5 books and is also editor of the journal *Psychiatric Rehabilitation Skills*.

David L. Penn, PhD, is assistant professor of psychology at the University of North Carolina–Chapel Hill. Dr. Penn received his PhD from the University of Nebraska–Lincoln in 1994 and subsequently completed his internship at the Medical College of Pennsylvania at Eastern Pennsylvania Psychiatric Institute. His research and clinical interests focus on stigma, social cognition, and psychosocial treatment for schizophrenia. Dr. Penn has received a Young Investigator Grant from the National Association for Research on Schizophrenia and Depression and fellowships from the Beck Institute and the British Psychological Society. In addition, Dr. Penn has published more than 60 articles and book chapters, and he is currently associate editor of the journal *Psychiatric Rehabilitation Skills*.